A Practical Introduction to Management Science

DONALD WATERS

Second Edition

To Elizabeth

A Practical

Introduction to

Management

Science

2nd Edition

DONALD WATERS
UNIVERSITY OF CALGARY

FINANCIAL TIMES
Prentice Hall

An imprint of **Pearson Education**

Harlow, England · London · New York · Reading, Massachusetts · San Francisco
Toronto · Don Mills, Ontario · Sydney · Tokyo · Singapore · Hong Kong · Seoul
Taipei · Cape Town · Madrid · Mexico City · Amsterdam · Munich · Paris · Milan

Pearson Education Limited
Edinburgh Gate
Harlow
Essex CM20 2JE
England

and Associated Companies throughout the world

Visit us on the World Wide Web at:
http://www.pearsoneduc.com

The programs in this book have been included for their instructional value. They have been tested with care but are not guaranteed for any particular purpose. The publisher does not offer any warranties or representations nor does it accept any liabilities with respect to the programs.

Many of the designations used by manufacturers and sellers to distinguish their products are claimed as trademarks. Addison Wesley Longman has made every attempt to supply trademark information about manufacturers and their products mentioned in this book.

Typeset by 32
Produced by Pearson Education Asia Pte Ltd
Printed in Singapore (COS)

First printed 1989
This edition 1998

ISBN 0-201-17847-8

British Library Cataloguing-in-Publication Data
A catalogue record for this book is available from the British Library

Library of Congress Cataloging-in-Publication Data is available

10 9 8 7 6 5 4 3 2
05 04 03 02 01

Contents

Chapter 4
Extensions to linear programming 99

Chapter 5
Scheduling and routing 141

Chapter 6
Forecasting 201

Chapter 10
Project management
392

Chapter 11
Inventory control
447

Preface

Approach of the book

This book gives an introduction to **management science**. It shows how managers can use scientific ideas and methods. We do not want a detailed discussion about 'What is science?' – but will say that it uses rational analyses and objective reasoning.

Managers can use scientific methods in many ways. We only have space to look at some of these, so we have decided to emphasize quantitative models. But even this is too broad an area, so we concentrate on applications rather than theory. We avoid formal proofs and derivations, and describe models by examples rather than theoretical argument. This practical approach is reinforced by real case examples and case studies.

The book takes a balanced look at many important topics. It does not emphasize one area, such as mathematical programming or statistics, at the expense of others. It describes a range of ideas that managers really use. We have, of course, had to omit a lot of material, but hope you agree that these are the less widely used topics, or the topics that are too complicated to deal with in a reasonable time.

Readers

The book gives a first course in management science. It assumes no previous knowledge, and can be used by a wide range of people. Perhaps the majority of readers are studying business or management. Almost all business courses include some core or optional material in management science – which may be called operational research, quantitative methods, decision analysis, or many other names.

Many people who are not students of management can also use the book. Those who are studying science, engineering, humanities, or any other area, can often take optional courses in management. This book gives them a useful introduction to management decisions. It can also be used by professionals in various fields, who want to develop their knowledge of the area.

Contents

The book takes the subject in a logical order. Chapter 1 introduces the basic ideas of management science, and shows how it tackles problems. Chapter 2 gives some illustrations of quantitative models in the important area of finance. This helps show that the ideas are widely used, and illustrates links with other subjects. The next few chapters look at specific areas. Chapter 3 introduces linear programming, Chapter 4 extends these ideas to other types of mathematical programming, Chapter 5 describes scheduling and Chapter 6 looks at forecasting.

These first six chapters describe deterministic models. However, there is often uncertainty, which is discussed in Chapter 7. Chapter 8 then looks at some common statistical analyses. The next few chapters look at some specific problem areas that can include uncertainty. Chapter 9 introduces decision analysis, Chapter 10 looks at project management, Chapter 11 describes some aspects of inventory control and Chapter 12 talks about simulation.

Format

Each chapter uses a consistent format which has:

- a table of contents
- the main material, divided into coherent sections
- worked examples to illustrate the methods described
- a summary at the end of each section
- self-assessment questions (with solutions in Appendix A) to test understanding of the material
- a review at the end of each chapter to summarize the main points of the material
- a set of key terms
- a case study to show how the ideas can be used in practice
- numerical problems
- discussion questions

Some references for additional reading are given in Appendix E.

Most people have access to a computer and there is no point in doing complicated arithmetic by hand. Although this book does not assume readers have a computer – and it certainly does not assume that they have a specific program or package – the results from calculations are often shown in computer printouts. Many packages, particularly spreadsheets, make these routine calculations very easy.

Because many of the calculations are done by computer, it is worth mentioning the notation used for arithmetic. Generally, we have given variables one- or two-character names and arithmetic operators (+, −, * and /) are written explicitly. This follows the pattern used by computers, and is generally clearer than traditional mathematical notation. So you will meet equations in the form:

$$VC = RC*D/Q + HC*Q/2$$

This notation has the advantages of:

- being easy to understand
- giving useful variable names
- making meanings clear

We are, however, flexible with the format. Many variables have commonly accepted names – such as α, μ or P_n – and we have continued to use these. Sometimes the computer style would make equations seem very complicated, so we have used a simpler form. Our aim is to make the meaning clear, rather than be pedantic over formats.

Changes to the second edition

There have been major changes to the second edition of this book. These have maintained the best points from the first edition, but have updated the material and made it easier to read. Some specific changes include:

- The text has been completely rewritten to make it clearer and easier to read.
- The contents have been adjusted. New topics – like dynamic programming and goal programming – have been added; some topics have been expanded – like simulation, statistical testing and integer programming; and some topics have been reduced – like basic models and queueing theory.
- The order of the text has been changed to provide a better development of ideas. There is no longer a clear break between deterministic and probabilistic models, so all material on a particular topic is in one chapter.
- There is much more use of computers and packages. Specialized software and spreadsheets are used for routine calculations, and to show typical printouts.
- Some areas have simpler formats – like chapter outlines and summaries which now use point form.
- New features have been added – such as case examples to illustrate real applications, new case studies, discussion questions, key terms and boxed features.

The whole book gives a solid foundation for understanding management science. We hope you enjoy using it, and we welcome your comments.

Introducing management science

1

CHAPTER OUTLINE

This chapter introduces the ideas of management science. It gives some definitions and describes a general approach to solving problems. After reading the chapter you should be able to:

- define management science
- say why scientific methods are used for tackling management problems
- discuss the benefits of quantitative analyses for management problems
- understand the use of models
- describe the overall approach of management science

(If you want to do some more reading, a list of selected references is given in Appendix E.)

1.1 | What is management science?

1.1.1 Managers and decisions

Every organization is run by *managers*. Their job is to make decisions in the organization. To be more specific, they:

- **Plan** – setting the organization's goals and showing how to achieve these.
- **Organize** – giving the organization the structure it needs to achieve its goals.
- **Employ staff** – making sure there are people to do all the jobs.
- **Direct** – telling people what jobs to do.
- **Motivate** – encouraging people to do their jobs well.
- **Allocate resources** – making sure the jobs have enough resources.
- **Monitor** – checking progress toward the organization's goals.
- **Control** – taking action to make sure the organization moves towards its goals.
- **Inform** – keeping everyone informed of progress.

All of these jobs involve decision-making – and *management science* uses scientific methods to help make decisions.

Managers make decisions.

Management science uses rational analyses to improve decision-making.

We usually assume that managers use proper analyses – and that their decisions are based on skills, knowledge and experience rather than guesswork. So we expect managers to use objective measures and analyses. They can get these by using *scientific methods*. A more formal justification for using scientific methods is shown in Figure 1.1.

In recent years organizations have tended to get bigger, and they have certainly become more complicated. It is difficult to make good decisions in these large, complex organizations. At the same time, international competition has increased and communications have improved. So decisions have to be made quickly. Now we have two factors – more difficult decisions and faster decisions – both of which increase the chance that managers will make mistakes.

Unfortunately, the costs of making mistakes can be high. Suppose Shell Oil has the chance of exploring for oil in the Canadian Arctic. Their decisions are complicated, taking into account finances, alternative uses of money, current operations, forecast demand for oil products, demand for crude oil, alternative sources of oil, chances of finding oil or gas, size of likely finds, refining capacity,

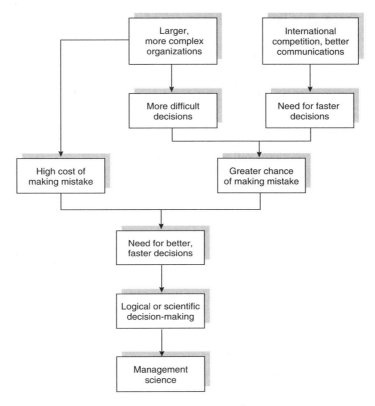

Figure 1.1 Reasons for using management science.

world oil prices, long-term company objectives, currency fluctuations, and so on. Unfortunately, Shell would have to make decisions quickly or competitors may take the exploration rights. If Shell make a bad decision, they could waste millions of pounds on fruitless exploration – or they could let other companies develop an area with high, long-term profits.

With this combination of risks and high costs, it is not surprising that managers look for ways of improving their decision-making. They want better, faster decisions – and one way of getting these is to use management science.

IN SUMMARY

Managers make the decisions within an organization. The aim of management science is to put their decision-making on a scientific, logical and rational basis.

1.1.2 Quantitative analyses

The aim of management science is to improve decision-making in an organization by using scientific methods. But what exactly are 'scientific methods'? We will look at this question later in the chapter – but can say here that they generally use mathematics. So we are going to develop a quantitative view of management problems.

You should not be surprised by this quantitative view, as we are surrounded by numbers. On a typical day the temperature might be 17°C, petrol costs 65 pence a litre, 2.3 million people are unemployed, gold costs $385 an ounce, a company made £24 million profit last year, bank rates are 7.3%, it is 520 kilometres from London to Land's End, and a cricket team scored 278 runs.

We use quantitative analyses on a small scale all the time. If we buy three bars of chocolate costing 30 pence each, we know that the total cost is 90 pence; if we pay with a £5 note we expect £4.10 in change. On a larger scale, we expect civil engineers to do calculations when they design bridges, doctors to prescribe measured quantities of drugs, accountants to describe a company's performance by numbers , banks to say how much money we have in an account, and so on. Unfortunately, some people do not realize that managers have to do similar analyses. They assume that managers somehow 'know' the right decisions intuitively. In this book we are trying to overcome this mistaken view, and show how managers can learn to make better decisions.

This does not, of course, mean that **all** management problems can be tackled scientifically, or that **all** scientific approaches use quantitative arguments. There are many areas – such as industrial relations, negotiations, recruiting, setting objectives and personal relations – which have hardly been touched by mathematics. You should also realize that no real problems are ever completely solved by mathematics. There are always factors that cannot be quantified, but they are still important. *Quantitative methods* can do some analyses and make suggestions – but managers always make the final decisions. They must look at all available information – both quantitative and qualitative – and then use their skills, knowledge and experience to make their decision (as shown in Figure 1.2).

Management science is not a new idea, as there are examples dating back to Archimedes and before. But it has really developed since the 1940s – and particularly since the arrival of cheap computers. The same methods are now

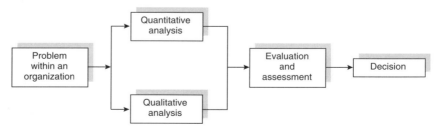

Figure 1.2 Qualitative and quantitative aspects of decisions.

known by a number of names including management science, operational research, operations research, quantitative methods, quantitative analysis and decision analysis.

IN SUMMARY

Management science often takes a quantitative view of decisions. This approach is known by several different names.

1.1.3 Different views of management science

We can look at management science in three different ways by describing:

- the types of problem it tackles
- the types of solution it uses
- the general approach

Taking the first of these, we can say that management science is used for forecasting demand, production planning, location decisions, and so on. The following table gives some examples of the problems it tackles. But remember that these are just illustrations and management science has been used to solve a huge range of problems.

Type of problem	Typical questions
Forecasting	How big will demand for products be, what are the patterns, how will this affect profits?
Finance	How much capital do we need, where can we get this, how much will it cost?
Manpower	How many employees do we need, what skills should they have, how long will they stay with us?
Scheduling	What work is most important, in what order should we do jobs?
Allocation	What resources are needed, are there shortages, how can we set priorities?
Replacement	How well is equipment working, how reliable is it, when should we replace it?
Stock control	How much stock should we hold, when do we order more, how much should we order?
Location	Where is the best location for operations, how big should facilities be?
Project planning	How long will a project take, what activities are most important, how should resources be used?
Queueing	How long are queues, how many servers should we use, what service level are we giving?

The second view of management science looks at the types of solution. The following table shows some ways of getting solutions, and again these are only illustrations of possible methods.

Solution	Typical approach
Linear programming	Optimization with linear objective and constraints
Goal programming	Finds a compromise between competing objectives
Forecasting	Projects time series, or finds causal relationships
Network analysis	Represents projects by networks of activities and events
Decision analysis	Compares consequences of alternative decisions
Inventory models	Minimizes the cost of holding stock
Statistics	Draws inferences about a population from a sample
Queueing theory	Analyses the characteristics of waiting lines
Simulation	Gives a dynamic view of complicated problems

The third view of management science describes a general approach to problems. We will discuss this view in the rest of the chapter.

IN SUMMARY

Three useful views of management science look at the problems it tackles, the types of solution it uses, or its general approach.

Self-assessment questions

(Solutions to all self-assessment questions are given in Appendix A.)

1.1   What is 'management science'?

1.2   What benefits would you expect from using management science?

1.3   Is management science a form of applied mathematics?

1.4   Does management science make decisions?

1.5   Why have quantitative analyses for management problems become more widely used in the past few years?

Case example

Safeway supermarkets

In November 1996 Safeway supermarkets had 7.8% of the British retail food market, made £230 million profit in six months, and raised sales to £14.63 a square foot. They were expanding their 'shop & go' operations (where customers scan their own goods), created 3250 jobs in the past year, opened small stores on BP's petrol forecourts, and were moving into banking services. As part of its expansion, they were opening ten new stores in the next six months, creating 5200 new jobs.

Supermarkets are fairly simple organizations. They buy goods from suppliers, and then sell the goods to customers. But when you walk around a Safeway store, you can see the results of a lot of management science.

- **Location.** The location of a store is chosen to attract large numbers of customers. It must be convenient for customers, far enough away from other Safeway stores, allow easy access, and be highly visible.

- **Capacity.** The store must be big enough to meet demand. So Safeway must forecast likely demand, and then design a store with enough capacity to meet this.

- **Financing.** Safeway must find the best way of raising money to finance the building and operations in the store.

- **Layout.** The layout of the store, car parks and other facilities must be easy for customers to use – and encourage them to buy goods.

- **Purchasing.** There must be a wide choice of goods available, so Safeway have to develop relationships with a large number of suppliers to guarantee deliveries, high quality and low prices.

- **Stock control.** Safeway forecast sales of all items they sell, then they make sure they have enough stock to cover these likely demands.

- **Logistics.** As well as buying the goods, Safeway make sure that everything is delivered from the supplier at the right times. For this they run a large transport fleet with operations throughout the country.

- **Staffing.** Staff schedules must ensure there are enough people working in the store at any time to deal with deliveries, stock rooms, stacking shelves, working at check-out counters, helping customers at special food counters, and doing any other work.

- **Pricing.** Safeway set the price of their goods so that they are comparable with competitors, but are still high enough to make a profit.

Questions

- What other types of decision do Safeway make in their stores?
- Give some examples of the decisions met in other organizations

1.2 | Management science methods

1.2.1 Using models

Scientific methods often use ***models***. Here we are not using the term 'model' to mean a toy, but any simplified view of a real situation.

> A **model**:
> - represents a real situation
> - is simplified with only relevant details included
> - has real properties represented by other properties in the model

There are three types of model:

- **Iconic models**, where properties in reality are represented by the same properties in the model, but on a different scale. A model car is an example of an iconic model. It has small wheels to represent real wheels, a small engine to represent a real engine, and so on. A manufacturer's prototype of a new product is an iconic model.

- **Analogue models**, which have properties in reality represented by other properties in the model. The time of day can be represented by the position of hands on a clock, temperature can be represented by the height of a column of mercury, speed can be represented by the position of a speedometer needle, and so on. The control room in a power station has many examples of analogue models.

- **Symbolic models**, which have properties in reality represented by some kind of symbol. The most common symbolic models for managers use mathematical equations, such as:

$$\text{Return on investment} = \text{annual profit/original capital}$$

Management science generally uses ***symbolic models***. So it uses equations to describe situations. If a company makes a product for £200 a unit and sells it for £300 a unit, a symbolic model of the profit would be:

$$\text{Profit} = \text{number sold} * (\text{selling price} - \text{cost})$$

or $\qquad\qquad\qquad P = N*(300 - 200)$

or, in general $\qquad\qquad P = N*(S - C)$

Now we have a model which shows the relationship between four variables, P, N, S and C. Some of these are ***decision variables*** that the managers give values to, like S. Others are ***external variables*** that are outside their control, like N. Symbolic models collect all the variables together into equations. We can then solve these equations to obtain useful results, as shown in Figure 1.3.

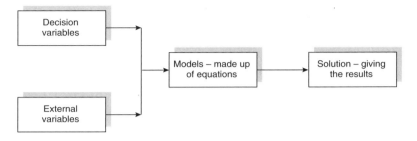

Figure 1.3 Using a model.

We can do experiments with models without affecting actual operations. If

$$P = N*(S - C)$$

we can substitute different values for N and calculate the corresponding values for P. We could, of course, experiment with real operations. In other words, we could change the actual production and find the resulting profit. This has the obvious disadvantages of being time-consuming, difficult, expensive, and damaging to the company. Sometimes it is also impossible. You could not, for example, find the best location for a factory by trying every possible location and keeping the best. So experiments with reality have major disadvantages – and the only feasible alternative is to build a model of the situation and experiment with this.

Models give simplified views of reality. Because they only include relevant features, they are always approximations. So there can be several equally good models for a situation, perhaps emphasizing different features, or making different assumptions. For example, several groups of economists have different models of the national economy which always give slightly different results.

WORKED EXAMPLE 1.1

Nancy is a retired civil servant living in the Channel Islands. She gets some of her income from a pension fund, some from a part-time job, and the rest from investments. A fixed amount of her income is tax-free, and she pays a standard rate of income tax on the rest. Build a model to find Nancy's net income.

Solution

Suppose Nancy gets an amount P from a pension fund, J from a job and I from investments. Her total income, TI, is:

$$TI = P + J + I$$

A fixed amount, F, is tax-free, and she pays income tax at a rate R on the rest. So her tax, X, is:

$$X = R * (TI - F) = R * (P + J + I - F)$$

and her net income, NI, is:

$$NI = TI - X = (P + J + I) - R * (P + J + I - F) = (P + J + I) * (1 - R) + R*F$$

WORKED EXAMPLE 1.2

James Morrisey is the operations manager for a parcel delivery service. He assumes that the cost of running a delivery van has three parts: a cost per kilometre to run the van, a cost per hour for the driver and a fixed cost for overheads.

(a) Build a model to describe this cost.

(b) Suppose the fixed cost is £40, the van costs £1 a kilometre, and the driver costs £20 an hour. How much would it cost to do a 60-kilometre journey at an average speed of 40 kilometres an hour?

Solution

(a) We can start by describing the cost as:

cost = fixed + number of hours * driver's hourly + number of kilometres * van's cost
　　　　 cost　　　　 driven　　　　　 cost　　　　　 driven　　　　 per kilometre

or　　　　$C = FC + (H*HC) + (K*KC)$

where　　C　= cost of running the van

　　　　　FC = fixed cost

　　　　　H　= hours of driving

　　　　　HC = hourly cost of driver

　　　　　K　= kilometres driven

　　　　　KC = cost per kilometre of the van

We can also use the average speed, as

　　　　　time = distance/speed

or　　　　$H = K/S$

so　　　　$C = FC + (K/S*HC) + (K*KC)$

(b) Now we know that $FC = 40$, $HC = 20$, $KC = 1$, $S = 40$ and $K = 60$. We can substitute these values to get:

$$C = FC + (K/S*HC) + (K*KC) = 40 + (60/40*20) + (60*1) = £130$$

Most business decisions are not isolated, but are part of a continuing management process. So it is important for managers to check the effects of earlier decisions. Then they can repeat good decisions, but avoid making the same mistakes again. This is the basis of *feedback*, as shown in Figure 1.4.

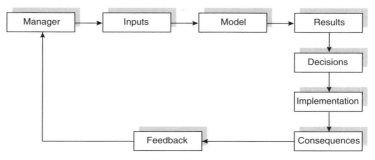

Figure 1.4   Feedback in decision-making.

IN SUMMARY

Models give a simplified view of real situations. They allow us to do experiments, without affecting real operations. Management science generally uses symbolic models.

Case example

Operating profit at Conrad Pfeiffer (Manufacturing) Inc.

Conrad Pfeiffer make a range of specialized pressure vessels. Their planned production for 1998 is 400 units, which is more than they have ever made before. One of their justifications for expanding production is the expected economies of scale. In other words, the more units they make, the lower is their unit cost.

The company did several analyses to support their claim. One of these is based on past profits, and can be summarized as follows. In 1995 they made 200 units with a gross profit of $3 million: in 1996 they made 250 units with a gross profit of $4 million. They believe that their gross profit, P, is related to the number of units made, N, by the equation:

$$P = 50*N^2 + 1000*N + 600\,000$$

So their gross profit with a production of 400 units is:

$$P = 50*400^2 + 1000*400 + 600\,000 = \$9 \text{ million}$$

Questions

- What other information can you get from the figures given?
- How reliable are the results?

1.2.2 The management science approach

Management science uses a wide range of symbolic models. Some of these are very simple and easy to work with: others are very complicated and take years to develop. Some situations are so complex that realistic models have never been built: some models are so complicated that they cannot be solved. Despite this great variety of models, management science has a standard approach – or *methodology* – for problems. This approach has four stages:

1   **Observation,** where managers examine the problem, collect data, identify details of the problem, set objectives, consider the context, and discuss various options.

2   **Modelling,** where they analyse data, build and test a model, and find initial solutions.

3   **Experimentation,** where they test solutions to see if they match predictions, search for optimal solutions, consider the effects of using other solutions, check alternative values for decision variables, collect other data, and make recommendations.

4   **Implementation,** where they make final decisions, set values for decision variables, implement these decisions, monitor actual performance, and keep models up to date.

There are different versions of these four stages. One popular version has six steps, and was described by Ackoff in 1962. This is not meant to be a recipe for all studies, but it does show some useful features:

1   Defining the problem
2   Building a model
3   Testing the model
4   Getting a solution to the problem
5   Implementing the solution
6   Controlling the solution

Defining the problem

This is the first stage of any project – and is the one where many go wrong. In this stage we describe the problem as fully as possible, typically giving:

- the real problem – which may not be the problem originally presented
- the decision makers – who may not be the people who present the problem
- their objectives – and how they measure success
- variables in the problem
- possible alternatives or courses of action
- the context of the problem

Building a model

Now we have a description of the problem, we can start building a model. For this we:

- identify and measure the relevant variables, and
- establish relationships between variables

So we build a model which relates the decision variables (which we can control, such as production quantity, selling price and advertising budget), and the external variables (which we cannot control, such as demand, raw material costs and competition). One useful approach to model building starts with simple models, tests them, and only adds more details if the results are not good enough.

Testing the model

We have to test the model to make sure that it gives a good enough view of the real situation. This testing is not a separate stage at the end of modelling, but is done continually as the model is built. Early tests might check separate parts of the model, with final testing of the model as a whole.

The usual way of testing a model is to use historical data. For this we substitute old data into the model and see how closely its predictions match actual outcomes. If the difference is reasonably small, we can accept the model and use its results. But if the model gives the wrong answers we have to make changes. Then we might find that:

- the model contains variables that are not relevant
- the model omits variables that are relevant
- there are mistakes in the functions relating variables, or
- some variables have been given the wrong numerical values

Getting a solution to the problem

After we have built a model, we must get a solution. In other words, we find the best values for the decision variables. There are several ways of doing this, including:

- **analytical methods** – which use a defined procedure to get a solution
- **numerical methods** – which iteratively improve numerical solutions
- **simulation methods** – which give a dynamic view of a problem.

We will meet these later in the book.

Sometimes it is too difficult to get an optimal solution to a problem, and then we have to use *heuristics*. These use rules of thumb and experience to give reasonable solutions – but with much less effort. Transport operators might, for example, use heuristics to find routes for their lorries; these routes might be 5% longer than optimal routes, but they take only one thousandth of the effort to find.

Implementing the solution

Even if we do the previous stages well, the work will be wasted unless we implement the results. But there are several reasons why even good results are not implemented:

- the new solution is not much better than the existing solution, and it is not worth making changes
- an organization may not have enough money for the investment needed
- the problem may change or go away
- managers may change their minds about the objectives
- the solution may not be presented well, so that managers are not convinced of its value

Controlling the solution

After the results are implemented, we can see how they work in practice. But it is difficult to judge them because:

- only one decision was implemented, and there is no way of knowing how well other decisions would have worked
- only some results can be measured, while others rely on subjective opinions
- the implementation might not have been done properly
- external factors might change
- there may be uncertainty which gives variable results

Control of the solution takes these factors into account, and adjusts the model to deal with changing circumstances.

IN SUMMARY

Management science often uses a standard approach to problems. We can consider this methodology in six steps – starting with formulating the problem and ending with implementing the solution.

Self-assessment questions

1.6 What is a model?

1.7 Why would you use a model?

1.8 What kind of model is most widely used in management science?

1.9 Is there a single correct model for any situation?

1.10 What are the four main stages in the management science approach?

CHAPTER REVIEW

This chapter introduced the scope and methods of management science. In particular it:

- defined management science as the application of scientific methods to the problems met by managers
- showed why management science is important for decision-making
- discussed management science in terms of the types of problems tackled, types of solutions used, and a general methodology
- discussed the importance of models
- described a general approach to solving problems

KEY TERMS

decision variables　　　*methodology*
external variables　　　*models*
feedback　　　　　　　*quantitative methods*
heuristics　　　　　　*scientific methods*
management science　*symbolic models*
managers

Case study

Perran Downs Pre-School Education Centre

The government has promised more resources for nursery education. This allows children to benefit from some formal education when they are still too young to go to school.

George and Daphne Phillips want to open a pre-school education centre in their local village. They think they can find suitable premises, but have to arrange a loan. Their bank manager will only give the loan if he is convinced that the centre will be a success. George and Daphne now have to make a convincing presentation about their centre.

Questions

- How should George and Daphne set about writing their presentation?
- What information do they need to support their case?
- What might their final presentation contain?

Problems

1.1 Last year's South European Tennis Championships had 1947 entries in the women's singles. If this was a standard knockout tournament, how many matches were played to find the champion?

1.2 A family of three is having grilled steak for dinner. They like their steaks grilled for 10 minutes on each side. Unfortunately, their grill pan is only big enough to grill one side of two steaks at a time. How long will it take to cook dinner?

1.3 A shopkeeper buys an article for £25. A customer buys it for £35 and pays with a £50 note. The shopkeeper does not have enough change, so he goes to a neighbour and changes the £50 note. A week later he is told the £50 note was a forgery, so he immediately repays his neighbour the £50. How much does the shopkeeper lose in this transaction?

1.4 Design a scheme for doctors to see how bad a stomach pain is.

1.5 The accounts for a small restaurant find that each customer pays an average of £15 for food and £8 for drinks. The food for each customer costs about £10 and the drinks cost £2. The restaurant also has fixed costs of £1000 a week for wages, rent, heat, and so on. At weekends the restaurant is about twice as busy as it is on weekdays. What information can you get from these figures?

Discussion questions

1.1 Managers often have little knowledge of science. How difficult do you think it is to convince them of the benefits of using scientific methods? How could you overcome these difficulties?

1.2 What is 'the scientific method'? Can it really be used for management problems?

1.3 Suppose you have a choice between: (a) a simple model that represents the real situation reasonably well, and (b) a sophisticated mathematical model that represents the real situation as accurately as possible. What are the benefits of each model?

1.4 Why is it important for a manager to understand both quantitative and qualitative aspects of decisions? Can you think of a real problem which does not involve both of these?

1.5 In 1981 only 47% of managers had any general training in management lasting more than a week. Do you think this situation has improved?

Financial models | 2

CHAPTER OUTLINE

Chapter 1 showed how management science uses quantitative models. In this chapter we are going to look at some models for finance. After reading the chapter you should be able to:

- calculate break-even points
- understand how the value of money changes over time
- calculate net present values and internal rates of return
- find the best time to replace equipment
- work with depreciated values and sinking funds.
- use scoring models

2.1 | Break-even point

2.1.1 Making a profit

Organizations usually want to make a ***profit***. This shows how much the organization's revenue is greater than its expenses:

> profit = total income − total costs

When a company makes a number of different products, it will want to know the profit on each one. Suppose we take one product that sells at a fixed price per unit. Then the income is:

income = price per unit * number of units sold

The costs are a little more awkward, as some are fixed regardless of the number of units made, while others vary with the output. If a company rents a machine to make a product, the cost of renting may be fixed regardless of the number of units made, but the cost of raw materials will vary. So we can divide the total cost into two parts:

total cost = fixed cost + variable cost
= fixed cost + (cost per unit * number of units made)

This total cost rises linearly with the number made, as shown in Figure 2.1.

You have probably met these costs with running a car. The total cost is a combination of fixed costs (payments on a car loan, road tax, insurance, etc.) and a variable cost for each kilometre travelled (for petrol, oil, tyres, depreciation, etc.).

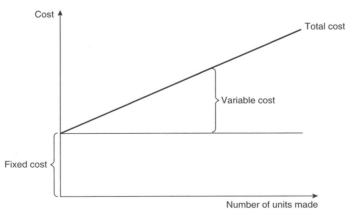

Figure 2.1 Variation of costs with number of units made.

Now we can compare the total cost of making N units of a product with the income from selling them. In particular, we can find the ***break-even point***, which is the number of units the company must sell before it starts to make a profit. Suppose a company spends £200 000 on research and development before selling a new product. During normal production each unit costs £20 to make and sells for £30. The company will only make a profit when it has recovered the original £200 000. This happens at the break-even point. In this example each unit sold contributes £30 − £20 = £10 to the company, so it must sell 200 000/10 = 20 000 units to cover the original investment.

We can define a break-even point when:

$$\text{income} = \text{total cost}$$

or

| price per unit | * | number of units sold | = | fixed cost | + | cost per unit | * | number of units made |

$$UP * N \qquad\qquad = FC + UC * N$$

where

FC = fixed cost
UC = variable cost of making a unit
UP = selling price of a unit
N = number of units made and sold

Rearranging this equation gives the break-even point as:

$$\textbf{break-even point} = N = \frac{FC}{UP - UC}$$

Both the income and total cost rise linearly with the number of units, so we can plot the graph shown in Figure 2.2.

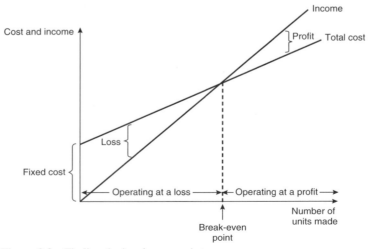

Figure 2.2 Finding the break-even point.

You can see from this graph that:

- if the number of units made equals the break-even point, the income exactly matches the costs
- if the number of units made is more than the break-even point, the company makes a profit of $N*(UP-UC) - FC$
- if the number of units made is less than the break-even point, the company makes a loss of $FC - N*(UP - UC)$

WORKED EXAMPLE 2.1

Altos Carparts sell an exhaust system for £130 a unit. The fixed costs for buildings, machines and employees are £6000 a week, while raw material and other variable costs are £50 a unit.

(a) What is the break-even point for the system?

(b) What is the profit if Altos sell 130 units a week?

(c) What is the profit if the selling price is lowered to £80 and sales rise to 250 a week?

Solution

(a) We know that:

$$FC = £6000 \text{ a week} = \text{fixed cost each week}$$
$$UC = £50 \text{ a unit} = \text{unit cost}$$
$$UP = £130 \text{ a unit} = \text{unit selling price}$$

So we can find the break-even point, N, by substituting in the equation:

$$N = \frac{FC}{UP - UC} = \frac{6000}{130 - 50} = 75 \text{ units}$$

If Altos sell 75 systems a week, their income exactly covers total cost (see Figure 2.3). If they sell less than 75 a week, they do not cover costs and make a loss of $6000 - (130 - 50)*N$. If they sell more than 75 units a week, they cover all costs and make a profit of $(130 - 50)*N - 6000$.

(b) If Altos sell 130 systems a week, this is more than the break-even point and they make a profit of:

$$(UP - UC)*N - FC = (130 - 50)*100 - 6000 = £2000 \text{ a week}$$

We can check this by finding:

- variable cost = cost per unit * units made = $UC*N = 50*100 = £5000$ a week
- total cost = fixed cost + variable cost = $6000 + 5000 = £11\,000$ a week

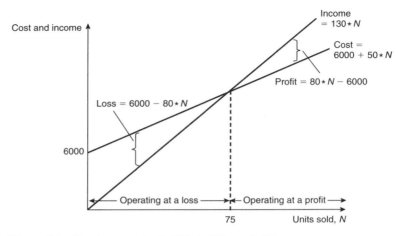

Figure 2.3 Break-even point for Worked Example 2.1.

- income = unit price * units sold = $UP * N$ = 130 * 100 = £13 000 a week
- profit = income − total cost = 13 000 − 11 000 = £2000 a week

(c) Now UP = £80 a unit = unit selling price

So the new break-even point, N, is:

$$N = \frac{FC}{UP - UC} = \frac{6000}{80 - 50} = 200 \text{ units}$$

Weekly sales, N, are 250 units which is above the break-even point of 200, so Altos make a profit of:

$$(UP - UC) * N - FC = (80 - 50) * 250 - 6000 = £1500 \text{ a week}$$

This shows that Altos can still make a profit with a low selling price provided their sales are high enough.

WORKED EXAMPLE 2.2

NorthAir is considering a new weekly service between Aberdeen and Calgary using its existing aeroplanes. Each of these has a capacity of 240 passengers, with fixed costs of £30 000 a flight and variable costs amounting to 50% of the ticket price. The airline is planning to sell tickets at £200 each. How many passengers will it need to break even on this route? Does this seem a reasonable number?

Solution

We can find the break-even point from:

$$N = FC/(UP - UC) = 30\,000/(200 - 100) = 300$$

Unfortunately, this break-even point is more than the aeroplane capacity of 240 passengers, so the route cannot run at a profit. If the airline could easily attract 240 passengers a week, it might increase prices to cover all costs. To break even with 240 passengers the airline needs to charge a new, higher price, *HP*, with:

$$N = FC/(HP - UC)$$

or $$240 = 30\,000/(HP - 0.5 * HP)$$

or $$HP = £250$$

A break-even analysis shows the number of units that must be sold to make a profit. It can also help with other types of decision, such as the choice between buying or leasing equipment, making sure new equipment has enough capacity, deciding whether to buy an item or make it within the company, and the choice between competitive tenders for services.

But there is one common problem with calculating the break-even point. If an organization makes several products, it can be difficult to find the amount of overheads to allocate to the fixed cost of each. This largely depends on the accounting conventions used. If an organization constantly changes its product mix, normal accounting practices will constantly change the amount of overheads assigned to each product. Then the costs of making a particular product can change, even though there has been no change in the product itself or the way it is made.

Case example

Electricity prices

There is no way of storing large amounts of electricity, so generating companies have to vary the amount of electricity they supply to match their customers' demands. This means that they close down generators when demand is low, and open them up again when demand is high. But they cannot just switch off generators and then restart them, so they keep the generators ticking over and giving a low output. At night, when demand is low, they actually generate more electricity than they need. Rather than waste this, they offer customers incentives to switch their demand to 'off-peak' times.

In 1995, one local electricity board offered a customer the choice of two alternative prices. The normal rate had standing charges of £18.20 a quarter, with each unit of electricity used costing £0.142. A special economy rate had standing charges of £22.70 a quarter, with each unit of electricity during the day costing £0.162, but each unit used during the night costing only £0.082.

If the consumer used an average of D units a quarter during the day and N units a quarter during the night, their costs were:

$$\text{normal rate:} \quad 18.20 + 0.142 * (D + N)$$
$$\text{economy rate:} \quad 22.70 + 0.162 * D + 0.082 * N$$

It was cheaper to use the economy rate when:

$$22.7 + 0.162 * D + 0.082 * N < 18.2 + 0.142 * (D+N)$$

$$4.5 < 0.06 * N - 0.02 * D$$

$$D < 3 * N - 225$$

In other words, if consumption during the day was less than three times the night consumption minus 225 units, it was cheaper to use the economy rate. These prices are shown in Figure 2.4. At any point below the line the economy rate is cheaper; at any point above the line the standard rate is cheaper; at any point on the line it does not matter which rate is used.

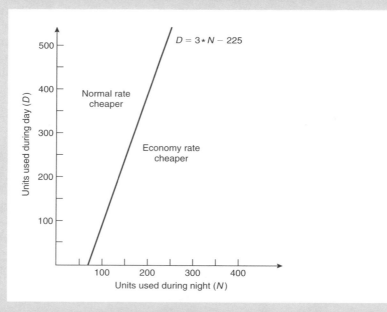

Figure 2.4 Break-even analysis for electricity supply.

> ## IN SUMMARY
>
> **We can classify costs as either fixed or variable. Income must cover both of these before a product makes a profit. The break-even point is the number of units that must be sold before an organization covers all costs and starts to make a profit.**

2.1.2 Economies of scale

Break-even analyses show one way in which organizations can get *economies of scale*, where the average cost per unit falls as the number of units made increases. We know that:

$$\text{total cost} = \text{fixed cost} + \text{variable cost}$$

or $$TC = FC + N * UC$$

So we can find the average cost of making a unit by dividing the total cost by the number of units, N:

$$\text{average cost per unit} = TC/N = FC/N + UC$$

As N increases, the average cost per unit falls, because a smaller proportion of the fixed cost is recovered by each unit sold (as shown in Figure 2.5).

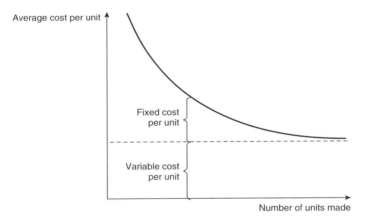

Figure 2.5 Variation of average cost with number of units made.

WORKED EXAMPLE 2.3

The Lombardi Restaurant serves 200 meals a day at an average price of £20. The variable cost of each meal is £10 and there are fixed costs of running the restaurant of £1750 a day.

(a) How much profit does the restaurant make?

(b) What is the average cost of a meal?

(c) How much does the average cost of a meal fall if the number served rises to 250 a day?

Solution

(a) The break-even point is:

$$N = FC/(UP - UC) = 1750/(20 - 10) = 175$$

Actual sales are above this, and the profit is:

$$\text{profit} = N*(UP-UC) - FC = 200*(20 - 10) - 1750 = £250 \text{ a day}$$

(b) The average cost of a meal is:

$$\text{average cost} = \text{total cost/number of meals}$$

$$TC/N = FC/N + UC = 1750/200 + 10 = £18.75 \text{ a meal}$$

(c) Serving 250 meals a day reduces the average cost to:

$$\text{average cost} = 1750/250 + 10 = £17 \text{ a meal}$$

In practice, spreading the fixed costs over more units is only one reason for economies of scale. The unit costs might go down because people become more familiar with the operations and work faster, specialized equipment can be bought, there are discounts on raw materials bought in bulk, marketing becomes more efficient, problems which disrupt operations are sorted out, and so on.

People often think that economies of scale mean that facilities should be as large as possible. But there can also be *diseconomies of scale*. Here the advantage of reduced unit cost is more than offset by increased bureaucracy, difficulties of communication, more complex management hierarchies, increased costs of supervision, perceived reduction in the importance of individuals, and so on. This usually means that there are economies of scale up to an optimal size, and then diseconomies of scale (as shown in Figure 2.6).

IN SUMMARY

Spreading fixed costs over more units – together with other effects – can give economies of scale. These reduce the unit cost as the number of units made increases. There may also be diseconomies of scale.

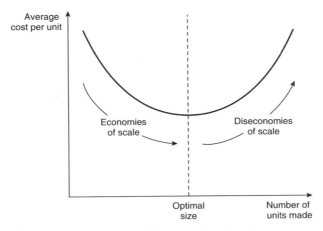

Figure 2.6   Economies and diseconomies of scale.

Self-assessment questions

2.1   What does the 'variable cost' vary with?

2.2   What is the 'break-even point'?

2.3   The break-even point for a product is 1500 units a week. What does it mean if actual production is 1200 units a week?

2.4   'Economies of scale mean that it is always better to have a single large factory than a number of smaller ones'. Do you think this is true?

‖ 2.2 ‖ Value of money over time

2.2.1 Interest rates

If you want to buy a house, there are several ways of paying for it. One option is to save enough money and then pay cash. Unfortunately, house prices always seem to rise faster than savings. A better option is to save a deposit and then borrow the rest of the money as a mortgage. You repay this mortgage over a long period – typically 25 years. Although the total repayments are two or three times the original amount you borrow, most people still think this is a good investment.

Anyone borrowing money must pay the lender *interest*. The amount borrowed is called the ***principal*** and the time for which it is borrowed is the duration of the loan. The amount of interest is usually quoted as an annual percentage of the principal, so a typical interest rate is 10% a year.

Suppose you put £1000 into a bank account, and it earns interest of 10% a year. At the end of the first year you have earned $1000 * 0.1 = £100$ interest, so you have the original investment of £1000 plus the interest of £100. In general, if you put an amount of money AP into a bank account and leave it untouched for a year earning interest at an annual rate I, at the end of the year you will have an amount:

$$AP * (1 + I)$$

where: AP = amount invested at present
   I = interest rate as a decimal fraction

With **compound interest**, if you leave this money untouched for a second year, you will earn interest not only on the initial amount deposited, but also on the interest earned in the first year. This amounts to:

$$\{AP * (1 + I)\} * (1 + I) \quad \text{or} \quad AP * (1 + I)^2$$

The amount of money increases in this compound way, so that at the end of 3 years there will be $AP * (1 + I)^3$ in the account. Then at any point N years in the future there will be AF in the account, where:

$$AF = AP * (1 + I)^N$$

Figure 2.7 shows AF – the amount of money in the future – for an initial investment of £1 and a range of interest rates.

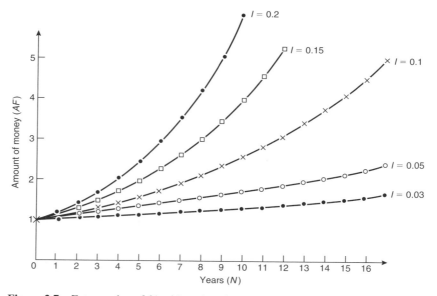

Figure 2.7   Future value of £1 with various interest rates.

WORKED EXAMPLE 2.4

If you leave £1000 in a bank account earning 5% compound interest a year, how much will be in the account at the end of 5 years? How much will there be at the end of 20 years?

Solution

We know that:

$$AP = £1000$$

$$I = 0.05$$

With compound interest the future amount in the account is $AF = AP * (1 + I)^N$

At the end of five years there will be:

$$AF = 1000 * (1 + 0.05)^5 = 1000 * 1.2763 = £1276$$

At the end of 20 years there will be:

$$AF = 1000 * (1 + 0.05)^{20} = 1000 * 2.6533 = £2653$$

Interest rates are usually quoted as annual figures, but we can use any convenient periods, such as 1% a month or 0.03% a day. There are several ways of calculating interest, and to avoid confusion lenders quote an ***annual percentage rate (APR)***. This is the true cost of borrowing. Suppose you borrow £100 with interest payable of 2% at the end of each month. Without doing the arithmetic, you might assume that this is the same as 2 * 12 = 24% a year. But it is not.

- Borrowing £100 at 24% APR raises the debt at the end of the year to:

$$AF = AP * (1 + I)^N = 100 * (1 + 0.24)^1 = £124$$

- Borrowing £100 at 2% a month raises the debt at the end of 12 months to:

$$AF = AP * (1 + I)^N = 100 * (1 + 0.02)^{12} = £126.82$$

IN SUMMARY

The value of money varies over time, and a given amount at present can generate a larger amount in the future. Money invested with compound interest increases over time so that $AF = AP * (1 + I)^N$.

2.2.2 Present value of money

An amount of money AP invested now will have a value of $AF = AP * (1 + I)^N$ at a time N periods in the future. Turning this around, we can say that an amount AF, N periods in the future, has a present value of AP, where:

$$AP = AF/(1 + I)^N = AF * (1 + I)^{-N}$$

Calculating the present value of an amount in the future is called ***discounting to present value***. We can use this discounting to compare amounts of money that are available at different times.

WORKED EXAMPLE 2.5

A company must choose one of two alternative new products. The profits from these products are phased over many years, but they can be summarized as:

● product 1 gives a profit of £300 000 in 5 years' time
● product 2 gives a profit of £500 000 in 10 years' time

Which product should the company choose if it uses a discounting rate of 20% a year?

Solution

The company wants to compare amounts of money available at different times. It can do this by finding the present value of both amounts.

Product 1: $\qquad AP = AF * (1 + I)^{-N} = 300\,000 * (1 + 0.2)^{-5} = £120\,563$

Product 2: $\qquad AP = AF * (1 + I)^{-N} = 500\,000 * (1 + 0.2)^{-10} = £80\,753$

Product 1 has a higher present value and is the better option.

Finding present values is particularly useful for large projects that have payments and incomes spread over long periods. Then we can discount all amounts to their present values, and subtracting the present value of all costs from the present value of all revenues gives a ***net present value***:

> **net present value** = sum of discounted revenues − sum of discounted costs

If the net present value is negative a project will make a loss and it should not be started. If different projects each have a positive net present value, the best is the one with the highest net present value.

WORKED EXAMPLE 2.6

Zbigniew Palucek's company wants to compare three projects with the following initial costs and revenues (each in thousands of pounds):

Project	Initial cost	Net revenue generated in each year				
		1	2	3	4	5
A	1000	500	400	300	200	100
B	1000	200	200	300	400	400
C	500	50	200	200	100	50

The company only has enough resources to start one project. If they use a discounting rate of 10%, which should they choose?

Solution

Conventional accounting often takes an **average rate of return**, which is the average annual revenue as a percentage of the initial investment. In this example the average rates of return are:

	Project A	Project B	Project C
Initial cost	1000	1000	500
Total revenue	1500	1500	600
Average annual revenue	300	300	120
Average rate of return	30%	30%	24%

Projects A and B have the same average rate of return, while project C is not as good. But if you look at the money flows for projects A and B, you can see that A offers more in early years while B offers more in later years. To give a better comparison Zbigniew should find the net present value of each project. So, for project A:

$$500 \text{ in year 1 has a present value of } 500/1.1 = 454.55$$
$$400 \text{ in year 2 has a present value of } 400/1.1^2 = 330.58$$
$$300 \text{ in year 3 has a present value of } 300/1.1^3 = 225.39$$

and so on. These calculations can easily be done on a spreadsheet, as shown in Figure 2.8.

Project A has the highest net present value and is the one that the company should start. Project C has a negative net present value – showing a loss – and the company should clearly avoid this alternative.

	A	B	C	D	E	F	G	H
1	**Net present value**							
2								
3			**Project A**		**Project B**		**Project C**	
4	**Year**	**Discount factor**	**Revenue**	**Present value**	**Revenue**	**Present value**	**Revenue**	**Present value**
5	1	1.1	500	454.55	200	181.82	50	45.45
6	2	1.21	400	330.58	200	165.29	200	165.29
7	3	1.331	300	225.39	300	225.39	200	150.26
8	4	1.4641	200	136.60	400	273.21	100	68.30
9	5	1.61051	100	62.09	400	248.37	50	31.05
10	**Totals**		**1500**	**1209.21**	**1500**	**1094.08**	**600**	**460.35**
11								
12	**Present values**							
13		**Revenues**		1209.21		1094.8		460.35
14		**Costs**		1000		1000		500
15								
16		**Net present values**		**209.21**		**94.08**		**-39.65**

Figure 2.8 Net present values for Worked Example 2.6.

IN SUMMARY

We can compare revenues and payments made at different times by discounting them to present values. The net present value shows the difference between the discounted costs and discounted benefits.

Case example

PowerGen/GEC Alsthom

GEC Alsthom is an Anglo-French supplier of equipment for power stations. In 1993 they won an order from PowerGen for a 1440 megawatt power station at Connah's Quay in North Wales. This project was due for completion in 1995. Usually in large construction projects the customer pays 10–20% of the cost up front, with progress payments during construction, and a final payment on completion. But in this case PowerGen paid the total cost of £450 million up front in exchange for a discount of about 7% from GEC Alsthom. This arrangement gave PowerGen the advantages of a price discount, together with some tax benefits in a year where they made pre-tax profits of £470 million. GEC Alsthom had the benefits of cash in hand from the start of the project.

Case example

Early retirement options

Henry Miller spent most of his working life as a school teacher in Yorkshire. For the past 10 years he has contributed to a 'with profits life endowment policy'. He is 55 years old and his employers have given him a generous incentive to take early retirement. Now he must decide what to do with his endowment policy. His income is much smaller than it was, so Henry does not want to continue paying premiums on the policy until it matures when he is 65. But the insurance company will give him a generous terminal bonus if he keeps up the policy.

Henry has just got some estimates of the policy's value. These estimated values are not guaranteed, but it seems that he could cash in the policy now and get £10 000, or he could keep it for the next 10 years and get around £20 000. Because Henry will pay very little in tax, he thinks that he can invest the money and get a tax-free return of around 10% a year. He did some calculations, and found the present values of the two amounts.

- Taking £10 000 now. This clearly has a present value of £10 000.
- Taking £20 000 in 10 years. Discounting this by 10% a year for 10 years gives a present value of $20\,000/(1 + 0.1)^{10} = £7711$.

Taking £10 000 now has a higher value, and this is the option that Henry should choose.

2.2.3 Internal rate of return

To compare the three projects in Worked Example 2.6 we took a fixed discounting rate and calculated three net present values. This approach needs a reasonable discounting rate. Using a simple interest rate is not good enough, as it ignores the effects of inflation, opportunity costs, taxes, changing rates, interest rates, exchange rates, risk, and everything else. In practice, it can be very difficult to find a discounting rate that takes all these factors into account.

An alternative approach finds the discounting rate that leads to a specified net present value. In other words, it keeps the same net present value for each project, and calculates three different discounting rates. Then the best project is the one with the highest discounting rate. Usually we find the discounting rate that gives a net present value of zero, and this is called the *internal rate of return* (*IRR*):

> The **internal rate of return** is the discounting rate that gives a net present value of zero.

A minor difficulty with internal rates of return is that there is no straightforward formula for calculating them. So we can use two approaches.

1 **Draw a graph of net present value against discounting rate**. This gives a straight line graph, and the internal rate of return is the point where this has the value zero – which is the point where it crosses the x-axis. Figure 2.9 shows a graph of net present value against discounting rate for Project B of Worked Example 2.6. As you can see, the internal rate of return is about 13%.

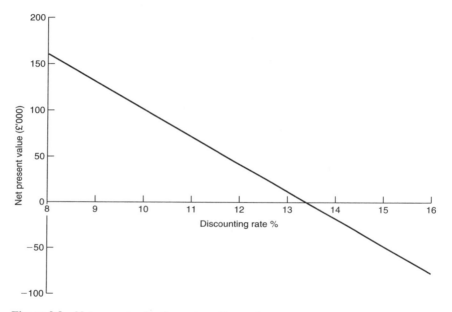

Figure 2.9 Net present value for various discounting rates.

2 **Use iterative calculations.** Looking again at Project B in Worked Example 2.6, if we use a discounting rate of 10% we get a net present value of £94 080. If we use a discounting rate of 14%, we get a net present value of −£23 600. So a discounting rate of 10% gives a positive net present value while a discounting rate of 14% gives a negative value; obviously the internal rate of return – which gives a net present value of zero – must lie between these two. Now we can do some more calculations to narrow the range until we get a reasonably accurate figure.

In practice, of course, we can easily do these calculations on a spreadsheet. Most spreadsheets have standard functions for internal rates of return, and one example is shown in Figure 2.10. Here the spreadsheet automatically calculates an internal rate of return of 13.14%. Then it discounts the values to check that the net present value is zero.

	A	B	C	D	E	F	G
1	**Internal rate of return**						
2							
3	**Calculation**			**Check**			
4							
5	**Year**	**Revenue**		**Discount rate**		**Discounted revenue**	
6	0	−1000		1		−1000.0	
7	1	200		1.1314		176.8	
8	2	200		1.280066		156.2	
9	3	300		1.448267		207.1	
10	4	400		1.638569		244.1	
11	5	400		1.853877		215.8	
12							
13	**IRR**	**13.14%**			**Total**	**0.0**	

Figure 2.10 Spreadsheet for internal rate of return calculation.

WORKED EXAMPLE 2.7

What is the internal rate of return for an investment which gives the following net cash flow:

Year	0	1	2	3	4	5	6	7	8
Net cash flow	−1200	−2000	−200	800	1800	2100	1500	800	450

Solution

Figure 2.11 shows the calculations for the internal rate of return on a spreadsheet.

	A	B	C	D	E	F	G
1	**Internal rate of return**						
2							
3	**Calculation**			**Check**			
4							
5	**Year**	**Revenue**		**Discount rate**		**Discounted revenue**	
6	0	−1200		1		−1200	
7	1	−2000		1.2		−1667	
8	2	−200		1.44		−139	
9	3	800		1.728		463	
10	4	1800		2.0736		868	
11	5	2100		2.48832		844	
12	6	1500		2.985984		502	
13	7	800		3.583181		223	
14	8	450		4.299817		105	
15							
16	**IRR**	**20.00%**			**Total**	**0**	

Figure 2.11 Internal rate of return for Worked Example 2.7.

The internal rate of return is the discounting rate that gives a net present value of zero. We can compare different investments by finding the internal rate of return for each. The best investment is the one with the highest internal rate of return.

2.2.4 Continuous discounting

If you leave money in a bank, the interest is often calculated at the end of every day. This calculation can become rather messy. With compounding every day, for example, the value of an amount AP in 10 years' time is $AF = AP * (1 + I)^{3650}$. As well as being messy, this kind of calculation is affected by rounding errors. So it is sometimes easier to use an approximation, and the best is:

$$AF = AP * e^{I * N}$$

where e is the exponential constant with value 2.71828.... This is the basis of **continuous discounting** or compounding. The calculations are exactly the same as for discrete discounting except:

$$(1 + I)^N \text{ is replaced by } e^{I * N}$$

WORKED EXAMPLE 2.8

How much will an initial investment of £1000 earning interest of 1% a month be worth at the end of 10 years?

Solution

Using discrete compounding:

$$AF = AP * (1 + I)^N = 1000 * (1.01)^{120} = £3300$$

Using continuous compounding:

$$AF = AP * e^{I * N} = 1000 * e^{0.01 * 120} = £3320$$

These answers are slightly different, but the continuous approximation seems to work well.

$\boxed{IN\ SUMMARY}$

The calculations for frequent compounding or discounting can become awkward. Continuous discounting gives an approximation for such calculations by replacing $(1 + I)^N$ by e^{I*N}.

Self-assessment questions

2.5 Is £1000 at present worth
(a) more than £1000 in 5 years' time
(b) less than £1000 in 5 years' time
(c) the same as £1000 in 5 years' time
(d) cannot say without more information?

2.6 Is an interest rate of 12% a year the same as 1% a month?

2.7 How can you compare the net benefits of two projects, one of which lasts for 5 years and the other for 7 years?

2.8 What is a discounting rate?

2.9 What is continuous discounting?

2.3 ‖ Replacing equipment

The performance of almost everything declines with age – cars go rusty, machines break down, computers get faults, opera singers lose their voices, and so on. Routine maintenance can keep equipment working efficiently, but there comes a point when the repairs are too expensive and it is cheaper to buy a replacement. In this section we will look at three questions about equipment replacement. When is the best time to replace equipment? How much is existing equipment worth? How can we save enough money to buy the replacement?

2.3.1 When is the best time to replace equipment?

Some replacement decisions – like building a new power station, office block, factory, aeroplane or ship – involve a lot of money. Other decisions are less expensive, but they still need careful planning. Figure 2.12 shows the effect of planned replacement. Equipment is replaced when its performance declines to the point where it is no longer acceptable – the output may be too low, quality too poor, breakdowns too frequent, costs too high, etc. One way of tackling replacement decisions is shown in the following example.

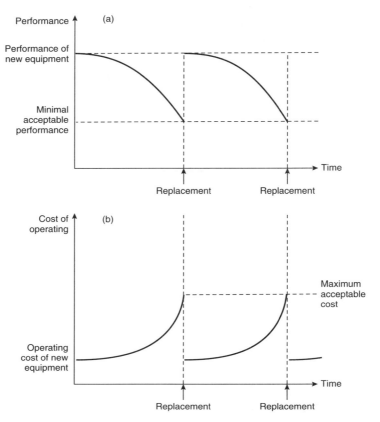

Figure 2.12 Performance and costs varying with age.

WORKED EXAMPLE 2.9

On the first of February each year Hamilton Brothers review the performance of their production machines so that they can get replacements before the end of the financial year. The cost of replacing each machine is £100 000. The following table shows the expected resale values and running costs for each year. What is the best age to replace the machines?

Age of machine (years)	1	2	3	4	5
Resale value (£)	50 000	30 000	15 000	10 000	5 000
Running cost in previous year (£)	5 000	9 000	15 000	60 000	

Solution

When Hamilton sell a machine, the total cost during its lifetime is in two parts:

- a capital cost, equal to the difference between the price of a new machine and the resale value of the old one
- a total running cost, which is the cumulative running cost over the machine's life

If Hamilton sell a machine after 1 year of use:

- capital cost is 100 000 – 50 000 = £50 000
- running cost is £5000

The total cost of using the machine for 1 year is £55 000.
If they sell a machine after 2 years:

- capital cost is 100 000 – 30 000 = £70 000
- running cost is £5000 in the first year plus £9000 in the second year

The total cost of using the machine for 2 years is £84 000, which gives an average of £42 000 a year.

Repeating these calculations for other ages of replacement gives the values shown in the spreadsheet in Figure 2.13.

	A	B	C	D	E	F	G	H
1	**Equipment replacement**							
2								
3	**Age of**	**Resale**	**Capital**	**Annual**	**Cumulative**	**Total**	**Average**	**Minimum**
4	**replacement**	**value**	**cost**	**running cost**	**running cost**	**cost**	**cost**	
5						**(C+E)**	**(F/A)**	
6								
7	0	100000	0	0	0			
8	1	50000	50000	5000	5000	55000	55000	
9	2	30000	70000	9000	14000	84000	42000	
10	3	15000	85000	15000	29000	114000	38000	******
11	4	10000	90000	41000	70000	160000	40000	
12	5	5000	95000	60000	130000	225000	45000	

Figure 2.13   Finding the best age to replace machines.

To get the lowest average annual cost Hamilton should replace the machines after 3 years, as shown in Figure 2.14.

For these results we have assumed that the value of money is constant over time. Earlier in the chapter we saw how to discount future amounts to their present value, so we can discount the values in this example to their present values. For this we will use a discounting rate of 1% a month.

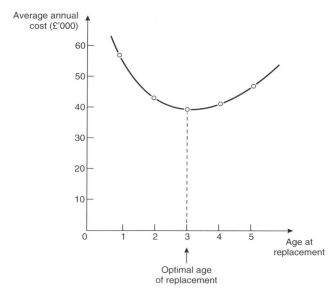

Figure 2.14 Average annual cost for Worked Example 2.9.

If Hamilton replace the machines after 1 year:

- The capital cost is the purchase price minus the resale value – but now they discount the resale value by 1.01^{12}.
- They have to discount running costs in the same way. As these occur more or less uniformly over the year, they can use an average discounting factor based on the middle of the year (i.e. month 6) equal to 1.01^{6}.

Then the total cost becomes:

- capital cost $= 100\,000 - 50\,000/1.01^{12} = 100\,000 - 44\,372 = £55\,628$
- running cost $= 5000/1.01^{6} = £4710$
- total cost $= 55\,628 + 4710 = £60\,338$

Similarly selling the machines after 2 years of operation has:

- capital cost $= 100\,000 - 30\,000/1.01^{24} = 100\,000 - 23\,627 = £76\,373$
- running cost $= 5000/1.01^{6} + 9000/1.01^{18} = 4710 + 7524 = £12\,234$
- total cost $= £88\,607$ or $£44\,304$ a year

Repeating these calculations for other operating periods gives the results shown in the spreadsheet in Figure 2.15.

Future costs have been discounted to give lower present values, and the best solution is to replace the machines every 4 years.

	A	B	C	D	E	F
1	**Equipment replacement**					
2						
3	**Age of**	**Resale**	**Capital**	**Discounting**	**Discounted**	
4	**replacement**	**value**	**cost**	**factor**	**capital cost**	
5	0	100000	0	1	0.00	
6	1	50000	50000	1.12682503	55627.54	
7	2	30000	70000	1.269734649	76373.02	
8	3	15000	85000	1.430768784	89516.13	
9	4	10000	90000	1.612226078	93797.40	
10	5	5000	95000	1.816696699	97247.75	
11						
12	**Age of**	**Running**	**Discounting**	**Discounted**	**Cumulative**	
13	**replacement**	**cost**	**factor**	**running cost**	**running cost**	
14	0	0	1	0.00	0.00	
15	1	5000	1.061520151	4710.23	4710.23	
16	2	9000	1.196147476	7524.16	12234.38	
17	3	15000	1.347848915	11128.84	23363.23	
18	4	41000	1.518789895	26995.18	50358.40	
19	5	60000	1.711410469	35058.80	85417.20	
20						
21	**Age of**	**Capital**	**Running**	**Total**	**Average**	**Minimum**
22	**replacement**	**cost**	**cost**	**cost**	**cost**	
23	0	0	0.00	0.00	0.00	
24	1	55627.53874	4710.23	60337.76	60337.76	
25	2	76373.01618	12234.38	88607.40	44303.70	
26	3	89516.12576	23363.23	112879.35	37626.45	
27	4	93797.39595	50358.40	144155.80	36038.95	******
28	5	97247.75192	85417.20	182664.95	36532.99	

Figure 2.15 Discounting the costs in Worked Example 2.9.

WORKED EXAMPLE 2.10

Belmont Leasing buy new cars for £18 000 each, and have the resale values and maintenance costs shown below. What is the best age to replace the cars if Belmont uses a continuous discounting rate of 1% a month?

Age of car (years)	1	2	3	4	5	6
Resale value (£)	12 000	9 000	5 000	3 000	1 200	600
Annual maintenance (£)	300	800	1 200	1 500	2 500	10 000

Solution

Continuous discounting, with I equal to 0.01, uses a factor of $e^{0.01*N}$. We can discount resale values for full years, and will assume that maintenance is notionally paid in the middle of the year. Then the discounting factor for the first year is $e^{0.06}$, for the second year is $e^{0.18}$ and so on. The calculations for this are shown in the spreadsheet in Figure 2.16. You can see from this that Belmont get a minimum average annual cost when they replace cars every 5 years.

	A	B	C	D	E	F	G
1	**Belmont Leasing**						
2							
3	**Age of car when sold**	**1**	**2**	**3**	**4**	**5**	**6**
4							
5	Resale value	12000	9000	5000	3000	1200	600
6	Discounting factor	1.1275	1.2712	1.4333	1.6161	1.8221	2.0544
7	Discounted resale value	10643.05	7079.65	3488.38	1856.35	658.57	292.05
8	Capital cost	7356.95	10920.35	14511.62	16143.65	17341.43	17707.95
9							
10	Maintenance cost	300	800	1200	1500	2500	10000
11	Discounting factor	1.0618	1.1972	1.3499	1.5220	1.7160	1.9348
12	Discounted maintenance cost	282.53	668.22	888.98	985.57	1456.87	5168.51
13	Cumulative maintenance	282.53	950.75	1839.73	2825.30	4282.17	9450.68
14							
15	Total discounted cost	7639.48	11871.09	16351.35	18968.95	21623.59	27158.63
16	Average annual cost	7639.48	5935.55	5450.45	4742.24	4324.72	4526.44
17							*****	

Figure 2.16 Cost of replacing cars at Belmont Leasing.

IN SUMMARY

The performance of almost everything declines with age. Maintenance can reduce the effects of ageing, but eventually equipment should be replaced. We can find the best time to replace equipment by minimizing the average annual cost.

2.3.2 How much is equipment worth?

Equipment forms part of an organization's assets. As its value falls with age, the accounts have to show a changing value over time. The way of doing this is to use *depreciation*:

> **Depreciation** measures the decline in
> value of an asset over time

Organizations **write down** the value of their assets each year. This means they reduce the book value of equipment and other assets, so they can record depreciation as an operating cost. The two most widely used methods of depreciating assets are the *straight-line method* and the *reducing-balance method*.

Straight-line method

This reduces the asset's value by the same amount every year. Then:

$$\text{annual depreciation} = \frac{\text{cost of equipment} - \text{resale value}}{\text{life of equipment}}$$

A machine costing £20 000 with a scrap value of £5000 and a useful life of 10 years has an annual depreciation of:

$$\text{annual depreciation} = \frac{20\,000 - 5000}{10} = £1500$$

Straight-line depreciation is easy to calculate, but it is not really accurate. Most equipment loses a lot of value in its first year, and will actually be worth less than its depreciated value.

Reducing-balance method

This writes off a fixed percentage of the equipment's value each year. Typically a piece of equipment has its book value reduced by 20% a year. This gives a more accurate value, with higher depreciation in the first few years.

For the reducing-balance method, we can calculate an asset's value by extending our work on discounting. We know that an amount AP which increases at a rate of I each year has a value after N years of:

$$AF = AP * (1 + I)^N$$

If the amount is decreasing by a fixed percentage, we simply subtract I instead of adding it. Then for a depreciation rate of I, equipment whose cost at present is AP has a depreciated value after N years of:

$$AF = AP * (1 - I)^N$$

WORKED EXAMPLE 2.11

Briggs-Henderson Holdings buy gas compressors for £10 000 each.

(a) Use the straight-line method to find the annual depreciation if the compressors have an expected life of 5 years and a scrap value of £1000.

(b) If Briggs-Henderson use the reducing-balance method with a depreciation rate of 30%, what is the value of a compressor after 5 years?

(c) With the reducing-balance method, what depreciation rate would reduce a compressor's value to £2000 after 3 years?

Solution

(a) For straight-line depreciation:

$$\text{annual depreciation} = \frac{\text{cost of equipment} - \text{scrap value}}{\text{life of equipment}}$$

so

$$\text{annual depreciation} = \frac{10\,000 - 1000}{5} = £1800$$

(b) For the reducing-balance method, the value after 5 years is:

$$AF = AP * (1 - I)^N = 10\,000 * (1 - 0.3)^5 = £1681$$

(c) We want AF to be £2000 in 3 years' time, so:

$$AF = AP * (1 - I)^N$$

or

$$2000 = 10\,000 * (1 - I)^3$$

$$0.2 = (1 - I)^3$$

$$0.585 = 1 - I$$

or

$$I = 0.415$$

giving a depreciation rate of 41.5%.

IN SUMMARY

The value of equipment decreases with its age. There are several ways of calculating depreciated values, with the straight-line and reducing-balance methods being widely used.

2.3.3 How can we save enough money to buy new equipment?

Organizations know that they must buy new equipment at some point in the future, so they have to set aside enough money for the purchases. Most organizations spread the payments over time, by putting regular payments into an account. This account grows so that it contains enough money to replace equipment when needed. Savings in this form are known as a ***sinking fund***.

Suppose you have an initial amount to invest, AP, which earns interest at a rate I, and you can add an additional fixed amount of F at the end of each period. Then the amount available N periods in the future is:

$$AF = AP^* (1 + I)^N + \frac{F^* (1 + I)^N - F}{I}$$

The first part of this equation shows the income from the original investment, and the second part shows the amount accumulated by regular payments. This is a standard result, so we will not worry about the details of the derivation.

WORKED EXAMPLE 2.12

An investor puts £1000 into a building society account which earns 10% interest a year. If the investor adds another £500 at the end of each year, how much will be in the account at the end of 5 years?

Solution

Listing the variables we are given:

$$
\begin{aligned}
AP &= \text{£1000} &&= \text{initial investment} \\
I &= 0.1 &&= \text{interest rate} \\
F &= \text{£500} &&= \text{fixed amount added each year} \\
N &= 5 &&= \text{number of years}
\end{aligned}
$$

We can find the value of AF from:

$$AF = AP * (1 + I)^N + \frac{F * (1 + I)^N - F}{I}$$

so

$$AF = 1000 * 1.1^5 + \frac{500 * 1.1^5 - 500}{0.1} = \text{£4663}$$

WORKED EXAMPLE 2.13

How much should a company invest each year to make sure a sinking fund has £20 000 at the end of 10 years, when expected interest rates are 15%?

Solution

Sinking funds usually have no initial payment, so $AP = 0$. Then we have:

$$AF = £20\,000$$
$$AP = £0$$
$$I = 0.15$$
$$N = 10$$

Substituting these values gives:

$$AF = AP * (1 + I)^N + \frac{F * (1 + I)^N - F}{I}$$

or

$$20\,000 = 0 + \frac{F * (1 + 0.15)^{10} - F}{0.15}$$

$$3000 = F * 4.046 - F$$

$$F = £985.04$$

The company should put £985.04 into the fund each year.

IN SUMMARY

Organizations can set up sinking funds to cover the cost of replacing equipment. We can calculate the value of an investment with regular additional payments from

$$AF = AP * (1 + I)^N + \frac{F * (1 + I)^N - F}{I}$$

Self-assessment questions

2.10   Is it likely that maintenance costs for a machine will decline over time?

2.11   When would you plan to replace a machine:
(a) when it breaks down and can no longer be repaired?
(b) when the operating costs rise above the cost of a new machine?

(c) when the average annual cost is a minimum?

(d) when the average annual cost rises above the resale value?

2.12 The best age to replace a machine has been calculated at 6 years. If future maintenance costs are now raised in line with expected inflation, how will this affect the calculation?

2.13 What is the difference between the straight-line and reducing-balance methods of calculating depreciation?

2.14 What is a sinking fund?

2.4 Scoring models

Most models for finance give a quantitative view – particularly looking at costs. But many decisions have to include a range of qualitative factors. If we want to compare three projects, we might find the internal rate of return of each, but before making a final decision we also have to consider a number of qualitative factors. One way of doing this uses *scoring models*. These can add a numerical view of qualitative information (harsher critics suggest it is a way of building a defence for decisions that may turn out to be wrong).

To build a scoring model, we have to identify the important factors in a decision. Then we show the relative importance of each factor by giving it a maximum possible score. We might think that financial factors are very important and give them a maximum score of 20, marketing factors are half as important so we give them a maximum score of 10, and so on. Then we look at each alternative, and give scores to show how well it performs on each factor. These scores are usually subjective views that are agreed after wide discussion. Then the alternative with the highest total is – all other things being equal – the most attractive.

Procedure for a **scoring model**:

1 decide the relevant factors in a decision

2 set a maximum score for each factor

3 take each alternative in turn

4 give each factor a score up to the maximum

5 add the total scores for each alternative

6 find the best alternative as the one with the highest score

7 discuss the results, look at other factors, and make a final decision

WORKED EXAMPLE 2.14

Almay Electronics is planning a new factory. A management team made a list of important factors for its location, and developed the scoring model shown in Figure 2.17. What does this show?

	A	B	C	D	E	F
1	**Scoring model**					
2						
3	**Factor**	**Maximum score**		**Points for each location**		
4				**A**	**B**	**C**
5	**Government grants**	10		8	8	5
6	**Community attitude**	10		8	7	5
7	**Electronic engineers**	15		10	8	8
8	**Experienced workforce**	20		20	15	15
9	**Nearby suppliers**	5		2	3	3
10	**Education centres**	10		8	6	5
11	**Housing**	5		2	3	5
12						
13	**Totals**	**85**		**58**	**50**	**46**

Figure 2.17 Scoring model for Almay Electronics.

Solution

The maximum score shows the relative importance of each factor. An experienced workforce is most important, followed by availability of electronic engineers; then come government grants, community attitude and education centres.

The actual scores show how well each location scores in each factor. Locations A and B qualified for the highest government grants and were given 8 points each, while location C qualified for a lower grant and was given 5 points.

The total scores show that A is the best location, followed by B.

Case example

Hambrox Engineering Works

Many factories have self-guided vehicles to move parts and products. Hambrox Engineering Works make a range of control units for these semi-automated vehicles. At the end of 1995 they were planning the replacement of one of their standard products. Most of the planning was done by a project team, which considered three main alternatives.

After a lot of discussion, this project team agreed a list of the most important factors, maximum scores and actual scores shown in the following table:

Factor	Points Maximum	A	B	C
Product:				
Time to develop product	10	8	4	7
Research and development effort	20	15	8	10
Experience with similar products	10	9	4	7
Similarity with existing products	10	9	2	5
Expected life	20	10	6	12
Ease of manufacture	25	20	12	18
Raw material needs	5	4	4	3
Finance:				
Research and development costs	20	18	14	17
Capital outlay	15	10	10	10
Return on investment	25	12	15	20
Net present value	20	10	17	18
Market:				
Existing demand	25	23	12	16
Marketing effort	10	10	4	7
Advertising effort	5	4	2	6
Competition	15	5	15	10
Stability of market	5	3	2	4
Market trends	10	4	9	7
Totals	**250**	**174**	**140**	**177**

The total points show that products A and C were about equally attractive, while product B was some way behind. Hambrox looked at other factors before finally choosing product A.

> ## IN SUMMARY
>
> **Many decisions need some subjective judgement. Scoring models are one way of allowing comparison of these opinions.**

Self-assessment questions

2.15 What is the main benefit of scoring models?

2.16 If a scoring model shows that a particular location is the best site for a new warehouse, would you need to do any other analyses?

CHAPTER REVIEW

This chapter described a number of quantitative models. Because of their importance, we concentrated on financial analyses. In particular we looked at:

- break-even analyses, which defined the number of units that have to be sold to make a profit
- the changing value of money over time
- the effects of discounting, including net present values and internal rates of return
- calculations for the best time to replace equipment
- straight-line and reducing-balance methods of depreciation
- sinking funds
- scoring models

KEY TERMS

annual percentage rate	internal rate of return
APR	IRR
break-even point	net present value
compound interest	principal
continuous discounting	profit
depreciation	reducing-balance method
discounting to present value	scoring models
diseconomies of scale	sinking fund
economies of scale	straight-line method
interest	write down

Case study

Manning-Gaumont plc

The board of directors of Manning-Gaumont were having a difficult meeting. For the past year they had been reorganizing their manufacturing operations to reduce costs and increase profits. Their meetings were full of phrases like 'downsizing', 'rightsizing', 'lean production', 'restructuring', 're-engineering', 'global positioning', 'quality' and 'world class'.

Now they were having another meeting to discuss the future of their seven smallest European plants. It seemed inevitable that they would make changes, but they could not agree on the type of changes. Some directors thought that they had already made enough changes in the past year, and should now have a period of stability. Others thought that they should continue aggressive new policies to reduce costs even further. The majority wanted to make smaller changes, perhaps concentrating production by closing one or two of their seven plants.

This raised the question of which plants might be closed. Paul Schenker said that they should simply shut the smallest plants as the others could get more economies of scale. Mary Martingale said that this was too simple, and they should close the plants that gave least profit. Geoffrey Brown said that the costs could be controlled, so they should close the plants that produced lowest revenues. Georgio Bellarossi took the opposite view and said that revenue could be controlled, so they should close the plants with the highest costs. Stefan Andersson said that they should maximize their return on investment.

The directors had many ideas, but Angelina Cambrussi was the only one who had collected any relevant figures. She presented the following data for the past year:

Plant	Units produced (thousands)	Sales revenue (million £)	Production costs (million £)	Capital investment (million £)	Other costs (million £)	Gross profit (million £)	Quality achieved	Annual assessment
A Sweden	20	28	13	6	6.5	2.5	99.7%	*****
B UK	30	28	12	10	5.2	0.8	99.1%	***
C Spain	25	32	11	5	5.5	10.5	99.3%	*
D Germany	35	38	14	12	3.5	8.5	99.8%	**
E Poland	25	24	12	4	4.8	3.2	98.4%	***
F UK	35	42	16	10	6.1	9.9	99.5%	****
G Italy	20	31	12	14	4.7	0.3	100%	**

Questions

- How could the directors approach their decision?
- What calculations might help them, and what would these suggest?
- What other information would be useful?

Problems

2.1   A taxi driver has fixed costs of £4500 a year. Each kilometre he drives costs 30 pence and he charges an average of 45 pence. How many kilometres a year does he need to travel before he starts to make a profit? If he drove 90 000 kilometres last year, what were his total and net incomes?

2.2   Ace Adventure Holiday Company sells an average of 100 holidays a month. The income generated has to cover fixed costs of £63 000 a month. Each holiday they sell has travel, accommodation and other variable costs of £500.

(a) Does the company make a profit if the price of a holiday is £1200?

(b) If the price of a holiday is reduced to £1000 and sales increase to 150 a month, does the company make a profit?

2.3   A company makes knives, forks and spoons. The variable costs, selling prices and production of each are given in the following table:

	Knives	Forks	Spoons
Variable cost (£)	2	2.50	1.50
Selling price (£)	4	5.25	4.50
Proportion of total production (%)	45	20	35

Fixed costs are £60 000 a year and the company has a target of making £30 000 a year profit. How many units should it make?

2.4   How much will an initial investment of £20 000, earning interest at 10%, be worth in 20 years' time?

2.5   A project has the following cash flows. What is the net present value with a discounting rate of 12% a year? What is the internal rate of return?

Year	Income (£)	Expenditure (£)
0	0	18 000
1	2 500	0
2	13 500	6 000
3	18 000	0
4	6 000	2 000
5	1 000	0

2.6   Use continuous discounting on the data for the last problem to see if there is much difference. Which of the two answers is more reliable?

2.7   The cash flows of three projects are given in the following table. Calculate the net present values using a discounting rate of 12% a year. What are the internal rates of return?

	Project A		Project B		Project C	
Year (£)	Income (£)	Expenditure (£)	Income (£)	Expenditure (£)	Income (£)	Expenditure (£)
0	0	18 000	0	24 000	0	21 000
1	2 500	0	2 000	10 000	0	12 000
2	13 500	6 000	10 000	6 000	20 000	5 000
3	18 000	0	20 000	2 000	20 000	1 000
4	6 000	2 000	30 000	2 000	30 000	0
5	1 000	0	30 000	2 000	30 000	0

2.8   What are the net present values and internal rate of return for a product that gives the following cash flows?

Year	1	2	3	4	5	6	7	8	9
Net cash flow (£)	−12 000	−4 000	−1 500	200	3 500	5 000	4 000	800	200

2.9   A company buys new vehicles for £15 000. If these have an expected life of 6 years, and a scrap value of £2000, use a straight-line method to find annual depreciation. If a reducing-balance method is used with a depreciation rate of 25%, what is the value of the vehicles after 6 years? What depreciation rate reduces the vehicles' value to £1000 after 4 years?

2.10   A company makes fixed annual payments into a sinking fund. They want to buy equipment costing £100 000 in 5 years' time. If interest rates are 12%, how much should each payment be?

2.11   A machine costs £75 000 with resale values and maintenance costs shown below:

Age of machine (years)	1	2	3	4	5	6	7
Resale value (£)	60 000	50 000	40 000	25 000	12 000	1 000	0
Maintenance in year (£)	5 000	7 000	9 000	15 000	20 000	60 000	140 000

What is the best age to replace the machine without discounting values? If values are discounted by 1.5% a month, how does this affect the calculations?

Discussion questions

2.1   Why are quantitative models so important in finance? Apart from those described, what other analyses would be useful for finance?

2.2   Why is it difficult to find a reasonable discounting rate? Do these difficulties mean that discounted values and related calculations are not very useful?

2.3   We have described net present values and internal rates of return for comparing different projects. What other methods could you use?

2.4   Planned replacement decisions can be rather inflexible. In practice, organizations have to respond to changing circumstances. For example, a company might plan to replace a machine after 5 years, but it develops a major fault and needs replacing after only 3 years. Do such effects make the models invalid?

2.5   To what extent do the results of financial analyses depend on the accounting conventions used?

Linear programming

3

CHAPTER OUTLINE

This chapter describes linear programming. This is a widely used method of finding optimal solutions to certain types of problem. Here 'programming' is used in its broad sense of 'planning' and has nothing to do with computer programming. After reading the chapter you should be able to:

- describe problems of constrained optimization and the use of linear programming
- formulate linear programmes
- discuss the assumptions made by linear programming
- use graphical methods to solve linear programmes with two decision variables
- do sensitivity analyses
- see how computers solve larger problems
- understand computer printouts from linear programming packages

3.1 | Introduction

Managers often try to make the best use of limited resources. Operations managers, for example, may want to make as many units as possible, but they have limited production facilities; marketing managers may want the most impact for their advertising campaigns, but they have limited budgets; finance managers may want to maximize their incomes, but they have limited funds; construction managers may want to minimize the cost of projects, but they have limited times to complete them. These problems have:

- an aim of optimizing – i.e. maximizing or minimizing – some *objective*
- *constraints* that limit the possible solutions.

For this reason they are called problems of *constrained optimization*.

> **Linear programming (LP)** is a way of solving problems of constrained optimization.

We should say straight away that linear programming was developed in the 1950s, when 'programming' meant 'planning'. It has nothing to do with 'computer programming'.

There are three stages in solving a linear programme:

- **formulation** – to get the problem in the right format
- **solution** – to find the optimal solution to the problem
- **sensitivity analysis** – to see what happens when the problem is changed

In practice, the first of these is the most difficult. Linear programmes can have many variables and it can be difficult to define these, or see how they are related. But once a problem is in the right format, the next step is easy. This is because linear programmes are **always** solved by computer. In this chapter, we are going to give some examples of formulations, and then show how a computer gets solutions to real problems.

IN SUMMARY

Managers often have problems of constrained optimization. Linear programming (LP) is a widely used method of solving these.

Self-assessment questions

3.1 What is constrained optimization?

3.2 What is linear programming?

3.2 | **Formulating linear programmes**

The first step in solving linear programmes is to describe the problem in a standard format. This is called *formulation*. We can give an example of formulation from production planning.

A small factory makes two types of liquid fertilizer, Growbig and Thrive. These are made on the same equipment for blending raw materials, distilling the mix and finishing (bottling, testing, weighing, etc.). The factory has a limited amount of equipment, so there are constraints on the time available for each process. In particular, there can be no more than 40 hours of blending in a week, 40 hours of distilling and 25 hours of finishing. We will assume that these are the only constraints and that there are no limits on, say, sales or raw materials.

The fertilizers are made in batches and each batch needs the following hours on each process:

Process	Growbig	Thrive
Blending	1	2
Distilling	2	1
Finishing	1	1

If the factory makes a net profit of £30 on each batch of Growbig and £20 on each batch of Thrive, how many batches of each should it make in a week?

Figure 3.1 gives a summary of this problem. We want to optimize an objective – i.e. maximize profit – when there are constraints on the capacity of each process. So we are talking about constrained optimization. To solve the problem, we want to find the number of batches of Growbig and Thrive that give the highest profit. So we can start by defining the two *decision variables*, G and T:

- let G be the number of batches of Growbig made in a week
- let T be the number of batches of Thrive made in a week

We can use any other names here – such as X and Y, X_1 and X_2, GROWBIG and THRIVE, or NumBatGro and NumBatThr. Each of these has advantages, but for the moment we will stick to the single letters.

Now we can look at the blending constraint. Each batch of Growbig uses 1 hour of blending, so G batches use $1 * G$ hours of blending; each batch of Thrive uses 2 hours of blending, so T batches use $2 * T$ hours. Adding these together gives the total amount of blending time used as $1 * G + 2 * T$. The maximum amount of blending time available is 40 hours, so the time used must be less than – or at worst equal to – this. So we have the first constraint:

$$1 * G + 2 * T \le 40 \qquad \text{blending constraint}$$

We can look at the distilling constraint in the same way. Each batch of Growbig uses 2 hours of distilling, so G batches use $2 * G$ hours; each batch of

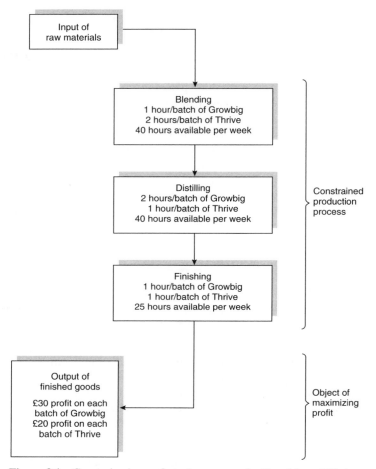

Figure 3.1 Constrained manufacturing process for Growbig and Thrive.

Thrive uses 1 hour of distilling, so T batches use $1 * T$ hours. Adding these together gives the total amount of distilling used. This must be less than – or at worst equal to – the amount of distilling available (40 hours). So the second constraint is:

$$2 * G + 1 * T \leq 40 \qquad \text{distilling constraint}$$

Now we can move on to the finishing constraint. Here the total time used for finishing is $1 * G$ for batches of Growbig plus $1 * T$ for batches of Thrive, and this must be less than or equal to the time available (25 hours). So the constraint is:

$$1 * G + 1 * T \leq 25 \qquad \text{finishing constraint}$$

These are the three constraints on the process. But the company cannot make a negative number of batches, so we can add the constraint that the number of batches of Growbig and Thrive must both be positive. These ***non-negativity constraints*** are a standard feature of linear programmes:

$$G \geq 0 \quad \text{and} \quad T \geq 0 \qquad \text{non-negativity constraints}$$

We have now listed all the constraints and can turn to the objective. In this case we want to maximize the profit. Each batch of Growbig makes £30 profit and the factory makes G batches, so the profit is $30 * G$: each batch of Thrive makes £20 profit and T batches are made, so the profit is $20 * T$. Adding these gives the total profit to be maximized. This is called the ***objective function***:

Maximize: $\quad 30 * G + 20 * T \qquad$ objective function

This finishes the formulation, and you can see that is has four parts:

> 1 decision variables
> 2 an objective function
> 3 a set of constraints
> 4 non-negativity constraints

For the problem of Growbig and Thrive the complete formulation is:

Let G be the number of batches of Growbig made $\quad \big\}$ decision variables
Let T be the number of batches of Thrive made

Maximize: $\quad 30 * G + 20 * T$
Subject to: $\quad 1 * G + 2 * T \leq 40$
$\qquad\qquad\quad 2 * G + 1 * T \leq 40 \quad \big\}$ objective function constraints
$\qquad\qquad\quad 1 * G + 1 * T \leq 25$
with $\qquad\quad G \geq 0$ and $T \geq 0 \qquad$ non-negativity constraints

The constraints are usually written in this way, with all the decision variables to the left of a $\leq$, $=$ or $\geq$, and a single number on the right-hand side.

It may not be obvious, but we have made a number of assumptions in this formulation. We have obviously assumed that there is reliable data and the model gives a reasonable view – but there are two other assumptions in every linear programme. Firstly, we assume that the amount of resources used is proportional to the number of units made: if production is doubled we double the resources used. This seems reasonable, but it might not be accurate. Increasing production may use larger batches and reduce set-up times; or faster throughput might produce more faults. Linear programmes assume that the data take these effects into account. Then the **proportionality assumption** is at least a reasonable approximation.

A second assumption is that adding the resources used for each product gives the total amount of resources used. Again, this may not be true. In a craft workshop, for example, the most skilled craftsmen do the most difficult jobs. If the workshop makes no complicated jobs in one period, the skilled craftsmen will do less complicated jobs, and they will do these jobs better or faster than usual. Again, LP assumes that such interactions are included in the data, and the **additivity assumption** is at least a reasonable approximation.

WORKED EXAMPLE 3.1

A political campaign wants to hire photocopying machines to produce leaflets for a local election. There are two suitable machines:

- ACTO costs £120 a month to rent, occupies 2.5 square metres of floor space and can make 15 000 copies a day
- ZENMAT costs £150 a month to rent, occupies 1.8 square metres of floor space and can make 18 500 copies a day.

The campaign can spend £1200 a month on copying machines, which it will put in a room of 19.2 square metres. Formulate this problem as a linear programme.

Solution

For the formulation we have to describe the decision variables, objective function and constraints. The decision variables are the things we can vary, which are the number of ACTO and ZENMAT machines rented. Let A be the number of ACTO machines rented, and let Z be the number of ZENMAT machines rented.

The objective is to make as many copies as possible:

Maximize: $15\,000 * A + 18\,500 * Z$ objective function

There are constraints on floor space and costs:

Subject to: $120 * A + 150 * Z \leq 1200$ cost constraint

$2.5 * A + 1.8 * Z \leq 19.2$ space constraint

with $A \geq 0$ and $Z \geq 0$ non-negativity constraint

WORKED EXAMPLE 3.2

The Excelsior Trust has £1 million to invest. It is considering six possible investments with the following characteristics:

Investment	% risk	% dividend	% growth	Rating
1	18	4	22	4
2	6	5	7	10
3	10	9	12	2
4	4	7	8	10
5	12	6	15	4
6	8	8	8	6

The Trust wants to invest the £1 million with minimum risk, but with a dividend of at least £70 000 a year, average growth of at least 12%, and average rating of at least 7. Formulate this problem as a linear programme.

Solution

The decision variables are the amount of money put into each investment:

Let X_1 be the amount of money put into investment 1
Let X_2 be the amount of money put into investment 2

and so on.

The objective is to minimize risk.

Minimize: $0.18 * X_1 + 0.06 * X_2 + 0.10 * X_3 + 0.04 * X_4 + 0.12 * X_5 + 0.08 * X_6$

The constraints are:

- the amount of money invested must equal £1 million

  $X_1 + X_2 + X_3 + X_4 + X_5 + X_6 = 1\,000\,000$

- the dividend must be at least 7% of a million pounds, which is £70 000

  $0.04 * X_1 + 0.05 * X_2 + 0.09 * X_3 + 0.07 * X_4 + 0.05 * X_5 + 0.08 * X_6 \geq 70\,000$

- average growth must be at least 12% of a million pounds, which is £120 000

  $0.22 * X_1 + 0.07 * X_2 + 0.12 * X_3 + 0.08 * X_4 + 0.15 * X_5 + 0.08 * X_6 \geq 120\,000$

- the average rating – weighted by the amount invested – must be at least 7

  $4 * X_1 + 10 * X_2 + 2 * X_3 + 10 * X_4 + 4 * X_5 + 6 * X_6 \geq 7\,000\,000$

The non-negativity constraints X_1, X_2, X_3, X_4, X_5 and $X_6 \geq 0$ complete the formulation.

WORKED EXAMPLE 3.3

Bentalls Oil makes two blends of fuel by mixing three oils. The costs of the oils and the amounts available each day are:

Oil	Cost (£/litre)	Amount available (litres)
A	0.25	10 000
B	0.28	15 000
C	0.35	20 000

There are constraints on the blends of fuel:

Blend 1	at most 25% of A
	at least 30% of B
	at most 40% of C
Blend 2	at least 20% of A
	at most 50% of B
	at least 30% of C

Bentalls can sell each litre of blend 1 for £0.60 and each litre of blend 2 for £0.70. They have long-term contracts to supply 10 000 litres of each blend. Formulate this blending problem as a linear programme.

Solution

The decision variables are the amount of each type of crude oil that is put into each blend:

$$\text{Let } A_1 \text{ be the amount of oil } A \text{ put into blend 1}$$
$$\text{Let } A_2 \text{ be the amount of oil } A \text{ put into blend 2}$$
$$\text{Let } B_1 \text{ be the amount of oil } B \text{ put into blend 1}$$

and so on.

The total amounts of blend 1 and blend 2 produced are:

blend 1: $\quad A_1 + B_1 + C_1$
blend 2: $\quad A_2 + B_2 + C_2$

and the amounts of each oil used are:

oil A: $\quad A_1 + A_2$
oil B: $\quad B_1 + B_2$
oil C: $\quad C_1 + C_2$

The objective is to maximize profit. The income from selling blends is:

$$0.6 * (A_1 + B_1 + C_1) + 0.7 * (A_2 + B_2 + C_2)$$

while the cost of buying oil is:

$$0.25 * (A_1 + A_2) + 0.28 * (B_1 + B_2) + 0.35 * (C_1 + C_2)$$

The profit is the difference between the income and the cost, which we can rearrange as the objective function:

Maximize:

$$0.35 * A_1 + 0.45 * A_2 + 0.32 * B_1 + 0.42 * B_2 + 0.25 * C_1 + 0.35 * C_2$$

There are constraints on the availability of oils:

$$A_1 + A_2 \leq 10\,000$$
$$B_1 + B_2 \leq 15\,000$$
$$C_1 + C_2 \leq 20\,000$$

There are also six blending constraints. The first of these says that blend 1 must be at most 25% of oil A. In other words:

$$A_1 \leq 0.25 * (A_1 + B_1 + C_1) \quad \text{or} \quad 0.75 * A_1 - 0.25 * B_1 - 0.25 * C_1 \leq 0$$

Similarly, for the other blends:

$$B_1 \geq 0.3 * (A_1 + B_1 + C_1) \quad \text{or} \quad 0.3 * A_1 - 0.7 * B_1 + 0.3 * C_1 \leq 0$$
$$C_1 \leq 0.4 * (A_1 + B_1 + C_1) \quad \text{or} \quad -0.4 * A_1 - 0.4 * B_1 + 0.6 * C_1 \leq 0$$
$$A_2 \geq 0.2 * (A_2 + B_2 + C_2) \quad \text{or} \quad -0.8 * A_2 + 0.2 * B_2 + 0.2 * C_2 \leq 0$$
$$B_2 \leq 0.5 * (A_2 + B_2 + C_2) \quad \text{or} \quad -0.5 * A_2 + 0.5 * B_2 - 0.5 * C_2 \leq 0$$
$$C_2 \geq 0.3 * (A_2 + B_2 + C_2) \quad \text{or} \quad 0.3 * A_2 + 0.3 * B_2 - 0.7 * C_2 \leq 0$$

Long-term contracts add the constraints:

$$A_1 + B_1 + C_1 \geq 10\,000$$
$$A_2 + B_2 + C_2 \geq 10\,000$$

The non-negativity conditions that all variables, A_1, A_2, B_1, etc. are greater than or equal to 0 completes the formulation.

IN SUMMARY

The first stage of solving linear programmes is to put the problem into a standard format. This is called formulation. An LP formulation consists of decision variables, an objective function, constraints and non-negativity constraints.

Self-assessment questions

3.3 What is meant by the 'formulation' of a linear programme?

3.4 What are the parts of an LP formulation?

3.5 What are the main assumptions of linear programming?

Case example

Sovereign Life Assurance

In 1996 Sovereign Life Assurance found that their reserves were not quite big enough to cover the life insurance policies they had issued, so they decided to transfer $20 million into their life policy reserves. The company wanted to maximize its returns on this new investment, but there were regulations and guidelines on the types of investment they could make. This was clearly a problem of constrained optimization, and the company used linear programming to suggest the best investment.

The main constraint was on the amount to be invested, which must give a total of $20 million. There were other constraints on the types of investment available. Sovereign would not make any investment that had a significant risk, so their choice was limited to bonds, common shares, preferred shares, property, mortgages and unclassified investments. Guidelines prevented them from buying common shares with a value greater than 25% of the total assets of the company. Similarly, property was limited to 15%, and unclassified investments to 2% of the total assets of the company. The final constraints were on the maximum amounts of each investment that were available at current rates of return.

The solution to this linear programme showed the best options at a particular time. But financial markets change very quickly, and the data used in the model had to be updated daily.

Case example

Mount Gibson Smelting

In recent years the demand for lead has fallen, as substitutes are used in petrol, paint and construction. But the supply of lead has grown and prices have fallen, putting pressure on supplier profits. Mount Gibson Smelting are major producers of lead in Australia. They use linear programming in several ways to maximize profit, with one model looking at production planning.

Mount Gibson mine their own ore, and buy smaller amounts from other suppliers. The ores have variable composition and costs, but are processed in the same way. They are crushed and prepared before a sintering plant removes sulphur and replaces it with oxygen. Then a blast furnace removes the oxygen and other impurities to leave lead bullion. This bullion still contains metallic impurities which are removed in a refinery. Mount Gibson can sell the impurities – which include copper, silver, arsenic and bismuth – along with other by-products like sulphuric acid.

The model of production plans has three types of decision variables:

- There are 22 different types of ore, and the first type of variable gives the amount of each ore used.

- There are 25 major products, and the second type of variable gives the amount of each product made.

- The third type of variable describes other conditions, such as the chemical composition of each ore.

Mount Gibson find their gross profit by subtracting the costs of all inputs from the revenues for all products. Their objective is to maximize this profit. The variables are combined into four types of constraint:

- The first type of constraint is on the preparation of the ores. There is always some variation in the incoming ores, but the smelters work best with fixed conditions. So the preparation of the ores includes blending to make the overall input reasonably consistent.

- The second type of constraint looks at the availability of different types of ore. It makes sure that the amounts of each ore used matches the supply.

- The third type of constraint looks at the different products. There is a varying demand for products, and Mount Gibson varies its supply to meet these.

- Finally there are constraints to match the total composition of the input to the outputs – so that no materials are lost in the process.

This basic production planning model has 214 decision variables and over a thousand constraints. Mount Gibson have several versions of the model for different time periods and production assumptions. The larger models have several hundred variables and thousands of constraints.

3.3 | Using graphs to solve linear programmes

Linear programmes are always solved by computer. There are many specialized LP packages, as well as LP functions in spreadsheets and other software. Most of these use a procedure called the ***simplex method***. It is not worth describing the calculations for simplex – which are easy but very tedious – but we can show the general approach. For this we will return to the earlier example with Growbig and Thrive.

Let G be the number of batches of Growbig made
Let T be the number of batches of Thrive made
} decision variables

Maximize: $\quad 30 * G + 20 * T \quad$ objective function

Subject to: $\quad 1 * G + 2 * T \leq 40 \quad$ blending constraint
$\qquad\qquad\quad 2 * G + 1 * T \leq 40 \quad$ distilling constraint
$\qquad\qquad\quad 1 * G + 1 * T \leq 25 \quad$ finishing constraint

with $\qquad G \geq 0$ and $T \geq 0 \quad$ non-negativity constraints

The blending constraint has $1 * G + 2 * T \leq 40$. If we look at the strict equality $1 * G + 2 * T = 40$, we can draw this as a straight line on a graph of G against T, as shown in Figure 3.2. The easiest way to draw such lines is to take two convenient points and draw a straight line through them. When $G = 0$, $2 * T = 40$ or $T = 20$; then when $T = 0$, $1 * G = 40$. So the constraint line passes through the points $G = 0$, $T = 20$ and $G = 40$, $T = 0$.

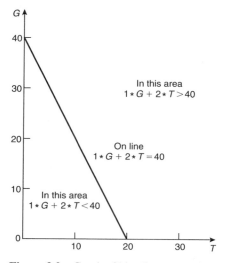

Figure 3.2 Graph of blending constraint.

In this graph, you can see that the blending constraint is broken for any point above the line, while it holds for any point on or below the line. You can check this by taking any random points. The point $G = 10$, $T = 10$, for example, is below the line and substitution into the constraint gives:

$$1 * 10 + 2 * 10 \leq 40$$

This is true and the constraint is not broken. On the other hand, the point $G = 20$, $T = 20$ is above the line and substitution gives:

$$1 * 20 + 2 * 20 \leq 40$$

This is not true and the constraint is broken. Points which are actually on the line satisfy the equality. For example, the point $G = 20$, $T = 10$ is on the line and substitution gives:

$$1 * 20 + 2 * 10 \leq 40$$

This is true and shows the extreme values allowed by the constraint. So the line divides the graph into two areas: all points above the line break the constraint, while all points on or below the line do not break the constraint (as shown in Figure 3.3).

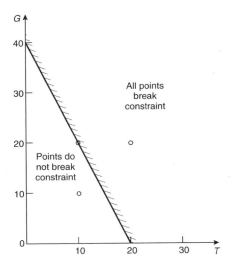

Figure 3.3 Blending constraint divides graph into two areas.

Now we can add the other two constraints to the same graph. The distilling constraint is the straight line through $G = 20$, $T = 0$ and $G = 0$, $T = 40$. As before, any point above the line breaks the constraint while any point on or below it does not break the constraint.

The finishing constraint is the straight line through the points $G = 0$, $T = 25$ to $G = 25$, $T = 0$. Again, any point above the line will break the constraint, as shown in Figure 3.4.

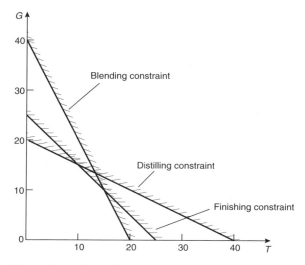

Figure 3.4 Graph showing the three constraints.

Any point below all three of the constraint lines represents a valid, feasible solution, but a point that is above any of the lines will break at least one of the constraints and will not represent a feasible solution. Now we can add the non-negativity constraints which limit feasible solutions to the positive quadrant of the graph. This completes a *feasible region*, which is the area in which all feasible solutions must lie. Any point inside the feasible region represents a valid solution to the problem, while any point outside the feasible region breaks at least one of the constraints (as shown in Figure 3.5).

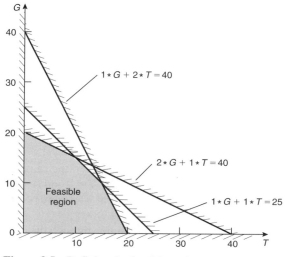

Figure 3.5 Defining the feasible region.

Now we have a feasible region that shows all the feasible solutions, and the next step is to see which solution is optimal. For this we use the objective function. We can plot the objective function on the graph of G against T in the same way as the constraints. We do not yet know the optimal value of the profit, but we can start by looking at an arbitrary value of, say, £600. Then we can draw the graph of $30 * G + 20 * T = 600$ as before. This line goes through the points $G = 0, T = 30$ and $G = 20, T = 0$. We chose a profit of £600 arbitrarily, and could draw similar lines for other arbitrary values for profit, giving the results shown in Figure 3.6.

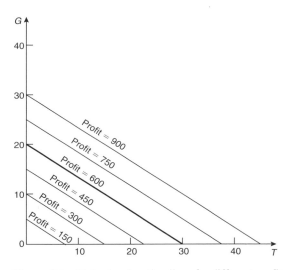

Figure 3.6 Objective function lines for different profits.

You can see that the lines for different profits are all parallel, and the ones with higher values are further away from the origin. We can use this observation to find the optimal solution. For this, we superimpose an objective function line onto the graph of constraints, so that it passes through the feasible region (as shown in Figure 3.7).

Then we move this objective function line away from the origin – the further it moves the higher is the profit. As the objective function line moves further out, it will pass through a smaller part of the feasible region. Eventually, it will just pass through a single point. This single point is the optimal solution, as shown in Figure 3.8.

You can see from the graph that the optimal solution is about the point $G = 15$, $T = 10$. This is the point where the distilling constraint crosses the finishing constraint. These are the **_limiting constraints_** which limit production. There is spare capacity in blending and this constraint does not limit production. We can find the optimal solution more accurately by solving the simultaneous equations of the limiting constraints:

$$2 * G + 1 * T = 40 \qquad \text{distilling}$$
$$1 * G + 1 * T = 25 \qquad \text{finishing}$$

These confirm the optimal solution as

$$G = 15 \quad \text{and} \quad T = 10.$$

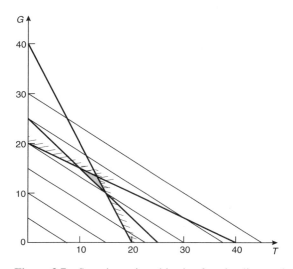

Figure 3.7 Superimposing objective function line on the constraints graph.

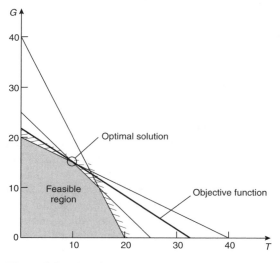

Figure 3.8 Identifying the optimal solution.

Substituting these values into the objective function gives:

$$30 * G + 20 * T = 30 * 15 + 20 * 10 = 650$$

So the maximum profit is £650.

We can also substitute $G = 15$ and $T = 12$ into the constraints to show the amounts of resources used:

Blending:

time available	= 40 hours
time used	= $1 * G + 2 * T = 1 * 15 + 2 * 10 = 35$
spare capacity	= $40 - 35 = 5$ hours

Distilling:

time available	= 40 hours
time used	= $2 * G + 1 * T = 2 * 15 + 1 * 10 = 40$
spare capacity	= 0

Finishing:

time available	= 25 hours
time used	= $1 * G + 1 * T = 1 * 15 + 1 * 10 = 25$
spare capacity	= 0

This gives a complete solution to the problem, with the optimal production, profit, resources used and spare capacities.

WORKED EXAMPLE 3.4

Elersome Manufacturing need weekly production schedules for two products X and Y. Each unit of X uses 1 component made in the factory, while each unit of Y uses 2 of the components. The factory has a maximum output of 80 components a week. Each unit of X and Y needs 10 hours of subcontracted work, and Elersome have signed agreements with subcontractors for a minimum of 200 hours and a maximum of 600 hours a week. The marketing department say they can sell all production of Y but only 50 units of X, despite one long-term contract for 10 units of X. The net profit on each unit of X and Y is £200 and £300 respectively.

Solution

The decision variables in this problem are the numbers of units of X and Y that Elersome should make in a week. Let X be the number of units of product X made in a week, and let Y be the number of units of product Y made in a week.

Then the formulation becomes:

Maximize: $200 * X + 300 * Y$ objective function

Subject to: $1 * X + 2 * Y \leq 80$ components available

$10 * X + 10 * Y \geq 200$ minimum subcontracted

$10 * X + 10 * Y \leq 600$ maximum subcontracted

$1 * X \leq 50$ maximum sales of X

$1 * X \geq 10$ long-term contract

$X, Y \geq 0$ non-negativity constraints

This formulation is drawn on the graph shown in Figure 3.9. Adding the objective function and moving it as far away from the origin as possible gives the last point it passes through in the feasible region as about $X = 40$ and $Y = 20$. Here the components available and maximum hours subcontracted are limiting:

$1 * X + 2 * Y = 80$ components available

$10 * X + 10 * Y = 600$ maximum subcontracted

Solving these simultaneous equations confirms the optimal solution as $X = 40$ and $Y = 20$. Substituting these values into the objective function gives a maximum weekly profit of $200 * 40 + 300 * 20 = £14\,000$.

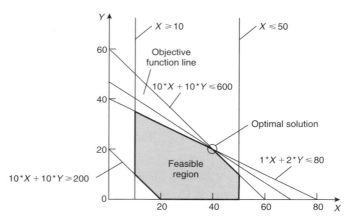

Figure 3.9 Graph for Worked Example 3.4.

In these two worked examples, you can see that the feasible region is convex – which means it is a polygon without any indentations. The optimal solution is at a corner or ***extreme point*** of the feasible region. This is not a coincidence but is a basic property of all linear programmes.

> **Optimal solutions** to linear programmes are always at
> an **extreme point** of the feasible region.

This is a very useful property as it shows how computers can tackle large problems. All they have to do is search the extreme points around the feasible region until they find an optimal value.

IN SUMMARY

We can draw linear programmes with two variables on a graph. The constraints identify a feasible region, which is convex. The objective function line shows which extreme point gives the optimal solution.

Self-assessment questions

3.6   What is the feasible region for a linear programme?

3.7   What is the role of the objective function in an LP model?

3.8   What are the extreme points of a feasible region and why are they important?

3.9   How can you identify the optimal solution on a graph?

3.4 ∥ Sensitivity analysis

Sometimes, managers may not want to use the exact solution they get from a linear programme – perhaps because they have some information that was not included in the model. So it would be useful to see how sensitive the optimal solution is to changes. This is the purpose of *sensitivity analysis*. In this section, we shall see how sensitive a solution is to changes in the objective function and available resources.

3.4.1 Changing the objective function

Going back to our problem with Growbig and Thrive, we have:

Maximize: $30 * G + 20 * T$

Subject to:
$1 * G + 2 * T \leq 40$ blending
$2 * G + 1 * T \leq 40$ distilling
$1 * G + 1 * T \leq 25$ finishing

with $G \geq 0$ and $T \geq 0$

Suppose a new accounting convention adjusts the profits to £20 for each batch of Growbig and £30 for each batch of Thrive. The objective function is now $20 * G + 30 * T$, but how does this affect the optimal solution? The graph of constraints is exactly the same as before and the feasible region is unchanged. But, adding the new objective function line and moving it as far away from the origin as possible gives a new optimal solution (as shown in Figure 3.10).

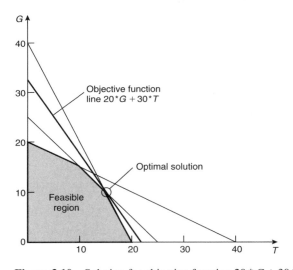

Figure 3.10 Solution for objective function $20 * G + 30 * T$.

The new optimal solution is the point where the blending constraint crosses the finishing constraint. These are the limiting constraints:

$1 * G + 2 * T = 40$ blending
$1 * G + 1 * T = 25$ finishing

We can solve these to get the optimal solution $G = 10$ and $T = 15$. Substituting these values into the objective function gives a profit of $20 * 10 + 30 * 15 = £650$.

Suppose the new accounting convention gave the profit on both Growbig and Thrive as £30 a batch. This objective function is now $30 * G + 30 * T$. We can draw this line on the feasible region as shown in Figure 3.11.

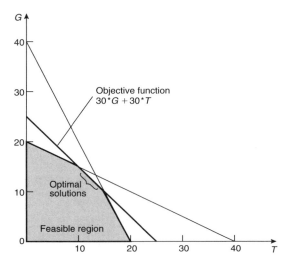

Figure 3.11 Multiple solutions for objective function $30 * G + 30 * T$.

This time the line of the objective function does not leave the feasible region at a single point. It is parallel to one of the limiting constraints and leaves the feasible region along one edge. When this happens any point along the edge is optimal and gives the same profit. You can check this by taking arbitrary points along the edge.

- At one extreme point of the edge $G = 15$, $T = 10$

  $$profit = 30 * 15 + 30 * 10 = £750$$

- At the other end of the edge $G = 10$ and $T = 15$

  $$profit = 30 * 10 + 30 * 15 = £750$$

- In the middle of the edge $G = 12.5$ and $T = 12.5$

  $$profit = 30 * 12.5 + 30 * 12.5 = £750$$

Now we can summarize these findings in three general statements:

- The optimal solution lies at an extreme point where two constraints cross.
- The gradient of the objective function has a value between the gradients of the two limiting constraints.
- If the gradient of the objective function changes so that it is no longer between these gradients, the optimal solution moves from one extreme point to another.

For equations with the form $a * G + b * T = c$, if we take G as the vertical axis, the gradient of the line is $-b/a$. In our original example, the gradients of the objective function and limiting constraints are:

$$\text{objective function} \quad = -30/20 = -0.667$$
$$\text{distilling} \quad = -1/2 = -0.5$$
$$\text{finishing} \quad = -1/1 = -1.0$$

If the gradient of the objective falls below -1.0 or rises above -0.5, the optimal solution will switch to another extreme point. Suppose we keep the coefficient of G constant while varying the coefficient of T, so that the objective function is $30 * G + b * T$. The optimal solution will change to another extreme point when:

$$\text{either} \quad -b/30 \geq -0.5 \quad \text{i.e. } b \leq 15$$
$$\text{or} \quad -b/30 \leq -1.0 \quad \text{i.e. } b \geq 30$$

This means that with a profit of £20 on a batch of Thrive, the optimal solution is $G = 15$ and $T = 10$, giving a total profit of $30 * 15 + 20 * 10 = £650$. If the profit on a batch of Thrive rises to £25, the optimal solution is still $G = 15$ and $T = 10$, giving a profit of $30 * 15 + 25 * 10 = £700$. But if the profit on a batch of Thrive falls below £15 or rises above £30, the optimal solution changes and we have to modify the formulation and solve a new problem.

We can see the same effect if we keep the coefficient of T constant, so that the objective function is $a * G + 20 * T$. Then the optimal solution changes to another extreme point when:

$$\text{either} \quad -20/a \geq -0.5 \quad \text{i.e. } a \geq 40$$
$$\text{or} \quad -20/a \leq -1.0 \quad \text{i.e. } a \leq 20$$

While the profit on a batch of Growbig stays between 20 and 40 the optimal solution stays at the same extreme point, and we can find the total profit by substitution. When the profit on a batch of Growbig moves outside this range, we have to modify the formulation and solve a new problem.

IN SUMMARY

Changing the profit on each product changes the gradient of the objective function. For small changes the optimal solution stays at the same extreme point. For larger changes the optimal solution moves to another point. Then we have to modify the formulation and solve a new problem.

3.4.2 Changing the resources available

Returning to the original problem, the limiting constraints were distilling and finishing and we found the optimal solution by solving:

$$2 * G + 1 * T = 40 \qquad \text{distilling constraint}$$
$$1 * G + 1 * T = 25 \qquad \text{finishing constraint}$$

Suppose we could buy some extra capacity for distilling. How much would it be worth? The answer comes from the marginal value of distilling, which in linear programmes is called the ***shadow price***. This is the value of one additional hour of distilling. We can find this by replacing the original constraint:

$$2 * G + 1 * T \leq 40 \qquad \text{original distilling constraint}$$
by $\qquad 2 * G + 1 * T \leq 41 \qquad \text{new distilling constraint}$

In practice, the feasible region expands by a very small amount, as shown in Figure 3.12.

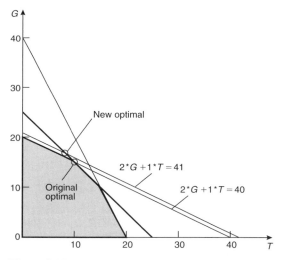

Figure 3.12 Effects of an extra hour of distilling.

For small increases of resources the same constraints are limiting, and the optimal solution stays at the same extreme point of the feasible region. Then we can find a new optimal solution by solving the equations:

$$2 * G + 1 * T = 41 \qquad \text{distilling constraint}$$
$$1 * G + 1 * T = 25 \qquad \text{finishing constraint}$$

to give $G = 16$ and $T = 9$. Substituting these values in the objective function gives a maximum profit of $30 * 16 + 20 * 9 = £660$. This is a rise of £10 from the original optimal solution and shows that distilling has a shadow price of £10 an hour. This is the most we should pay for one extra hour of distilling.

We can use a similar argument to show that the shadow price is also the cost of losing one hour of distilling. If equipment breaks down for an hour, we can get a revised solution by solving:

$$2 * G + T = 39 \qquad \text{distilling constraint}$$
$$G + T = 25 \qquad \text{finishing constraint}$$

This gives $G = 14$ and $T = 11$, with a profit of $30 * 14 + 20 * 11 = £640$. The profit has fallen by £10, which confirms the value of the shadow price.

For small changes in resources, the objective function alters by the shadow price multiplied by the change. If, for example, we can have an extra 3 hours of distilling its value is $3 * 10 = £30$: if equipment breaks down for an hour and a half, the cost is $1.5 * 10 = £15$. But the shadow price is only valid for small changes. An extra hour of distilling is worth £10, but there are limits and an extra 1000 hours is certainly not worth £10 000. Suppose we can have an extra 20 hours of distilling, so the constraint $2 * G + 1 * T \leq 40$ becomes $2 * G + 1 * T \leq 60$, as shown in Figure 3.13.

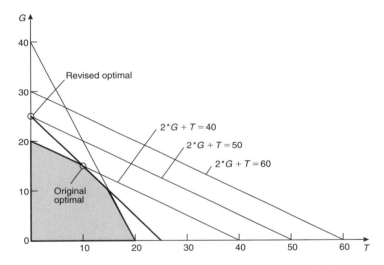

Figure 3.13 Revised optimal solution when distilling is not limiting.

Distilling now has so much capacity that the constraint has moved up the graph and is no longer limiting. Production is only limited by the constraints on finishing, $G + T \leq 25$ and the non-negativity constraint, $T \geq 0$. So distilling stops being limiting when the amount available increases beyond 25 hours. Any increase beyond this only adds spare capacity. It is worth paying £10 for each extra hour of distilling up to a maximum of 25 hours.

We can do a similar analysis to find the shadow price of finishing. Now we can find the value of an extra hour by replacing the original limiting constraints by:

$$2 * G + 1 * T = 40 \qquad \text{distilling constraint}$$
$$1 * G + 1 * T = 26 \qquad \text{new finishing constraint}$$

Solving these equations gives $G = 14$ and $T = 12$. Substituting these values into the objective function gives an optimal value of $30 * 14 + 20 * 12 = £660$, which is an increase of £10 over the original optimal solution. The shadow price for finishing – which is the most we should pay for an extra hour of capacity – is £10. (It is just a coincidence that this is the same as the shadow price for distilling.) This value holds for small changes, but if there is a bigger increase in the capacity, the constraint line moves up the graph and is no longer limiting. The limiting constraints become blending (with $G + 2 * T \le 40$) and distilling (with $2 * G + T \le 40$). At this point both G and T equal 13.33, so the maximum useful amount of finishing is $G + T = 26.7$ hours (see Figure 3.14).

Obviously, if a process already has spare capacity there is no point in getting more, so the shadow prices of non-limiting resources are zero. In this example there is spare capacity in blending so the shadow price is zero.

Now we have the shadow prices for the three processes separately as:

blending $= £0$ an hour

distilling $= £10$ an hour

finishing $= £10$ an hour.

But what happens when we have an extra hour of both distilling and finishing? We can find the value of this by replacing the original constraints by:

$2 * G + 1 * T = 41$ new distilling constraint

$1 * G + 1 * T = 26$ new finishing constraint

Solving these gives $G = 15$ and $T = 11$, and substituting in the objective function gives a maximum profit of $30 * 15 + 20 * 11 = £670$. This is £20 more than the

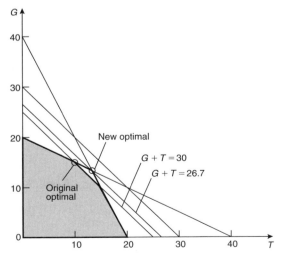

Figure 3.14   Revised optimal solution when finishing is not limiting.

original optimal solution, and is also the sum of the shadow prices when the increases were taken separately. So for small changes in resources, the total benefit is the sum of the separate benefits of increasing each resource separately.

We can use this result to see how new products would compete for resources with existing ones. Suppose we can make a new fertilizer, Vegup, in addition to Growbig and Thrive. Vegup uses 2 hours of blending, 2 hours of distilling and 2 hours of packing for each batch and contributes £50 to profits. Should we introduce this new product?

If we make one batch of Vegup, we have to make less Growbig and Thrive. We can use the shadow prices to find the cost of this reduced production. A batch of Vegup uses 2 hours of blending. This means that Growbig and Thrive will have 2 hours less blending available. As the shadow price is £10, this will cost £20. So the total cost of producing one batch of Vegup is:

Process	Hours used	Shadow price	Total cost
Blending	2	0	0
Distilling	2	10	20
Finishing	2	10	20
Total			40

The total cost of reducing existing production is £40. But the batch of Vegup gives an extra profit of £50, so there is a net benefit of $50 - 40 = £10$. This means that we should certainly make some Vegup. Unfortunately, the only way of finding how much Vegup to make is to revise the formulation and solve a new problem.

IN SUMMARY

For small changes in resources the optimal solution stays at the same extreme point. The shadow price then gives the cost or benefit of each unit of change. For larger changes the optimal solution moves and we have to revise the formulation and solve a new problem.

Self-assessment questions

3.10 What is meant by 'sensitivity analysis' in LP problems?

3.11 How much can the coefficients of the objective function vary without changing the position of the optimal solution?

3.12 What are 'shadow prices' in linear programming?

3.13 Within what limits are the shadow prices valid?

3.5 | Solving real problems

We have seen how to solve linear programmes with two variables. But real problems can have thousands of variables and so they are obviously solved by computer. The usual procedure for this is called the **simplex method**.

Throughout this chapter we have done calculations on the production planning problem of Growbig and Thrive. Now we should check these calculations by looking at the printout from a computer package.

Returning to the original formulation:

Maximize: $30 * G + 20 * T$

subject to: $1 * G + 2 * T \leq 40$

$2 * G + 1 * T \leq 40$

$1 * G + 1 * T \leq 25$

with $G \geq 0$ and $T \geq 0$

Many packages want the data in a matrix, so we can rewrite this as:

	G	T		
Maximize:	30	20		
subject to:	1	2	$\leq$	40
	2	1	$\leq$	40
	1	1	$\leq$	25

This data was put into a standard package with the results shown in Figure 3.15. The first part of these results shows the original data. The next part shows the main results, with optimal values, slack resources, shadow prices and objective function. The 'reduced cost' is used for variables that have the value zero – so they are not made. It shows how much the unit profit must rise before they are made – or how much the current profit declines if we decide to make a unit.

The next part of the printout shows the sensitivity analysis. The original profit on each batch of Growbig is £30, and this can vary between £20 and £40 without changing the optimal solution. Similarly, the profit on each batch of Thrive can vary between £15 and £30 without changing the optimal solution.

The final table shows the sensitivity of the right-hand side of constraints. It shows how much the right-hand side can vary and still keep the same shadow price. So distilling has a shadow price of £10, provided there is between 35 and 50 hours available. Similarly the shadow price of blending is zero provided there is more than 35 hours available.

PROBLEM ENTERED – Growbig and Thrive

Maximise:
    30 G + 20 T

Subject to:
    1) blending   G + 2 T < = 40
    2) distilling   2 G + T < = 40
    3) finishing   G + T < = 25

END OF INPUT

SOLUTION – LP OPTIMUM FOUND AT STEP 2

Objective function value = 650.0000

Variable	Value	Reduced Cost
G	15.0000	.0000
T	10.0000	.0000

Constraint	Stack Or Surplus	Shadow Prices
1) blending	5.0000	.0000
2) distilling	.0000	10.0000
3) finishing	.0000	10.0000

NO. ITERATIONS= 2

SENSITIVITY ANALYSIS – RANGES IN WHICH THE BASIS IS UNCHANGED

Objective Function Coefficient Ranges

Variable	Current Coefficient	Allowable Increase	Allowable Decrease
G	30.0000	10.0000	10.0000
T	20.0000	10.0000	5.0000

Righthand Side Ranges

Constraint	Current Rhs	Allowable Increase	Allowable Decrease
1) blending	40.0000	INFINITY	5.0000
2) distilling	40.0000	10.0000	5.0000
3) finishing	25.0000	1.6667	5.0000

END OF RESULTS

Figure 3.15 Computer printout for Growbig and Thrive.

WORKED EXAMPLE 3.5

West Coast Wood Products Ltd make four types of pressed panels from pine and spruce. Each sheet of panel must be cut and pressed. The following table shows the hours needed to produce a batch of each type of panel and the hours available each week:

Panel type	Hours of cutting	Hours of pressing
Classic	1	1
Western	1	4
Nouveau	2	3
East Coast	2	2
Available	80	100

West Coast have a limited amount of wood. The amounts needed for each type of panel, and total amount available each week, are given below:

Panel	Classic	Western	Nouveau	East Coast	Available
Pine	50	40	30	40	2500
Spruce	20	30	50	20	2000

The net profit on each batch of panel is £40 for Classic, £110 for Western, £75 for Nouveau and £35 for East Coast.

(a) Formulate this as a linear programme.

(b) A computer program gave the results shown in Figure 3.16. What do these figures show?

Solution

(a) We can start by defining the decision variables as the number of batches of each type of panelling to make a week (CLS, WST, NOU and EST). Then we get the formulation shown in the following matrix:

	CLS	WST	NOU	EST			
Maximize:	40	110	75	35			
subject to:	50	40	30	40	≤	2500	pine
	20	30	50	20	≤	2000	spruce
	1	1	2	2	≤	80	cutting
	1	4	3	2	≤	100	pressing

with CLS, WST, NOU and $EST \geq 0$

(b)

` PROBLEM ENTERED – West Coast Wood Products Ltd

Maximise:
$40\,CLS + 110\,WST + 75\,NOU + 35\,EST$

Subject to:
1) pine	$50\,CLS + 40\,WST + 30\,NOU + 40\,EST <= 2500$
2) spruce	$20\,CLS + 30\,WST + 50\,NOU + 20\,EST <= 2000$
3) cutting	$CLS + WST + 2\,NOU + 2\,EST <= 80$
4) pressing	$CLS + 4\,WST + 3\,NOU + 2\,EST <= 100$

END OF INPUT

SOLUTION – LP OPTIMUM FOUND AT STEP 2

Objective function value = 3218.7500

Variable	Value	Reduced Cost
CLS	37.5000	.0000
WST	15.6250	.0000
NOU	.0000	7.5000
EST	.0000	26.2500

Constraint	Stack Or Surplus	Shadow Prices
1) pine	.0000	.3125
2) spruce	781.2500	.0000
3) cutting	26.8750	.0000
4) pressing	.0000	24.3750

NO. ITERATIONS = 2

SENSITIVITY ANALYSIS – RANGES IN WHICH THE BASIS IS UNCHANGED

Objective Function Coefficient Ranges

Variable	Current Coefficient	Allowable Increase	Allowable Decrease
CLS	40.0000	97.5000	12.5000
WST	110.0000	50.0000	10.0000
NOU	75.0000	7.5000	INFINITY
EST	35.0000	26.2500	INFINITY

Righthand Side Ranges

Constraint	Current Rhs	Allowable Increase	Allowable Decrease
1) pine	2500.0000	1433.3330	1500.0000
2) spruce	2000.0000	INFINITY	781.2500
3) cutting	80.0000	INFINITY	26.8750
4) pressing	100.0000	150.0000	50.0000

END OF RESULTS

Figure 3.16 Computer printout for Worked Example 3.7.

The results show that the optimal solution is to make 37.5 batches of Classic a week, 15.625 batches of Western and none of the others. This gives a profit of £3218.75. Making a batch of Nouveau would reduce profit by £7.50, while a batch of East Coast would reduce profit by £26.25.

The limiting constraints are pine and pressing, with spare capacity in spruce (781.25) and cutting (26.875 hours). This remains true while the amount of spruce remains over 1218.75 and the amount of cutting remains above 53.125 hours. The shadow price of pine is £0.312 (valid for amounts between 1000 and 3933.333) and of pressing is £24.375 (valid for between 50 and 250 hours).

The profit for each batch of Classic can vary between £27.50 and £137.50 without changing the position of the optimal solution, while the profit on Western can vary between £100.00 and £160.00. The profits on Nouveau and East Coast must remain below £82.50 and £61.25 respectively.

WORKED EXAMPLE 3.6

A manufacturer makes four models of metal filing cabinet, A to D. Each of these has four stages in manufacturing: cutting, stamping, assembly and packing. The following table shows the times needed for each stage, together with the times available each week:

Model	Hours needed per unit				Number of machines	Hours available per machine per week
	A	B	C	D		
Cutting	2	3	4	4	10	40
Stamping	1	2	2	3	6	36
Assembly	3	3	2	4	12	38
Packing	2	3	3	3	8	40

The fixed cost of production is £30 000 a year. Selling prices are £25, £28, £34 and £40 respectively for each cabinet, with direct costs of £16, £18, £22 and £25 respectively. On average the cutting machines need 10% of their total time for maintenance, stamping machines need 16.667%, assembly machines 25% and packing machines 10%. The company works a standard 48-week year.

(a) Formulate this problem as a linear programme.

(b) The solution to this problem is given in Figure 3.17. What does this show?

(c) How would you interpret a solution that gave non-integer values for the number of cabinets?

(d) Why does the company not produce any of cabinet model B?

(e) What would be the effect on the company's profit if all maintenance is reduced to 10% of available machine time?

Solution

(a) Let A be the number of filing cabinets of type A made each week, B be the number of filing cabinets of type B made each week, and so on.

The profit on each cabinet is:

Model	A	B	C	D
Selling price	25	28	34	40
Direct costs	16	18	22	25
Profit	9	10	12	15

The weekly times available for each process are:

	Machines	Hours	Utilization	Net hours/week
Cutting	10	40	0.9	360
Stamping	6	36	0.833	180
Assembly	12	38	0.75	342
Packing	8	40	0.9	288

So the formulation becomes:

Maximize: $\quad 9*A + 10*B + 12*C + 15*D \qquad$ objective function

subject to: $\quad 2*A + 3*B + 4*C + 4*D \leq 360 \qquad$ cutting

$\qquad\qquad\quad 1*A + 2*B + 2*C + 3*D \leq 180 \qquad$ stamping

$\qquad\qquad\quad 3*A + 3*B + 2*C + 4*D \leq 342 \qquad$ assembly

$\qquad\qquad\quad 2*A + 3*B + 3*C + 3*D \leq 288 \qquad$ packing

with $\qquad A, B, C$ and $D \geq 0 \qquad\qquad\quad$ non-negativity

(b)

```
PROBLEM ENTERED - Filing cabinets

Maximise:
9A + 10B + 12C + 15D

Subject to:
1) cutting       2A + 3B + 4C + 4D <= 360
2) stamping      A + 2B + 2C + 3D <= 180
3) assembly      3A + 3B + 2C + 4D <= 342
4) packing       2A + 3B + 3C + 3D <= 288

END OF INPUT
```

Figure 3.17   continued overleaf

SOLUTION – LP OPTIMUM FOUND AT STEP 3

Objective function value = 1265.1430

VARIABLE	VALUE	REDUCED COST
A	74.5714	.0000
B	.0000	2.8571
C	33.4286	.0000
D	12.8571	.0000

Constraint	Stack Or Surplus	Shadow Prices
1) cutting	25.7143	.0000
2) stamping	.0000	1.2857
3) assembly	.0000	.8571
4) packing	.0000	2.5714

NO. ITERATIONS = 3

SENSITIVITY ANALYSIS – RANGES IN WHICH THE BASIS IS UNCHANGED

Objective Function Coefficient Ranges

Variable	Current Coefficient	Allowable Increase	Allowable Decrease
A	9.0000	1.5000	2.0000
B	10.0000	2.8571	INFINITY
C	12.0000	2.0000	3.6000
D	15.0000	4.5000	1.8000

Righthand Side Ranges

Constraint	Current Rhs	Allowable Increase	Allowable Decrease
1) cutting	360.0000	INFINITY	25.7143
2) stamping	180.0000	45.0000	18.0000
3) assembly	342.0000	78.0000	90.0000
4) packing	288.0000	22.5000	46.8000

END OF RESULTS

Figure 3.17 Computer printout for Worked Example 3.8.

The optimal solution is to make 74.57 cabinets of type A a week, no cabinets of type B, 33.43 of type *C* and 12.86 of type D. This gives a profit of £1265.14 a week – or £60 726.72 in a 48-week year. The fixed costs of £30 000 have to be subtracted from this.

This solution has 25.71 hours of spare cutting, but all other processes are fully used with shadow prices of 1.29, 0.86 and 2.57 respectively.

(c) The optimal solution has 74.57 cabinets of type A to be made a week. This simply means that a cabinet is left partly finished at the end of a week. If this is not possible, we can define the problem as an 'integer linear programme', which we will describe in the next chapter.

(d) Making one cabinet of type B would reduce profits by £2.86. We can confirm this from the shadow prices. The costs of making a unit of B are:

Process	Hours needed	Shadow price	Cost
Cutting	3	0	0
Stamping	2	1.2857	2.5714
Assembly	3	0.8571	2.5713
Packing	3	2.5714	7.7142
Total cost			12.8569

Subtracting the profit of £10 from this gives the reduction in profits for each unit of B made.

(e) There is already 25.71 spare hours of cutting so reducing the maintenance would have no effect. The other three processes are fully used and extra capacity will increase profits.

Reducing the maintenance for stamping will increase the amount available each week by $6*36*(0.9-0.833) = 14.47$ hours. Stamping has a shadow price of 1.29, so the extra weekly profit is $1.29*14.47 = £18.67$ a week.

Similarly, reducing the maintenance for assembly gives an extra profit of $12*38*(0.9-0.75)*0.86 = £58.82$. Packing already has maintenance of 10% so there would be no change there. These effects are additive so the overall effect is a rise in profit of $18.67 + 58.82 = £77.49$ a week or about 6%.

LP formulations can have thousands of variables and constraints. With these large and complicated models, it is easy to make a mistake in the formulation. Computer software will find these mistakes and give messages about:

- **unbound solution** – which means the constraints do not limit the solution, and the feasible region effectively extends to infinity
- **infeasible solution** – which means the constraints are too limiting and have left no feasible region
- **redundancy** – when some constraints are not needed as there are other, more severe ones

When you get these results you have to check the model and data carefully to make sure there are no mistakes.

> *IN SUMMARY*

Real linear programmes are always solved by computer. These generally use the simplex method to get solutions.

Self-assessment questions

3.14   Why are computers always used to solve linear programmes?

3.15   What information might be given in a computer printout for a linear programme?

Case example

PetroCanada

PetroCanada is Canada's largest oil company. It was formed as a federal crown corporation in 1976, to concentrate the Canadian oil industry and provide more competition to US companies. By the 1980s it was involved in all aspects of the industry from initial exploration, through production and refining, and on to retail sales. It operated seven major refineries and 5000 service stations throughout Canada. In 1986 alone, it spent $6.5 billion acquiring five other oil companies. Then government policies changed, and PetroCanada was privatized in the late 1980s.

PetroCanada use linear programming for many purposes, including capital investment decisions, marketing strategies, raw material purchases, inventory policy, refinery configuration, feasibility studies, logistics planning and blending problems. One important use optimizes refinery operations, so that specified market demands are met at minimum cost. This problem requires decisions at various levels. Strategic decisions have effects over many years – such as the type of products to be made and the plants operated. Tactical decisions have effects in the next year – such as the annual production of different types of product. Operational decisions have effects over the next few weeks – such as weekly production targets for individual products.

One way in which LP helps with this production planning is to show managers the effects of their proposed plans. Managers can suggest an outline plan, perhaps describing overall production for the next year. An LP model then adds the details to this plan, using two types of data:

- **fixed data**, such as refinery capacity and operating characteristics, market demand, blending coefficients, transfer options, yield models
- **variable data**, such as prices of crude oil, amounts purchased, constraints on raw materials, sales and purchase options, plant shut-downs, and inventories

The LP model finds the optimal production for the year. Managers can look at the results, adjust the plans, and re-run the linear programme. They might, for example, suggest closing one of the smaller refineries. Then they can run the LP model to find the optimal profit with the refinery open, and re-run it to find the optimal profit with the refinery closed.

A typical production planning model in PetroCanada has 37 000 variables with 10 000 constraints, and generates 5000 lines of report.

CHAPTER REVIEW

Many problems in business can be described as constrained optimization. Linear programming can solve certain problems of constrained optimization. This chapter described the approach of linear programming, and in particular it:

- discussed problems of constrained optimization
- listed the three stages in solving a linear programme, i.e. formulation, solution and sensitivity analysis
- described problem formulation
- showed how problems with two variables can be solved by graphs
- described sensitivity analysis
- discussed the results from computer packages

KEY TERMS

constrained optimization
constraints
decision variables
extreme point
feasible region
formulation
limiting constraints
linear programming

LP
non-negativity constraints
objective
objective function
sensitivity analysis
shadow price
simplex method

Case study

Smithers Engineering Company

In the 1930s George Smithers started to supply parts to car manufacturers in the West Midlands. As Smithers Engineering grew it opened new factories and bought several other manufacturers. John Smithers took control of the company when his father retired in 1964. Everything ran smoothly until the early 1970s when the economy began to decline and the traditional engineering centres of the West Midlands were badly affected by recession. Smithers closed several of their older factories and concentrated production on a few of their most successful products. Things continued badly until the early 1990s when the period of continuous contraction seemed to be ending. The company could now do some serious planning for the future.

Strategic planning in Smithers looked at the period between 1 and 5 years in the future. A small Tactical Planning Group was formed to bridge the gap between these strategic plans and daily operations. The group's first job was to design an annual plan for their eight main products, which were made in three factories and sold in seven regional markets. They wanted to find how much of each product to make at each factory and ship to each market.

Because they had dramatically reduced production in their factories, there was some free space, but this was kept in mothballs and was not normally maintained. If sales increased beyond normal capacities, this space could be used, but it would have higher production costs. So the most relevant variables for the annual plan were:

- the quantity of each product to make at each factory and sent to each market
- the amount of higher cost capacity to use at each factory
- the advertising budget for each product
- the price of each product

The Tactical Planning Group started to build a linear programming model of operations for the current year. One part of the group set about building a model, while the other part collected data.

The modelling group soon established a series of rules:

- The main objective is to maximize total profit. This is:

  selling price – production costs – cost of transport – cost of selling

- Production levels for each product in each factory must be between upper and lower limits.

- Total production at each factory – including use of higher cost expansions – must not be more than the available capacity.
- Deliveries between factories and markets are limited by available transport.
- Sales of each product in each market must lie between upper and lower limits.
- Total sales must not exceed total production.
- Total production of any product must not exceed maximum possible sales for that product.
- Advertising expenditure must not exceed its budget.
- Cash needed for advertising and expanding production must be less than the money available.

Unfortunately the data collection did not go well. After a lot of effort, they had only collected data from one factory making four products for one market, as follows.

Production

Four products A, B, C and D are made on two assembly lines in the factory: A and B are made on the first line while C and D are made on the second. The following table shows the amount of standard and higher cost capacity of the factory:

Production line	[Standard capacity] cost per unit	capacity per year	[Higher cost capacity] cost per unit	capacity per year
1	16.00	2000	18.40	600
2	12.00	1800	14.00	400

Product	A	B	C	D
Material cost per unit	64	84	72	28

Marketing

Each £5000 spent on advertising increases sales by the following percentages:

Product	A	B	C	D
Percentage increase in demand for £5000 in advertising	5.0	14.0	4.2	16.5

Estimates were also made of the effect of selling price on sales:

Product	Selling price (£)	Estimated annual sales (£)
A	120	64 000
B	120	18 000
	130	11 000
C	120	30 000
D	70	60 000
	80	90 000

The total advertising budget for the year was £70 000.

There was a lot less data than the Group hoped for, but in their first report they could still:

- describe a linear programme formulation for tactical planning when they get enough data
- demonstrate this formulation with the limited data available
- describe plans for expanding the model in future years

Problems

3.1   Find the optimal solution to the following linear programme:

Minimise $2 * Q + 1 * R$

subject to: $1 * Q + 1 * R \leq 10$ (1)

$1 * Q - 1 * R \leq 2$ (2)

$1 * Q \geq 4$ (3)

$1 * R \leq 5$ (4)

with Q and R greater than or equal to zero.

3.2   Two additives X1 and X2 can increase the octane number of petrol. One kilogramme of X1 in 5000 litres of petrol will increase the octane number by 10, while one kilogramme of X2 in 5000 litres will increase the octane number by 20. The total additives must increase the octane number by at least 5, but a total of no more than half a kilogramme can be added to 5000 litres and the amount of X2 plus twice the amount of X1 must be at least half a kilogramme. If X1 costs £30 a kilogramme and X2 costs £40 a kilogramme, formulate this problem as a linear programme. What is the optimal solution?

3.3 A diet needs a daily intake of at least 3000 calories and 160 units of protein. Seven basic foods can be used in the diet with characteristics as follows:

Food	Calories per kg	Protein per kg	Cost (pence per kg)
1	600	4	40
2	50	16	20
3	500	20	50
4	800	6	60
5	1000	0	80
6	30	30	100
7	200	10	30

Formulate this as a linear programme. What is the optimal solution?

3.4 Novacook Ltd makes two types of cooker, one electric and one gas. There are four stages in the production of each of these, with details given below.

Manufacturing stage	Time required (hours per unit)		Total time available (hours a week)
	Electric	Gas	
Forming	4	2	3 600
Machine shop	10	8	12 000
Assembly	6	4	6 000
Testing	2	2	2 800

The electric cooker has variable costs of £200 a unit and a selling price of £300 while the gas cooker has variable costs of £160 and a selling price of £240 a unit. Fixed overheads are £60 000 a week and the company works a 50-week year. The marketing department suggest maximum sales of 800 electric and 1250 gas cookers a week.

Formulate this as a profit-maximizing linear programme. What is the optimal solution and annual profit? If an outside consultant offers his testing services to the company, how much is this worth and how much should they use?

Novacook is considering a new cooker that will use the manufacturing stages for 4, 6, 6 and 2 hours respectively. At what selling price is it worth making this cooker if the other variable costs are £168 a unit?

3.5 A manufacturer makes five types of electrical tester – Standard 1 and 2, Normal 1 and 2, and Super. The production time (in hours per hundred units) of each type and the capacity of each production process are given below. All testers can be sold, and the profits on each unit are £6, £7, £8, £9 and £11 respectively.

Process	Standard 1	Standard 2	Normal 1	Normal 2	Super	Capacity (hours per month)
Pressing	2	2	4	5	6	160
Wiring	6	3	5	4	7	240
Assembly	4	4	6	7	8	200

What is the maximum monthly profit? What would be the effect of raising the selling price of Standard testers by 20%? A new tester is proposed that could go through each of Pressing, Wiring and Assembly at a rate of 50 units an hour. What profit is needed before it is worth making the new tester?

3.6 Figure 3.18 shows the printout from a linear programming package. What information can you get from this?

3.7 Figure 3.19 shows the printout from another linear programming package. What information can you get from this?

3.8 Figure 3.20 shows a printout from a linear programming package. Make sure you can understand all of this and can explain the results.

3.9 A manufacturing company has forecast the numbers of a component it will need each month. Unfortunately, the cost of the component is rising fairly quickly. The following table shows the forecast needs and cost:

Month	Jan	Feb	Mar	Apr	May	Jun	Jul	Aug	Sep	Oct	Nov	Dec
Demand	100	90	80	60	50	50	70	90	100	100	110	110
Cost (£)	200	200	205	205	210	210	210	220	220	230	230	240

The company can buy components ahead of time to avoid the price increases, but there is a cost of £2 a unit for carrying stock from one period to the next. What is the best pattern for ordering the component?

```
PROBLEM

MIN
    14 A + 10 B + 7 C + 6 D + 12 E + 7 F

SUBJECT TO
    2)  A − B − 4 C − 10 D <= 100
    3)  10 A + 7 B + 4 C + 18 D + 6 E + 8 F >= 1200
    4)  6 A + 3 C + 8 E <= 150
    5)  D + E + 10 F <= 50
    6)  4 C − 3 D − 2 E − 5 F >= 140
    7)  10 A + 6 E + 10 F >= 80
END

LP OPTIMUM FOUND AT STEP 5

OBJECTIVE FUNCTION VALUE
    1)  1682.6670
```

VARIABLE	VALUE	REDUCED COST
A	3.333333	.000000
B	128.000000	.000000
C	43.333330	.000000
D	3.333333	.000000
E	.000000	50.270420
F	4.666667	.000000

ROW	SLACK OR SURPLUS	SHADOW PRICES
2)	431.333300	.000000
3)	.000000	−1.428571
4)	.000000	7.473304
5)	.000000	1.935065
6)	.000000	−5.926407
7)	.000000	−4.455411

```
NO. ITERATIONS=  5

RANGES IN WHICH THE SOLUTION IS UNCHANGED:

OBJ COEFFICIENT RANGES
```

VARIABLE	CURRENT COEF	ALLOWABLE INCREASE	ALLOWABLE DECREASE
A	14.000000	67.253660	21.285710
B	10.000000	INFINITY	6.208333
C	7.000000	10.642860	97.785710
D	6.000000	18.378570	INFINITY
E	12.000000	INFINITY	50.270420
F	7.000000	21.285710	183.785700

RIGHTHAND SIDE RANGES

ROW	CURRENT RHS	ALLOWABLE INCREASE	ALLOWABLE DECREASE
2	100.000000	INFINITY	431.333300
3	1200.000000	INFINITY	895.999900
4	150.000000	107.130400	8.250000
5	50.000000	36.666660	36.666660
6	140.000000	11.000000	154.000000
7	80.000000	13.750000	44.000000

Figure 3.18 Computer printout for Problem 3.6.

Program: Linear Programming

Problem Title: Problem 3.7

***** Input Data *****
Max. $Z = 10x1 + 7x2 + 5x3 + 8x4 + 14x5 + 22x6$

Subject to
C1 $2x1 - 3x2 - 2x3 + 4x4 + 5x5 - 6x6 <= 250$
C2 $4x1 + 3x2 + 7x3 + 6x4 + 9x5 + 12x6 <= 500$
C3 $-3x1 + 5x2 + 4x3 + 6x4 - 2x5 + 4x6 >= 120$
C4 $7x1 + 5x2 + 9x3 - 8x4 - 5x5 + 6x6 >= 200$
C5 $-1x1 + 3x2 + 4x3 + 6x4 - 3x5 - 5x6 <= 550$
C6 $-4x1 + 3x2 + 2x3 + 1x4 + 6x5 + 6x6 >= 250$
C7 $6x1 - 8x2 + 6x3 - 3x4 + 2x5 + 2x6 <= 400$

***** Program Output *****

Final Optimal Solution At Simplex Tableau: 8
$Z = 1187.500$

Variable	Value	Reduced Cost
x1	31.250	0.000
x2	125.000	0.000
x3	0.000	11.750
x4	0.000	6.417
x5	0.000	7.250
x6	0.000	6.500

Constraint	Slack/Surplus	Shadow Price
C1	562.500	0.000
C2	0.000	2.417
C3	411.250	0.000
C4	643.750	0.000
C5	206.250	0.000
C6	0.000	−0.083
C7	1212.500	0.000

Objective Coefficient Ranges

Variables	Lower Limit	Current Values	Upper Limit	Allowable Increase	Allowable Decrease
x1	9.333	10.000	No limit	No limit	0.667
x2	4.833	7.000	7.500	0.500	2.167
x3	No limit	5.000	16.750	11.750	No limit
x4	No limit	8.000	14.417	6.417	No limit
x5	No limit	14.000	21.250	7.250	No limit
x6	No limit	22.000	28.500	6.500	No limit

Righthand Side Ranges

Constraints	Lower Limit	Current Values	Upper Limit	Allowable Increase	Allowable Decrease
C1	−312.500	250.000	No limit	No limit	562.500
C2	250.000	500.000	1050.000	550.000	250.000
C3	No limit	120.000	531.250	411.250	No limit
C4	No limit	200.000	843.750	643.750	No limit
C5	343.750	550.000	No limit	No limit	206.250
C6	−90.345	250.000	500.000	250.000	340.345
C7	−812.500	400.000	No limit	No limit	1212.500

***** End of Output *****

Figure 3.19   Computer printout for Problem 3.7.

```
Program: Linear Programming

Problem Title: Problem 3.8

***** Input Data *****

Min. Z = 4 x 1 + 6 x 2 + 8 x 3 + 2 x 4

Subject to
    C1  1 x 1 + 6 x 2 + 5 x 3 + 8 x 4 <= 120
    C2  -2 x 1 - 3 x 2 + 1 x 3 + 1 x 4 >= 60
    C3  5 x 1 + 1 x 2 - 3 x 3 - 2 x 4 <= 100
    C4  -4 x 1 - 1 x 2 - 1 x 3 + 4 x 4 >= 20

***** Program Output *****

Infeasible Solution

Artificial variables remain in the final tableau.

Check data and constraints for errors.

***** End of Output *****
```

Figure 3.20   Computer printout for Problem 3.8.

Discussion questions

3.1   Linear programming assumes that all aspects of a problem are linear. But in the real world there are many non-linearities. How much do you think this limits the use of LP?

3.2   LP requires a huge amount of data. This will inevitably contain approximations – and possibly errors. So it is optimistic to suggest that LP finds an 'optimal solution'. Do you agree with this?

3.3   It always takes a lot of effort to solve a linear programme. But there are other methods – based on heuristics – that can give good solutions with much less effort. When is it worth putting in the extra effort to get optimal rather than good solutions?

3.4   Managers find it difficult to understand linear programmes. Often the printouts are too complicated and come with little explanation. How might this affect the implementation of LP results?

3.5   Linear programmes are often designed and run by specialized groups, who are separate from both the problem and the managers responsible. What difficulties might this cause?

Extensions to linear programming

4

CHAPTER OUTLINE

Linear programming is the most widely used member of a family of mathematical programming models. In this chapter we are going to look at some other members of this family. After reading the chapter you should be able to:

- discuss different types of mathematical programming
- formulate integer linear programmes
- understand the purpose of zero-one programming
- formulate goal programmes
- understand the approach of dynamic programming
- interpret the results from mathematical programming software

4.1 | Integer linear programming

4.1.1 Mathematical programming

In the last chapter we saw how linear programming can solve problems of constrained optimization. But we can only use LP for certain types of problem. In particular, the objective function and constraints must be linear functions of the decision variables. Now we are going to extend the ideas of LP to look at a family of related models. These models are generally called *mathematical programmes*.

An obvious extension of LP looks at problems that are not linear. Suppose an organization can get economies of scale – so the production costs do not rise linearly with the amount it produces. If the organization tries to minimize costs, it will have a problem with a non-linear objective function. Other problems can also have non-linear constraints.

Unfortunately, such non-linear problems are much more difficult to solve than standard linear programmes. In practice, they are so difficult that we can only get optimal solutions to a few special types of *non-linear programmes*. These are not widely used, so we will look at another area where there has been more success. This concerns *integer programming*.

IN SUMMARY

There are many extensions to linear programming, which form a family of mathematical programmes. These are generally much more difficult to solve than linear programmes.

4.1.2 Integer decision variables

Integer linear programming – which is sometimes abbreviated to **integer programming** – is used for problems where some of the decision variables must be integers. You can meet problems like this when finding, for example, the best number of machines to buy, shops to open, people to employ, cars to drive, ships to build, or factories to run.

> For **integer programmes**, some – or all of the decision variables are constrained to integer values.

To get an integer solution, we have to solve a large number of related linear programmes. This means that integer linear programmes are much more difficult to solve than standard linear programmes. In practice, it is difficult to solve integer linear programmes with more than a few hundred variables.

If integer linear programmes are so much more difficult to solve, you might ask why we bother. Why do we not simply use a standard linear programme and round the answers to the nearest integers? Unfortunately, there are two problems with this:

- the rounded solution may be infeasible
- rounding may not give an optimal solution

WORKED EXAMPLE 4.1

Palladin Construction is looking at two types of production machines. Each machine of type A costs £20 000, can make 9000 units and needs 40 hours of maintenance a month. Each machine of type B costs £10 000, can make 7000 units and needs 50 hours of maintenance a month. The company can spend £100 000 on machines, and it has 400 hours of maintenance available each month. What mix of machines should it buy?

Solution

The number of machines Palladin buy must be integer, so this is clearly a problem of integer programming. But suppose we ignore the integer values and treat it as a standard linear programme.

Let	A = the number of machines of type A Palladin buy	
Let	B = the number of machines of type B	
Maximize:	$9000*A - 7000*B$	production
subject to:	$20*A + 10*B \leq 100$	cost
	$40*A + 50*B \leq 400$	maintenance
	$A, B \geq 0$	non-negativity

This linear programme has the optimal solution $A = 1.67$ and $B = 6.67$. Total production is $9000 * 1.67 + 7000 * 6.67 = 61\,667$ units a month.

But the variables A and B should be integer, as it makes no sense to buy 1.67 or 6.67 machines. So we can try rounding the answers to the nearest integers, to give $A = 2$ and $B = 7$. Unfortunately this breaks the constraints:

cost: $20*A + 10*B = 20*2 + 10*7 = 110$

This is not less than 100, so the solution breaks the first constraint.

maintenance: $40*A + 50*B = 40*2 + 50*7 = 430$

This is not less that 400, so the solution also breaks the second constraint.

This first solution did not work, as we rounded both A and B up. We could try rounding A down to 1, to give the solution $A = 1$ and $B = 7$. This does not break the constraints:

$$\text{cost:} \qquad 20 * A + 10 * B = 20 * 1 + 10 * 7 = 90$$

This is less than 100 and does not break the first constraint.

$$\text{maintenance:} \qquad 40 * A + 50 * B = 40 * 1 + 50 * 7 = 390$$

This is less than 400 and does not break the second constraint.

Substituting these values into the objective function gives a total production of:

$$9000 * A + 7000 * B = 9000 * 1 + 7000 * 7 = 58\,000 \text{ units a month}$$

But this is not the optimal solution. Taking $A = 2$ and $B = 6$ gives a production of 60 000 a month and still does not break the constraints (as shown in Figure 4.1).

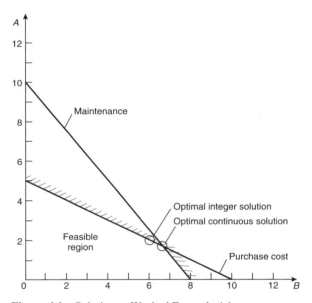

Figure 4.1 Solution to Worked Example 4.1.

This example shows that rounding the results from a standard linear programme does not necessarily give an optimal – or even feasible – solution for an integer linear programme. In practice, the solution may be good enough, particularly if the decision variables are large or the costs are small. If a fast food company uses LP to find the number of plastic cups to buy, it might get an answer of 15 904.3 cups. Rounding this to 15 904 – or even 16 000 – will have very little effect on costs, and will certainly be easier than solving the equivalent integer linear programme.

$\boxed{IN\ SUMMARY}$

Standard LP assumes that decision variables are continuous. Many problems need integer variables. Rounding the results from linear programmes can give reasonable answers, but to guarantee optimal solutions we have to use integer linear programming (ILP).

4.1.3 Formulating integer linear programmes

The overall approach of ILP is similar to the approach of linear programming. This starts by formulating the problem to get it into a standard form.

WORKED EXAMPLE 4.2

Gem Furniture Warehouses want to run a short advertising campaign. They can use several types of advertisement, with costs and likely audiences shown in the following table. To spread the advertisements around, they have set a maximum number of each type. If the budget for the campaign is £30 000, formulate this problem as an integer linear programme.

	Cost	Audience (in units)	Maximum number
Daytime TV on Channel 3	2000	30	3
Evening TV on Channel 3	5000	70	3
Daytime TV on Channel 4	1000	10	3
Evening TV on Channel 4	2000	20	3
Local radio	500	10	6
Weekly newspaper	200	20	4
Weekend newspaper	400	35	4

Solution

We can define the decision variables as follows:

Let: $D3$ and $D4$ be the number of advertisements on daytime TV for Channels 3 and 4

$E3$ and $E4$ be the number of advertisements on evening TV for Channels 3 and 4

R be the number of advertisements on local radio

NW and NE be the number of advertisements in the weekly and evening newspapers

The objective is to maximize the audience:

Maximize:

$$30 * D3 + 70 * E3 + 10 * D4 + 20 * E4 + 10 * R + 20 * NW + 35 * NE$$

There are constraints on the amount of money Gem spend:

$$2000 * D3 + 5000 * E3 + 1000 * D4 + 2000 * E4 + 500 * R + 200 * NW + 400 * NE$$
$$\leq 30\,000$$

and the number of advertisements of each type:

$$D3 \leq 3$$
$$E3 \leq 3$$
$$D4 \leq 3$$
$$E4 \leq 3$$
$$R \leq 5$$
$$NW \leq 4$$
$$NE \leq 4$$

Then there are the integer constraints which say that Gem cannot buy fractions of advertisements:

$$D3, E3, D4, E4, R, NW \text{ and } NE \quad \text{are integer}$$

Finally, we have the non-negativity constraints:

$$D3, E3, D4, E4, R, NW \text{ and } NE \geq 0$$

WORKED EXAMPLE 4.3

Edward Reynolds is moving to a village in the Highlands, and wants to invest £100 000 in the local economy. He finds three attractive alternatives:

- A developer is selling up to 10 holiday cottages for £30 000 each, with a profit of £6000 a year.
- A farmer is selling up to 25 acres of land for £3000 an acre and a profit of £800 a year.
- A business is looking for partners willing to buy up to six shares for £1000 each, with a profit of £200 a year. Edward liked this project and decided to buy at least one share in the partnership.

Any money that Edward did not spend on these investments would buy shares in local companies, with an average profit of 10%. Formulate Edward's investment problem as an integer programme.

Solution

We can start by defining the decision variables.

Let: HC = the number of holiday cottages Edward buys

L = the number of acres of land he buys

SP = the number of shares bought in the partnership

SS = the amount spent on stocks and shares

This is an integer programme, because HC and SP must be integer. L and SS can take any value, so we have a ***mixed integer programme.*** The last worked example was a ***pure integer programme*** where all the variables were integer.

The objective function is to maximize the gross profits:

Maximize: $6000 * HC + 800 * L + 200 * SP + 0.1 * SS$

There are constraints on:

$HC \leq 10$	number of holiday cottages available
$L \leq 25$	area of land available
$SP \geq 1$	buying at least one share in the partnership
$SP \leq 6$	available shares in the partnership
$30\,000 * HC + 3000 * L$ $+ 1000 * SP + SS = 100\,000$	total investment
HC and SH = integers	integer constraints
HC, L, SH and $SS \geq 0$	non-negativity constraints

IN SUMMARY

The first step in solving an integer linear programme is the formulation. This puts the problem into a standard format.

4.1.4 Solving integer linear programmes

Integer linear programmes are always solved by computer. There is no point in going through the arithmetic, but we can show how a ***branch and bound*** method works. This divides all solutions to a problem into sets, then looks at each set to see if it is likely to contain the optimal solution, or if it can be ignored. Suppose you are looking for the fastest route between London and Copenhagen. There are many possible routes, some of which include the link from Brussels and Bonn, and some of which do not. It might take so long to get from Brussels and Bonn that any route which includes this link is unlikely to be the fastest. Then you can ignore all of these and concentrate on the other routes. This is the basis of branch and bound methods, which we can illustrate by the following example.

WORKED EXAMPLE 4.4

Use a branch and bound method to solve the following problem:

$$\text{Maximize:} \quad 3*X+4*Y$$

$$\begin{array}{lll} \text{subject to:} & 100*X+60*Y & \leq \ 800 \\ & 4*X+7*Y & \leq \ 75 \\ & X \text{ and } Y & \geq \ 0, \text{ and are integer} \end{array}$$

Solution

We will start by ignoring the integer constraint and solving the ordinary linear programme. This has an optimal solution of:

$$X = 2.39 \quad Y = 9.35 \qquad \text{objective function} = 44.57$$

Now this ordinary linear programme is exactly the same as the integer linear programme, except it has ignored the integer constraints. When we return the integer constraints, we are adding more conditions. A more constrained problem cannot have a better solution than a less constrained one, so the best possible optimal solution for the integer linear programme is 44.57. In other words, we have found an *upper bound* on the optimal solution. Whatever the values of X and Y, the optimal value of the objective function cannot be greater than 44.57.

We can also find a *lower bound* on the optimal solution. If we round down the ordinary LP answers we get:

$$X = 2 \quad Y = 9 \qquad \text{objective function} = 42$$

So now we know that the optimal solution must lie between these two bounds, 42 and 44.57.

The ordinary LP solution has $Y = 9.35$. But in the final solution, we know that Y must be integer, so it cannot be between 9 and 10. Then there are two alternatives:

- either Y is less than or equal to 9
- or Y is greater than or equal to 10

The next step is to see which of these two alternatives is likely to be true. We can do this by adding constraints to give two versions of the problem, and solving the resulting linear programmes.

Version 2

Add the constraint that *Y* is less than or equal to 9.

Maximize: $3 * X + 4 * Y$

subject to:
$$100 * X + 60 * Y \leq 800$$
$$4 * X + 7 * Y \leq 75$$
$$Y \leq 9$$

This has the optimal solution:

$$X = 2.6 \quad Y = 9 \qquad \text{objective function} = 43.8$$

Version 3

Add the constraint that *Y* is greater than or equal to 10.

Maximize: $3 * X + 4 * Y$

subject to:
$$100 * X + 60 * Y \leq 800$$
$$4 * X + 7 * Y \leq 75$$
$$Y \geq 10$$

This has the optimal solution:

$$X = 1.25 \quad Y = 10 \qquad \text{objective function} = 43.75$$

These two solutions give a revised upper bound for when *Y* is 9 or less, and when *Y* is 10 or more, as shown in Figure 4.2.

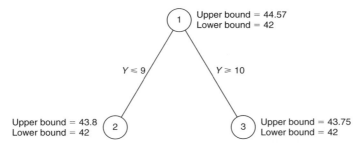

Figure 4.2 Branch and bound values for Worked Example 4.4.

It is more likely that the branch with the higher upper bound contains the optimal solution, so we will look at version 2 of the problem. This has a value of *X* of 2.6. But we know that in the final solution *X* must be an integer, and cannot lie between 2 and 3. So there are two alternatives:

- either *X* is less than or equal to 2
- or *X* is greater than or equal to 3.

We can add these constraints to version 2 of the problem, to get two further versions.

Version 4

Adding the constraint that X is less than or equal to 2.

Maximize: $3 * X + 4 * Y$

subject to: $100 * X + 60 * Y \leq 800$
$4 * X + 7 * Y \leq 75$
$Y \leq 9$
$X \leq 2$

This has the optimal solution:

$X = 2 \quad Y = 9 \qquad$ objective function $= 42$

Version 5

Adding the constraint that X is greater than or equal to 3.

Maximize: $3 * X + 4 * Y$

subject to: $100 * X + 60 * Y \leq 800$
$4 * X + 7 * Y \leq 75$
$Y \leq 9$
$X \geq 3$

This has the optimal solution:

$X = 3 \quad Y = 8.33 \qquad$ objective function $= 42.33$

Version 4 gives an integer solution with a value of 42. Version 5 does not have an integer solution, but has a higher upper bound. So we can now look at this solution and add constraints to form two more versions, with Y as either less than or equal to 8, or Y as greater than or equal to 9 (as shown in Figure 4.3).

If we continue adding constraints in this way, we will eventually find the optimal solution. This happens when we get a feasible integer solution that is greater than the upper bound on any other solution. Here the optimal solution is:

$X = 1 \quad Y = 10 \qquad$ objective function $= 43$

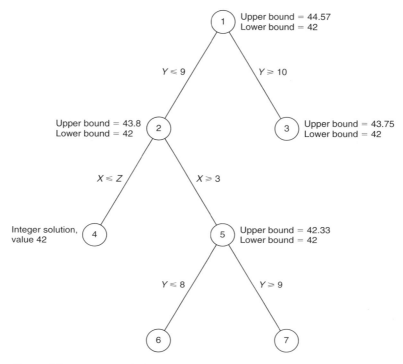

Figure 4.3 Extending the branch and bound procedure.

WORKED EXAMPLE 4.5

Worked Example 4.2 described the advertising campaign for Gem Furniture Warehouses. What is the optimal solution to this problem? What would happen if the advertising budget fell from £30 000 to £25 000?

Solution

Figure 4.4 shows a printout from an ILP package. This shows the largest audience of 610 by using all the advertising on Channel 3 and in the newspapers, five radio advertisements, and two evening advertisements on Channel 4.

ILP packages usually give a brief commentary on how they found the solution. They may not give a sensitivity analysis, which is quite difficult to interpret in ILP. If you want to find the effects of changes, it is usually better to revise the problem and find a new solution. In this case, when the budget constraint is tightened, the audience is reduced to 550, as shown in Figure 4.5.

INTEGER PROGRAMMING
Gem Furniture Warehouses
Advertising Campaign

PROBLEM ENTERED

MAXIMIZE
  1)   30 D3 + 70 E3 + 10 D4 + 20 E4 + 10 R + 20 NW + 35 NE

SUBJECT TO
  2)   2000 D3 + 5000 E3 + 1000 D4 + 2000 E4 + 500 R + 200 NW + 400 NE <= 30000
  3)   D3 <= 3
  4)   E3 <= 3
  5)   D4 <= 3
  6)   E4 <= 3
  7)   R <= 6
  8)   NW <= 4
  9)   NE <= 4

INTEGER VARIABLES
      D3   E3   D4   E4   R   NW   NE

SOLUTION

ILP OPTIMUM FOUND AT STEP   6   OBJECTIVE VALUE =   616.00
NEW INTEGER SOLUTION OF   585.000000   AT BRANCH   4 PIVOT   21
NEW INTEGER SOLUTION OF   610.000000   AT BRANCH   6 PIVOT   33
ENUMERATION COMPLETE. BRANCHES=   12 PIVOTS=   60

LAST INTEGER SOLUTION IS THE BEST FOUND

    OBJECTIVE FUNCTION VALUE

  1)   610.00000

VARIABLE	VALUE	REDUCED COST
D3	3.000000	−30.000000
E3	3.000000	−70.000000
D4	.000000	−10.000000
E4	2.000000	−20.000000
R	5.000000	−10.000000
NW	4.000000	−20.000000
NE	4.000000	−35.000000

NO. ITERATIONS =   61

Figure 4.4   Computer printout for Worked Example 4.5.

INTEGER PROGRAMMING
Gem Furniture Warehouses
Reduced Budget Advertising Campaign

PROBLEM ENTERED

MAXIMIZE
1) $30\,D3 + 70\,E3 + 10\,D4 + 20\,E4 + 10\,R + 20\,NW + 35\,NE$

SUBJECT TO
2) $2000\,D3 + 5000\,E3 + 1000\,D4 + 2000\,E4 + 500\,R + 200\,NW + 400\,NE <= \quad 25000$
3) $D3 <= \quad 3$
4) $E3 <= \quad 3$
5) $D4 <= \quad 3$
6) $E4 <= \quad 3$
7) $R <= \quad 6$
8) $NW <= \quad 4$
9) $NE <= \quad 4$

INTEGER VARIABLES
        D3   E3   D4   E4   R   NW   NE

SOLUTION

ILP OPTIMUM FOUND AT STEP   58   OBJECTIVE VALUE =   560.40
NEW INTEGER SOLUTION OF   555.000000   AT BRANCH   13 PIVOT   69

LAST INTEGER SOLUTION IS THE BEST FOUND

   OBJECTIVE FUNCTION VALUE

   1)   550.00000

VARIABLE	VALUE	REDUCED COST
D3	2.000000	−30.000000
E3	3.000000	−70.000000
D4	.000000	−10.000000
E4	.000000	−20.000000
R	6.000000	−10.000000
NW	4.000000	−20.000000
NE	4.000000	−35.000000

NO. ITERATIONS =   99

Figure 4.5   Computer printout for reduced budget in Worked Example 4.5.

WORKED EXAMPLE 4.6

In Worked Example 4.3 we formulated Edward Reynolds' investment problem. What is the optimal solution to this problem?

Solution

A printout for this problem is shown in Figure 4.6. The optimal solution is to buy one holiday cottage, one share of the partnership and 23 acres of land. This gives a profit of £24 600 a year.

```
INTEGER PROGRAMMING
Edward Reynolds
Investment Problem


PROBLEM ENTERED

MAXIMIZE
   1)   6000 HC + 800 L + 200 SP + 0.1 SS

SUBJECT TO
   2)   HC <=  10
   3)   L <=  25
   4)   SP >=  1
   5)   SP <=  6
   6)   30000 HC + 3000 L + 1000 SP + SS =   100000

INTEGER VARIABLES
        HC      SP

NON-INTEGER VARIABLES
        L       SS

SOLUTION

ILP OPTIMUM FOUND AT STEP   7
NEW INTEGER SOLUTION OF   24600.0000   AT BRANCH   2 PIVOT   11

LAST INTEGER SOLUTION IS THE BEST FOUND

    OBJECTIVE FUNCTION VALUE

   1)   24600.000

VARIABLE          VALUE            REDUCED COST
   HC            1.000000             .000000
   L            23.000000         - 200.000000
   SP            1.000000             .000000
   SS             .000000             .100000

NO. ITERATIONS =   16
```

Figure 4.6   Computer printout for Worked Example 4.6.

> **IN SUMMARY**
>
> **A common method of solving integer linear programmes uses a branch and bound approach. This has to solve a lot of related linear programmes to get an integer solution.**

Self-assessment questions

4.1 'Mathematical programming is another name for linear programming.' Is this true?

4.2 How would you solve non-linear programmes?

4.3 What is the main feature of integer programmes?

4.4 What is meant by 'branch and bound'?

4.5 Why does the solution to a linear programme form a bound on the solution to the equivalent integer linear programme?

∥ 4.2 ∥ Zero-one programming

A particularly useful type of integer programme has some variables that can only have the values zero or one. This is called *zero-one programming*.

> With **zero-one programming** some variables are constrained to have the values zero or one.

At first sight, this may not seem particularly useful – but it is one of the most common types of mathematical programming. Suppose you are thinking of opening a new shop. You may decide to open the shop, or not, and we could describe this decision using a zero-one variable X. Then X has the value '1' if you open the shop, and '0' if you do not. We can formulate many other problems using zero-one variables in this way. For example, should we use a piece of equipment or not; should a vehicle travel between two towns or not; should we make a product or not; should we do one job immediately after another or not?

WORKED EXAMPLE 4.7

A holiday resort can spend £500 000 on improving its facilities. Four plans have been suggested, for a swimming pool, gymnasium, squash courts and tennis centre. The costs, land needed and likely visitors to each of these are shown below. If the resort has 7 hectares of land for development, formulate their problem as a zero-one programme.

Development	Cost (£'000)	Number of visitors (people a day)	Area needed (hectares)
Swimming pool	350	400	3
Gymnasium	250	600	4
Squash courts	150	150	2
Tennis centre	100	100	4

Solution

We can start by defining the variables. Let:

$X_1 = 1$ if the resort builds a swimming pool, and $= 0$ if it does not

$X_2 = 1$ if the resort builds a gymnasium, and $= 0$ if it does not

$X_3 = 1$ if the resort builds squash courts, and $= 0$ if it does not

$X_4 = 1$ if the resort builds a tennis centre, and $= 0$ if it does not

The objective is to maximize the number of visitors

Maximize: $400 * X_1 + 600 * X_2 + 150 * X_3 + 100 * X_4$

When facilities are built, the corresponding X_i equals one, and the value is included in the objective function; but when facilities are not built the corresponding X_i equals zero and the value is not added to the objective function.

Now there are constraints on the money:

$$350 * X_1 + 250 * X_2 + 150 * X_3 + 100 * X_4 \leq 500$$

Again, the values are only used in the constraint if the corresponding X_i equals one; otherwise the X_i equals zero and the cost is not counted. Similarly, the constraint on land is:

$$3 * X_1 + 4 * X_2 + 2 * X_3 + 4 * X_4 \leq 7$$

Finally, we can add explicitly the zero-one constraint:

$$X_i = 0 \text{ or } 1 \quad \text{for } i = 1 \text{ to } 4$$

WORKED EXAMPLE 4.8

Snack-Products are looking at six research projects for new savoury snacks. The following table shows the capital, research staff and expected net present values of each project.

Project	Capital (£'000)	Research staff	Net present value (£'000)
1	500	11	650
2	650	16	900
3	450	9	800
4	550	7	900
5	400	5	600
6	900	24	1100

The company want to maximize the net present value of the projects, but only have £1.7 million of capital and 35 research staff. It is not worth doing part of a project, so each is either started, or it is not. Projects 5 and 4 are connected, so that if project 5 is done, project 4 must also be done. If projects 2 and 3 are done, project 4 must also be done. To spread the risk, only two out of projects 1, 4 and 6 can be done. Because they have long-term importance, at least one of projects 3, 4 and 5 must be done. Formulate this problem as a linear programme.

Solution

There are six projects, each of which is either started, or it is not. So we can define the following zero-one variables:

Let $X_1 = 1$ if project 1 is started, and $= 0$ if it is not started

$X_2 = 1$ if project 2 is started, and $= 0$ if it is not started

and so on.

The objective is to maximize the net present value:

Maximize:

$$650 * X_1 + 900 * X_2 + 800 * X_3 + 900 * X_4 + 600 * X_5 + 1100 * X_6$$

If a project is started the relevant X_i has a value 1 and its net present value is added to the objective function; if a project is not started the relevant X_i has a value 0 and the net present value is not added.

There are constraints on the amount of capital (in thousands of pounds):

$$500 * X_1 + 650 * X_2 + 450 * X_3 + 550 * X_4 + 400 * X_5 + 900 * X_6 \le 1700$$

Again, if the project is started the relevant $X_i = 1$ and the capital needed is added to the constraint; otherwise the relevant $X = 0$ and the capital is ignored. The next constraint is on research staff:

$$11 * X_1 + 16 * X_2 + 9 * X_3 + 7 * X_4 + 5 * X_5 + 24 * X_6 \leq 35$$

We also know that project 4 must be done if project 5 is done. This means:

if $X_5 = 1$, X_4 must also equal one

if $X_5 = 0$, X_4 can be either zero or one

We can write this constraint as:

$$X_4 \geq X_5 \quad \text{or} \quad X_4 - X_5 \geq 0$$

Project 4 must be done if both projects 2 and 3 are done. In other words:

if $X_2 = 1$ and $X_3 = 1$ then $X_4 = 1$

if either $X_2 = 0$ or $X_3 = 0$ then X_4 can be either zero or one

We can write this as:

$$X_4 \geq X_2 + X_3 - 1 \quad \text{or} \quad -X_2 - X_3 + X_4 \geq -1$$

At most two of projects 1, 4 and 6 are done. So:

$$X_1 + X_4 + X_6 \leq 2$$

The company must do at least one of projects 3, 4 and 5, or:

$$X_3 + X_4 + X_5 \geq 1$$

To complete the formulation we state explicitly that:

$$X_i = 0 \text{ or } 1 \quad \text{for} \quad i = 1 \text{ to } 6$$

Like other integer linear programmes, zero-one programmes are often solved by branch and bound methods. Because there are only a few integer values the solutions can be much faster, and we can solve bigger problems.

WORKED EXAMPLE 4.9

The printout in Figure 4.7 shows the result for Worked Example 4.8. What can you find from the printout?

INTEGER PROGRAMMING
Gem Furniture Warehouses
Reduced Budget Advertising Campaign

PROBLEM ENTERED

MAXIMIZE
 1) $650 X1 + 900 X2 + 800 X3 + 900 X4 + 600 X5 + 1100 X6$

SUBJECT TO
 2) $500 X1 + 650 X2 + 450 X3 + 550 X4 + 400 X5 + 900 X6 <=$ 1700
 3) $11 X1 + 16 X2 + 9 X3 + 7 X4 + 5 X5 + 24 X6 <=$ 35
 4) $X4 - X5 >=$ 0
 5) $-X2 - X3 + X4 >=$ -1
 6) $X1 + X4 + X6 <=$ 2
 7) $X3 + X4 + X5 >=$ 1

ZERO-ONE VARIABLES
      X1   X2   X3   X4   X5   X6

SOLUTION

LP OPTIMUM FOUND AT STEP   4
OBJECTIVE VALUE =   2715.38500
NEW INTEGER SOLUTION OF   2600.00000   AT BRANCH   11 PIVOT   52

LAST INTEGER SOLUTION IS THE BEST FOUND

    OBJECTIVE FUNCTION VALUE

 1)   2600.0000

VARIABLE	VALUE	REDUCED COST
X1	.000000	−650.000000
X2	1.000000	−900.000000
X3	1.000000	−800.000000
X4	1.000000	−900.000000
X5	.000000	−600.000000
X6	.000000	−1100.000000

NO. ITERATIONS =   59

Figure 4.7   Computer printout for Worked Example 4.9.

Solution

The printout starts by describing the problem entered, including the six zero-one variables. Then it gives the optimal solution. This has X_2, X_3 and X_4 equal to one, so Snack-Products should go ahead with projects 2, 3 and 4. X_1, X_5 and X_6 equal zero, so the company should not do projects 1, 5 and 6. This gives a net present value of £2 600 000.

> ### IN SUMMARY
>
> **Zero-one programming is a useful extension to integer programming. As its name suggests, this has some variables that are constrained to take the values either zero or one. This is particularly useful for describing problems that include logical relationships.**

Self-assessment questions

4.6   What do you think 'binary variables' are?

4.7   'In zero-one programmes **all** the decision variables have the values zero or one'. Is this true?

4.8   Why is zero-one programming so useful?

Case example

Amoco's NGL system

Natural gas liquids (NGL) are the propane, butane and condensate that are extracted from natural gas before it is sold. Amoco's Canadian distribution system can handle over 250 000 barrels of NGL a day. This system moves products from wells in Alberta to fractionation facilities – which split the NGL into propane and butane components. To serve its Eastern markets, Amoco operate the largest fractionation facility in North America – with a capacity of 130 000 barrels a day – at Sarnia, Ontario. There are storage and terminal facilities at Sarnia, Windsor, Ontario and St Clair, Michigan.

Amoco's production of NGL can be formulated as a linear programme. They want to maximize the profit from sales of NGL products. But there are constraints on the supply of feedstock (the raw materials), the feedstock composition, customer demand, capacity of fractionation towers and butane splitting unit, capacity of the pipelines connecting operations, storage capacity and withdrawal rates at the different locations and products that can be formed from the feedstock used. Some of the variables in this programme are zero-one, and these typically show whether a particular pipeline is used, or whether a facility is used for a particular product.

4.3 | Goal programming

So far we have looked at problems that have a single objective. But in practice, many problems have a range of different *goals*. A financial planner might want to get high returns on investments with reasonable security, long-term growth, and a spread over different industries. A production planner might have the goals of satisfying customer demand, minimizing production costs, limiting hours of overtime and improving productivity. In these cases, we want to find the solution that gives the best results when judged by several different criteria.

WORKED EXAMPLE 4.10

Joan Petri has opened a pottery in St Ives. She specializes in making two types of garden pots, and can sell up to 70 of these a week. It takes 1 hour to make the first kind of pot, and 2 hours to make the second kind. Joan and an assistant are willing to work up to 60 hours each a week. There is one other constraint, as they have signed a long-term contract to buy at least 240 kilogrammes of clay a week. The first type of pot uses 3 kg of clay, and the second type uses 2 kg. The profits on pots are £15 each for the first type and £20 each for the second type. Can linear programming find the best mix of pots?

Solution

We can formulate this problem as a linear programme.

Let X = the number of the first type of pot Joan makes each week, and Y = the number of the second type of pot she makes each week.

The objective function is:

Maximize:	$15 * X + 20 * Y$	gross profit
subject to:	$X + Y \leq 70$	sales constraint
	$X + 2 * Y \leq 120$	hours worked constraint
	$3 * X + 2 * Y \geq 240$	supply of clay constraint
	$X \geq 0, Y \geq 0$	non-negativity constraints

This formulation seems reasonable, but if you try to solve it you will see that there is no feasible region (as shown in Figure 4.8).

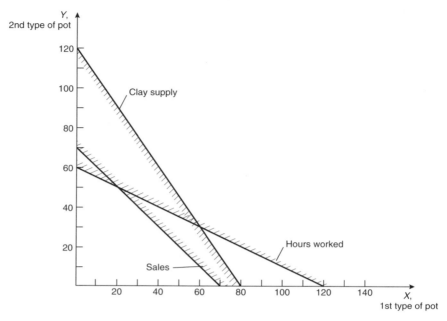

Figure 4.8 Constraints for Worked Example 4.10 with no feasible region.

The linear programme described in the last worked example has no solution. If we want to go further with this problem, we have to compromise. Although there is no solution that satisfies all the constraints, we can look for one that comes close to satisfying most of them. In other words, we are not looking for an optimal solution, but a 'satisfying' one. Ideally, Joan Petri wants to make less than 70 pots a week, but she might accept a solution that is close to this. Or they might ideally work less than 120 hours a week, but will accept a solution that is close to this.

Now the constraints become target values. The inflexible constraints of linear programming become more flexible goals that we are aiming for. We can tackle this kind of problem using *goal programming*:

> **Goal programming** looks for the compromise solution that comes closest to achieving a set of goals.

The first step in solving a goal programme is the formulation, to get the problem into a standard format.

WORKED EXAMPLE 4.11

Formulate Joan Petri's problem described in Worked Example 4.10 as a goal programme.

Solution

We can start as before by defining the same variables. Let X = the number of the first type of pot Joan makes each week, and Y = the number of the second type of pot she makes each week.

Now we can look at the old constraints and phrase these in terms of goals. The first constraint was on sales:

$$X + Y \leq 70 \qquad \text{sales constraint}$$

If this is no longer a rigid constraint, but a goal that can be broken, we can define two other variables. Let d_1^+ be the number of excess pots (above 70) that Joan makes, and d_1^- be the number of pots short (below 70) that Joan makes.

Here the 'd' stands for 'deviation', the subscript '1' shows that we are working on the first goal, and the '$+$' or '$-$' show whether we are over- or under-achieving the goal. Then we can write the goal as:

$$X + Y - d_1^+ + d_1^- = 70 \qquad \text{sales goal}$$

Goals are always written as equations. If the solution makes 80 jugs, the over-supply, d_1^+, equals 10, while the under-supply, d_1^-, equals zero. If the solution makes 60 jugs, the under-supply, d_1^-, equals 10, while the over-supply, d_1^+, equals zero. The final solution will only give a positive value to either d_1^+ or d_1^-, and the other is zero.

Now we can deal with the second constraint in the same way. We can convert it into another goal using the variables d_2^+ and d_2^- for over- and under-supply:

$$X + 2 * Y - d_2^+ + d_2^- = 120 \qquad \text{hours worked goal}$$

The supply of clay constraint becomes the goal:

$$3 * X + 2 * Y - d_3^+ + d_3^- = 240 \qquad \text{clay supply goal}$$

This deals with all the original constraints, but we have not yet included the old objective function. We can do this by describing it as another goal. Suppose Joan thinks that a gross profit of £1000 a week is reasonable, then we can define a fourth goal based on the old objective function:

$$15 * X + 20 * Y - d_4^+ + d_4^- = 1000 \qquad \text{gross profit goal}$$

Now we have four goals. Each of these is an equation that contains terms for both under- and over-supply. A reasonable solution would minimize the deviation from these goals. In other words, we can form a new objective that minimizes some function of the d_i^+ and d_i^-.

Some goals are more important than others. Joan might think it is very important to make a gross profit of £1000, but less important to use 240 kg of clay. So we must include the relative importance of each goal in the objective function. There are two ways of doing this:

- *give each goal a weight* – with more important goals having a higher weight. This only really works if the units in each goal are the same. So we cannot use weights here as we have mixed units of pounds, hours and kilogrammes.

- *rank the goals* – assigning a priority, P_i, to each goal. In this case, Joan might think that making a gross profit of £1000 is most important, so it gets the priority P_1. Then working 120 hours a week is second most important, and gets a priority P_2. Then sales and matching clay supplies get priorities P_3 and P_4 respectively.

The objective is to minimize the deviations from the goals, weighted by the priorities. So we can write the objective function as:

Minimize:

$$P_3 * d_1{}^+ + P_3 * d_1{}^- + P_2 * d_2{}^+ + P_2 * d_2{}^- + P_4 * d_3{}^+ + P_4 * d_3{}^- + P_1 * d_4{}^+ + P_1 * d_4{}^-$$

This finishes the formulation. The only thing to remember is that the non-negativity conditions still apply to all the variables X, Y, $d_i{}^+$, $d_i{}^-$ and P_i.

As usual, we are going to solve this problem using a standard package. A printout for the solution is given in Figure 4.9.

This printout starts with a description of the problem entered. Variables like '$d+1$' describe the deviation from the target, and '$P3$' show the priorities. Then it solves the problem and lists the solution, which has $X = 0$, which says that Joan should make none of the first type of pot, and $Y = 50$, which says that she should make 50 of the second type. Then the solution lists the deviations to show how closely the goals were achieved. Finally, it lists the priorities. The first priority was to make a gross profit of £1000, and this was completely achieved. The second priority was to work for 120 hours a week, but the result was 20 hours under this; the goal of 70 pots was missed by 20, and the least important goal of using 240 kg of clay was missed by 140 kg. The 'non-achievement' of the goals increases as their importance decreases.

Sometimes, we do not mind if a target is exceeded, but would like it to be at least reached. Joan Petri, for example, would not mind if her profit is more than £1000, so the goal is really to make at least £1000. This means that we need not put the deviation for over-achievement into the objective function. On the other hand, Joan may not mind working less than her goal of 120 hours, but would prefer not to work more – so we can omit the deviation for working less hours. Her contract for clay means that she does not want to use less than 240 kg, but can

```
Program:          Goal Programming
Problem Title:    Joan Petri's Pottery


***** Input Data *****

Minimize
   P3*d+1 + P3*d−1 + P2*d+2 + P2*d−2 + P4*d+3 + P4*d−3 + P1*d+4 + P1*d−4

Subject to:
   Goal 1        1 x 1 + 1 x 2 + d − 1 − d + 1 = 70
   Goal 2        1 x 1 + 2 x 2 + d − 2 − d + 2 = 120
   Goal 3        3 x 1 + 2 x 2 + d − 3 − d + 3 = 240
   Goal 4        15 x 1 + 20 x 2 + d − 4 − d + 4 = 1000

***** Program Output *****

Analysis of decision variables
```

Variable	Solution Value
X1	0.000
X2	50.000

Analysis of deviations

Variable	Value	Variable	Value
d−1	20	d+1	0
d−2	20	d+2	0
d−3	140	d+3	0
d−4	0	d+4	0

Analysis of the objective function

Priority	Nonachievement
P1	0.000
P2	20.000
P3	20.000
P4	140.000

```
***** End of Output *****
```

Figure 4.9 Computer printout for goal programming.

use more, so we can omit the deviation for over-supply. Then the revised objective function is:

$$\text{Minimize:} \quad P_3 * d_1^+ + P_3 * d_1^- + P_2 * d_2^+ + P_4 * d_3^- + P_1 * d_4^-$$

As Joan's main priority is now to make more money, the solution is to make 66.67 of the first type of pot. This shows how the solutions to goal programmes can be very sensitive to changes – a small change in the goals can give a completely different solution.

WORKED EXAMPLE 4.12

The Konigsveldt National Forest has 30 000 hectares which is used by ramblers, for other leisure activities, as special habitat for elk, and for logging. Each hectare of the forest can support 150 visitor-days for ramblers, 300 visitor-days for other leisure uses, 1 elk or 1500 cubic metres of wood. The annual costs of maintaining an acre of forest are £100 for ramblers, £400 for other leisure and £50 for elk. Any forest cut for timber gives an income of £2000, and this must cover all costs of the forest.

The wardens of the forest have a number of goals. In order of priority, they want to:

- have at least two million visitor-days of ramblers
- have at least six million visitor-days of other leisure
- support 3000 elk
- cut no more than 6 million cubic metres of timber

Formulate this problem as a goal programme.

Solution

We can define the decision variables as follows. Let:

$x1$ = the area set aside for ramblers
$x2$ = the area set aside for other leisure activities
$x3$ = the area set aside for elk
$x4$ = the area set aside for logging

There are two hard constraints:

1   the forest has a limited area

$$x1 + x2 + x3 + x4 \leq 30\,000 \qquad \text{area constraint}$$

2   the income from logging must cover all costs

$$2000 * x4 \geq 100 * x1 + 400 * x2 + 50 * x3$$

or $100 * x1 + 400 * x2 + 50 * x3 - 2000 * x4 \leq 0 \qquad \text{cost constraint}$

There is also a series of goals:

3       $150 * x1 \geq 2\,000\,000$

or $150 * x1 + d_3^- - d_3^+ = 2\,000\,000 \qquad \text{rambler goal}$

4       $300 * x2 \geq 5\,000\,000$

or $300 * x2 + d_4^- - d_4^+ = 5\,000\,000 \qquad \text{leisure activities goal}$

5             $x3 = 3000$

   or $x3 + d_5^- - d_5^+ = 3000$ elk goal

6             $1500 * x4 \leq 6\,000\,000$

   or $1500 * x4 + d_6^- - d_6^+ = 6\,000\,000$ logging constraint

Now we have two constraints and four goals, and we need an objective function. This is to minimize a function of the deviations from goals. The wardens have goals for minimum numbers of visitors, but they do not mind if these are exceeded. So we put in the objective function the deviations for under-achievement (d_3^- and d_4^-), but do not bother with the over-achievement (d_3^+ and d_4^+). The elk goal is a more definite target, so we include the deviation for both under- and over-achievement (d_5^- and d_5^+). With the area set aside for logging, the wardens have specified a maximum, so we put the over-achievement d_6^+ in the objective function, and ignore the under-achievement d_6^-. Adding the priorities gives the objective function:

   Minimize: $P_1 * d_3^- + P_2 * d_4^- + P_3 * d_5^- + P_3 * d_5^+ + P_4 * d_6^+$

Figure 4.10 shows a printout for this problem.

   You can see here that the solution is to set aside 13 333 hectares for ramblers, 13 333.33 hectares for other leisure activities, nothing for elk and 3333.33 hectares for logging. This satisfies both the constraints, and one of the goals. Unfortunately the solution only gives 4 000 000 user-days for other leisure activities, and it does not leave any room for elk.

IN SUMMARY

Sometimes the constraints of linear programming can be viewed as goals. We can then solve these problems using goal programming. This adds variables to measure the deviation from target values, and the objective is to minimize the weighted value of these deviations.

Self-assessment questions

4.9   What is the main difference between constraints and goals?

4.10 A goal programme gave the result that $d_4^+ = 20$. What does this mean?

4.11 If you got a solution which included the results $d_5^- = 10$ and $d_5^+ = 20$, what would it mean?

4.12 What is in the objective function of goal programmes?

Program: **Goal Programming**
Problem Title: **Konigsveldt National Forest**

***** Input Data *****

Minimize
$$P1*d-3 + P*2d-4 + P*3d+5 + P*3d-5 + P4*d+6$$

Subject to

Constraint 1	$1x1 + 1x2 + 1x3 + 1x4 <= 30000$
Constraint 2	$100x1 + 400x2 + 50x3 - 2000x4 <= 5$
Goal 3	$150x1 + d-3 - d+3 = 2000000$
Goal 4	$300x2 + d-4 - d+4 = 5000000$
Goal 5	$1x3 + d-5 - d+5 = 3000$
Goal 6	$1500x4 + d-6 - d+6 = 6000000$

***** Program Output *****

Analysis of deviations

Constraint	RHS Value	d+	d-
Constraint 1	30000.000	0.000	0.000
Constraint 2	0.000	0.000	0.000
Goal 3	2000000.000	0.000	0.000
Goal 4	5000000.000	0.000	1000000.000
Goal 5	3000.000	0.000	3000.000
Goal 6	6000000.000	0.000	1000000.000

Analysis of decision variables

Variable	Solution Value
X1	13333.333
X2	13333.333
X3	0.000
X4	3333.333

Analysis of the objective function

Priority	Nonachievement
P1	0.000
P2	1000000.000
P3	3000.00
P4	1000000.000

***** End of Output *****

Figure 4.10   Computer printout for Konigsveldt National Forest.

4.4 ‖ Dynamic programming

So far we have looked at problems that need a single decision. But many problems occur in stages and require a series of related decisions. In manpower planning, for example, an organization will find the numbers of people it must recruit, train, promote, or dismiss each period. But the most important factor affecting the number of people working in any period is the number of people who were working in the previous period. So the organization does not want a single decision relating to a particular period – but the best series of related decisions. *Dynamic programming* can solve this kind of problem.

Dynamic programmes are not as well-structured as other types of mathematical programmes. There is no standard formulation, and no single method of solution. It is really an approach to solving problems rather than a single method.

> **Dynamic programming** provides an approach to solving problems that need a series of related decisions.

Dynamic programming (DP) breaks down a problem into a series of **stages**. At each stage we have a simpler problem – and the solution to one stage affects the solution at the following stage.

We can use a simple problem to illustrate this approach. A chef has two cups, one of which holds 8 ounces and the other holds 5 ounces. The chef has a recipe that needs 7 ounces. How can she measure this? The answer comes by realizing that she needs 2 ounces in the larger cup, so that she can add 5 ounces from the smaller cup. So now the chef's problem is how to get 2 ounces into the larger cup. There is no way of removing 6 ounces from the large cup, so the chef has to get 2 ounces in the smaller cup, and then transfer this to the larger cup. But the chef can easily get 2 ounces in the smaller cup. She fills it once and pours the contents into the larger cup; then she refills the smaller cup and pours as much as she can into the larger cup. The larger cup is full after 3 ounces, and this leaves 2 ounces in the smaller cup. We can summarize these stages as:

Action	Amount in 5 ounce cup	Amount in 8 ounce cup
fill smaller cup	5	0
transfer to larger cup	0	5
fill smaller cup	5	5
transfer 3 ounces to larger cup	2	8
empty larger cup	2	0
transfer 2 ounces to larger cup	0	2
fill smaller cup	5	2
transfer to larger cup	0	7

This is not a very useful problem, but it shows how dynamic programming tackles a problem. The chef took the original problem and divided it into stages. She went to the end to see the result she wanted, and then she worked backwards to look at the type of decision she needed at each stage. Eventually she reached a starting point where she could solve the initial problem. Then she used this to work forwards to find the best decision at each stage.

Approach of **dynamic programming**:
- divide the whole problem into a number of stages
- find the end-point that you want to reach
- work backwards from this end-point, taking each stage in turn and finding the type of decision you need
- continue working backwards until you reach a starting point where you can solve the initial problem
- find this initial solution, and work forwards to find the best decision at each stage.

WORKED EXAMPLE 4.13

Figure 4.11 shows the roads and distances between Glasgow and London. Use dynamic programming to find the shortest route between these two.

Solution

The complete problem here is to find the shortest route from Glasgow to London, but we can break this down into stages. Each stage will find the best routes between towns. The end-point we want to reach is London, so this is where dynamic programming starts. Remember that the first stage shows how to reach the final solution, and we are working backwards – so later stages describe earlier decisions.

Stage 1

Stage 1 looks at ways of reaching the final point – which are the ways of reaching London. For this we can travel directly from towns 6, 7, 8 or 9. If earlier decisions get us to town 6, our best route is obviously to travel directly to London with a distance of 125 miles. We can use the same reasoning for the other towns, to give the following decisions in stage 1:

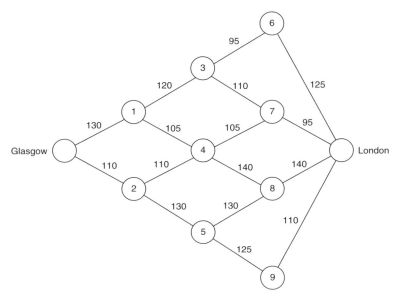

Figure 4.11 Road network between Glasgow and London.

Town reached	Routes to London	Distance
6	6–London	125
7	7–London	95
8	8–London	140
9	9–London	110

Now we can move on to stage 2.

Stage 2

Stage 2 looks at the different ways of reaching the towns considered in stage 1. So it looks at the ways of reaching towns 6, 7, 8 and 9. We can reach these directly from towns 3, 4 or 5. From town 3, we can go to either of towns 6 or 7. So the shortest distance from town 3 to London is:

- the distance from town 3 to town 6, plus the shortest distance from town 6 to London, or

- the distance from town 3 to town 7, plus the shortest distance from town 7 to London

But we already know the shortest distance from towns 6 and 7 to London from stage 1. Using this approach we can work out the distances from all towns in stage 2, to give the following summary of decisions:

Town in stage 2	Route from town in stage 2	Distance in this stage	Best distance from stage 1 town to London	Total distance from stage 2 town to London	Best route
3	3–6	95	125	220	
3	3–7	110	95	205	****
4	4–7	105	95	200	****
4	4–8	140	140	280	
5	5–8	130	140	270	
5	5–9	125	110	235	****

Now we have found the best distance from each stage 2 town to London. If, for example, we got to town 4, the best route to London is through town 7 with a distance of 200 miles. This is the end of the stage, and we can move on to stage 3.

Stage 3

Stage 3 looks at the different ways of reaching the towns considered in stage 2. So it looks at the ways of reaching towns 3, 4 and 5. We can reach these directly from towns 1 and 2. From town 1 we can go to either of towns 3 or 4. So the shortest distance from town 1 to London is:

- the distance from town 1 to town 3, plus the shortest distance from town 3 to London, or

- the distance from town 1 to town 4, plus the shortest distance from town 4 to London

But we already know the shortest distance from towns 3 and 4 to London from stage 2. Using this approach we can work out the distances from all towns in stage 3, to give the following summary of decisions:

Town in stage 3	Route from town in stage 3	Distance in this stage	Best distance from stage 2 town to London	Total distance from stage 3 town to London	Best route
1	1–3	120	205	325	
1	1–4	105	200	305	****
2	2–4	110	200	310	****
2	2–5	130	235	365	

Now we have found the best distance from each stage 3 town to London. If, for example, we got to town 1, the best route to London is through town 4 with a distance of 305 miles. This is the end of the stage, and we can move on to stage 4.

Stage 4

Stage 4 is the final stage and looks at the different ways of reaching towns considered in stage 3. So it looks at the ways of reaching towns 1 and 2 from Glasgow. Using the same reasoning as before, we can summarize the decisions for stage 4 as follows:

Town in stage 4	Route from town in stage 4	Distance in this stage	Best distance from stage 3 town to London	Total distance from stage 4 town to London	Best route
Glasgow	Glasgow–1	130	305	435	
	Glasgow–2	110	310	420	****

This gives the best distance from Glasgow to London. Working forwards to check the solution we have:

Stage	Route	Distance
4	Glasgow–2	110
3	2–4	110
2	4–7	105
1	7–London	95
Total		420

You can see from this worked example that dynamic programming is not easy. It is often difficult to formulate problems, and then difficult to solve them. As there is not a standard format, there is little standard software. You can guess that dynamic programming is not as widely used as other types of mathematical programming. Nonetheless, it can be very useful for certain types of problems.

You can see some useful points in the last worked example. It relies on the fact that when we got to, say, town 4 it did not matter how we got there – all we needed was the shortest distance from town 4 to London. Then if the optimal solution goes through town 4, it will include the shortest distance from town 4 to London. A general statement of this idea is given in the ***principle of optimality***:

> The **principle of optimality** states that it does not matter what decisions were made to get to a particular stage, the remaining decisions must form an optimal policy to get from that stage to the final solution.

Another feature in the worked example is the relationship that connects each stage. Here we had:

distance from a = distance from the town + distance from the
town in this   to a town in the   town in the previous
stage to London   previous stage   stage to London

Dynamic programmes always have this kind of ***recursive relationship*** to link the different stages.

WORKED EXAMPLE 4.14

A hospital has 5 nurses to assign to 3 wards. The following table shows the benefits of assigning different numbers of nurses to each ward. So assigning 3 nurses to ward Y has a benefit of 13. Use dynamic programing to maximize the overall benefit.

Number of nurses	Benefit in ward		
	X	Y	Z
0	0	0	0
1	4	4	6
2	6	8	9
3	10	13	13
4	14	15	16
5	16	16	17

Solution

We have to start by dividing the whole problem into a number of stages. So we will look at the assignment of nurses to each ward as a separate problem. This gives a series of three smaller problems of assigning nurses to ward X, then assigning nurses to ward Y and finally assigning nurses to ward Z.

The end-point that we want to reach is to assign the remaining nurses to ward Z. So working backwards, we have stage 1 that assigns nurses to ward Z, then stage 2 that assigns nurses to ward Y, then stage 1 that assigns nurses to ward X. Now we can define a recursive relationship to link these stages. At each stage, the number of nurses we can assign is the number we could assign in the previous stage, minus the number we actually assigned:

$$C_{i-1} = C_i - A_i$$

where: C_i = the number of nurses we could assign in stage i

                      A_i = the number of nurses we actually assigned in stage i.

Stage 1 – assigning nurses to ward Z

The number of nurses to assign is between 0 and 5, depending on how many are assigned to wards Y and X. So C_1 is essentially fixed by the other decisions:

$$C_1 = C_2 - A_2$$

But we know the benefit of assigning nurses to ward Z. If we assign 0 nurses we get 0 benefit, if we assign 1 nurse we get 6 benefit, and so on. So the decisions are:

Number of nurses we could assign, C_1	Immediate benefit	Best decision – to actually assign, A_1	Overall benefit
0	0	0	0
1	6	1	6
2	9	2	9
3	13	3	13
4	16	4	16
5	17	5	17

The best decision is to assign all the nurses that are available, so that $A_1 = C_1$. The overall benefit – which shows the total benefit so far – is just the immediate benefit from this decision. Now we have the best decisions at stage 1, and can move on to stage 2.

Stage 2 – assigning nurses to ward Y

We know that:

$$C_2 = C_3 - A_3$$

The number of nurses we could assign in stage 2 depends on the number that are actually assigned in stage 3. The following table shows the benefits from different combinations:

Number of nurses we could assign, C_2	Benefits of assigning nurses, A_2						Best decision, to actually assign, A_2	Overall benefit
	0	1	2	3	4	5		
0	0 + 0	–	–	–	–	–	0	0
1	0 + 6	4 + 0	–	–	–	–	1	6
2	0 + 9	4 + 6	8 + 0	–	–	–	1	10
3	0 + 13	4 + 9	8 + 6	13 + 0	–	–	2	14
4	0 + 16	4 + 13	8 + 9	13 + 6	15 + 0	–	3	19
5	0 + 17	4 + 16	8 + 13	13 + 9	15 + 6	16 + 0	3	22

This table shows the benefit of assigning nurses to ward Y. Obviously A_2 cannot be bigger than C_2, so these entries are blank. The other figures have two entries.

The first shows the immediate benefit of assigning different numbers of nurses, A_2, to ward Y. The second shows the best return from different C_1 values in stage 1. We know that $C_1 = C_2 - A_2$, so each combination of C_2 and A_2 gives a value for C_1, and we can look up the benefit for this value from stage 1. For example, taking $C_2 = 4$ and $A_2 = 2$ gives an immediate benefit of 8 – which is the benefit of assigning 2 nurses to ward Y. Then we add the benefit from $C_1 = C_2 - A_2 = 4 - 2 = 2$ in stage 1. This is 9, so the total benefit is $8 + 9 = 17$. Repeating these calculations gives the other entries in the table.

Now we can go along the rows for each value of C_2 to find the best choice of A_2. This comes from the highest value in the row. If $C_2 = 4$ the highest value comes from $A_2 = 3$, which gives an overall benefit of 19.

Now we have the solution to stage 2, and can move on to stage 3.

Stage 3 – assigning nurses to ward X
This is the start of the problem. At this point, we could assign 5 nurses, so $C_5 = 5$. Now we can build a table to show the benefits of actually assigning nurses:

Number of nurses we could assign, C_3	Benefits of assigning nurses, A_3						Best decision, to actually assign, A_3	Overall benefit
	0	*1*	*2*	*3*	*4*	*5*		
5	0 + 22	4 + 19	6 + 14	10 + 10	14 + 6	16 + 0	1	23

Again the entries in this table show the immediate benefit of assigning nurses to ward X, plus the benefits from stage 2. We know that $C_2 = C_3 - A_3$, so each combination of C_3 and A_3 gives a value for C_2. We can look up the benefit for this value from stage 2. For example, taking $C_3 = 5$ and $A_3 = 2$ gives an immediate benefit of 6 – which is the benefit of allocating 2 nurses to ward X. Then we add the benefit of allocating $C_2 = C_3 - A_3 = 5 - 2 = 3$ in stage 2. This is 14, so the overall benefit is $6 + 14 = 20$.

The last step in this problem is to work forward and identify the best decision at each stage. Starting with stage 3, the best decision is to assign 1 nurse to ward X. Then $C_3 = 5$ and $A_3 = 1$. But $C_2 = C_3 - A_3 = 5 - 1 = 4$, and the best decision with $C_2 = 4$ is $A_2 = 3$. So we assign three nurses to ward Y. Then $C_1 = C_2 - A_2 = 4 - 3 = 1$, and the best decision with $C_1 = 1$ is $A_1 = 1$. So we assign 1 nurse to ward Z. This gives the overall solution:

Ward	Nurses	Benefit
X	1	6
Y	3	13
Z	1	4
Total	5	23

IN SUMMARY

Dynamic programming provides a way of tackling certain problems. It divides the whole problem into a series of stages, each of which is easier to solve. These stages are linked by recursive relationships. DP is not a single procedure, but an overall approach to tackling problems.

Self-assessment questions

4.13 'In common with all mathematical programmes, dynamic programmes use standard software to solve problems.' Is this true?

4.14 Why is it so difficult to formulate dynamic programmes?

4.15 What is a recursive relationship?

CHAPTER REVIEW

This chapter described several types of mathematical programming. In particular it:

- showed how there are several extensions to linear programming that form the broader subject of mathematical programming
- described integer linear programmes, where some of the variables are constrained to be integers
- looked at branch and bound methods to solve integer linear programmes
- described zero-one programming, where some variables are constrained to have the values zero or one
- outlined the way in which constraints of linear programming may really be goals
- discussed the approach of goal programming
- showed how dynamic programming can tackle certain types of problems

KEY TERMS

branch and bound
dynamic programming
goals
goal programming
integer linear programming
integer programming
lower bound
mathematical programmes

mixed integer programme
non-linear programmes
principle of optimality
pure integer programme
recursive relationship
upper bound
zero-one programming

Case study

Alberta Research Council

The Alberta Research Council has a 'Technology Help Line' that gives companies help with a range of technological problems. Last year Mike Cooper was passed a problem from a manufacturer of aluminium extrusions. The manufacturer had a large extrusion press that formed lengths of aluminium bars with various cross-sections, or profiles. These bars were treated, cut to length, drilled, machined and assembled into windows for office blocks.

As the bars came from the extrusion press, they were put into batches for the next stages of treatment. This treatment typically started with stretching, heat treating and anodizing. It was expensive to adjust the equipment for different lengths, so only one standard length of extrusion was produced for each profile run. The maximum length of extrusion was 27 feet, which was the length of the anodizing tank.

After coming from the anodizing tank, the extrusions were cut to the different lengths shown on design drawings. But each time an extrusion was cut, there would be some scrap. The company wanted to find the lengths of extrusions that would minimize the total amount of scrap. They had been offered some commercial software, but did not know how good this was. So they telephoned the Alberta Research Council for advice.

The Council recognized this as a 'stock cutting problem' which could be solved using integer programming. The company would have to run the program several times a day to deal with the different profiles. To test the results, they collected one day's demand for one profile as shown in the following table:

Part	Length (inches)	Quantity
1	235.72	38
2	219.97	38
3	212.63	14
4	211.38	2
5	172.72	35
6	152.97	19
7	89.28	35
8	76.31	6
9	28.13	48
10	26.42	14

Each time a length was cut, the saw blade lost 0.25 inches, so this was added to each cut, and in a typical day 20 to 30 profiles of this kind were made.

The company currently had a scrap rate of 15%. Suppliers of the commercial software said that it typically reduced scrap to around 9%. But the company thought that it could do better than this, and was aiming for 7% or less.

Questions

- What exactly are the operations in the company?
- How could the company use mathematical programming to minimize its scrap?
- Could heuristics give reasonable results with less effort?

Problems

4.1   What is the solution to the following linear programme?

Maximize: $2*x1 + x2 + 3*x3$

subject to: $x1 - 3*x2 - x3 \geq -4$

$2*x2 - x3 \leq 2$

$x1 - 2*x2 + 3*x3 \leq 4$

with $x1, x2$ and $x3 \geq 0$

What solution would you get by rounding the continuous variables to integers? What is the optimal integer solution? What is the optimal solution if the variables must all take values of zero or one?

4.2   The following table shows the minimum number of crews needed by an emergency ambulance service in each four-hour period:

Time period	Crews needed
midnight – 4 am	12
4–8 am	8
8–12 am	28
12–4 pm	16
4–8 pm	24
8 pm – midnight	32

Each crew works a continuous eight-hour shift. Formulate the problem of scheduling crews as an integer linear programme. What is the optimal solution?

4.3 A transport company wants to find the best composition for its fleet next year. The table below shows the types of vehicle, fixed costs, annual tonne-kilometres of load moved, minimum numbers available from the existing fleet, and numbers of drivers. Expected business this year will need at least 30 million tonne-kilometres of goods moved. Formulate this as an integer programme. What is the optimal solution?

Vehicle	Fixed costs (£)	Tonne-kilometres	Minimum number	Drivers available
1.5 tonne	21 000	40 000	6	no limit
5 tonne	24 000	80 000	3	no limit
10 tonne	28 000	170 000	6	12
20 tonne	30 000	350 000	10	20
32 tonne	37 000	500 000	15	16
36 tonne	42 000	600 000	20	24

4.4 Conway Financial Services are compiling an investment portfolio for a group of clients. They have £250 000 to invest, and have chosen six options for investment. Now they want to find the mix of investments that gives the highest return.

Investment	Cost (£)	Return	Maximum allowed
Personal saving plan	any amount	8%	£10 000
Commercial property	10 000	10%	–
Residential property	20 000	8%	–
Preferred shares	10	10% of par value	2000 shares
Ordinary shares	varies	5% of par value	–

The cost of ordinary shares is £10 if the client buys less than 100, and £9 if they buy at least 100 shares. Par values for preferred shares is £10, and £5 for ordinary shares. The clients want to diversify their investments and will not invest in both properties. Formulate this problem as an integer programme. What is the optimal solution?

4.5 Next month Geo-maritime want to make 1000 units of a product. They have four available machines with costs shown below. Formulate this problem, and find the optimal solution.

Machine	Set-up cost (£)	Production cost for each unit (£)	Maximum production
1	1000	100	450
2	2500	40	600
3	2000	50	800
4	2500	30	200

4.6   A company has two factories and three warehouses. The following table shows the cost of shipping a unit between the two, capacity of each factory and demand of each warehouse.

	Factory 1	Factory 2	Factory 3	Supply
Warehouse 1	100	45	120	1500
Warehouse 2	85	110	35	2000
Demand	1000	800	1500	

Formulate this problem as an integer programme and find the optimal solution.

4.7   A company makes two products. Each week they try to make 8 of the first product and 11 of the second. They have a fixed order for 8 of the second product. The production process works best when about equal numbers of units are made for each product. If these goals are given in order of importance, what is the best production plan?

4.8   Find the optimal solution for the holiday resort in Worked Example 4.7. How sensitive is this solution to changes?

4.9   Formulate Problem 4.6 as a goal programme, with the goals of:
- meeting all the demands of Factory 3
- meeting at least 75% of demand from each factory
- minimizing the total cost of transport
- shipping at least 500 units between Warehouse 1 and Factory 1

4.10   An operations manager has to schedule jobs for the next month. There are four types of job with completion times and values for each job shown in the following table:

Type of job	Number of jobs to be done	Duration	Value
1	6	1	3
2	6	3	8
3	4	5	12
4	3	7	18

Use dynamic programming to find the jobs that give the highest total value.

Discussion questions

4.1   Mathematical programmes give optimal solutions, but they are always difficult to solve. When would it be better to use heuristics that give reasonable solutions with less effort?

4.2   Linear programming can give a reasonable approximation to other types of mathematical programming. So why are the more complicated forms used?

4.3   Integer solutions can be found by rounding solutions to linear programmes. When is this a reasonable approach? What are the problems and advantages?

4.4   Some people have suggested that zero-one programming is – or should be – the most common type of mathematical programming. Why is this?

4.5   The solution to a goal problem is satisfactory rather than optimal. How are the two different? What are the real differences between goals and constraints?

4.6   Why is dynamic programming not more widely used in practice?

Scheduling and routing

5

CHAPTER OUTLINE

This chapter describes some common problems of scheduling and routing. After reading the chapter you should be able to:

- discuss different types of scheduling problems
- use permutations and combinations
- understand the difficulty of finding optimal solutions to scheduling problems
- use a variety of scheduling rules
- formulate and solve assignment problems
- formulate and solve transportation problems
- find the shortest path through a network
- calculate the maximum flow through a network

5.1 | Background to scheduling

Schedules tell you when things happen. A railway timetable gives a schedule of train departures, factories have production schedules, lectures are scheduled at certain times, restaurants use schedules for meals, debts have scheduled repayments, and so on. You need a schedule whenever there is:

- a number of activities that can be done in different orders, and
- the order in which the activities are done affects the overall performance

The order that milkmen visit customers will affect the time they need for deliveries; the order in which jobs are done on a machine will affect the overall processing time; the way a restaurant schedules employees' shifts will affect the service it can give.

Strictly speaking there is a difference between *schedules* and *sequences*:

- A **sequence** shows the order in which activities are done
- A **schedule** shows the time when each activity is done

Finding the best order for milkmen to visit customers is really a sequencing problem; finding the times when they arrive at each customer is a scheduling problem. In practice, there is little difference between the two and most people use the terms to mean the same thing.

With scheduling problems, we are looking for the best sequence of activities. This is surprisingly difficult to find, mainly because of the large number of possible sequences. If you have n activities to schedule, you can choose the first as any one of the n. Then you can choose the second activity as any one of the remaining $(n-1)$, so there are $n*(n-1)$ possible sequences for the first two activities. Then you can choose the third activity as any one of the remaining $(n-2)$, the fourth any of $(n-3)$, and so on.

The **number of possible sequences** of n activities
$$= n*(n-1)*(n-2)*(n-3) \ldots *3*2*1$$
$$= n!$$

Even a small problem with 15 activities has $15! = 1.3 * 10^{12}$ possible sequences. Two other useful calculations for scheduling find the number of *combinations* and *permutations*.

Suppose we have n activities that are distinct – in other words we can tell the difference between them – and we want to choose r of these. How many ways can we choose them? If we are **not** interested in the order we choose the r things, the answer is the combination of r things from n, which is written as ^nC_r.

The number of ways of choosing r things from n – when the order of selection is not important – is the **combination** of r from n, which is:

$$^nC_r = \frac{n!}{r! * (n - r)!}$$

If there is a pool of 10 cars and 3 customers arrive to use them there are $^{10}C_3 = 10!/(3! * 7!) = 120$ ways of allocating cars to customers. When you buy a national lottery ticket there are $^{49}C_6 = 49!/(6!*43!) =$ about fourteen million combinations of numbers.

If the order we choose the r things **is** important, we must find the permutation of r things from n, which is written as ^nP_r.

The number of ways of choosing r things from n – when the order of selection is important – is the **permutation** of r from n, which is:

$$^nP_r = \frac{n!}{(n - r)!}$$

Suppose there are 10 applicants for a social club committee consisting of a chairman, deputy chairman, secretary and treasurer. We want to choose 4 people from 10, but the order in which we choose them is important as it corresponds to the different jobs. The number of ways we can choose the committee of 4 is $^nP_r = n!/(n - r)! = 10!/6! = 5040$. If we want to choose 4 ordinary committee members – so the order we choose them is not important – the number of ways we can choose the committee is $^nC_r = 10! / (4!*6!) = 210$.

Permutations depend on order of choice and combinations do not – so there are always a lot more permutations than combinations. There are almost 14 million combinations of six lottery numbers from 49; but if the order of choosing numbers is important, there are 10^9 permutations.

WORKED EXAMPLE 5.1

(a) Able Enterprises has 8 applicants to fill 8 different jobs. How many ways can they assign applicants to jobs?

(b) There is a sudden reorganization in Able, and the number of jobs falls to 6. How many different ways can they assign the 6 jobs to 8 applicants?

(c) Suppose the reorganization leads to a reclassification of jobs and the 6 jobs are now identical. How many different ways can they be filled?

Solution

(a) This asks, 'How many different ways can 8 people be sequenced' – and the answer is 8!. Able can assign applicants to jobs in $8! = 40\,320$ different ways.

(b) Now Able want to choose 6 people from 8. As the jobs are different, the order of selection is important, so we want the permutation, $^8P_6$:

$$^nP_r = \frac{n!}{(n-r)!} = \frac{8!}{(8-6)!} = 20\,160$$

(c) Now Able want to choose 6 people from 8, but this time the jobs are the same. The order of selection is not important, so we want the combination, $^8C_6$:

$$^nC_r = \frac{n!}{r! * (n-r)!} = \frac{8!}{6! * (8-6)!} = 28$$

WORKED EXAMPLE 5.2

Twelve areas in the North Sea have just been opened for oil exploration. A government policy of encouraging competition means that it will only allocate one area to any exploration company.

(a) If 12 exploration companies bid for the areas, how many ways are there of allocating the areas to companies?

(b) Forecasts now show that each area is equally likely to produce oil, and 20 exploration companies put in bids. How many ways are there of allocating areas to companies?

(c) A later report revises the probabilities of major oil discoveries in each area. Based on this, 4 companies withdraw their bid. How many ways can the areas be allocated to the remaining companies?

Solution

(a) Twelve companies will get one area each, so the companies can be sequenced in 12! possible ways, or $4.79 * 10^8$.

(b) The government will choose 12 of the 20 companies. As the areas are equally attractive, it does not matter in which order the companies are chosen. The number of combinations is:

$$^nC_r = \frac{n!}{r! * (n - r)!} = \frac{20!}{12! * (20 - 12)!} = 125\,970$$

(c) Now the areas are different, and the order of choosing 12 of the 16 remaining companies is important. The number of permutations is:

$$^nP_r = \frac{n!}{(n - r)!} = \frac{16!}{(16 - 12)!} = 8.71 * 10^{11}$$

IN SUMMARY

- **There are $n!$ possible sequences of n different things.**
- **If the order of selection is *not* important, we can choose r things from n in ^nC_r different ways (combinations).**
- **If the order of selection is important, we can choose r things from n in ^nP_r different ways (permutations).**

Self-assessment questions

5.1 What is the difference between sequencing and scheduling?

5.2 How many ways are there of scheduling n different activities?

5.3 What is the difference between a permutation and a combination?

5.4 When choosing r things from n, are there more combinations than permutations, or vice versa?

5.2 | Scheduling jobs on machines

A common scheduling problem has a queue of jobs waiting to be processed on machines. Although we talk about 'jobs' and 'machines' you can see many forms of this problem with, for example, different material waiting to be printed on the same press, cars waiting for petrol pumps, different blends of whisky waiting to use the same bottling machine, customers waiting at a post office counter, and aeroplanes waiting to use airport terminals (see Figure 5.1).

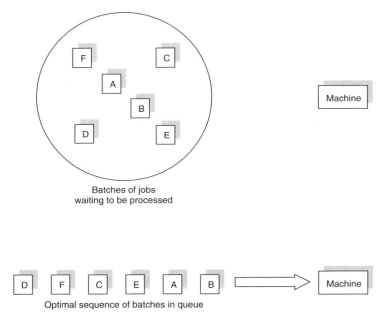

Figure 5.1   Scheduling jobs on a machine.

The problem here is to find the best schedule for the jobs. If the time for each job is constant – and is not affected by the job that was done before – the total time needed to finish all jobs is fixed and is not affected by the order in which the jobs are done. But other factors may be important. If stocks of one product are low, the job that replenishes these stocks will have a high priority; it may be better to have a few, bigger jobs in the queue than to have more, smaller jobs; it might be useful to minimize the average time spent in the queue; if there are delays it may be better to have one job very late, than to have several jobs a bit late. Simple *scheduling rules* can deal with this kind of problem.

WORKED EXAMPLE 5.3

Six parts are made in batches on the same piece of equipment. At some point, average weekly demands, stock levels and times to make a batch of each part are as follows:

Part	A	B	C	D	E	F
Average demand	10	4	26	34	7	3
Current stock	72	21	48	92	28	23
Production time	2.0	1.5	0.5	0.5	1.0	1.5

In what order would you make one batch of each part?

Solution

We can see how long the stock of each part will last by dividing the current stock by the average demand. Then it makes sense to schedule the jobs in the order 'most urgent first'. Scheduling jobs in the order the parts will run out gives:

C, D, E, B, A and F

Taking the start time for the first batch as time 0, a batch of item C will be finished at time 0.5. Then a batch of D can start, and this will finish 0.5 later at time 1.0.

	A	B	C	D	E	F	G
1	**Most Urgent First**						
2							
3	**Data**						
4	Item	A	B	C	D	E	F
5	Current stock	72	21	48	92	28	23
6	Average demand	10	4	26	34	7	3
7	Runout time	7.20	5.25	1.85	2.71	4.00	7.67
8							
9	**Sorted data**						
10	Runout time	1.85	2.71	4.00	5.25	7.20	7.67
11	Item	C	D	E	B	A	F
12	Current stock	48	92	28	21	72	23
13	Average demand	26	34	7	4	10	3
14							
15	Production time	0.5	0.5	1.0	1.5	2.0	1.5
16	Start production	0.0	0.5	1.0	2.0	3.5	5.5
17	Finish production	0.5	1.0	2.0	3.5	5.5	7.0
18	Spare time	1.4	1.7	2.0	1.8	1.7	0.7

Figure 5.2 Schedule for Worked Example 5.3.

Next a batch of E can start, and this will finish at time 2.0, and so on. The spreadsheet in Figure 5.2 shows the time at which each batch is finished, and the time the part will run out. As you can see, none of the parts actually run out before the next batch is finished.

Different scheduling rules achieve different objectives. Suppose, for example, we want to minimize the time a job spends in the system, where:

- **processing time** = the time machines actually work on the job
- **time in the queue** = the time a job waits before processing begins
- **time in the system** = processing time plus time in the queue

If a job needs 2 days on a piece of equipment, but has to wait in a queue for 3 days before processing starts, the processing time is 2 days, time in the queue is 3 days and time in the system is 5 days.

If a series of jobs have different processing times, taking them in the order 'shortest first' will minimize the average time in the system. The time each job spends in the queue is set by the time taken by preceding jobs, so taking the shortest jobs first will minimize the average waiting time and hence the average time in the system.

If the jobs each have a date when they are due to be finished, a reasonable objective is to minimize the average lateness of jobs. The rule for this is to schedule jobs in the order, 'earliest due date first'.

WORKED EXAMPLE 5.4

Eight jobs are waiting to be processed on a single machine, with processing times and due dates shown in the following table:

Job	A	B	C	D	E	F	G	H
Processing time	2	5	3	8	4	7	2	3
Due date	13	7	8	30	14	20	2	36

(a) What order of jobs will minimize the average queueing time?

(b) What order will minimize the average lateness?

Solution

(a) The average queueing time is minimized by taking jobs in the order 'shortest first'. If several jobs have the same processing time, we can take these in any convenient order. This gives the sequence A, G, C, H, E, B, F and D. Setting the start time for the first job as 0, the start and finish times of other jobs are shown in Figure 5.3.

	A	B	C	D	E	F	G	H	I
1	**Shortest First**								
2									
3	**Data**								
4	Job	A	B	C	D	E	F	G	H
5	Processing time	2	5	3	8	4	7	2	3
6									
7	**Sorted data**								
8	Job	A	G	C	H	E	B	F	D
9	Processing time	2	2	3	3	4	5	7	8
10									
11	Start production	0.0	2.0	4.0	7.0	10.0	14.0	19.0	26.0
12	Finish production	2.0	4.0	7.0	10.0	14.0	19.0	26.0	34.0

Figure 5.3 Shortest first rule for Worked Example 5.4 (a).

The average waiting time is found by adding the start times and dividing by the number of jobs. This gives $82/8 = 10.25$.

(b) The average lateness is minimized by taking jobs in order of increasing due date. This gives the sequence G, B, C, A, E, F, D and H, with the schedule shown in Figure 5.4.

	A	B	C	D	E	F	G	H	I
1	**Nearest Due Date First**								
2									
3	**Data**								
4	Job	A	B	C	D	E	F	G	H
5	Due date	13	7	8	30	14	20	2	36
6									
7	**Sorted data**								
8	Job	G	B	C	A	E	F	D	H
9	Due date	2	7	8	13	14	20	30	36
10									
11	Processing time	2	5	3	2	4	7	8	3
12	Start production	0.0	2.0	7.0	10.0	12.0	16.0	23.0	31.0
13	Finish production	2.0	7.0	10.0	12.0	16.0	23.0	31.0	34.0
14									
15	Lateness	0.0	0.0	2.0	0.0	2.0	3.0	1.0	0.0

Figure 5.4 Schedule for Worked Example 5.4 (b).

The average lateness is $(2 + 2 + 3 + 1)/8 = 1$ day.

Although both of these rules give the same total processing time of 34 days, they have different characteristics. For example:

- The first solution has an average wait of 10.25 days; the second has $101/8 = 12.625$ days.

- The first solution has 4 jobs late (B, D, F and G), with an average lateness of $(12 + 4 + 6 + 2)/8 = 3$ days; the second has 4 jobs late and an average lateness of 1 day.

Rather than minimize the average lateness, we may want to minimize the number of jobs that are late. We can do this using the following five steps.

Step 1. Use the earliest due date to find an initial sequence of jobs. If no job is late this is the optimal solution, otherwise move on to step 2.

Step 2. Find the first late job in the schedule.

Step 3. Find the longest job preceding (and including) the job found in step 2.

Step 4. Remove this longest job from the schedule and update the times. If there are still late jobs go to step 2, otherwise continue to step 5.

Step 5. Add the jobs removed in step 4 to the end of the schedule.

WORKED EXAMPLE 5.5

Take the 8 jobs described in Worked Example 5.4 and find the sequence that minimizes the number of late jobs.

Solution

For this we have to use the five steps described above.

Job	A	B	C	D	E	F	G	H
Processing time	2	5	3	8	4	7	2	3
Due date	13	7	8	30	14	20	2	36

Step 1

Taking the jobs in order of due date gives the solution:

Job	G	B	C	A	E	F	D	H
Due date	2	7	8	13	14	20	30	36
Start processing	0	2	7	10	12	16	23	31
Processing time	2	5	3	2	4	7	8	3
Finish processing	2	7	10	12	16	23	31	34
Late jobs			*		*	*	*	

Step 2

The first late job in the schedule is C.

Step 3

The longest job up to and including C is B, with a processing time of 5.

Step 4

Remove job B from the schedule and update the times:

Job	G	C	A	E	F	D	H
Due date	2	8	13	14	20	30	36
Start processing	0	2	5	7	11	18	26
Processing time	2	3	2	4	7	8	3
Finish processing	2	5	7	11	18	26	29

Step 5

There are no jobs late now so we add job B to the end of the schedule:

Job	G	C	A	E	F	D	H	B
Due date	2	8	13	14	20	30	36	7
Start processing	0	2	5	7	11	18	26	29
Processing time	2	3	2	4	7	8	3	5
Finish processing	2	5	7	11	18	26	29	34

Now there is only one job late, the average queueing time is 98/8 = 12.25 and the average lateness is 27/8 = 3.375 days.

There are many scheduling rules for different circumstances. Some useful ones take jobs in the order:

- *arrival time* – or 'first come first served'
- *least slack time* – where slack time = time to due date − processing time
- *most nearly finished*
- *fewest remaining operations before completion*
- *shortest queue at next operation*
- *lowest critical ratio* – which equals (time to due date) / (time needed to finish job)
- *highest priority*
- *least changeover cost.*

These rules assume that jobs are queueing at a single machine. A useful extension would look at jobs that are processed on several machines. Unfortunately, this kind of problem soon becomes very complicated. One simple rule looks at a *flowshop*, where jobs move through a set of machines in the same order, as shown in Figure 5.5.

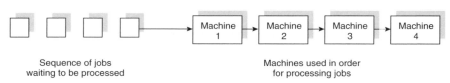

Sequence of jobs   Machines used in order
waiting to be processed   for processing jobs

Figure 5.5   Jobs moving through a flowshop.

The simplest flowshop problem has two machines, with each job moving from machine 1 to machine 2. To minimize the total time spent in the system – which is the time between starting the first job on machine 1 and finishing the last job on machine 2 – we can use *Johnson's Rule*:

> ### *Johnson's Rule*:
>
> *Step 1.* List the jobs and their processing time on each machine.
>
> *Step 2.* Find the job with the next smallest processing time on either machine.
>
> *Step 3.* If this time is on machine 1 schedule the job as early as possible; if it is on machine 2 schedule the job as late as possible. Always work inwards from the ends of the schedule, adding new jobs nearer the middle.
>
> *Step 4.* Do not consider this job again, and go to step 2. If there are no more jobs, this is the optimal solution.

WORKED EXAMPLE 5.6

Seven jobs must be processed on machine 1 followed by machine 2. The time needed by each job on each machine is as follows:

Job	A	B	C	D	E	F	G
Machine 1	2	5	10	8	4	12	9
Machine 2	14	7	3	10	5	6	6

What schedule maximizes the machine utilizations?

Solution

To maximize machine utilizations, we want the jobs to spend as short a time as possible in the system, so we can use Johnson's Rule to find the best sequence.

Step 1

The processing times are given in the table above.

Step 2

The shortest processing time is 2, which is the time job A spends on machine 1.

Step 3

This time is on machine 1, so we schedule the job as early as possible (in this case first):

> Sequence: A ....

Step 4

There are still unscheduled jobs, so we go back to step 2.

Step 2

The shortest remaining processing time is 3, which is the time job C takes on machine 2.

Step 3

This time is on machine 2, so we schedule the job as late as possible (in this case last):

> Sequence: A C

Step 4

There are still unscheduled jobs, so go back to step 2.

Step 2

The shortest remaining processing time is 4, which is the time job E takes on machine 1.

Step 3

This time is on machine 1, so we schedule the job as early as possible (in this case after A):

Sequence: A   E C

Repeating this procedure until all jobs have been allocated to the sequence – in the order B, F then G – gives the sequence A E B D G F C, as shown in Figure 5.6.

	A	B	C	D	E	F	G	H
1	**Johnson's Rule**							
2								
3	Job	A	B	C	D	E	F	G
4	Time on machine 1	2	5	10	8	4	12	9
5	Time on machine 2	14	7	3	10	5	6	6
6								
7	Best sequence	A	E	B	D	G	F	C
8	Start on machine 1	0	2	6	11	19	28	40
9	Finish on machine 1	2	6	11	19	28	40	50
10	Start on machine 2	2	16	21	28	38	44	50
11	Finish on machine 2	16	21	28	38	44	50	53

Figure 5.6   Spreadsheet showing calculations for Worked Example 5.6.

IN SUMMARY

Scheduling rules provide an effective way of scheduling 'jobs' on 'machines'. This type of problem occurs in many different forms. There are many rules for different circumstances.

Self-assessment questions

5.5   What is a 'scheduling rule'?

5.6   How should jobs be scheduled on a single machine to minimize average waiting time?

5.7   How should jobs be scheduled on a single machine to minimize average lateness?

5.8   When would you use Johnson's Rule?

Case example

The Foothills Hospital

The Foothills Hospital does 18 500 surgical operations a year in its 16 theatres. Each theatre is used on about 230 working days a year, and is open between 8.00 am and 3.00 pm on Monday to Friday. Six theatres are kept open until 6.00 pm and two are open until 11.00 pm. The Director of Nursing and two clerical assistants schedule patients into these times to achieve three goals:

- never to compromise the health or life of a patient
- minimize the cost of running the theatres
- use all resources efficiently.

Before scheduling a patient, the Director of Nursing checks the following questions:

- Is there time on the right floor of the hospital? Some large equipment, such as X-ray machines and lasers, can move between theatres on the same floor, but cannot move to another floor.

- Is there time in the right theatre? Some theatres are dedicated to specific types of operation, such as ophthalmology, cardiovascular surgery and arthroscopy. Other operations need theatres of a certain size.

- Is the patient's surgeon available? Surgeons are usually assigned blocks of time in a specific theatre.

- Are more than one surgeon needed? These operations are usually scheduled at the start of the day.

- Is an anaesthetist available?

- Is the necessary mobile equipment available – such as c-arm X-rays?

- Are technical staff available to work the equipment?

- Are the other equipment and instruments available in the theatre?

- Is a pathology specimen needed? This must be arranged so the specimen can be analysed before the laboratory closes.

- Is the patient an in-patient or day patient? Day patients must be scheduled early enough for them to recover before going home.

- Is the patient travelling a long way to the hospital? These patients are usually scheduled later to allow for possible delays.

- Has all the necessary patient assessment and preparation been done?

- Does the patient have other conditions that need special attention – such as diabetes or a heart problem? These patients are usually scheduled earlier in the day.
- Does the surgeon have preferred times for operations?

After answering these questions, the Director of Nursing can find the best time to schedule the patients – and all related services. But each operation is different, and the times needed can vary quite widely. There is also an unknown number of emergencies that have to be added to the schedule.

This is a complicated scheduling problem. Traditionally it has been solved by hand, with the Director of Nursing using experience and a set of scheduling rules. More recently, special software provides initial solutions, which the Director of Nursing can update to get a final solution. This software still uses a series of scheduling rules and approximations. The expected time for an operation, for example, is taken as the average time the surgeon has taken for the past ten similar operations.

5.3 | The Assignment Problem

Different people have different skills and abilities, so the way we assign people to different jobs will affect the overall performance. The way managers assign football players to positions, for example, affects the number of games they win. This is the idea behind the *Assignment Problem*. This generally talks about assigning 'operators' to 'machines', but it can be used for many problems – such as assigning the output from factories to markets, assigning books to editors, assigning salesmen to geographical areas, assigning construction projects to companies, and so on.

> The **Assignment Problem** finds the allocation of operators to machines that minimizes the total cost.

This problem assigns one operator to each machine, and we can start by defining C_{ij} as the cost of assigning operator i to machine j. Now the problem becomes a zero-one programme which we discussed in the previous chapter.

Let: $\qquad X_{ij} = 1$ if we assign operator i to machine j

$\qquad\qquad\quad = 0$ otherwise.

One valid allocation of operators to machines is shown in the following table of X_{ij}:

		Machine					
		1	2	3	4	5	6
	1	0	1	0	0	0	0
	2	0	0	0	1	0	0
	3	1	0	0	0	0	0
Operator	4	0	0	0	0	0	1
	5	0	0	0	0	1	0
	6	0	0	1	0	0	0

You can see that operator 1 is assigned to machine 2, operator 2 is assigned to machine 4, operator 3 is assigned to machine 1, and so on. Every row and every column has a single '1' to identify the assignment, and the rest of the entries are zero. So the constraints are that:

- there is only one entry in each row:

$$\sum_{j=1}^{n} X_{ij} = 1 \quad \text{for } i = 1, \ldots, n$$

- there is only one entry in each column:

$$\sum_{i=1}^{n} X_{ij} = 1 \quad \text{for } j = 1, \ldots, n$$

The cost of assigning an operator to a job is $X_{ij} * C_{ij}$. If the operator is assigned to this job, $X_{ij} = 1$ and the cost is C_{ij}; if the operator is not assigned to this job, $X_{ij} = 0$ and the cost is ignored. So the objective function is:

Minimize: $$\sum_{i=1}^{n} \sum_{j=1}^{n} X_{ij} * C_{ij}$$

with $\qquad C_{ij} \geq 0 \qquad$ for $i = 1, \ldots, n$ and $j = 1, \ldots, n$

Although this is a relatively simple formulation, mathematical programmes always need a lot of computing. We can avoid this by using a special procedure, called the ***Hungarian Method***. This uses the following iterative procedure:

Step 1. Form a cost matrix, C_{ij}, with the number of rows equal to the number of columns.

Step 2. Reduce the cost matrix. This means subtracting the smallest element in each row from all elements in the row, then subtracting the smallest element in each column from all elements in the column. There should now be at least one zero in each row and one in each column.

Step 3. Cross out all the zeros with the minimum number of horizontal and vertical straight lines. If this minimum number of lines equals the number of rows we have found an optimal solution, so go to step 5. Otherwise continue to step 4.

Step 4. Find the smallest uncovered (i.e. not crossed out) element. Subtract this from all uncovered elements and add it to those elements that are crossed out twice. Go to step 3.

Step 5. Identify the optimal assignment from the position of the zeros.

This may seem a strange procedure, but it is based on good theoretical reasoning.

WORKED EXAMPLE 5.7

Five ships have to be unloaded at 5 berths. Each berth has different facilities, and the costs of unloading are given below (in thousands of pounds). What assignment of ships to berths minimizes the total cost?

		Berths				
		1	2	3	4	5
	1	8	10	9	3	6
	2	7	8	11	2	9
Ships	3	2	4	6	4	4
	4	7	7	5	2	7
	5	10	8	10	3	11

Solution

Following the steps described in the Hungarian Method:

Step 1

We already have the cost matrix C_{ij}.

Step 2

Reduce the matrix by subtracting the smallest element in each row from all elements in the row:

	1	2	3	4	5	Smallest
1	8	10	9	3	6	3
2	7	8	11	2	9	2
3	2	4	6	4	4	2
4	7	7	5	2	7	2
5	10	8	10	3	11	3

Then subtract the smallest element in each column from all elements in the column:

	1	2	3	4	5
1	5	7	6	0	3
2	5	6	9	0	7
3	0	2	4	2	2
4	5	5	3	0	5
5	7	5	7	0	8
Smallest	0	2	3	0	2

This gives the reduced cost matrix:

	1	2	3	4	5
1	5	5	3	0	1
2	5	4	6	0	5
3	0	0	1	2	0
4	5	3	0	0	3
5	7	3	4	0	6

Step 3

Now we cross out all the zeros with the minimum number of straight – either horizontal or vertical – lines. In this case the minimum number of lines is three. This does not equal the number of rows so we go to step 4.

	1	2	3	4	5
1	5	5	3	0	1*
2	5	4	6	0	5
3	0	0	1	2	0
4	5	3	0	0	3
5	7	3	4	0	6

Step 4

The smallest number not crossed out is 1 in row 1 column 5. We subtract this from all other numbers that are not crossed out, and added it to all the numbers that are crossed out twice. Then return to step 3.

Step 3

The minimum number of straight lines needed to cross out all the zeros is now four.

	1	2	3	4	5
1	4	4	2	0	0
2	4	3	5	0	4
3	0	0	1	3	0
4	5	3	0	1	3
5	6	2*	3	0	5

This is not equal to the number of rows so we find the smallest number not crossed out (2 in row 5 column 2), subtract this from all numbers not crossed out and add it to those crossed out twice.

	1	2	3	4	5
1	4	4	2	2	0
2	2	1	3	0	2
3	0	0	1	5	0
4	5	3	0	3	3
5	4	0	1	0	3

Step 4

This time we need five lines to cross out all the zeros. This means we have found an optimal solution and can move to step 5.

	1	2	3	4	5
1	4	4	2	2	0
2	2	1	3	0	2
3	0	0	1	5	0
4	5	3	0	3	3
5	4	0	1	0	3

Step 5

The zeros identify the optimal assignment of ships to berths. There are eight zeros, so we have to find the five that identify the optimal. Each ship must be assigned to a berth and each berth must have a ship assigned to it – so we are looking for one zero in each row and one in each column. We can start by finding the rows and columns with only a single zero. Ship 1 must be assigned to berth 5, ship 2 must be assigned to berth 4, and ship 4 must be assigned to berth 3. Similarly berth 1 must have ship 3 assigned to it. This leaves ship 5 which might be assigned to berth 2 or 4. But ship 2 is already assigned to berth 4, so ship 5 must be assigned to berth 2.

	1	2	3	4	5
1	4	4	2	2	0*
2	2	1	3	0*	2
3	0*	0	1	5	0
4	5	3	0*	3	3
5	4	0*	1	0	3

We can find the cost of this assignment by substituting values for C_{ij} from the original cost matrix. The optimal assignment has a cost of $(6 + 2 + 5 + 8 + 2) = £23\,000$.

WORKED EXAMPLE 5. 8

Use a computer package to confirm the solution to Worked Example 5.7.

Solution

Figure 5.7 shows a printout from a typical package. This shows the problem and solutions, which confirm the previous results.

ASSIGNMENT PROBLEM – SOLUTION
PROBLEM: Ship Berth

ORIGINAL PROBLEM DATA

	Berth 1	Berth 2	Berth 3	Berth 4	Berth 5	Totals
Ship 1 :	8.00	10.00	9.00	3.00	6.00	: 1
Ship 2 :	7.00	8.00	11.00	2.00	9.00	: 1
Ship 3 :	2.00	4.00	6.00	4.00	4.00	: 1
Ship 4 :	7.00	7.00	5.00	2.00	7.00	: 1
Ship 5 :	10.00	8.00	10.00	3.00	11.00	: 1
Totals :	1	1	1	1	1	: 5

REDUCED MATRIX

	Berth 1	Berth 2	Berth 3	Berth 4	Berth 5	Totals
Ship 1 :	5.00	5.00	3.00	0.00	1.00	: 1
Ship 2 :	5.00	4.00	6.00	0.00	5.00	: 1
Ship 3 :	0.00	0.00	1.00	2.00	0.00	: 1
Ship 4 :	5.00	3.00	0.00	0.00	3.00	: 1
Ship 5 :	7.00	3.00	4.00	0.00	6.00	: 1
Totals :	1	1	1	1	1	: 5

Figure 5.7 continued overleaf

OPTIMAL SOLUTION

	Berth 1	Berth 2	Berth 3	Berth 4	Berth 5	Totals
Ship 1 :	0.00	0.00	0.00	0.00	1.00	: 1
Ship 2 :	0.00	0.00	0.00	0.00	0.00	: 1
Ship 3 :	1.00	0.00	0.00	0.00	0.00	: 1
Ship 4 :	0.00	0.00	1.00	0.00	0.00	: 1
Ship 5 :	0.00	1.00	0.00	0.00	0.00	:
Totals :	1	1	1	1	1	: 5

Assign	To
Ship 1	Berth 5
Ship 2	Berth 4
Ship 3	Berth 1
Ship 4	Berth 3
Ship 5	Berth 2

Minimum cost is C = 23

Figure 5.7 Computer printout for Worked Example 5.8.

WORKED EXAMPLE 5.9

A sales manager has to assign six salesmen to different territories. The salesmen have different contacts and techniques, and their expected monthly sales (in thousands of pounds) are shown in the following table. What assignment would maximize the monthly income?

		Territory					
		1	2	3	4	5	6
	1	17	24	41	19	33	28
	2	22	22	31	14	27	26
Salesman	3	9	33	25	26	30	31
	4	29	43	45	8	22	20
	5	39	19	17	30	32	30
	6	31	37	27	23	37	10

Solution

The Hungarian Method will only deal with minimising problems, and this problem wants to maximize the income. So we must form a cost matrix. The easiest way of doing this is to find the biggest element in the matrix, and then subtract all other elements from it. Here the largest element is 45, and subtracting each entry in the original matrix from this gives a revised cost matrix. Standard programs will deal with this automatically, as shown in Figure 5.8.

ASSIGNMENT PROBLEM – SOLUTION
PROBLEM: Sales Manager

ORIGINAL PROBLEM DATA

	Territory1	Territory2	Territory3	Territory4	Territory5	Territory6	:	Totals
Salesm1 :	17.00	24.00	41.00	19.00	33.00	28.00	:	1
Salesm2 :	22.00	22.00	31.00	14.00	27.00	26.00	:	1
Salesm3 :	9.00	33.00	25.00	26.00	30.00	31.00	:	1
Salesm4 :	29.00	43.00	45.00	8.00	22.00	20.00	:	1
Salesm5 :	39.00	19.00	17.00	30.00	32.00	30.00	:	1
Salesm6 :	31.00	37.00	27.00	23.00	37.00	10.00	:	1
Totals :	1	1	1	1	1	1	:	6

REVISED COST DATA

	Territory1	Territory2	Territory3	Territory4	Territory5	Territory6	:	Totals
Salesm1 :	28.00	21.00	4.00	26.00	12.00	17.00	:	1
Salesm2 :	23.00	23.00	14.00	31.00	18.00	19.00	:	1
Salesm3 :	36.00	12.00	20.00	19.00	15.00	14.00	:	1
Salesm4 :	16.00	2.00	0.00	37.00	23.00	25.00	:	1
Salesm5 :	6.00	26.00	28.00	15.00	13.00	15.00	:	1
Salesm6 :	14.00	8.00	18.00	22.00	8.00	35.00	:	1
Totals :	1	1	1	1	1	1	:	6

REDUCED MATRIX

	Territory1	Territory2	Territory3	Territory4	Territory5	Territory6	:	Totals
Salesm1 :	24.00	17.00	0.00	15.00	8.00	11.00	:	1
Salesm2 :	9.00	9.00	0.00	10.00	4.00	3.00	:	1
Salesm3 :	24.00	0.00	8.00	0.00	3.00	0.00	:	1
Salesm4 :	16.00	2.00	0.00	30.00	23.00	23.00	:	1
Salesm5 :	0.00	20.00	22.00	2.00	7.00	7.00	:	1
Salesm6 :	6.00	0.00	10.00	7.00	0.00	25.00	:	1
Totals :	1	1	1	1	1	1	:	6

OPTIMAL SOLUTION

	Territory1	Territory2	Territory3	Territory4	Territory5	Territory6	:	Totals
Salesm1 :	0.00	0.00	1.00	0.00	0.00	0.00	:	1
Salesm2 :	0.00	0.00	0.00	0.00	0.00	1.00	:	1
Salesm3 :	0.00	0.00	0.00	1.00	0.00	0.00	:	1
Salesm4 :	0.00	1.00	0.00	0.00	0.00	0.00	:	1
Salesm5 :	1.00	0.00	0.00	0.00	0.00	0.00	:	1
Salesm6 :	0.00	0.00	0.00	0.00	1.00	0.00	:	1
Totals :	1	1	1	1	1	1	:	6

Assign	To
Salesm1	Territory3
Salesm2	Territory6
Salesm3	Territory4
Salesm4	Territory2
Salesm5	Territory1
Salesm6	Territory5

Minimum profit is P = 212

Figure 5.8 Computer printout for Worked Example 5.9.

IN SUMMARY

The Assignment Problem finds the assignment of 'operators' to 'machines' that minimizes costs. It can be formulated as a zero-one programme, but the Hungarian Method is a more efficient procedure.

Self-assessment questions

5.9 What is the 'Assignment Problem'?

5.10 'Mathematical programming can be used to solve the Assignment Problem.' Is this true?

5.11 How would you identify the optimal solution in the Hungarian Method?

5.4 | The Transportation Problem

The *Transportation Problem* finds the best way of moving goods between sources and destinations – perhaps from factories to warehouses. So it has:

- a number of sources, each of which can supply a known amount of goods
- a number of destinations, each of which has a demand for goods
- costs of moving one unit of goods between any source and destination
- an objective of meeting all demands at minimum total cost

We can describe this problem in the following matrix:

		Destinations						Supply
		1	2	3	.	.	n	
	1	.	.	.				S_1
	2	.	.					S_2
Sources	3	.	.	costs C_{ij}	.			.
	.	.	.					.
	.	.	.					.
	m							S_m
Demand		D_1	D_2	.	.	.	D_n	Total

where: S_i = supply of goods from source i

D_j = demand for goods at destination j

C_{ij} = cost of transporting one unit of goods from source i to destination j

Like the Assignment Problem, the Transportation Problem is used in many situations – it is only for convenience that we talk about goods being moved. We can formulate this general problem as a linear programme. Setting X_{ij} as the amount of goods moved from source i to destination j gives the objective of minimizing the total cost:

Minimize: $\displaystyle\sum_{i=1}^{m} \sum_{j=1}^{n} X_{ij} * C_{ij}$

There is a maximum supply from each source:

$$\sum_{j=1}^{n} X_{ij} = S_i \qquad \text{for } i = 1 \text{ to } m$$

and a demand at each destination:

$$\sum_{i=1}^{m} X_{ij} = D_j \qquad \text{for } j = 1 \text{ to } n$$

As usual: $\qquad X_{ij} \geq 0 \qquad\qquad$ for $i = 1 \ldots m$ and $j = 1 \ldots n$

But there is an easier way of solving this problem, which is a specialized procedure called the ***Transportation Algorithm***. This has two parts:

- *Part 1*, which finds an initial feasible solution
- *Part 2*, which iteratively improves this initial solution until it reaches an optimum

A good way of finding an initial solution uses ***Vogel's Approximation Method*** (***VAM***). This usually gives results that are close to optimal, and reduces the effort needed in the second part of the algorithm. VAM realizes that if the cheapest option is not used in any row or column then, at best, the second cheapest must be used. Then there is a penalty cost that is at least as big as the difference between the cheapest and second cheapest element in the row or column. In detail, the procedure is as follows:

Step 1. Describe the problem in terms of a cost matrix with the format shown above.

Step 2. Calculate the penalty cost for each row, as the difference between lowest cost in the row and the second lowest cost.

Step 3. Calculate the penalty cost for each column as the difference between the lowest cost in the column and the second lowest cost.

Step 4. Find the maximum value for this penalty cost, and find the element in this row or column with the lowest cost.

Step 5. Assign as much as possible to this element – with the amount limited by the available supply or remaining demand.

Step 6. Adjust the unmet supply and demand by subtracting the amount assigned in this round. Then ignore any column with no remaining demand or row with no remaining supply. Repeat this procedure until all supply has been used and all demands met.

This procedure seems quite complicated when it is written down, but is really quite straightforward.

WORKED EXAMPLE 5.10

Use Vogel's Approximation Method to find an initial solution to the following transportation matrix:

		To destination				
		1	2	3	4	Supply
	1	10	12	20	10	60
From	2	16	6	10	22	30
source	3	18	14	10	16	25
	4	2	16	18	14	45
Demand		40	40	40	40	160

Solution

Step 1 has already been done, so we can move on to *steps 2* and *3* to calculate the penalty cost for each row and column. For this we subtract the lowest cost from the second lowest in each row, and the lowest cost from the second lowest in each column:

		To destination					Penalty
		1	2	3	4	Supply	cost
	1	10	12	20	10	60	0
From	2	16	6	10	22	30	4
source	3	18	14	10	16	25	4
	4	2	16	18	14	45	12 <
Demand		40	40	40	40	160	
Penalty cost		8	6	0	4		

Step 4 finds the highest penalty cost, which is 12 in row 4. The lowest cost in row 4 is 2 in column 1.

Step 5 assigns as much as possible to this element. This is the lower of the remaining supply in row 4 – which is 45 – and demand in column 1 – which is 40. So we assign 40 to travel between source 4 and destination 1, and enter this amount in the matrix with an asterisk to show it is an assignment and not a cost.

Step 6 updates the supply and demand by reducing the remaining supply in row 4 to 5 and the unmet demand in column 1 to zero. Then column 1 is not considered again.

We keep on repeating this procedure until we get an optimal solution:

		To destination				Remaining	Penalty
		1	2	3	4	supply	cost
	1	–	12	20	10	60	2
From	2	–	6	10	22	30	4
source	3	–	14	10	16	25	4
	4	40*	16	18	14	5	2
Unmet demand		0	40	40	40	120	
Penalty cost		–	6	0	4		
			∧				

This time the highest penalty cost is 6 for column 2. The lowest cost in this column is in row 2. So we assign as much as possible to this element. This is 30 units, which is the supply from source 2. Then we update the supply and demand, and do not consider row 2 again.

		To destination				Remaining	Penalty
		1	2	3	4	supply	cost
	1	–	12	20	10	60	2
From	2	–	30*	–	–	0	–
source	3	–	14	10	16	25	4
	4	40*	16	18	14	5	2
Unmet demand		0	10	40	40	90	
Penalty cost		–	2	8	4		
				∧			

Repeating this procedure gives the following tables:

		To destination				Remaining	Penalty
		1	2	3	4	supply	cost
	1	–	12	20	10	60	2
From	2	–	30 *	–	–	0	–
source	3	–	–	25*	–	0	–
	4	40*	16	18	14	5	2
Unmet demand		0	10	15	40	65	
Penalty cost		–	4	2	4		
			∧				

		To destination				Remaining supply	Penalty cost
		1	2	3	4		
	1	–	10*	20	10	50	10 <
From	2	–	30*	–	–	0	–
source	3	–	–	25*	–	0	–
	4	40*	–	18	14	5	4
Unmet demand		0	0	15	40	55	
Penalty cost		–	–	2	4		

		To destination				Remaining supply	Penalty cost
		1	2	3	4		
	1	–	10*	20	40*	10	–
From	2	–	30*	–	–	0	–
source	3	–	–	25*	–	0	–
	4	40*	–	18	–	5	–
Unmet demand		0	0	15	0	15	
Penalty cost		–	–	2	–		
				∧			

		To destination				Remaining supply
		1	2	3	4	
	1	–	10*	10*	40*	0
From	2	–	30*	–	–	0
source	3	–	–	25*	–	0
	4	40*	–	5*	–	0
Unmet demand		0	0	0	0	0

Now we have an initial feasible solution, and can find the cost of this from the original matrix:

$$(10 * 12) + (10 * 20) + (40 * 10) + (30 * 6) + (25 * 10) + (40 * 2) + (5 * 18) = 1320$$

The next step in the Transportation Algorithm uses an iterative procedure to improve this initial solution. For this, we put all the information into a single matrix, as shown below. The figures in the body of each box show the amounts moved in the initial solution; the figures in the top right-hand corners are the costs.

	1	2	3	4	Supply
	[10]	[12]	[20]	[10]	
1	0	10	10	40	60
	[16]	[6]	[10]	[22]	
2	0	30	0	0	30
	[18]	[14]	[10]	[16]	
3	0	0	25	0	25
	[2]	[16]	[18]	[14]	10
4	40	0	5	0	45
Demand	40	40	40	40	160

We are now going to calculate a shadow price for each element in the matrix where no goods are moved. You can think of this shadow price as the cost we are willing to pay to move goods between two points. If the actual cost is more than this shadow price, we should not move any goods; if the actual cost is less than this shadow price, we should move as many goods as possible.

For every element of the matrix that actually has goods moved, we can separate the cost of going between i and j, C_{ij}, into two elements:

- a cost u_i of coming from i
- a cost v_j of going to j

Then for every element of the matrix with a positive amount moved:

$$C_{ij} = u_i + v_j$$

But we know C_{ij} for every entry, so if we know either u_i or v_j we can find the value of the other. To start the process we will arbitrarily set u_1 as 0. Then taking the first element with a positive amount moved, we have $C_{12} = 12$. So we have:

$$C_{12} = 12 = u_1 + v_2$$

and we have now set $u_1 = 0$, so v_2 must equal 12

Moving to the next element with a positive entry:

$$C_{13} = 20 = u_1 + v_3 = 0 + v_3$$

and $\qquad v_3 = 20$

then: $\qquad C_{14} = 10 = u_1 + v_4 = 0 + v_4$

and $\qquad v_4 = 10$

$$C_{22} = 6 = u_2 + v_2 = u_2 + 12$$

and $\qquad u_2 = -6$

$$C_{33} = 10 = u_3 + v_3 = u_3 + 20$$
$$u_3 = -10$$

Continuing these calculations give values to every u_i and v_j, as shown in the following matrix. Sometimes the procedure might stop before it gives all the values, in which case we arbitrarily set another u_i to zero.

	1	2	3	4	Supply	u_i
	10	12	20	10		0
1	0	10	10	40	60	
	16	6	10	22		−6
2	0	30	0	0	30	
	18	14	10	16		−10
3	0	0	25	0	25	
	2	16	18	14		−2
4	40	0	5	0	45	
Demand	40	40	40	40	160	
v_j	4	12	20	10		

Now we can calculate a shadow price for each element of the matrix that has nothing moved. The price we are willing to pay to use the element is the sum of the relevant u_i and v_j, so this shadow price is:

$$C'_{ij} = u_i + v_j$$

Starting at the top we have:

$$C'_{11} = u_1 + v_1$$

but we know that $u_1 = 0$ and $v_1 = 4$, so:

$$C'_{11} = u_1 + v_1 = 0 + 4 = 4$$

Then:

$$C'_{21} = u_2 + v_1 = -6 + 4 = -2$$
$$C'_{23} = u_2 + v_3 = -6 + 20 = 14$$

and so on.

Adding these shadow prices to the top left-hand corners of the elements gives the following matrix:

	1	2	3	4	Supply	u_i
1	4 10	12	20	10		0
	0	10	10	40	60	
2	−2 16	6	14 10	4 22		−6
	0	30	0	0	30	
3	−6 18	2 14	10	0 16		−10
	0	0	25	0	25	
4	2	10 16	18	8 14		−2
	40	0	5	0	45	
Demand	40	40	40	40	160	
v_j	4	12	20	10		

Now the elements with no goods moved have two costs:

- an actual cost that we are asked to pay, C_{ij}
- a shadow price that we are willing to pay, C'_{ij}

If we are asked to pay more than we are prepared to pay, we will not move goods using the element. But if we are willing to pay more than we are asked to pay, we will move as much as possible. So the next step in the algorithm finds the element where we are prepared to pay most above the actual price, i.e. the maximum value of $C'_{ij} - C_{ij}$. In this example there is only one element $(2, 3)$ where C'_{ij} is greater than C_{ij}, so we move as much as possible using this element.

Suppose we move an amount X from source 2 to destination 3. We must make some other changes or we would have $30 + X$ coming from source 2 and $40 + X$ going to destination 3. So we must reduce the amounts already moved from source 2 and to destination 3 by X, as shown below.

	1	2	3	4	Supply	u_i
1	4 10	12	20	10		0
	0	10	10 − X	40	60	
2	−2 16	6	14 10	4 22		−6
	0	30 − X	X	0	30	
3	−6 18	2 14	10	0 16		−10
	0	0	25	0	25	
4	2	10 16	18	8 14		−2
	40	0	5	0	45	
Demand	40	40	40	40	160	
v_j	4	12	20	10		

Unfortunately, this does not solve the problem, as we have now reduced row 1 and column 2 by X, and this demand and supply are no longer properly met. So we must add an amount X from source 1 to destination 2, and the sums now add properly.

	1	2	3	4	Supply	u_i
1	4 ⌐10⌐ 0	⌐12⌐ $10 + X$	⌐20⌐ $10 - X$	⌐10⌐ 40	60	0
2	−2 ⌐16⌐ 0	6⌐14 $30 - X$	⌐10⌐ 4 X	⌐22⌐ 0	30	−6
3	−6 ⌐18⌐ 0	2⌐14 0	⌐10⌐ 0 25	⌐16⌐ 0	25	−10
4	2⌐10⌐ 40	⌐16⌐ 0	⌐18⌐ 8 5	⌐14⌐ 0	45	−2
Demand	40	40	40	40	160	
v_j	4	12	20	10		

Notice that after we added X to the initial element, we only adjust elements that already had goods assigned to them. These changes form a circuit through the matrix – and the rows and columns still add properly because we add and subtract an equal amount from each column and row.

Finally, we have to set a value for X. We want to make it as big as possible, but there is a limit. This limit comes from the restriction that the amount of goods moved cannot be negative. So we must look at those elements where X is subtracted from the amount already transported – and the value of X must still leave these non-negative. In this case if X is more than 10 the entry in (1,3) will become negative. Setting X to 10 gives the revised plan:

	1	2	3	4	Supply
1	⌐10⌐ 0	⌐12⌐ 20	⌐20⌐ 0	⌐10⌐ 40	60
2	⌐16⌐ 0	⌐6⌐ 20	⌐10⌐ 10	⌐22⌐ 0	30
3	⌐18⌐ 0	⌐14⌐ 0	⌐10⌐ 25	⌐16⌐ 0	25
4	⌐2⌐ 40	⌐16⌐ 0	⌐18⌐ 5	⌐14⌐ 0	45
Demand	40	40	40	40	160

This completes one iteration of the algorithm. The cost of this revised solution has fallen from 1320 to 1280. To find an optimal solution we have to repeat this improving procedure until all the values of $C'_{ij} - C_{ij}$ are negative. The following matrix shows the next iteration for this problem:

	1	2	3	4	Supply	u_i
1	[4] [10] 0	[12] 20	[16] [20] 0	[10] 40	60	0
2	[−2] [16] 0	[6] 20	[10] 10	[4] [22] 0	30	−6
3	[−6] [18] 0	[6] [14] 0	[10] 25	[4] [16] 0	25	−6
4	[2] 40	[14] [16] 0	[18] 5	[12] [14] 0	45	−2
Demand	40	40	40	40	160	
v_j	0	12	16	10		

As you can see, every value for the actual price is higher than the price we are willing to pay – so we have found an optimal solution. The amounts moved are given in the body of the boxes, and we can find the total cost by adding individual costs from the original C_{ij}:

$$(20 * 12) + (40 * 10) + (20 * 6) + (10 * 10) + (25 * 10) + (40 * 2) + (5 * 18) = 1280$$

In practice, all these calculations are done with a computer, with a typical printout shown in Figure 5.9. This simply shows the initial problem, the initial solution and the final solutions. As you can see, the improving procedure is sometimes called MODI.

Program: Transportation problem
Problem Title: Transportation Example

***** Input Data *****

Minimization Problem:

	1	2	3	4	Supply
1	10.0	12.0	20.0	10.0	60.0
2	16.0	6.0	10.0	22.0	30.0
3	18.0	14.0	10.0	16.0	25.0
4	2.0	16.0	18.0	14.0	45.0
Demand	40.0	40.0	40.0	40.0	

***** Program Results *****

Initial Solution using Vogel's Approximation Method

	1	2	3	4	Supply
1	0.0	10.0	10.0	40.0	60.0
2	0.0	30.0	0.0	0.0	30.0
3	0.0	0.0	25.0	0.0	25.0
4	40.0	0.0	5.0	0.0	45.0
Demand	40.0	40.0	40.0	40.0	160.0

Initial Solution : 1320.0

Optimal Solution by MODI

	1	2	3	4	Supply
1	0.0	20.0	0.0	40.0	60.0
2	0.0	20.0	10.0	0.0	30.0
3	0.0	0.0	25.0	0.0	25.0
4	40.0	0.0	5.0	0.0	45.0
Demand	40.0	40.0	40.0	40.0	160.0

Optimal Solution : 1280.0

***** End of Output *****

Figure 5.9 Computer printout for Transportation Problem.

WORKED EXAMPLE 5.11

Find the minimum cost of moving goods between sources and destinations, with
the following costs, supplies and demands:

		To destination			
		1	2	3	Supply
From	1	10	8	9	100
source	2	8	10	11	150
	3	6	7	9	200
Demand		50	225	175	450

Solution

Firstly, we use Vogel's Approximation Method to find an initial solution. In this problem, there are many equally good results, and you can check one of them is as follows:

		To destination 1	2	3	Remaining supply
From source	1	–	75*	25*	0
	2	–	–	150*	0
	3	50*	150*	–	0
Unmet demand		0	0	0	175

Now we use the iterative procedure to improve this initial solution. The first iteration is shown in the following matrix:

	1	2	3	Supply	u_i
1	[7] [10] 0	[8] $75 - X$	[9] $25 + X$	100	0
2	[9] [8] $0 + X$	[10] [10] 0	[11] $150 - X$	150	2
3	[6] $50 - X$	[7] [8] $150 + X$	[9] 0	200	–1
Demand	50	225	175	450	
v_j	7	8	9		

We should move some goods from source 2 to destination 1, where we are willing to pay more than we are asked. If we move X on this route, we have to make adjustments in a circuit to make sure all rows and columns add up properly – but remember that we can only adjust elements with positive entries. So the maximum value of X is 50 (set by the quantity from 3 to 1) and the revised matrix is shown below.

	1	2	3	Supply	u_i
1	[6] [10] 0	[8] 25	[9] 75	100	0
2	[8] [10] 50	[10] 0	[11] 100	150	2
3	[5] [6] 0	[7] [8] 200	[9] 0	200	–1
Demand	50	225	175	450	
v_j	6	8	9		

The actual price is now always greater than the shadow price, so we have found an optimal solution. The cost of this is:

$$(25 * 8) + (75 * 9) + (50 * 8) + (100 * 11) + (200 * 7) = 3775$$

A typical printout for this problem is shown in Figure 5.10.

Program: Transportation problem
Problem Title: Worked Example 5.11

***** Input Data *****

Minimization Problem:

	1	2	3	Supply
1	10.0	8.0	9.0	100.0
2	8.0	10.0	11.0	150.0
3	6.0	7.0	9.0	200.0
Demand	50.0	225.0	175.0	

***** Program Results *****

Initial Solution using Vogel's Approximation Method

	1	2	3	Supply
1	0.0	0.0	100.0	100.0
2	0.0	75.0	75.0	150.0
3	50.0	150.0	0.0	200.0
Demand	50.0	225.0	175.0	450.0

Initial Solution :   3825.0

Optimal Solution by MODI

	1	2	3	Supply
1	0.0	0.0	100.0	100.0
2	50.0	25.0	75.0	150.0
3	0.0	200.0	0.0	200.0
Demand	50.0	225.0	175.0	450.0

Optimal Solution :   3775.0

***** End of Output *****

Figure 5.10   Computer printout for Worked Example 5.11.

IN SUMMARY

The Transportation Problem finds the lowest cost of moving goods from sources to destinations. We can solve this scheduling problem using linear programming. A simpler method uses two steps to find an initial solution, and iteratively improves this.

Self-assessment questions

5.12 What are the characteristics of a Transportation Problem?

5.13 What is the penalty cost in Vogel's Approximation Method?

5.14 In the Transportation Algorithm, where does the relationship

$$\text{actual cost} = C_{ij} = u_i + v_j$$

hold?

5.15 What is C'_{ij}?

5.5 | Shortest paths through a network

The Transportation Algorithm needs a matrix of costs for moving goods between sources and destinations, but sometimes it is difficult to find these costs. Suppose, for example, the sources and destinations are joined by a complex *network* of roads. How could we find the shortest path through the network? There is a useful method for this, which we can describe by an example.

Figure 5.11 shows a road network where the nodes – or circles – are towns and the numbers on the lines are distances. Now we want to find the *shortest path* between node 1 and every other node.

The method gives each node a label that shows the shortest distance found to it, and the previous node on the route. The label [20,6] on a node would show the shortest route from node 1 is 20 and the previous node on the route is node 6.

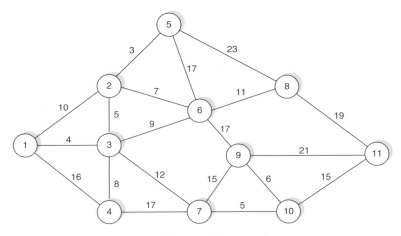

Figure 5.11 Road network to illustrate shortest path.

Initially, we put temporary labels on the nodes, but the method iteratively improves these until we find the best distance and the labels are made permanent. The steps for this are as follows:

Step 1. Put the permanent label $[0, s]$ on the starting node and the temporary labels $[T, -]$ on all other nodes.

Step 2. Define L_{ij} as the distance between nodes i and j. Then find the nodes directly connected to the starting node and put the label $[L_{1j}, 1]$ on each. Make the label on the node nearest to the starting node permanent by adding an asterisk.

Step 3. Find all the nodes, j, that can be reached directly from the new permanently labelled node, i – but do not include any permanently labelled nodes. For each of these find the minimum of the existing distance and the distance through node i. This is:

$$MIN[D_j, D_i + L_{ij}].$$

If the distance through node i is lower, change the label to $[D_i + L_{ij}, i]$.

Step 4. Find the temporary label with the lowest distance D_j and make the node permanent by adding an asterisk.

Step 5. If all nodes have permanent labels we have found the optimal solution. Otherwise, go to step 3.

WORKED EXAMPLE 5.12

Find the shortest path between node 1 and every other node in the network shown in Figure 5.12.

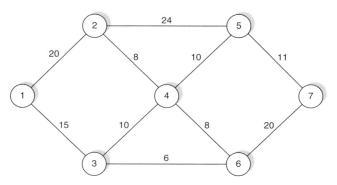

Figure 5.12 Network for Worked Example 5.12.

Solution

We can solve this problem using the steps described above. You can see how these labels develop in Figure 5.13.

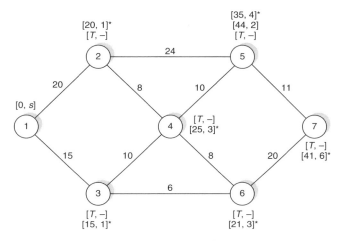

Figure 5.13   Solution to Worked Example 5.12.

Step 1

Put the permanent label [0, *s*] on node 1 and temporary labels [*T*, −] on all other nodes.

Step 2

There are two nodes reached directly from node 1. So we put the labels [20, 1] and [15, 1] on nodes 2 and 3 respectively. As node 3 is closer to node 1 we make this label permanent by adding an asterisk.

Step 3

Nodes 4 and 6 can be reached directly from node 3 (which is the node with a new permanent label). The shortest known route to both of these comes through node 3, so we label these [25, 3] and [21, 3] respectively.

Step 4

Nodes 2, 4 and 6 have temporary labels. The label on node 2 has the shortest distance, so we make this permanent by adding an asterisk.

Step 5

Four nodes are still not permanently labelled so we return to step 3.

Step 3

Nodes 4 and 5 can be reached directly from node 2. The distance to node 5 through node 2 is 44, so we change the label to [44, 2]. The distance to node 4 through node 2 is 32. This is greater than the distance on the existing label so we do not change the label.

Step 4

Nodes 4, 5 and 6 have temporary labels and the shortest distance on these is 21 on node 6. So we make this label permanent by adding an asterisk.

Step 5

Three nodes are still not permanently labelled so we return to step 3.

Step 3

Nodes 4 and 7 can be reached directly from node 6. The shortest path to node 7 is 41 from node 6, so we change the label to [41, 6]. The shortest path to node 4 is still through node 3 so we do not change the label.

Step 4

Nodes 4, 5 and 7 have temporary labels. The distance to node 4 is smallest, so we make the label permanent.

Step 5

Two nodes are still not permanently labelled so we return to step 3.

Repeating this procedure twice more gives all nodes permanent labels. The shortest distances can then be read from the nodes, and the routes found by tracing backwards through the network.

Node	Shortest distance from node 1	Route
2	20	1–2
3	15	1–3
4	25	1–3–4
5	35	1–3–4–5
6	21	1–3–6
7	41	1–3–6–7

There are many programmes that can do these calculations, with a typical printout shown in Figure 5.14.

Program: Network Models / Shortest Route
Problem Title: Worked Example 5.12

***** Input Data *****

Start node <---> End node	Distance
1 <---> 2	20.00
1 <---> 3	15.00
2 <---> 4	8.00
3 <---> 4	10.00
2 <---> 5	24.00
3 <---> 6	6.00
4 <---> 5	10.00
4 <---> 6	8.00
5 <---> 7	11.00
6 <---> 7	20.00

***** Program Results *****

Start node <---> End node	Distance
1 <---> 3	15.00
3 <---> 6	6.00
6 <---> 7	20.00

Shortest Path is:

1 <---> 3 <---> 6 <---> 7

Total Shortest Distance :   41.000

***** End of Output *****

Figure 5.14   Computer printout for shortest path in Worked Example 5.12.

WORKED EXAMPLE 5.13

Figure 5.15 shows the travel times between a central warehouse (1) and a number of customers. What is the shortest travel time from the warehouse to all customers?

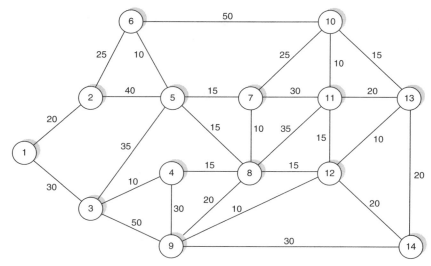

Figure 5.15 Network for Worked Example 5.13.

Solution

Using the procedure described above, we get the labels as shown in Figure 5.16. The nodes are permanently labelled in the order:

1, 2, 3, 4, 6, 5, 8, 7, 9, 12, 13, 11, 10, 14

and the solution is:

Node	Shortest distance	Route
2	20	1–2
3	30	1–3
4	40	1–3–4
5	55	1–2–6–5
6	45	1–2–6
7	65	1–3–4–8–7
8	55	1–3–4–8
9	70	1–3–4–9
10	90	1–3–4–8–7–10
11	85	1–3–4–8–12–11
12	70	1–3–4–8–12
13	80	1–3–4–8–12–13
14	90	1–3–4–8–12–14

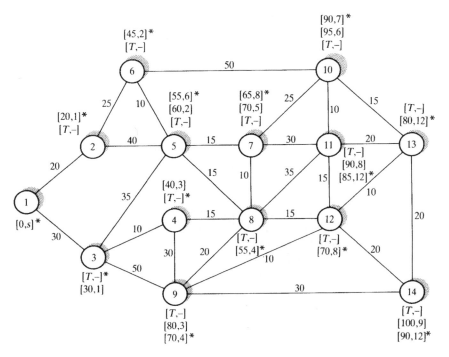

Figure 5.16 Solution to Worked Example 5.13.

IN SUMMARY

A simple labelling method can show the shortest path between two points in a network.

Self-assessment questions

5.16 What does the label $[D_j, n]$ mean when we are looking for the shortest path?

5.17 How does a labelling method find the nodes that are on the shortest paths?

Case example

Road networks

The roads in Britain are among the most congested in the world. Old cities – particularly London and Cambridge – were not designed to handle heavy traffic, and it is now often faster to walk than to drive.

An obvious solution to the congestion is to build more roads. For a period up to the early 1990s the government built many new road schemes, including motorways and bypasses. Unfortunately, these often did not ease the congestion, and sometimes made it worse. The explanation is that drivers always follow the shortest route – not in distance but in time. When a new road is built to reduce the congestion on an old road, its capacity is set to cover existing traffic plus expected growth over the next few years. But another set of traffic also uses the new road – those who find it faster to divert from their existing route. The result is that the new road soon gets as congested as the old road.

Many people believe that new roads do not solve existing traffic problems, but create new traffic. This is one reason why the government changed its policies in the early 1990s and substantially reduced its road-building programmes.

5.6 | Maximum flow through a network

Many scheduling problems can be viewed as flows through a network – such as traffic along roads, gas through pipelines, telephone calls along optical fibres, or products along a factory assembly line. But each link in the network has a maximum capacity. So how can we find the maximum possible flow between two points in a network? This is the *Maximum Flow Problem*.

We can tackle the Maximum Flow Problem using another labelling method. In this, we label each node with the flow into the node, and the node from which this flow comes. So the label [20,6] shows a node with a flow of 20 coming in from node 6. Then the steps in the algorithm are as follows:

Step 1. Label the source $[\infty, s]$

Step 2. Choose any labelled node, i, and examine the unlabelled nodes, j, that can be reached directly from it.

Step 3. For each unlabelled node, j, calculate the maximum flow that can go between i and j. This is the lower of the capacity of the link between i and j, and the amount that is flowing into i. Call this flow F and label the nodes j $[F, i]$. If there are no possible flows between labelled and unlabelled nodes, we have an optimal solution. Then go to step 5. Otherwise continue to step 4.

Step 4. If the terminal node is not labelled go to step 2. If the terminal node is labelled calculate the additional flow through the network. Subtract this amount from the link capacities and go to step 1.

Step 5. Now we have the answer, and can find the maximum flow through the network by adding the separate flows identified in step 4.

WORKED EXAMPLE 5.14

Figure 5.17 shows a network of connected pipes with the capacity given on each section. What is the maximum possible flow between nodes 1 and 7?

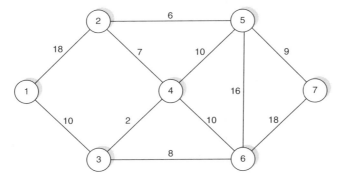

Figure 5.17   Network capacities for Worked Example 5.14.

Solution

You can follow progress through the steps described above in Figure 5.18.

Step 1
Label the source node $[\infty, s]$.

Step 2
There is only a label on node 1, so we consider the unlabelled nodes connected directly to this, i.e. nodes 2 and 3.

Step 3

The maximum amount that can flow from 1 to 2 is 18 and from 1 to 3 is 10. Both of these are set by the capacity of the connecting pipes. So we label these nodes [18, 1] and [10, 1] respectively.

Step 4

The terminal node (7) is not labelled so we return to step 2.

Step 2

Now we take the labelled node 2 and consider unlabelled nodes connected directly to this (i.e. 4 and 5).

Step 3

The maximum flow from 2 to 4 is 7, and the maximum flow from 2 to 5 is 6. Both of these are set by the capacity of the connecting pipes. So we put labels [7, 2] and [6, 2] respectively on nodes 4 and 5.

Step 4

The terminal node is not labelled so we return to step 2.

Step 2

Next we take the labelled node 5 and consider the unlabelled nodes connected directly to it, i.e. nodes 6 and 7.

Step 3

The maximum flow from 5 to 6 is 6 and from 5 to 7 is 6. Both of these are set by the flow into 5. Now we put labels [6,5] on both nodes 6 and 7.

Step 4

The terminal node has now been labelled, so we can find the flow through the network. As you can see, we have defined a flow of 6 through the path 1–2–5–7. So we reduce the capacity of these pipes by 6 and repeat the procedure from step 1.

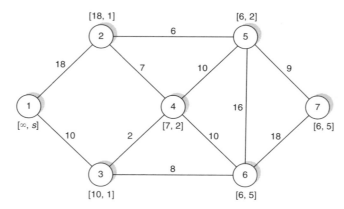

Figure 5.18 Solution to Worked Example 5.14.

As you can see from Figure 5.19, repeating this procedure gives, in order,

- flow of 3 through 1–2–4–5–7
- flow of 8 through 1–3–6–7
- flow of 4 through 1–2–4–6–7
- flow of 2 through 1–3–4–6–7

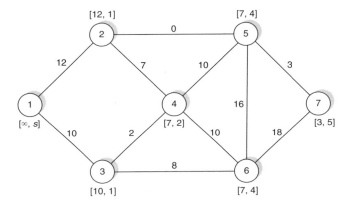

(a)

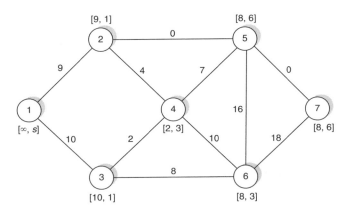

(b)

Figure 5.19 continued overleaf

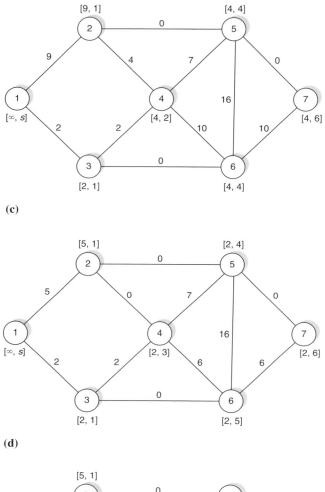

(c)

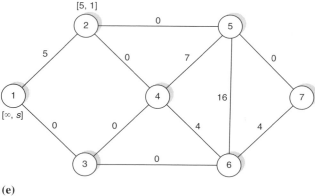

(d)

(e)

Figure 5.19 (a)–(e)   Further iterations for the solution to Worked Example 5.14.

At this point we cannot label any more flows all the way from the origin to the terminal node, so we have found the optimal solution. The labels on the pipes after the final iteration show the spare capacities. The maximum flow from node 1 to node 7 is the total of flows calculated in steps 4, which is 23, with flows in each link shown in Figure 5.20.

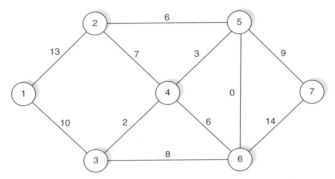

Figure 5.20   Optimal solution for maximum flow in Worked Example 5.14.

WORKED EXAMPLE 5.15

The roads between a city centre and an airport are shown in Figure 5.21. If the number on each link is the maximum number of cars (in thousands per hour) that can use a road, what is the maximum number of vehicles that can travel between the city centre and the airport?

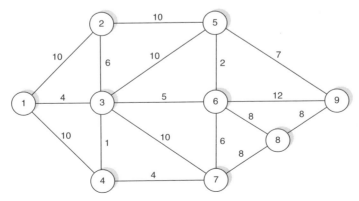

Figure 5.21   Flows along the road network for Worked Example 5.15.

Solution

We can use the procedure described above to find the separate flows in the network. First we can find a flow of 7 through 1–2–5–9, as shown in Figure 5.22.

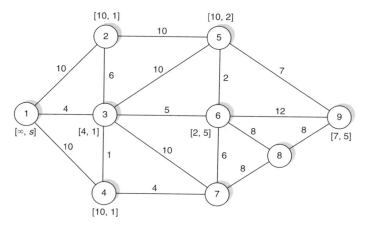

Figure 5.22 First iteration of solution for Worked Example 5.15.

We can use the same approach to find:

- flow of 4 through 1–4–7–8–9
- flow of 4 through 1–3–6–9
- flow of 2 through 1–2–5–6–9
- flow of 1 through 1–2–3–6–9
- flow of 1 through 1–4–3–7–8–9

The maximum number of cars is the sum of these flows, which is 19 000 an hour. We can confirm this result using a computer, with a typical printout shown in Figure 5.23.

IN SUMMARY

Many scheduling problems can be represented as flows through a network. If each link in the network has a fixed capacity, a labelling method gives the maximum flow through the network.

Program: Network Models / Maximum Flow
Problem Title: Worked Example 5.15

***** Input Data *****

Start node ---> End node	Capacity
1 ----> 2	10.00
1 ----> 3	4.00
1 ----> 4	10.00
2 ----> 3	6.00
3 ----> 4	1.00
2 ----> 5	10.00
3 ----> 5	10.00
3 ----> 6	5.00
3 ----> 7	10.00
4 ----> 7	4.00
5 ----> 6	2.00
6 ----> 7	6.00
5 ----> 9	7.00
6 ----> 9	12.00
6 ----> 8	8.00
7 ----> 8	8.00
8 ----> 9	8.00

***** Program Results *****

Start node ---> End node	Flow
1 ----> 2	10.000
1 ----> 3	4.000
1 ----> 4	5.000
2 ----> 3	1.000
4 ----> 3	1.000
2 ----> 5	9.000
3 ----> 6	5.000
3 ----> 7	1.000
4 ----> 7	4.000
5 ----> 6	2.000
5 ----> 9	7.000
6 ----> 9	7.000
7 ----> 8	5.000
8 ----> 9	5.000

Total Maximum Flow :   19.000

***** End of Output *****

Figure 5.23   Computer printout of results for Worked Example 5.15.

Self-assessment questions

5.18 In a maximum flow labelling algorithm what does the node label $[F, n]$ mean?

5.19 How many iterations of the maximum flow algorithm do you need to find an optimal solution?

CHAPTER REVIEW

This chapter has looked at a number of scheduling problems. In particular it:

● explained how scheduling problems look for the best sequence of activities

● showed how the number of possible solutions make scheduling problems very difficult to solve

● did calculations with combinations and permutations

● described some scheduling rules

● showed how to solve the Assignment Problem using the Hungarian Method

● described the Transportation Problem

● used a labelling method to find the shortest path through a network

● found the maximum flow through a network

KEY TERMS

Assignment Problem
combinations
flowshop
Hungarian Method
Johnson's Rule
Maximum Flow Problem
network
permutations

schedules
scheduling rules
sequences
shortest path
Transportation Algorithm
Transportation Problem
Vogel's Approximation Method
VAM

Case study

International Electronic Trading Corporation

International Electronic Trading Corporation (IETC) has subsidiaries in over 30 countries and marketing operations in a further 90. They started making cash registers on the West Coast of America in the 1920s, and now make a wide range of electronic office equipment.

IETC was primarily a manufacturing company until the 1960s. Most of its production was in the West Coast of America, with smaller factories nearer the main markets in the Eastern United States and Europe. In the 1960s the company noticed a lot of changes – particularly the development of computers and the growth of manufacturing centres in the Far East. Competition increased, not only from established rivals, but also from new companies based in Japan and Singapore.

IETC made a major change in direction in the mid-1970s. The company felt that it could no longer compete with new manufacturers, and it became more of a trading company. It had 50 years of experience in marketing office equipment and had a well-respected name throughout the world. Using these strengths, the company started licensing other companies in the Far East and South America to build its equipment.

This change was successful and profits increased by an average of 7% a year through the 1980s. But there were still reminders of the previous operations of the company. These were most obvious in the distribution system.

All the products made by IETC were passed from a factory to an adjacent Central Finished Goods Warehouse (CFGW). Any imported items for the local market were brought to the same warehouse. From here, any goods for the domestic market were moved to a regional warehouse and then on to customers. Goods for export were sent to the relevant CFGW, and then on to a regional warehouse and customers.

For some time it was clear to IETC that this pattern of movements could be improved, and there was no need to move all goods through CFGWs. In practice, urgent or important orders were often sent directly to regional warehouses. Large orders were occasionally sent directly to customers. Those countries that had more than one factory also had more than one CFGW, while countries without a factory had imported goods diverted through the CFGW in another country.

To see if it could improve matters, the West European Division of IETC looked at the goods moved during the past year. This Division manufactured at three factories: in Peterborough in the United Kingdom, Toulouse in France, and Brussels in Belgium. Over 3000 tonnes of goods were made in these factories, while almost 1800 tonnes of equipment were imported.

Goods flowing into Europe, both imported and manufactured, were shipped to 17 countries.

Company records gave the total weights moved in the past year between factories, CFGWs and regional warehouses in each country. However, these figures should be viewed with some caution. There is no guarantee that historical movements will give an accurate picture of future movements and, perhaps more importantly, there seem to be inconsistencies in the figures.

The following tables show the amounts shipped in kilogrammes. Movements between, say, Peterborough and Peterborough refer to the amounts shipped between the factory and the CFGW on the same site. All other entries are shipments from the CFGW to regional warehouses.

From \ To	Central warehouses			Regional warehouse	
	Peterborough	*Toulouse*	*Brussels*	*Austria*	*Belgium*
Peterborough	520 002	65 712	261 081	1645	0
Toulouse	103 676	351 772	171 734	637	216 090
Brussels	187 134	7078	0	0	0
USA West Coast	124 279	306 111	103 692	1295	0
USA North East	285 572	70 124	36 746	760	0
USA South East	125 184	30 064	69 950	22	0
USA Central	25 644	10 549	7519	344	0
Japan	107 570	2450	350	0	0
Brazil	3557	25 282	19 023	0	0
Mexico	5860	0	0	0	0
Canada	27 622	46 287	20 326	0	0

From \ To	Regional warehouses					
	Denmark	*Finland*	*France*	*Germany*	*Greece*	*Holland*
Peterborough	10 563	22 013	0	118 855	7966	44 948
Toulouse	10 727	9494	0	18 212	487	64 767
Brussels	160	3228	736 439	1713	4300	1432
USA West Coast	7770	21 916	0	52 453	1482	22 599
USA North East	12 409	2675	0	6460	1467	5933
USA South East	570	7000	0	3084	16	8719
USA Central	5	327	0	3511	20	1161
Japan	225	350	0	992	0	10 257
Brazil	1056	470	0	41	1172	0
Mexico	0	0	0	0	0	0
Canada	2547	3100	0	1709	863	5952

From \ To	Regional warehouses				
	Iceland	*Italy*	*Luxembourg*	*Norway*	*Portugal*
Peterborough	3196	126 891	0	19 861	12 067
Toulouse	5	10 376	3684	5802	20
Brussels	210	3727	0	128	316
USA West Coast	0	4956	0	3482	1593
USA North East	484	4874	22	151	1386
USA South East	2	2418	0	879	84
USA Central	0	16 370	0	3415	1029
Japan	0	0	1164	0	0
Brazil	0	269	0	293	0
Mexico	0	0	0	0	0
Canada	0	1552	0	1120	0

From \ To	Regional warehouses				
	Spain	*Sweden*	*Switzerland*	*UK*	*Rest of World*
Peterborough	39 037	33 957	42 724	950 631	2 260 427
Toulouse	6348	10 910	30 126	0	248 334
Brussels	61	2624	2999	0	237 591
USA West Coast	1139	6599	15 560	0	438 564
USA North East	4265	7167	12 375	0	383 132
USA South East	847	2734	4629	0	322 219
USA Central	1039	905	527	0	134 337
Japan	0	7583	5228	0	37 479
Brazil	0	940	0	0	169 914
Mexico	0	0	0	0	111 350
Canada	1743	1408	0	0	107 242

Over 1700 tonnes of goods were imported to Europe by air. Although more expensive than sea, IETC liked the speed of service and felt the extra cost was a relatively small part of the overall price. They also argued that the shorter lead time reduced stock levels. A comparison of average costs of transport to European destinations is given in the following table:

Source	Cost	(US $/kg)
	Air	Surface
USA West Coast	3.30	0.75
USA North East	2.40	0.45
USA South East	2.40	0.45
USA Central	2.50	0.52
Japan	8.79	0.67
Brazil	4.88	0.85
Mexico	3.30	0.75
Canada	2.74	0.60

Within Europe 90% of IETC's goods are moved by road. It is difficult to be specific about freight rates as these are highly variable. IETC has long-term arrangements with several haulage contractors, but they often use other companies that give cheaper rates for a particular delivery. The typical range of quotations from different haulage companies for delivery from Peterborough to regional warehouses is given below (values in US cents per kg):

Destination	Minimum rate	Maximum rate
Austria	32.0	139.9
Belgium	18.4	76.2
Denmark	28.8	133.5
France	20.8	99.7
Germany	25.9	129.0
Holland	14.9	92.1
Italy	26.4	158.0
Norway	18.7	211.1
Portugal	40.0	176.7
Spain	40.0	190.4
Sweden	16.0	198.2
Switzerland	28.8	101.7
UK	3.7	33.7

IETC is thinking about closing CFGWs near some factories. They could, perhaps, replace these by a small number of Logistics Centres. All production from European factories and all imports would be sent to these centres and either passed on to regional warehouses within Europe or exported to markets outside.

There are many possible locations for logistics centres in Europe. There is even space in some of IETC's existing facilities. At Peterborough, for example, they could extend the warehouse at very little cost. Brussels has some space but would need extra facilities costing $80 000 a year. Toulouse would need some expansion at a cost of $120 000 a year. Other attractive options might be new sites at Amsterdam (with costs of $330 000 a year), Southampton ($430 000 a year), Hamburg ($560 000 a year) or Genoa ($460 000 a year).

Questions

- How effective is IETC's current logistics system?
- Should IETC change its transport?
- What are the benefits of setting up European Logistics Centres? Where might they be located?

Problems

5.1 Part of a stockroom has 8 bins to hold 8 different items. In how many ways can the items be assigned to bins? In how many ways can the items be assigned if the number of bins is increased to 11?

5.2 An open-plan office has 10 desks. If 10 clerks work in the area, how many different seating arrangements are there? If two of the clerks leave, how many seating arrangements are there? How many different arrangements are there for the two empty desks?

5.3 Seven items are made in batches on a machine. Current stocks, average demands and production times are given below. Design a schedule for the machine that makes sure no item runs out of stock.

Item	A	B	C	D	E	F	G
Average demand	20	15	10	4	15	25	14
Current stock	72	20	50	24	32	100	68
Production time	1	1.5	0.5	1	0.5	1.0	0.5

5.4. Seven jobs are waiting to be processed on a single machine with the following processing times:

Job	A	B	C	D	E	F	G
Processing time	20	17	6	30	25	12	34

What sequence of jobs minimizes the mean queueing time? If each job has the following due date, what order will minimize the average lateness?

Job	A	B	C	D	E	F	G
Due date	48	80	45	25	130	120	70

What sequence minimizes the number of late jobs?

5.5 Ten jobs are to be processed on machine 1 followed by machine 2 with expected times as follows. What sequence of jobs maximizes machine utilization?

Job	A	B	C	D	E	F	G	H	I	J
Machine 1	14	19	24	22	6	40	20	4	1	25
Machine 2	2	10	8	32	35	18	30	6	35	28

5.6 Use the Hungarian Method to confirm the solution to Worked Example 5.9.

5.7 The costs of assigning seven jobs to equipment are given in the following table. Find the assignment that minimizes the total cost.

		Equipment						
		1	2	3	4	5	6	7
	1	68	48	57	48	84	10	77
	2	14	64	71	50	24	10	84
	3	54	10	54	13	8	9	8
Tasks	4	15	12	55	54	46	45	87
	5	55	78	12	84	84	54	48
	6	19	8	48	54	84	62	45
	7	44	12	48	77	43	46	52

5.8 Solve the Transportation Problem described by the following matrix:

		Demand							
---	---	1	2	3	4	5	6	7	Supply
	1	41	62	84	12	55	30	50	150
	2	44	46	83	91	10	90	71	200
	3	55	31	10	15	51	47	47	200
Supply	4	64	49	21	29	27	73	50	350
	5	80	19	46	56	68	70	46	150
	6	71	18	82	46	28	55	49	50
	7	76	38	42	67	13	49	86	50
Demand		75	225	175	275	125	150	125	1150

5.9 Look again at the network shown in Figure 5.11. Use a labelling algorithm to find the shortest route between node 1 and all other nodes. Check your results using a computer.

5.10 Figure 5.24 shows a network of roads with distances marked on links. Find the shortest distance from node 1 to all other nodes.

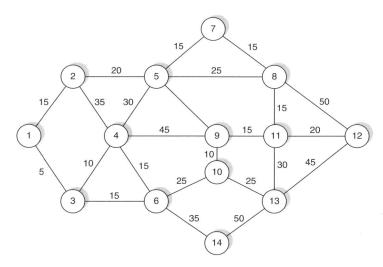

Figure 5.24 Road network for Problem 5.10.

5.11 Figure 5.25 shows a network of pipes with maximum capacities marked on each link. Find the maximum flow between nodes 1 and 14.

5.12 Look again at the network shown in Figure 5.11. If the numbers on the links show the capacity, use a labelling algorithm to find the maximum flow through the network.

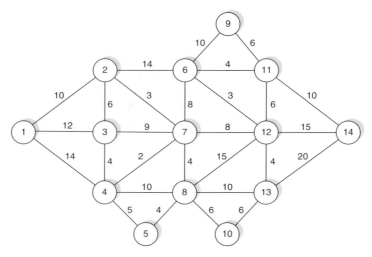

Figure 5.25   Network of pipes for Problem 5.11.

Discussion questions

5.1   Why are scheduling problems so difficult to solve?

5.2   'Mathematical programming is the only reliable way of scheduling.' Do you think this is true? How are scheduling problems tackled in practice?

5.3   This chapter has described some general scheduling problems. What other types of scheduling problem do organizations face?

5.4   'Scheduling is the most common problem faced by management.' Do you agree with this? What other problems might be more common?

Forecasting

6

CHAPTER OUTLINE

All management decisions rely on forecasts of future circumstances. This chapter describes the most common methods of forecasting, which include judgemental, projective and causal methods. After reading the chapter you should be able to:

- understand the importance of forecasting
- discuss different approaches to forecasting
- describe a variety of judgemental forecasting methods
- define 'time series' and understand their importance
- calculate errors in forecasts
- describe the characteristics of causal forecasts
- find lines of best fit using linear regression
- describe the characteristics of projective forecasting
- forecast using actual averages, moving averages and exponential smoothing
- forecast series with seasonality and trend

| 6.1 | Forecasting within an organization

All management decisions are based on *forecasts*. Every decision becomes effective at some point in the future, so it should be based on forecasts of future conditions. When British Aerospace plans its production, it does not make enough aeroplanes to meet current demand, but enough to meet forecast demand when the planes are ready for sale.

> Every decision in an organization is based on **forecasts** of future conditions.

The list of things that are forecast is endless: demand for products, interest rates, productivity, output, resources needed, manpower available, time to finish a job, production rates, weather, share prices, costs of raw materials, and so on. In this chapter we will often talk about 'demand' being forecast, but this is just for convenience. You can think of it as a general term for everything that could be forecast.

Forecasts are needed throughout an organization – and they should certainly not be produced by an isolated group of specialists. Neither is forecasting ever 'finished'. Forecasts are needed continually, and as time moves on, actual performance is compared with forecasts, original forecasts are updated, plans are modified, and so on. This process is shown in Figure 6.1.

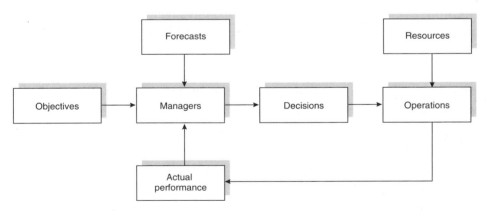

Figure 6.1 Forecasting and decisions.

In many ways, work on forecasting has been disappointing. It is still difficult to get a reliable weather forecast; we cannot tell which horse will win a race; the price of gold still seems to fluctuate randomly; we buy too much food for a party;

shops have sales of excess stock, and so on. But we can get quite good forecasts if we use the right method. Unfortunately, there is no single method that is always best – so we have to look at a number of models and see when each can be used.

We can classify forecasting models in several ways. We can, for example, look at the time in the future covered by the forecasts:

- **Long-term forecasts** look ahead several years – the time typically needed to build a new factory.

- **Medium-term forecasts** look ahead between 3 months and 2 years – the time typically needed to replace an old product by a new one.

- **Short-term forecasts** cover the next few weeks – describing the continuing demand for a product.

The time horizon affects the choice of forecasting method because of the availability of historical data, how relevant this is for the future, the time available to make the forecast, the cost involved, the seriousness of any errors, the effort considered worthwhile, and so on.

Another classification of forecasting methods shows the difference between qualitative and quantitative approaches (as shown in Figure 6.2).

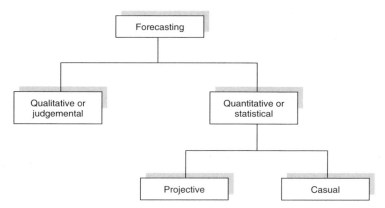

Figure 6.2   A classification of forecasting methods.

If an organization is already making a product it will have records of past demand. Then it can use a quantitative method for forecasting future demand. There are two ways of doing this:

- *projective forecasting* – which looks at the pattern of past demand and extends this into the future. If demand in the last 4 weeks has been 10, 20, 30 and 40, we can project this pattern into the future and suggest that demand in the next week will be around 50.

- *causal forecasting* – which looks at outside influences and uses these to forecast. The productivity of a factory might depend on the bonus rates paid to employees. Then we can forecast future productivity from the planned bonus rate.

Both of these approaches rely on accurate, numerical data. But if an organization is introducing an entirely new product, it will have no past demand figures to project into the future, and it will not yet know the outside influences that affect demand. So the organization does not have the data for a quantitative method. The only option is to use a qualitative method. Such methods are generally called *judgemental forecasting*, and they rely on subjective views and opinions.

This classification of methods does not mean that each is independent and must be used in isolation. Managers should look at all available information and then make the decision they feel is best. This means that any forecast should have a subjective review before it is used, as shown in Figure 6.3.

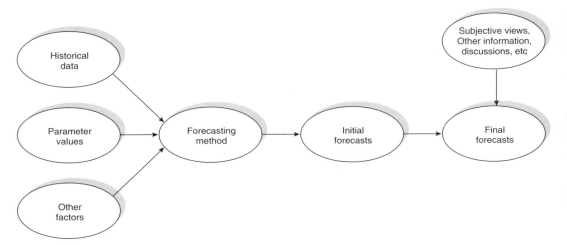

Figure 6.3   Overall approach to forecasting.

IN SUMMARY

Forecasting is an important part of every business decision. There are many ways of forecasting, and none is best in all circumstances. Available methods can be classified in several ways.

Case example

Euro Disney

Euro Disney runs the major theme park outside Paris. In the early years after it opened, the park had continuous financial problems. By March 1994 it faced permanent closure. At this time its owners, 61 banks and other investors, agreed a rescue package valued at F 13 billion.

The basic problem was that Euro Disney's income was not meeting its costs. The capacity of the park, the number of people employed, the number of rides, and almost every other aspect of operations were based on forecasts of the number of visitors. There were no other Disney parks in Europe, so these forecasts were based largely on American experiences. Unfortunately, later results showed that there were significant differences between operations in America and Europe.

In 1993 Euro Disney attracted nearly 10 million visitors, which was 13% fewer than expected. At the same time, each visitor spent at least 10% less than forecast. The result was an annual loss of F 5.34 billion, which grew worse when 1994 saw less than 9 million visitors.

So all decisions about Euro Disney were based on faulty forecasts. When actual performance became known, the theme park had to make significant changes to operations. They tried to attract more visitors, by cutting prices in the park, reducing hotel costs, seasonal pricing in the autumn and winter when only 30% of visitors came, special deals for pensioners, school groups and 'kids-free' packages, more emphasis on short packages, and more promotion in Britain. Several other measures were agreed with Walt Disney, who own 49% of Euro Disney. These include F 1.1 billion of extra credit, selling F 1.4 billion of assets to Walt Disney and leasing them back at favourable terms, waiving of royalties on entry fees, food and merchandise, and suspending management fees. Other plans included greater cost control, a new shopping mall, multiplex cinema, new restaurants, more convention facilities, high-speed rail link and improved access. These measures aimed at making the park financially secure by 1997.

Self-assessment questions

6.1 Why is forecasting important to an organization?

6.2 'Forecasting is best done by a group of experts working in isolation.' Do you think this is true?

6.3 List three different approaches to forecasting.

6.2 || Judgemental forecasting

> **Judgemental forecasting** methods are subjective views, often based on the opinions of experts. These are sometimes called qualitative or subjective methods.

Suppose a company is about to market an entirely new product, or a medical team is considering a new organ transplant, or a manufacturer wants to develop new batteries to power cars, or a board of directors is considering plans for 25 years in the future. These decisions need forecasts of future conditions, but there is no relevant historical data. This means that they cannot use quantitative forecasting methods, and must use judgemental methods. Here we will consider five methods of judgemental forecasting:

- *personal insight*
- *panel consensus*
- *market surveys*
- *historical analogy*
- *Delphi method*

6.2.1 Personal insight

This uses a single person who is familiar with the situation to produce a forecast based on their own judgement. This is the most widely used forecasting method – and is the one that managers should try to avoid. It relies entirely on one person's judgement – as well as their opinions, prejudices and ignorance. It can give good forecasts, but can also give very bad ones. The major weakness of this method is its unreliability.

Comparisons of forecasting methods clearly show that someone who is familiar with a situation, using experience and subjective opinions to forecast, will consistently produce **worse** forecasts than someone who knows nothing about the situation but uses a more formal method.

6.2.2 Panel consensus

One person can easily make a mistake, but collecting together a group of people should give a consensus that is more reliable. If there is no secrecy and the panel talk freely and openly, they may find a genuine consensus. But it can be difficult to combine the views of different people when they cannot reach a consensus.

Although it is more reliable than one person's insight, panel consensus still has the major weakness that everybody, even experts, can make mistakes. There are also problems of group working, where 'he who shouts loudest gets his way', everyone tries to please the boss, some people do not speak well in groups, and so on. Overall, panel consensus is better than personal insight, but you should be cautious about the results from either method.

6.2.3 Market surveys

Sometimes, even groups of experts do not have sufficient knowledge to give a reasonable forecast. This happens, for example, with the launch of a new product. Then market surveys collect data from a sample of potential customers, analyse their views and make inferences about the population at large.

Market surveys can give useful information but they tend to be expensive and time-consuming. They are also prone to errors as they rely on:

- a sample of customers that accurately represents the population
- useful, unbiased questions
- fair and honest answers
- reliable analyses of the answers
- valid conclusions drawn from the analyses

6.2.4 Historical analogy

Demands for most products follow a common pattern through their lifetime. Most sales go through periods of:

- introduction
- growth
- maturity
- decline
- withdrawal

These give the general pattern of demand shown in Figure 6.4.

If an organization is introducing a new product, it might have a similar product that was launched recently, and can assume that demand for the new product will follow the same pattern. A publisher, for example, might forecast the likely sales of a new book from the actual sales of a similar book it published earlier.

Historical analogy can only be used if a similar product has been introduced fairly recently. In practice, it is often difficult to find such similar products, or to fit the characteristic life-cycle curve.

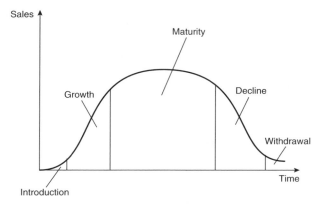

Figure 6.4   Stages in a product life cycle.

6.2.5 Delphi method

This is the most formal of the judgemental methods and has a well-defined procedure. A number of experts are contacted by post and each is given a questionnaire to complete. The replies from these questionnaires are analysed and summaries are passed back to the experts. Each expert is then asked to reconsider their original reply in the light of the summarized replies from others. Each reply is anonymous to avoid any undue influences of status and the pressures of face-to-face discussions. This process of modifying responses in the light of replies made by the rest of the group is repeated several times – usually between three and six. By this time, the range of opinions should be narrow enough to help with decisions.

We can illustrate the Delphi method by an example from offshore oil fields. Suppose a company wants to know when underwater inspections on platforms will be done entirely by robots rather than divers. They will contact a number of experts to start the Delphi forecast. These experts come from various backgrounds, including divers, technical staff from oil companies, ships' captains, maintenance engineers and robot designers. The company will explain the overall problem, and then ask each of the experts when they think robots will replace divers. The initial returns probably give a wide range of dates from, say, 1998 to 2050. The company summarizes these replies and passes the results back to the experts. Then it asks if they would like to change their answer in the light of other replies. After repeating this several times, views might converge so that 80% of replies give a date between 2005 and 2015. This is close enough to help planning.

6.2.6 Comparison of methods

Each of these judgemental methods works best in different circumstances. If you want a quick reply, personal insight is the fastest and cheapest method. If you want a reliable forecast, it may be worth organising a market survey or Delphi method. A general comparison of methods is shown below.

Method	Accuracy in term			Cost
	Short	Medium	Long	
Personal insight	Poor	Poor	Poor	Low
Panel consensus	Poor to fair	Poor to fair	Poor	Low
Market survey	Very good	Good	Fair	High
Historical analogy	Poor	Fair to good	Fair to good	Medium
Delphi method	Fair to very good	Fair to very good	Fair to very good	Medium to high

IN SUMMARY

We can classify forecasting methods as judgemental, projective or causal. Judgemental forecasts rely on subjective views. The most common methods are personal insight, panel consensus, market surveys, historical analogy and the Delphi method. Each of these is useful in different circumstances.

Self-assessment questions

6.4   What are 'judgemental forecasts'?

6.5   List five types of judgemental forecast.

6.6   What is the main problem with judgemental forecasts?

6.3 | Time series and forecast errors

Quantitative forecasting models often look at *time series*. These are series of observations taken at regular intervals, like the sales of newspapers each day, weekly production figures, number of shifts worked each month, quarterly profit, annual rainfall, and population reported in the ten-year census.

If you have a time series, it is always useful to draw a graph to show any underlying patterns. The three most common patterns in time series are shown in Figure 6.5 as:

- **constant series** – where values stay roughly the same over time, such as annual rainfall

- **series with a trend** – which either rise or fall steadily, such as the gross national product per capita
- **seasonal series** – which have cycles, such as weekly sales of soft drinks

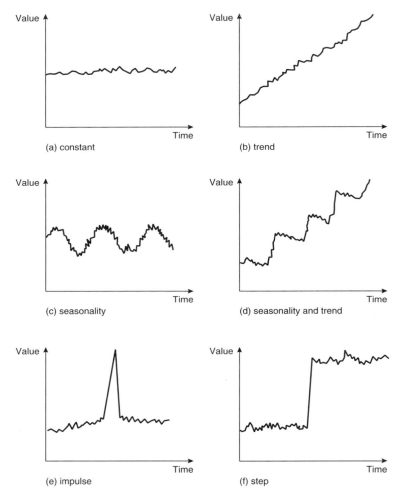

Figure 6.5 Common patterns in a time series.

If observations followed these simple patterns we would have no problems with forecasting. Unfortunately, there are always differences between actual observations and the underlying pattern. These differences appear as a random *noise* which is superimposed on the underlying pattern. Then a constant series, for example, does not always have exactly the same value, but is somewhere close. So:

    200   205   194   195   208   203   200   193   201   198

is a constant series of 200 with superimposed noise.

actual value = underlying pattern + random noise

The noise is a completely random effect that is caused by many factors, such as variations in demand from customers, hours worked by employees, speed of working, weather conditions, rejection rates at inspections, and so on. It is the noise that makes forecasting difficult. If the noise is relatively small we can make good forecasts, but if there is a lot of noise it hides the underlying pattern and forecasting becomes very difficult (see Figure 6.6).

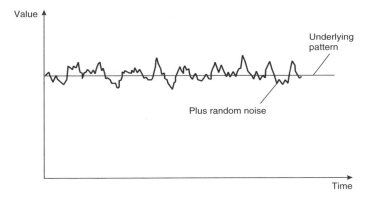

Figure 6.6   A constant time series with random noise.

Because of the noise, there are almost always errors in forecasts. In other words, there is a difference between the forecast and actual values. If we measure these errors, we have a way of:

- measuring the accuracy of the forecast
- minimizing the errors
- showing how confident we are in the forecast
- monitoring forecasts to make sure they do not go seriously wrong
- comparing different forecasting methods.

A number of different measures have been developed and three of these are described below. For these we will use the convention:

$$t \quad = \text{time}$$
$$D(t) = \text{demand at time } t$$
$$F(t) = \text{forecast } \textbf{for} \text{ time } t \text{ (not the forecast made } \textbf{at} \text{ time } t)$$

6.3.1 Mean error

If a forecast, $F(t)$, is made for the demand at some time t, and the actual demand turns out to be $D(t)$, there is an error of:

$$E(t) = D(t) - F(t)$$

If this is repeated for a number of periods, n, an obvious measure of forecast error is the ***mean error***:

$$mean\ error = \frac{\sum E(t)}{n} = \frac{\sum [D(t) - F(t)]}{n}$$

The drawback with this measure is that positive and negative errors cancel each other, and very poor forecasts can have low mean errors. If you look at the following values, the demand pattern is clear, but the forecasts are obviously very poor:

t	1	2	3	4
$D(t)$	100	200	300	400
$F(t)$	0	0	0	1000

If we calculate the mean error, we get:

$$(100 + 200 + 300 - 600)/6 = 0$$

This shows that the mean error does not really measure forecast accuracy, but it measures bias. If the mean error has a positive value, the forecast is consistently too low; if it has a negative value, the forecast is consistently too high.

6.3.2 Mean absolute deviation and mean squared error

The mean error allows positive and negative errors to cancel each other. There are two ways around this problem. We could take absolute values of the errors (ignoring any negative signs) and calculate the ***mean absolute deviation***, or, we could square the errors and calculate the ***mean squared error***:

$$mean\ absolute\ deviation = \frac{\sum |E(t)|}{n} = \frac{\sum |[D(t) - F(t)|}{n}$$

$$mean\ squared\ error = \frac{\sum E(t)^2}{n} = \frac{\sum [D(t) - F(t)]^2}{n}$$

The mean absolute deviation has an obvious meaning; when it takes a value of, say, 2.5, the forecast is on average 2.5 away from actual demand. The mean squared error does not have a clear meaning, but it is useful for some statistical analyses. The larger the value of either measure, the worse is the forecast.

WORKED EXAMPLE 6.1

The Excalibur Hotel has forecast the number of rooms needed for a week, and compares these with actual bookings. What are the errors? What do these errors show?

t	1	2	3	4	5	6	7
Demand, $D(t)$	20	34	39	35	22	15	11
Forecast, $F(t)$	19	31	43	37	25	16	12

Solution

The error for each week is:

$$E(t) = D(t) - F(t)$$

so for the first day

$$E(1) = D(1) - F(1) = 10 - 9 = 1$$

and so on.

t	1	2	3	4	5	6	7
Demand, $D(t)$	20	34	39	35	22	15	11
Forecast, $F(t)$	19	31	43	37	25	16	12
Error, $E(t)$	1	3	-4	-2	-3	-1	-1

Calculating the errors gives:

- mean error $= (1 + 3 - 4 - 2 - 3 - 1 - 1)/7 = -1$
- mean absolute deviation $= (1 + 3 + 4 + 2 + 3 + 1 + 1)/7 = 2.14$
- mean squared error $= (1 + 9 + 16 + 4 + 9 + 1 + 1)/7 = 5.86$

The mean error of -1 shows that the hotel expects one more room to be filled than it actually has. The mean absolute deviation shows that the forecast is, on average, 2.14 away from the actual bookings. The mean squared error does not have such a specific meaning.

WORKED EXAMPLE 6.2

What are the errors in the following time series?

t	1	2	3	4	5	6	7	8
$D(t)$	122	135	142	156	156	161	169	177
$F(t)$	112	120	131	144	157	168	176	180

Solution

Figure 6.7 shows a spreadsheet for these calculations.

	A	B	C	D	E	F
1	**Forecast Error**					
2						
3	**Observation**	**Demand**	**Forecast**	**Error**	**Absolute error**	**Error squared**
4	1	122	112	10	10	100
5	2	135	120	15	15	225
6	3	142	131	11	11	121
7	4	156	144	12	12	144
8	5	156	157	−1	1	1
9	6	161	168	−7	7	49
10	7	169	176	−7	7	49
11	8	177	180	−3	3	9
12						
13	**Sum**	1218	1188	30	66	698
14	**Mean**	174.00	169.71	4.29	9.43	99.71

Figure 6.7 Calculations for Worked Example 6.2.

IN SUMMARY

Forecasts often deal with time series, which are observations taken at regular intervals. There are several common patterns in time series. Actual observations have a random noise superimposed onto this underlying pattern. The noise means that forecasts contain errors. There are several ways of measuring these errors, including mean error, mean absolute deviation and mean squared error.

Self-assessment questions

6.7   Why do forecasts always have errors?

6.8   What is the mean error of a forecast and why is it of limited value?

6.9   How would you compare different forecasting methods?

6.4 | Causal forecasting

> **Causal forecasting** looks for a cause or relationship that can be used to forecast.

The sales of a product might depend on the price being charged. So we can find the relationship between price and sales, and use this to forecast future sales at a proposed price. There might be similar relationships between the speed of a machine and its output, bonus payments and productivity, interest rates and amount of money borrowed, amount of fertilizer used and crop size, and so on. These are examples of true relationships where changes in the first, *independent variable* actually cause changes in the second, *dependent variable*.

6.4.1 Linear regression

We shall illustrate causal forecasting by *linear regression*. This assumes the dependent variable is linearly related to the independent one, as shown in Figure 6.8.

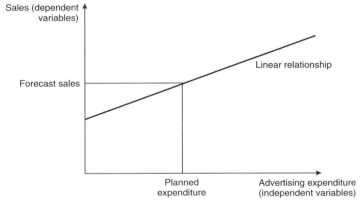

Figure 6.8   Linear relationship between dependent and independent variables.

WORKED EXAMPLE 6.3

A factory has the following shifts worked each month and output. If the factory needs 400 units next month, how many shifts should it work?

Month	1	2	3	4	5	6	7	8	9
Shifts worked	50	70	25	55	20	60	40	25	35
Output	352	555	207	508	48	498	310	153	264

Solution

When you have a time series, it is always worth drawing a graph. A scatter diagram of shifts worked (the independent variable) and units made (the dependent variable) shows a clear linear relationship (Figure 6.9).

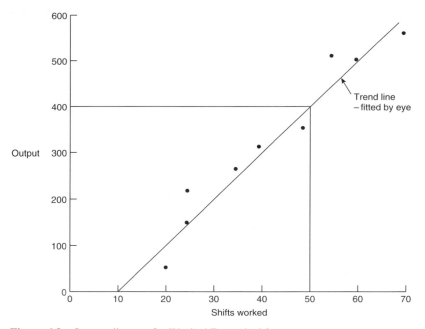

Figure 6.9   Scatter diagram for Worked Example 6.3.

We can draw by eye a reasonable straight line through the data. This shows that about 50 shifts are needed to make 400 units.

In this worked example, we drew a scatter diagram, noticed a linear relationship and then drew a **line of best fit** by eye. This informal approach can work quite well, but it would be more reliable to find the equation for the line of best fit. In other words, we want the values for the constants a and b in the equation:

$$\text{dependent variable} = a + b * \text{independent variable}$$

or $\qquad Y = a + b * X$

where: $\qquad X$ = value of independent variable

$\qquad\qquad Y$ = value of dependent variable

$\qquad\qquad a$ = point where the line crosses the Y-axis

$\qquad\qquad b$ = gradient of the line.

Because of the random noise, even the line of best fit through the data will not be a perfect fit. There is always likely to be an error, so the ith observation is really:

$$Y(i) = a + b * X(i) + E(i)$$

The line of best fit will minimize some measure of these errors, $E(i)$. We saw earlier that simply adding the errors and finding the mean allows positive and negative errors to cancel. So it would be better to minimize the mean absolute deviation or mean squared error. Because it allows other statistical analyses, the mean squared error is usually used.

It is easy to derive the equation for the line of best fit, but we are only really interested in the results. As you can see, these are rather messy.

$$
\begin{array}{c}
\text{For the line of best fit:} \\[4pt]
Y = a + b * X \\[6pt]
b = \dfrac{n * \sum X * Y - \sum X * \sum Y}{n * \sum X^2 - (\sum X)^2} \\[10pt]
a = \dfrac{\sum Y}{n} - b * \dfrac{\sum X}{n} = \overline{Y} - b * \overline{X}
\end{array}
$$

In these equations:

$$\sum X = \sum_{i=1}^{n} X$$

$$\overline{X} = \text{mean value of } X = \frac{\sum X}{n}$$

$$\overline{Y} = \text{mean value of } Y = \frac{\sum Y}{n}$$

WORKED EXAMPLE 6.4

Swincert Trading did ten experiments to see if the bonus rates paid to salesmen had any effect on their sales. What is the line of best fit through their results?

% bonus	0	1	2	3	4	5	6	7	8	9
Sales	3	4	8	10	15	18	20	22	27	28

Solution

The independent variable, X, is the bonus rate and the dependent variable, Y, is the sales. So we have:

											Totals
X	0	1	2	3	4	5	6	7	8	9	45
Y	3	4	8	10	15	18	20	22	27	28	155
$X*Y$	0	4	16	30	60	90	120	154	216	252	942
X^2	0	1	4	9	16	25	36	49	64	81	285

With $n = 10$, we can substitute these values into the linear regression equations to give:

$$b = [n * \sum (X*Y) - \sum X * \sum Y] / [n * \sum X^2 - (\sum X)^2]$$
$$= (10*942 - 45*155)/(10*285 - 45*45) = 2.96$$
$$a = \sum Y/n - b * \sum X = 155/10 - 2.96*45/10 = 2.18$$

So the line of best fit (shown in Figure 6.10) is:

$$Y = 2.18 + 2.96 * X$$

or: $$\text{sales} = 2.18 + 2.96 * \text{bonus percentage}$$

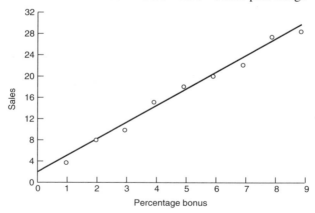

Figure 6.10 Relationship between scales and bonus rate for Worked Example 6.4.

WORKED EXAMPLE 6.5

Helford Chemicals is about to change the way it inspects one of its products. They have done some experiments with different numbers of inspections, and have found the corresponding numbers of defects:

Inspections	0	1	2	3	4	5	6	7	8	9	10
Defects	92	86	81	72	67	59	53	43	32	24	12

If Helford plan to use 6 inspections, how many defects should they expect? What is the effect of doing 20 inspections?

Solution

The independent variable, X, is the number of inspections and the dependent variable, Y, is the corresponding number of defects. The graph in Figure 6.11 shows a clear linear relationship between these, and the calculations are shown in the spreadsheet.

	A	B	C	D	E	F	G
1	**Linear regression**						
2							
3		**Inspections**	**Defects**				
4		**X**	**Y**	**X*Y**	**X^2**		
5		0	92	0	0		
6		1	86	86	1		
7		2	81	162	4		
8		3	72	216	9		
9		4	67	268	16		
10		5	59	295	25		
11		6	53	318	36		
12		7	43	301	49		
13		8	32	256	64		
14		9	24	216	81		
15		10	12	120	100		
16	**Sums**	55	621	2238	385		
17							
18							
19	**Calculated values**						
20	a	95.86					
21	b	−7.88					

Figure 6.11 continued overleaf

22
23
24
25
26
27
28
29
30
31
32
33
34
35
36
37
38
39
40

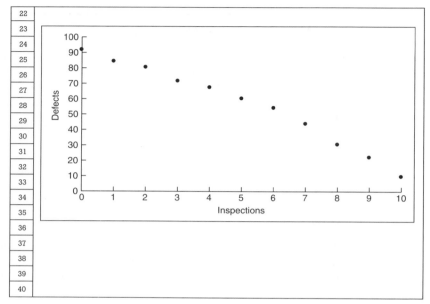

Figure 6.11 Spreadsheet showing results for Worked Example 6.5.

The spreadsheet has automatically calculated values for *a* and *b*. We can check these, as:

$$n = 11$$

$$b = (n * \sum X * Y - \sum X * \sum Y)/(n * \sum X^2 - \sum X * \sum X)$$

$$= (11 * 2238 - 55 * 621)/(11 * 385 - 55 \times 55) = -7.88$$

$$a = \sum Y/n - b * \sum X/n = 621/11 + 7.88 * 55/11 = 95.86$$

The line of best fit is:

$$Y = 95.85 - 7.88 * X$$

or   defects $= 95.85 - 7.88 *$ number of inspections

With 6 inspections Helford would forecast $95.85 - 7.88 * 6 = 48.57$ defects. With 20 inspections we have to be a bit more careful as substitution gives $95.85 - 7.88 * 20 = -61.75$. Obviously, there cannot be a negative number of defects, so we would simply forecast zero defects.

IN SUMMARY

Causal forecasting is based on relationships between variables. Then we take values of one variable to forecast values of a second variable. Linear regression – which finds the line of best fit through a set of data – is an example of causal forecasting.

6.4.2 Coefficient of determination

Linear regression finds the line of best fit through a set of data, but we really need some way of saying how good this line is. If the errors are small the line is a good fit, but if the errors are large even the best line is not very good. To measure the goodness of fit, we will use a measure called the *coefficient of determination*. This looks at the way the independent variable is scattered around its mean value.

If we take a set of independent observations, $Y(i)$, we can calculate a mean value $\overline{Y}$. The observations vary around this mean value, and we can find the total sum of squared errors (SSE):

$$\text{total SSE} = \sum [Y(i) - \overline{Y}]^2$$

Now we can use a regression model to estimate values, $Y'(i)$, when all noise is eliminated. So the regression model explains some of the variation from the mean:

$$\text{explained SSE} = \sum [Y'(i) - \overline{Y}]^2$$

But there is random noise in the observations, so the regression model does not explain all the variation. There are some residual variations that are unexplained:

$$\text{unexplained SSE} = \sum [Y(i) - Y'(i)]^2$$

With a little algebra we can show that:

$$\text{total SSE} = \text{explained SSE} + \text{unexplained SSE}$$

as shown in Figure 6.12.

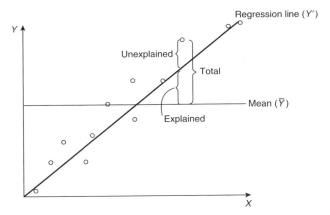

Figure 6.12 Relationship between total, explained and unexplained variations.

The greater the amount of the total variation explained by the regression, the more accurate is the linear relationship. So the coefficient of determination measures the proportion of total SSE explained by the regression model.

$$\text{coefficient of determination} = \frac{\text{explained SSE}}{\text{total SSE}}$$

This coefficient has a value between zero and one: if it is near to one, most of the variation is explained by the regression and the straight line is a good fit. If it is near to zero, most of the variation is unexplained and the line is not a good fit.

The easiest way of calculating the coefficient of determination is the rather messy-looking equation:

$$\text{coefficient of determination} = \left[\frac{n * \sum (X * Y) - \sum X * \sum Y}{\sqrt{[n * \sum X^2 - (\sum X)^2] * [n * \sum Y^2 - (\sum Y)^2]}} \right]^2$$

WORKED EXAMPLE 6.6

Find the coefficient of determination for the data in Worked Example 6.5.

Solution

Expanding the previous spreadsheet gives the results in Figure 6.13.

	A	B	C	D	E	F
1	**Linear regression**					
2						
3		Inspections	Defects			
4		**X**	**Y**	**X*Y**	**X^2**	**Y^2**
5		0	92	0	0	8464
6		1	86	86	1	7396
7		2	81	162	4	6561
8		3	72	216	9	5184
9		4	67	268	16	4489
10		5	59	295	25	3481
11		6	53	318	36	2809
12		7	43	301	49	1849
13		8	32	256	64	1024
14		9	24	216	81	576
15		10	12	120	100	144
16	**Sums**	**55**	**621**	**2238**	**385**	**41977**
17						
18						
19	**Calculated values**			**Coefficient of determination**		
20	a	95.86		0.9877		
21	b	−7.88				

Figure 6.13 Spreadsheet showing calculations for Worked Example 6.6.

We already know the line of best fit through this data is $Y = 95.86 - 7.88 * X$. Now we are seeing how well this line fits the data. The spreadsheet automatically gives a value for the coefficient of determination, but we can check this from:

$$\text{Coefficient of determination} = \left[\frac{n * \sum (X * Y) - \sum X * \sum Y}{\sqrt{[n * \sum X^2 - (\sum X)^2] \times [n * \sum Y^2 - (\sum Y)^2]}} \right]^2$$

$$= \left[\frac{11 \times 2238 - 55 \times 621}{\sqrt{[11 \times 385 - 55 \times 55] \times [11 \times 41\,977 - 621 \times 621]}} \right]^2$$

$$= [-0.9938]^2$$

$$= 0.9876$$

This is very close to 1, so the line is a very good fit. Normally any value for the coefficient of determination above about 0.5 is considered good.

IN SUMMARY

The coefficient of determination shows how well the line of best fit describes the data. It measures the proportion of squared variation from the mean that is explained by the regression line.

6.4.3 Coefficient of correlation

A second useful measure is the *coefficient of correlation* which asks the question 'are X and Y linearly related?'. The coefficients of correlation and determination answer very similar questions, and a standard calculation – which we need not describe – shows:

coefficient of correlation $= \sqrt{\text{coefficient of determination}}$

The coefficient of determination is usually called r^2 and the coefficient of correlation is r. The coefficient of correlation has a value between $+1$ and -1.

- A value of $r = 1$ shows that the two variables have a perfect linear relationship with no noise at all, and as one increases so does the other.
- A small positive value of r shows a weak linear relationship.
- A value of $r = 0$ shows that there is no correlation at all between the two variables and no linear relationship.

- A small negative value of r shows a weak linear relationship.
- A value of $r = -1$ shows the two variables have a perfect linear relationship and as one increases the other decreases.

With correlation coefficients near to $+1$ or -1 there is a strong linear relationship between the two variables. When r is between 0.7 and -0.7 the coefficient of determination is less than 0.49 and less than half the variation is explained by the regression. So linear regression is only reliable when the coefficient of correlation is between about 0.7 and -0.7 (see Figure 6.14).

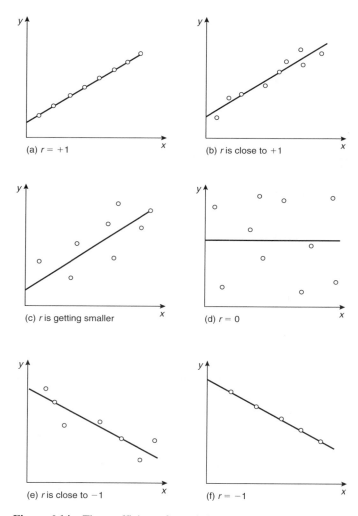

(a) $r = +1$

(b) r is close to $+1$

(c) r is getting smaller

(d) $r = 0$

(e) r is close to -1

(f) $r = -1$

Figure 6.14 The coefficient of correlation.

WORKED EXAMPLE 6.7

In the past 10 months, the amount of electricity used in one section of a steel works is related to the amount of steel produced, as follows:

Output of works ('00 tonnes)	15	13	14	10	6	8	11	13	14	12
Electricity used ('00 kWh)	105	99	102	83	52	67	79	97	100	93

(a) Draw a scatter diagram to show the relationship between electricity consumption and output.

(b) Calculate the coefficients of determination and correlation.

(c) Find the line of best fit through the data. What do the values of a and b represent?

(d) How much electricity does the works need to make 2000 tonnes of steel a month?

Solution

(a) The independent variable, X, is the steel output and the dependent variable, Y, is the electricity consumption. The scatter diagram in Figure 6.15 shows a clear linear relationship.

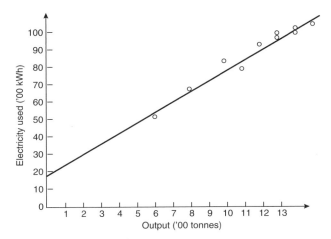

Figure 6.15 Scatter diagram for Worked Example 6.7.

(b) The calculations have been done automatically in the spreadsheet in Figure 6.16. This shows that the coefficient of correlation is 0.9838, and the coefficient of determination is 0.9679.

	A	B	C	D	E	F
1	**Linear regression**					
2						
3	**Observations**			**Calculations**		
4						
5	**Output**	**Electricity**		**Summary results**		
6	**('00 tonnes)**	**('00 kWh)**				
7	15	105		*Regression Statistics*		
8	13	99		Correlation	0.983844	
9	14	102		Determination	0.967948	
10	10	83		Adjusted r Square	0.963942	
11	6	52		Observations	10	
12	8	67				
13	11	79				
14	13	97		*Coefficients*		
15	14	100		Intercept, a	18.97312	
16	12	93		Gradient, b	5.924731	
17						
18	**Forecasts**					
19	20	137.4677				

Figure 6.16 Spreadsheet showing calculations for Worked Example 6.7.

We can check these calculations as:

$$\sum X = 116 \quad \sum X^2 = 1420 \quad \sum X*Y = 10\,614 \quad \overline{X} = 11.6$$

$$\sum Y = 877 \quad \sum Y^2 = 79\,611 \quad N = 10 \quad \overline{Y} = 87.7$$

Coefficient of correlation, $r = \dfrac{10*10\,614 - 116*877}{\sqrt{[\{10*1420 - 116*116\} * \{10*79\,611 - 877*877\}]}} = 0.9838$

This suggests a very strong linear relationship. The coefficient of determination is:

coefficient of determination, $r^2 = 0.9838^2 = 0.9679$

This shows that 96.79% of the variation is explained by the regression, and only 3.21% is residual noise. Sometimes the coefficient of determination is a bit optimistic – especially when there are only a few data points. So the computer has calculated an 'Adjusted r Square' which gives a slightly more realistic value.

(c) The spreadsheet has automatically calculated the line of best fit, but we can check the results:

$$b = \frac{10 * 10\,614 - 116 * 877}{10 * 1420 - 116 * 116} = 5.925$$

$$a = 87.7 - 5.925 * 11.6 = 18.97$$

so: electricity used $= 18.97 + 5.925 *$ output

a is the amount of electricity (1897 kWh) needed to keep the works going without making any steel; b (592.5 kWh) is the amount of electricity needed to make each tonne of steel.

(d) The forecast amount of electricity needed to make 2000 tonnes (so $X = 20$) is:

$$Y = 18.97 + 5.925 * 20 = 137.47$$

or 13 747 kWh a month.

IN SUMMARY

The coefficient of correlation shows how strong a linear relationship is. It is equal to the square root of the coefficient of determination.

Self-assessment questions

6.10   What is 'linear regression'?

6.11   Define each of the terms in the equation $Y(i) = a + b * X(i) + E(i)$.

6.12   What is measured by the coefficient of determination?

6.13   What values can be taken by the coefficient of correlation?

‖ 6.5 ‖ Projective forecasting

Causal forecasting is **extrinsic**, as it forecasts demand by looking at other variables. Projective forecasting is **intrinsic**, as it uses historical values of demand to forecast future values. We will describe four methods of this type:

- *simple averages*
- *moving averages*
- *exponential smoothing*
- *models for seasonality and trend*

6.5.1 Simple averages

Suppose you are going away on holiday and want to know how much sunshine to expect. The easiest way of finding this is to look up records for previous years and take an average. If your holiday starts on July 1st, you could find the average hours of sunshine on July 1st over, say, the past 10 years. This forecasting uses a simple average with:

$$F(t+1) = \sum_{t=1}^{n} D(t)$$

where: n = number of periods of historical data

t = time period

$D(t)$ = demand in period t

$F(t)$ = forecast for period t

WORKED EXAMPLE 6.8

Use a simple average to forecast demand for period 6 of the following time series. What are the forecasts for period 24?

Period, t	1	2	3	4	5
Series 1, $D(t)$	98	100	98	104	100
Series 2, $D(t)$	140	66	152	58	84

Solution

For series 1 $F(6) = 1/n * \sum_{t=1}^{n} D(t) = 1/5 * \sum_{t=1}^{5} D(t) = 100$

For series 2 $F(6) = 1/5 * \sum_{t=1}^{5} D(t) = 100$

Although the forecasts are the same, there is clearly more noise in the second series than the first. So you would be more confident in the first forecast and expect the error to be smaller.

Simple averages assume the demand is constant, so forecasts for period 24 are the same as forecasts for period 6, i.e. 100.

Using simple averages to forecast demand is easy and can work well for constant demands. Unfortunately, if there is a change in the demand pattern, older data tends to swamp the latest figures and the forecast is very unresponsive to changes. Suppose weekly demand for an item has been constant at 100 units for the past 2 years. Simple averages give a forecast demand for week 105 of 100 units. If the demand suddenly rises to 200 in week 105, simple averages give a forecast of:

$$F(106) = (104 * 100 + 200)/105 = 100.95$$

A rise in demand of 100 leads to an increase of 0.95 in the forecast. If demand continued at 200 units a week, the following forecasts are:

$$F(107) = 101.89 \quad F(108) = 102.80 \quad F(109) = 103.70, \text{ and so on}$$

The forecasts are rising but the response is very slow. Very few time series are stable over long periods, so we usually need a forecast that is more sensitive to changes. As simple averages can only be used for constant series, they are not widely used.

IN SUMMARY

Simple averages can give reasonable forecasts if demand is constant. For any other pattern of demand we have to use some other method.

6.5.2 Moving averages

The problem with simple averages is that old data – which may be out of date – tends to swamp newer, more relevant data. One way around this is to ignore old data and only use a number of the most recent values. We might, for example, forecast demand from the average weekly demand over the past 12 weeks. Then we simply ignore any data older than 12 weeks. This is the basis of **moving averages**:

$$F(t+1) = \text{average of } N \text{ most recent pieces of data}$$
$$= [\text{latest data} + \text{next latest} + \dots N\text{th latest}]/N$$
$$= [D(t) + D(t-1) + \dots D(t-N+1)]/N$$

WORKED EXAMPLE 6.9

The demand for an item over the past 6 months is as follows:

t	1	2	3	4	5	6
$D(t)$	425	500	475	525	525	450

The market for the item is unstable, and any data over 3 months old is no longer reliable. Use a moving average to forecast demand for the item.

Solution

Only data more recent than 3 months is reliable, so we can use a 3-month moving average for the forecast. If we consider the situation at the end of period 3, the forecast for period 4 is:

$$F(4) = [D(1) + D(2) + D(3)]/3 = (425 + 500 + 475)/3 = 466.7$$

At the end of period 4, when actual demand is known to be 525, we can update this forecast to give:

$$F(5) = [D(2) + D(3) + D(4)]/3 = (500 + 475 + 525)/3 = 500.0$$

Then $$F(6) = [D(3) + D(4) + D(5)]/3 = (475 + 525 + 525)/3 = 508.3$$

and $$F(7) = [D(4) + D(5) + D(6)]/3 = (525 + 525 + 450)/3 = 500.0$$

In the last example, the forecast is clearly responding to changes, with a high demand moving the forecast upwards and low demand moving it downwards. At the same time the forecast is smoothing out variations, so the forecast does not blindly follow changes in the random noise.

We can adjust the rate at which a moving average forecast responds to changes by altering the value of N. A high value of N takes the average of a large number of observations and will be unresponsive: the forecast will smooth out random variations, but may not follow genuine changes. On the other hand, a low value of N will give a responsive forecast; it will follow genuine changes in demand, but may be too sensitive to random fluctuations. To get reasonable results we need a compromise value of N, and a moving average of about six periods is often useful.

WORKED EXAMPLE 6.10

The following table shows the monthly demand for a product over the past year. Use moving averages with $N = 3$, $N = 6$ and $N = 9$ to give one-period-ahead forecasts.

Month	1	2	3	4	5	6	7	8	9	10	11	12
Demand	16	14	12	15	18	21	23	24	25	26	37	38

Solution

The earliest forecast we can make using a three-period moving average (i.e. $N = 3$) is:

$$F(4) = [D(1) + D(2) + D(3)]/3 = [16 + 14 + 12]/3 = 14$$

Similarly, the earliest forecast for a six- and nine-period moving average are $F(7)$ and $F(10)$ respectively. The results from these calculations are shown in the spreadsheet in Figure 6.17.

	A	B	C	D	E
1	**Moving Averages**				
2					
3			**Forecasts**		
4	**Month**	**Demand**	**N = 3**	**N = 6**	**N = 9**
5	1	16			
6	2	14			
7	3	12			
8	4	15	14.00		
9	5	18	13.67		
10	6	21	15.00		
11	7	23	18.00	16.00	
12	8	24	20.67	17.17	
13	9	25	22.67	18.83	
14	10	26	24.00	21.00	18.67
15	11	37	25.00	22.83	19.78
16	12	38	29.33	26.00	22.33
17	13		33.67	28.83	25.22

Figure 6.17   Moving average forecasts for Worked Example 6.10.

Plotting these forecasts in Figure 6.18 shows how the three-month moving average is most responsive to change, while the nine-month moving average is least responsive.

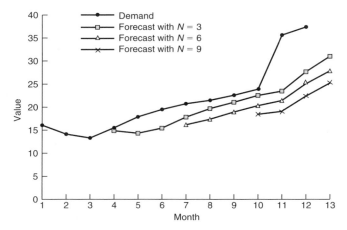

Figure 6.18   Graph of moving average forecasts for Worked Example 6.10.

Moving averages have a useful property when they forecast demands with strong seasonal variations. If we choose N to equal the number of periods in a season, a moving average will completely deseasonalize the data.

WORKED EXAMPLE 6.11

The average share price of J. Oxborough (Holdings) plc over the past 12 months is given below. Use a moving average with 2, 4 and 6 periods to find the one-month-ahead forecasts of share price.

Month	1	2	3	4	5	6	7	8	9	10	11	12
Price	100	50	20	150	110	55	25	140	95	45	30	145

Solution

The results for moving averages are shown in Figure 6.19. There is a clear seasonal pattern, with a peak every fourth month, shown in Figure 6.20.

	A	B	C	D	E
1	**Moving Averages**				
2					
3			**Forecasts**		
4	**Month**	**Demand**	**N = 2**	**N = 4**	**N = 6**
5	1	100			
6	2	50			
7	3	20	75		
8	4	150	35		
9	5	110	85	80.00	
10	6	55	130	82.50	
11	7	25	82.5	83.75	80.83
12	8	140	40	85.00	68.33
13	9	95	82.5	82.50	83.33
14	10	45	117.5	78.75	95.83
15	11	30	70	76.25	78.33
16	12	145	37.5	77.50	65.00
17	13		87.5	78.75	80.00

Figure 6.19   Spreadsheet showing forecasts for Worked Example 6.11.

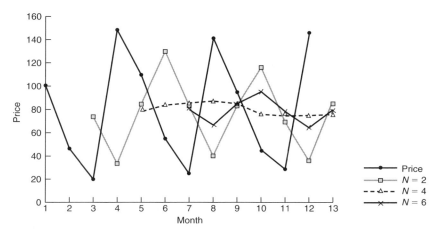

Figure 6.20   Graph of results for Worked Example 6.11.

The moving average with both $N = 2$ and $N = 6$ has responded to the peaks and troughs of demand, but neither has got the timing right – both forecasts lag behind demand. As expected, the two-period moving average is much more responsive than the six-period one. The most interesting result is the four-period moving average. This has completely deseasonalized the data.

Although moving averages overcome some of the problems with simple averages, they still have three drawbacks:

- all historical values are given the same weight
- the method only works well with constant demand – as we have seen it either removes seasonal factors or gets the timing wrong
- a large amount of historical data must be stored to update forecasts

These problems are overcome by exponential smoothing, which we describe in the following section.

IN SUMMARY

Moving average forecasts use the latest data and ignore any older values. Their sensitivity can be adjusted by changing the value of N. Time series can be deseasonalized by setting N to the number of periods in the season.

6.5.3 Exponential smoothing

Exponential smoothing assumes that old data becomes less relevant and should be given less weight. In particular, it gives a declining weight to data, as shown in Figure 6.21.

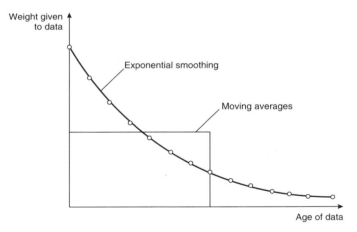

Figure 6.21 The weight given to data changes with its age.

We can get this declining weight using only the latest demand figure and the previous forecast. To be specific, we calculate a new forecast by taking a proportion, α, of the latest demand and adding a proportion, $1 - \alpha$, of the previous forecast:

$$\boxed{\begin{array}{c} \text{new forecast} = \alpha * \text{latest demand} + (1 - \alpha) * \text{last forecast} \\ F(t+1) = \alpha * D(t) + (1 - \alpha) * F(t) \end{array}}$$

where α is the **smoothing constant** and generally takes a value around 0.2.

We can show how exponential smoothing adapts to changes in demand, by looking at a forecast which was optimistic and suggested a value of 110 for a demand which actually turns out to be 100. With a value of $\alpha = 0.2$, the forecast for the next period is:

$$F(t+1) = \alpha * D(t) + (1 - \alpha) * F(t) = 0.2 * 100 + (1 - 0.2) * 110 = 108$$

The optimistic forecast is noted and the value for the next period is adjusted downwards. The reason for this adjustment is clear if we rearrange the exponential smoothing formula:

$$F(t+1) = \alpha * D(t) + (1 - \alpha) * F(t) = F(t) + \alpha * [D(t) - F(t)]$$

but the error is $\quad E(t) = D(t) - F(t)$

so $\quad\quad\quad\quad F(t+1) = F(t) + \alpha * E(t)$

The error in each forecast is noted and a proportion is added to adjust the next forecast. The larger the error in the last forecast the greater is the adjustment to the next forecast.

WORKED EXAMPLE 6.12

Use exponential smoothing with $\alpha = 0.3$ and an initial value of $F(1) = 84$ to give one-period-ahead forecasts for the following time series:

Month	1	2	3	4	5	6	7	8	9	10	11	12
Demand	89	90	78	75	81	79	77	66	72	69	63	73

Solution

We know that $F(1) = 84$ and $\alpha = 0.3$. Substituting these values gives:

$$F(2) = \alpha * D(1) + (1 - \alpha) * F(1) = 0.3 * 89 + 0.7 * 84 = 85.5$$

$$F(3) = \alpha * D(2) + (1 - \alpha) * F(2) = 0.3 * 90 + 0.7 * 85.5 = 86.85$$

$$F(4) = \alpha * D(3) + (1 - \alpha) * F(3) = 0.3 * 78 + 0.7 * 86.85 = 84.2$$

and so on, as shown in the spreadsheet in Figure 6.22.

	A	B	C
1	**Exponential Smoothing**		
2			
3	**Month**	**Demand**	**Forecasts**
4	1	89	84.00
5	2	90	85.50
6	3	78	86.85
7	4	75	84.20
8	5	81	81.44
9	6	79	81.31
10	7	77	80.61
11	8	66	79.53
12	9	72	75.47
13	10	69	74.43
14	11	63	72.80
15	12	73	69.86
16	13		70.80

Figure 6.22 Spreadsheet of results for Worked Example 6.12.

The value of the smoothing constant, α, is important in setting the sensitivity of the forecasts:

- a high value of α – say 0.3 to 0.35 – puts more weight on the latest demand and gives a responsive forecast
- a lower value of α – say 0.1 to 0.15 – puts more weight on the previous forecast and gives a less responsive forecast

We usually compromise by giving α a value around 0.15 or 0.2.

Although we have shown how it works, it may not be obvious that exponential smoothing actually does give less weight to data as it gets older. We can show that it does, by taking an arbitrary value for α, say 0.2. Then:

$$F(t + 1) = 0.2 * D(t) + 0.8 * F(t)$$

But substituting $t - 1$ for t gives:

$$F(t) = 0.2 * D(t\text{-}1) + 0.8 * F(t\text{-}1)$$

and using this in the first equation gives:

$$F(t + 1) = 0.2 * D(t) + 0.8 * [0.2 * D(t - 1) + 0.8 * F(t - 1)]$$
$$= 0.2 * D(t) + 0.16 * D(t - 1) + 0.64 * F(t - 1)$$

But $F(t-1) = 0.2*D(t-2) + 0.8*F(t-2)$

so $F(t+1) = 0.2*D(t) + 0.16*D(t-1) + 0.64*[0.2*D(t-2) + 0.8*F(t-2)]$

$\qquad = 0.2*D(t) + 0.16*D(t-1) + 0.128*D(t-2) + 0.512*F(t-2)$

As you can see, the weight put on older data gets progressively less. If we continue these calculations we get the following weights:

Age of data	Weight
0	0.2
1	0.16
2	0.128
3	0.1024
4	0.08192
5	0.065536
6	0.0524288
etc.	etc.

We took an arbitrary value of $\alpha = 0.2$ here, but any other value gives similar results.

WORKED EXAMPLE 6.13

The following time series has a clear step upwards in demand in month 3. Use an initial forecast of 500 to compare exponential smoothing forecasts with various values of α.

Period	1	2	3	4	5	6	7	8	9	10	11
Value	480	500	1500	1450	1550	1500	1480	1520	1500	1490	1500

Solution

Taking values of $\alpha = 0.1$, 0.2, 0.3 and 0.4 gives the results shown in the spreadsheet in Figure 6.23.

	A	B	C	D	E	F
1	**Exponential Smoothing**					
2						
3			**Forecasts**			
4	**Month**	**Demand**	**α = 0.1**	**α = 0.2**	**α = 0.3**	**α = 0.4**
5	1	480	500.00	500.00	500.00	500.00
6	2	500	498.00	496.00	494.00	492.00
7	3	1500	498.20	496.80	495.80	495.20
8	4	1450	598.38	697.44	797.06	897.12
9	5	1550	683.54	847.95	992.94	1118.27
10	6	1500	770.19	988.36	1160.06	1290.96
11	7	1480	843.17	1090.69	1262.04	1374.58
12	8	1520	906.85	1168.55	1327.43	1416.75
13	9	1500	968.17	1238.84	1385.20	1458.05
14	10	1490	1021.35	1291.07	1419.64	1474.83
15	11	1500	1068.22	1330.86	1440.75	1480.90
16	12		1111.39	1364.69	1458.52	1488.54

Figure 6.23   Varying forecast sensitivity with different values of α.

All these forecasts would eventually follow the sharp step and raise forecasts to around 1500. Higher values of α make this adjustment more quickly and give a more responsive forecast, as shown in Figure 6.24 .

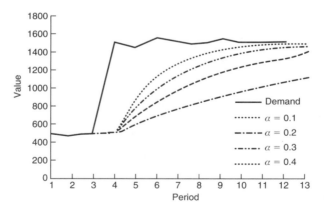

Figure 6.24   Exponential smoothing with different smoothing constants.

Exponential smoothing is the most widely used type of projective forecasting. It works well for relatively stable time series, but can produce large errors if there is some other pattern. In the following section we shall see how to forecast when the demand has some more complicated underlying pattern.

IN SUMMARY

Exponential smoothing reduces the weight given to data as its age increases. It does this by balancing the latest demand with the previous forecast. The sensitivity of the forecast is adjusted by the value given to the smoothing constant, α.

6.5.4 Models for seasonality and trend

The methods described so far can only really be used with constant time series. In this section we shall develop a model for data that has both **seasonality** and **trend**.

Trend is the amount that demand grows between two consecutive periods. If two periods have demands of 100 and 120, the trend is 20: if two consecutive periods have demands of 100 and 80, the trend is -20. Many time series have trends, including GNP per capita, sales of telephones, use of electricity, long-term decline in beer production, numbers of people getting higher education, and the increasing proportion of small car sales.

Seasonality is a regular cyclical pattern, but it is not necessarily annual. It is measured by seasonal indices, which are the amounts deseasonalized values must be multiplied by to get seasonal values:

$$\text{seasonal index} = \frac{\text{seasonal value}}{\text{deseasonalized value}}$$

Suppose a newspaper has average daily sales of 1000 copies in a particular area, but this rises to 2000 copies on Saturday and falls to 500 copies on Monday and Tuesday. The deseasonalized value is 1000, the seasonal index for Saturday is $2000/1000 = 2.0$, the seasonal indices for Monday and Tuesday are $500/1000 = 0.5$, and seasonal indices for other days are $1000/1000 = 1.0$. As you can imagine, many products have this kind of seasonal demand, ranging from ice-cream to office blocks.

The easiest way of forecasting complex time series is to split observations into separate components, and then forecast each component separately. Then we get the final forecast by recombining the separate components. Here we are going to split demand into four components:

- **Underlying value**, $U(t)$, which is the basic demand that must be adjusted for seasonality and trend.

- **Trend**, $T(t)$, which is an adjustment to allow for the long-term upward or downward movement of the series.

- **Seasonal index**, $I(n)$, which allows for a regular variation around the trend. As we are looking at cycles, we have to multiply the deseasonalized value by the seasonal index for the appropriate period in the cycle, n.
- **Noise**, $N(t)$, which is the random noise whose effects we cannot forecast.

We can forecast these separately, except for the random noise. So our forecasts will come from a trend added to the underlying value, and multiplied by the appropriate seasonal index (see Figure 6.25):

$$F(t + 1) = [U(t) + T(t)] * I(n)$$

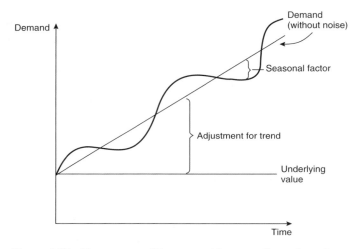

Figure 6.25 Components of forecasts with seasonality and trend.

Our approach is to forecast separately $U(t)$, $T(t)$ and $I(t)$, using exponential smoothing on each. Then the overall procedure is as follows:

Step 1. Deseasonalize observations to find the underlying values. Then use exponential smoothing to give the smoothed underlying values.

Step 2. Find the trend in each period. Then use exponential smoothing to give the smoothed trend.

Step 3. Find the seasonal index for each period. Then use exponential smoothing to give the smoothed indices.

Step 4. Add the trend to the underlying value and multiply by the appropriate seasonal index to give the forecast.

This may seem a little complicated, but it is really quite straightforward – and the calculations are always done on a computer.

WORKED EXAMPLE 6.14

You have twelve periods of demand data which show a season of two periods. This kind of forecast needs some initial values, so the first eight periods have been used to find:

- seasonal index for first period in cycle = 1.2
- seasonal index for second period in cycle = 0.8
- underlying demand, $U(8) = 100$
- trend, $T(8) = 10$
- a smoothing constant of 0.15 gives reasonable answers

Use the remaining data to run-in these values, and forecast demand for the next four periods.

Period	9	10	11	12
Period in cycle	1	2	1	2
Demand	130	96	160	110

Solution

We can start forecasting from period 8 using:

$$F(t + 1) = [U(t) + T(t)] * I(n)$$

Then setting $t = 8$, we can forecast for period 9, which is the first period in a cycle:

$$F(9) = [U(8) + T(8)] * I(1) = (100 + 10) * 1.2 = 132$$

Now we can use this forecast for period 9, together with the actual demand, to update the variables, i.e. underlying value, trend and seasonal index. For this we use the procedure described above.

Step 1

The latest demand is $D(9) = 130$. The seasonal index for the first period of the cycle is $I(1) = 1.2$, so the latest deseasonalized demand is $130/1.2 = 108.333$. The last underlying demand was $U(8) = 100$, so we can use exponential smoothing to update the smoothed underlying value:

$$U(9) = \alpha * [D(9)/I(1)] + (1 - \alpha) * [U(8) + T(8)]$$
$$= 0.15 * 108.333 + 0.85 * 110$$
$$= 109.750$$

In general this calculation is:

$$U(t) = \alpha * [D(t)/I(n)] + (1 - \alpha) * [U(t - 1) + T(t - 1)]$$

Step 2

The latest value for trend is the difference between the last two underlying values. So the latest trend is $U(9) - U(8) = 109.750 - 100 = 9.750$. The last value for trend was 10, so exponential smoothing gives the updated value:

$$T(9) = \alpha * [U(9) - U(8)] + (1 - \alpha) * T(8)$$
$$= 0.15 * 9.750 + 0.85 * 10$$
$$= 9.963$$

In general this calculation is:

$$T(t) = \alpha * [U(t) - U(t-1)] + (1 - \alpha) * T(t-1)$$

Step 3

The latest figure for the underlying value is $U(9) = 109.750$. The actual demand for period 9, $D(9)$, is 130. So the latest seasonal index for the first period in the cycle is $130/109.750 = 1.185$. The last value for $I(1)$ was 1.2. So exponential smoothing gives the updated value for the seasonal index as:

$$I(1) = \alpha * [D(9)/U(9)] + (1 - \alpha) * \text{last value for } I(1)$$
$$= 0.15 * [130/109.750] + 0.85 * 1.2$$
$$= 1.198$$

In general this calculation is:

$$I(n) = \alpha * [D(t)/U(t)] + (1 - \alpha) * I'(n)$$

where $I'(n)$ is the previous value of the seasonal index.

Step 4

$$F(t + 1) = [U(t) + T(t)] * I(n)$$

So:
$$F(10) = [U(9) + T(9)] * I(2)$$
$$= [109.750 + 9.963] * 0.8$$
$$= 95.770$$

Notice that period 10 is the second period in a cycle, so we have to use $I(2)$ and not the value of $I(1)$ that we have just calculated.

Now we can repeat this procedure for the next period:

Step 1

Latest figure for underlying value:

$$U(t) = \alpha * [D(t)/I(n)] + (1 - \alpha) * [U(t-1) + T(t-1)]$$
$$U(10) = \alpha * [D(10)/I(2)] + (1 - \alpha) * [U(9) + T(9)]$$
$$= 0.15 * [96/0.8] + 0.85 * [109.750 + 9.963]$$
$$= 119.756$$

Step 2

Latest figure for trend:

$$T(t) = \alpha * [U(t) - U(t-1)] + (1 - \alpha) * T(t-1)$$
$$T(10) = \alpha * [U(10) - U(9)] + (1 - \alpha) * T(9)$$
$$= 0.15[119.756 - 109.750] + 0.85 * 9.963$$
$$= 9.969$$

Step 3

Latest figure for seasonal index for the second period of the cycle:

$$I(n) = \alpha * [D(t)/U(t)] + (1 - \alpha) * I'(n)$$
$$I(2) = \alpha * [D(10)/U(10)] + (1 - \alpha) * I'(2)$$
$$= 0.15 * [96/119.756] + 0.85 * 0.8 = 0.800$$

Step 4

Next forecast:

$$F(t + 1) = [U(t) + T(t)] * I(n)$$
$$F(11) = [U(10) + T(10)] * I(1)$$
$$= [119.756 + 9.969] * 1.198 = 155.368 \text{ (after rounding)}$$

We can repeat these calculations for two more periods, until we run out of data. These results are shown in the spreadsheet in Figure 6.26.

	A	B	C	D	E	F	G	H	I	J
1	**Seasonality and trend**									
2										
3	Period	Demand	Period in cycle	Actual deseasonalized demand	Forecast underlying demand	Actual seasonal index	Forecast seasonal index	Actual trend	Forecast trend	Forecast
4	1									
5	2									
6	3									
7	4									
8	5									
9	6									
10	7		1							
11	8		2		100.000				10.000	
12	9	130	1	108.333	109.750	1.185	1.200	9.750	9.963	132.000
13	10	96	2	120.000	119.756	0.802	0.800	10.006	9.969	95.770
14	11	160	1	133.592	130.305	1.228	1.198	10.549	10.056	155.368
15	12	110	2	137.458	139.925	0.786	0.800	9.621	9.991	112.323
16	13		1		149.916		1.198		9.991	179.551
17	14		2		159.907		0.800		9.991	127.964
18	15		1		169.897		1.198		9.991	203.482
19	16		2		179.888		0.800		9.991	143.954
20										
21	**Calculation**									
22			1,2	B/G	0.15*D + 0.85*(E+I)	B/D	0.15*F + 0.85*G	G-G'	0.15*H + 0.85*I	(E+I)*G

Figure 6.26 Spreadsheet for forecasting with seasonality and trend.

At period 12 we can forecast demand for periods 13 to 16. Using the latest values for underlying demand, trend and seasonal indices we have:

$$F(13) = [U(12) + T(12)] * I(1) = [139.925 + 9.991] * 1.198 = 179.551$$
$$F(14) = [U(13) + T(13)] * I(2)$$

Using the best estimates available this is:

$$= [U(12) + 2 * T(12)] * I(2) = 159.907 * 0.800 = 127.964$$
$$F(15) = [U(12) + 3 * T(12)] * I(1) = 169.897 * 1.198 = 203.482$$
$$F(16) = [U(12) + 4 * T(12)] * I(2) = 179.888 * 0.800 = 143.954$$

There are three obvious problems with this approach. Firstly, the calculations are messy – so you should always use a computer. Secondly, we have to find initial values for the variables. For this we can use some of the historical data to get reasonable initial estimates, and the rest of the data to run the system in. In the last worked example, we used the first two-thirds of the data to get initial estimates, and then refined these using the last third of the data. Thirdly, we have to find a suitable value for α. A reasonable value is around 0.15, but we do not have to use this, or even use the same value for all updates. We could, for example, use a forecast that is more responsive to changes in underlying values than to trend. The best way of finding good values is to use a series of trials with historical data and choose the smoothing constants that give the smallest errors.

WORKED EXAMPLE 6.15

Quarterly demand for a product has been recorded over the past 3 years as follows:

Quarter	1	2	3	4	5	6	7	8	9	10	11	12
Demand	182	105	77	168	210	126	119	161	217	140	133	189

Use a smoothing constant of $\alpha = 0.15$ to get forecasts for the next year's demand.

Solution

We can use the first two-thirds of the data to get initial estimates for the variables, and refine these using the last third of the data.

Linear regression will find the line of best fit through the first eight points. This gives a line of about:

$$demand = 125 + 5.25 * period$$

From this we can get an initial estimate for trend of 5.25. We can also use the regression line to give deseasonalized demand. Then dividing the actual demands in each period by these deseasonalized values gives estimates of the seasonal indices. These, together with the graph in Figure 6.27, show that there are four periods in a season:

Period t	Demand D(t)	Deseasonalized value from regression	Seasonal index
1	182	125.00	1.46
2	105	130.25	0.81
3	77	135.50	0.57
4	168	140.75	1.19
5	210	146.00	1.44
6	126	151.25	0.83
7	119	156.50	0.76
8	161	161.75	1.00

The average seasonal index for the first period in the cycle is $(1.46 + 1.44)/2 = 1.45$. Similarly, the average seasonal indices for the other periods are 0.82, 0.67 and 1.10 respectively.

This gives all the initial estimates, and the next step is to use the updating procedure to refine these in the last third of the data.

Period, Demand	t $D(t)$	8 161	9 217	10 140	11 133	12 189
Underlying value,	$U(t)$	161.75	164.40	169.48	177.99	181.69
Trend,	$T(t)$	5.25	4.86	4.89	5.44	5.17
Seasonal index,	$I(n)$	1.45	0.82	0.67	1.10	1.43
Forecast,	$F(t)$			138.79	116.83	201.77

The updated seasonal indices are 1.43, 0.82, 0.68 and 1.09 respectively. Now we have good initial values and can forecast next year's figures (shown in Figure 6.27):

$$F(13) = [U(12) + T(12)] * I(1) = [181.69 + 5.17] * 1.43 = 267.21$$

$$F(14) = [U(12) + 2 * T(12)] * I(2) = (181.69 + 10.34) * 0.82 = 157.46$$

$$F(15) = [U(12) + 3 * T(12)] * I(3) = (181.69 + 15.51) * 0.68 = 134.10$$

$$F(16) = [U(12) + 4 * T(12)] * I(4) = (181.69 + 20.68) * 1.09 = 220.58$$

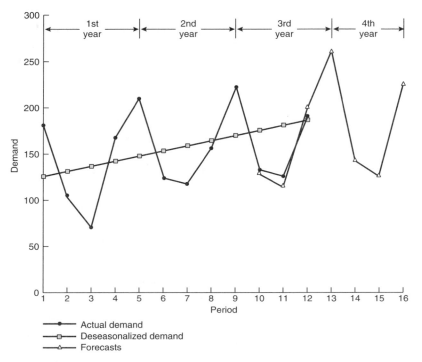

Figure 6.27 Demand for Worked Example 6.16.

Case example

Generating electricity

Forecasting the demand for electricity is notoriously difficult. Electricity cannot be stored – except in very small quantities using batteries – so all demand must be exactly matched by the supply from generators in power stations. Generating too little electricity would cause power cuts – which is not acceptable to consumers – while generating too much would waste expensive resources.

The long-term demand for electricity is expected to rise steadily. So enough power stations must be built to meet this demand. Planning and building a nuclear power station can take 20 years and cost billions of pounds. Conventional stations, particularly gas-fired ones, can be built faster and cheaper, but they are still based on forecast demand 10 or 20 years into the future.

In the shorter term, demand for electricity follows an annual cycle, with demand generally heavier in winter when people turn on their heating systems. There are also short irregular periods when demand surges, notably during very cold periods. There are also cycles during the week, with lower demand at the weekends when industry is not working so intensely. On top of this are cycles during the day, with lighter demand during the night when most of us are asleep. Finally, there are irregular peaks during the day, perhaps corresponding to breaks in television programmes when people turn on their electric kettles for tea.

Power stations need 'warming up' before they can start supplying electricity. So a stable demand would make operations much easier to manage. Electricity suppliers try to stabilize demand by giving off-peak price incentives, but these do not solve the problems of variable demand. In practice, they must still forecast demands with long-term trend, annual cycle, periods with changes, weekly cycles, daily cycles and short-term fluctuations. Electricity generators must then match their supply to this ever-changing demand from the cheapest possible sources.

IN SUMMARY

We can forecast patterns with seasonality and trend by splitting the demand into different components and forecasting each separately. The final forecast comes from recombining these parts.

Self-assessment questions

6.14 Why are simple averages of limited use for forecasting?

6.15 How would you make a moving average forecast more responsive?

6.16 How can you deseasonalize data using moving averages?

6.17 Why is the forecasting method called 'exponential smoothing'?

6.18 How would you make an exponential smoothing forecast more responsive?

6.19 Define all the terms in the equation

$$F(t + 1) = [U(t) + T(t)] * I(n)$$

CHAPTER REVIEW

This chapter described various aspects of forecasting. In particular it:

- showed why forecasting is important in all organizations
- discussed different methods of forecasting
- described judgemental forecasts, which are based on opinions and qualitative considerations
- illustrated judgemental forecasts by methods ranging from personal insight to the more formal Delphi method
- described noise and forecast errors in time series
- discussed causal forecasting, which looks for relationships between variables
- described linear regression to find the line of best fit through a set of data
- showed how projective forecasting looks at the patterns in historical data and projects these into the future
- illustrated projective forecasting by simple averages, moving averages, exponential smoothing and models for seasonality and trend

KEY TERMS

causal forecasting
coefficient of correlation
coefficient of determination
Delphi method
dependent variable
exponential smoothing
forecasts
historical analogy
independent variable
judgemental forecasting
linear regression
market surveys

mean absolute deviation
mean error
mean squared error
models for seasonality and trend
moving averages
noise
panel consensus
personal insight
projective forecasting
simple averages
time series

Case study

Loch Erichsae Knitwear Company

Hamish Macdonald started manufacturing knitwear in the Scottish borders in 1883. The company has continued to operate in the same location and is still run by the Macdonald family. Their main products are high-quality lambswool sweaters, aimed at the golf and other sports markets.

Sales of sweaters have risen steadily in recent years as more people have taken up leisure activities and sweaters have become increasingly popular. The highest sales are for a plain sweater, which is available in two styles (roll collar and V-neck), twelve colours and seven sizes. This accounts for 70% of sales while other styles (sports shirts, intarsias, sleeveless pullovers, speciality sweaters and special orders) make up the remaining 30%.

The premises occupied by the company for the past 100 years are now in need of major renovation. The company is reluctant to spend so much money on an old building. An alternative has been suggested by a local construction company. The factory is near the town centre and is now surrounded by modern houses. The construction company would buy the site, demolish the factory and build more houses. In return they would give Macdonald new custom-built premises on a nearby industrial estate.

Macdonald's first problem is to see how big a new factory should be. It should clearly be big enough to cover expected demand for some time in the future. At the same time the company does not want to run a factory which is too large for their needs, and the construction company would be reluctant to finance a very large expansion. Although the demand for sweaters is rising, there have been long periods in the past when demand has fallen.

Another problem at Macdonald's is the variation in demand, with peaks in the summer (when more outdoor sports are played) and near Christmas (where high-quality sweaters are a popular present). This gives a fluctuating demand which makes production planning difficult. One way around this is to keep large stocks of finished sweaters, but this has proved expensive. An alternative is to develop an export market. By selling goods around the world they can reduce the effects of seasons. Export sales are less reliable than domestic ones since they depend on the value of international currencies and the competition from cheaper, lower-quality products from the Far East. At one time the company tried importing finished sweaters to meet fluctuating demand but the quality was not reliable and the experiment was quickly stopped. Another way of stabilizing demand is to sell sweaters in bulk to clubs, associations, etc.

There are several views within the company about the size of a new factory. James Macdonald, the present company chairman, says the current premises are 50 000 square feet: this has been big enough for the last 100 years and the company should, therefore, move into new premises of the same size. An alternative view from the factory manager says that 2 years ago the company was producing 2000 sweaters a month, last year it was 3000 a month, now it is 4000 a month. In 3 years they could be making 7000 sweaters a month and should, therefore, move into a factory of at least 50 000/4000 * 7000 = 87 500 square feet.

To help planning, the actual sales of sweaters over the past 2 years have been collected for the domestic, export and bulk markets. The following table shows monthly sales for domestic and export, and average monthly sales for bulk calculated every quarter:

Month	Domestic	Export	Bulk
1	804	1108	174
2	680	974	
3	711	1072	
4	775	944	215
5	1014	996	
6	1480	1073	
7	1407	1044	293
8	1283	927	
9	1206	1020	
10	1333	1003	348
11	1622	838	
12	1947	902	
13	1830	805	406
14	1644	884	
15	1504	1055	
16	1613	967	485
17	1821	1036	
18	1941	1077	
19	1802	906	566
20	1664	732	
21	1598	763	
22	1712	719	617
23	2028	751	
24	2573	918	
25	2349	870	682

The company auditor found that the factory has 6000 square feet of offices, reception areas, cafeteria, etc.; 22 000 square feet for production on the factory floor; 16 000 square feet for stocks and a factory shop, and

6000 square feet which is unused or unusable. Based on this, and some estimates from past years, he suggests that they need 20 000 square feet to keep the factory running and a variable amount of space for production. He says that a year ago the factory effectively used 70% of its available space, while this year effective utilization was up to 80%.

The sales manager added to the discussion by saying that he was not only interested in the overall number of sweaters made, but also the distribution of sizes, colours and quantities ordered. If the product range is reduced then stock levels, production set-up times and space needed could all be reduced. He collected the following figures for sales and order quantities over a typical period:

Colour	Size						
	XXS	XS	S	M	L	XL	XXL
White	0	1	6	15	17	9	1
Grey	0	1	6	18	19	9	1
Black	0	2	7	23	23	10	2
Dark blue	1	4	20	59	68	41	4
Mid blue	0	1	4	12	12	7	2
Light blue	1	4	12	25	28	15	2
Bright red	0	3	9	21	20	13	3
Dark red	0	2	7	20	22	11	1
Cream	0	2	10	24	25	11	1
Fawn	0	0	3	8	7	4	1
Brown	0	0	4	5	7	5	1
Green	0	1	6	17	21	10	1

Units per order	% of orders	% of units
0–10	52.5	11.4
11–20	21.5	15.1
21–30	9.1	10.7
31–40	5.7	9.5
41–50	4.3	9.5
51–60	2.3	6.1
61–70	0.9	2.9
71–100	1.5	5.9
101–200	1.5	9.6
201+	0.6	19.2

The Macdonald family have now asked for your advice on all their options. What would you say to them?

Problems

6.1 The productivity of Semantic Services Inc. has been recorded over a 10-month period, together with forecasts made the previous month by the operations manager, the supervisor and the management services department. How could you compare the three sets of forecasts?

Month	1	2	3	4	5	6	7	8	9	10
Productivity	22	24	28	27	23	24	20	18	20	23
Operations manager	23	26	32	28	20	26	24	16	21	23
Supervisor	22	28	29	29	24	26	21	21	24	25
Management services	21	25	26	27	24	23	20	20	19	24

6.2 The number of accident-free shifts worked in a company over the past 10 months are shown below. Use linear regression to forecast the number of accident-free shifts for the next 6 months. How reliable are these figures?

Month	1	2	3	4	5	6	7	8	9	10
Shifts	6	21	41	75	98	132	153	189	211	243

6.3 The number of shifts worked in a factory and the total output are shown in the following table. If 400 units are needed next month, how many shifts should be planned? How reliable is this result?

Month	1	2	3	4	5	6	7	8
Shifts worked	50	70	25	55	20	60	40	25
Units made	352	555	207	508	48	498	310	153

6.4 Figures for the demand and cost of an item have been collected from five suppliers as follows:

Supplier	1	2	3	4	5
Cost	14	25	18	28	20
Demand	24	18	20	16	20

The demand seems to be related to the cost by the equation:

$$\text{demand} = a + b/\text{cost}$$

Use linear regression to forecast demand for a cost of 16.

6.5 Find the 2, 3 and 4-period moving average for the following time series, and say which gives the best results.

t	1	2	3	4	5	6	7	8	9
$D(t)$	140	120	180	170	150	110	100	180	210

6.6 The following figures show the number of road accidents per quarter in New Lansbury. Deseasonalize the data and find the underlying trend.

Quarter	1	2	3	4	5	6	7	8	9	10	11	12
Number of accidents	750	300	520	880	320	530	900	300	560	960	340	600

6.7 Use exponential smoothing with $\alpha = 0.1$, 0.2, 0.3 and 0.4 to get one-period-ahead forecasts for the following time series. Use an initial value of $F(1) = 208$ and say which value of α is best.

t	1	2	3	4	5	6	7	8
$D(t)$	212	216	424	486	212	208	208	204

6.8 Use exponential smoothing with smoothing constant equal to 0.1 and 0.2, to get one-period-ahead forecasts for the following time series. Use an initial value of $F(1) = 10.4$ and say which value of α is best.

t	1	2	3	4	5	6	7	8	9
$D(t)$	10.6	10.8	21.2	24.3	10.6	10.4	10.4	10.2	10.8

6.9 Forecast values for periods 10 to 15 of the following time series using a smoothing constant of 0.15 where appropriate:

t	1	2	3	4	5	6	7	8	9
$D(t)$	112	151	142	174	207	212	247	283	268

6.10 The following data has a trend but no seasonality. Use values of $\alpha = 0.2$, $F(1) = 100$ and initial trend = 15 to give forecasts for period 10 to 13:

t	1	2	3	4	5	6
$D(t)$	100	120	135	140	155	170

6.11 The demand for a product is shown below. What forecasts would you give for demand in the following year?

Month	Jan	Feb	Mar	Apr	May	June	July	Aug	Sept	Oct	Nov	Dec
Year 1	100	87	86	75	92	107	115	131	120	118	120	142
Year 2	123	101	105	93	121	136	130	155	158	142	147	181

Discussion questions

6.1 Is forecasting really essential for all decisions? Can you give examples where it is not needed?

6.2 How might poor forecasts affect an organization's performance? Give some examples to support your views.

6.3 What factors should you consider when choosing a forecasting method?

6.4 What are the assumptions of linear regression? Are these generally realistic?

6.5 If you have some data with seasonality and trend, a simple way of forecasting would use linear regression to find the line of best fit. This gives the underlying values and trend. Variations from the line give the seasonal indices. So we could forecast by projecting the regression line, and multiplying by the relevant seasonal indices. Would this method give good results? What other methods can you suggest?

6.6 Projective forecasting cannot deal with sudden, unexpected changes. In July 1993, for example, the Times had 15% of the quality daily newspaper market in Britain. The owner of the Times was Rupert Murdoch's News International, who decided to boost sales and cut the price from 45p a day to 30p.

Average daily sales (thousands of copies) of quality newspapers between June 1993 and April 1994 are shown below:

Month	June	July	Aug	Sept	Oct	Nov	Dec	Jan	Feb	March	April
Daily Telegraph	1012	1017	1028	1008	1011	1032	1008	1033	1015	1001	999
Financial Times	283	288	275	287	288	294	294	284	300	304	299
Guardian	407	403	392	404	403	402	389	406	405	403	397
Independent	339	335	326	332	329	314	302	291	292	277	271
Times	362	360	354	442	445	445	439	456	468	471	478
Total	2403	2403	2375	2474	2475	2487	2433	2470	2481	2455	2445

How could newspapers forecast their demands? Is it possible to forecast the effects of a sudden drop in price of the Times?

Probability and probability distributions

7

CHAPTER OUTLINE

This chapter introduces the ideas of statistics. It shows how to deal with situations involving uncertainty. It is important for you to understand this material, as it is used widely in the rest of the book. After reading the chapter you should be able to:

- understand the purpose of data reduction
- calculate the mean, median and mode of a set of data
- calculate the range, mean absolute deviation, variance and standard deviation
- work with probabilities and understand their meaning
- use Bayes' theorem
- understand when and how to use the binomial distribution
- understand when and how to use the Poisson distribution
- understand when and how to use the normal distribution

| 7.1 | | Describing data

There is a difference between data and information. Data are the raw numbers that are processed to give information in a useful form. So 78, 64, 36, 70 and 52 are data we can process to give the information that the average mark of five students sitting an exam is 60% (see Figure 7.1).

Figure 7.1   Relationship between data and information.

To make decisions, managers must continually collect data – and much of this is numerical. Provided it comes in small amounts, numerical data is easy to understand. We know what it means when petrol costs 65 pence a litre, a building is 60 metres tall, a Member of Parliament had a majority of 10 547, the family next door has three cars, and so on. But we have problems if there is a lot of data and we get swamped by the detail. Suppose the sales of a product in the past year are:

$$
\begin{array}{cccccccccccccc}
54 & 84 & 35 & 12 & 65 & 22 & 09 & 45 & 57 & 66 & 50 & 80 & 88 \\
06 & 05 & 12 & 28 & 39 & 55 & 69 & 84 & 89 & 95 & 92 & 82 & 76 \\
74 & 70 & 66 & 67 & 68 & 51 & 32 & 31 & 30 & 24 & 17 & 08 & 06 \\
57 & 68 & 15 & 35 & 26 & 49 & 58 & 60 & 30 & 22 & 21 & 87 & 42
\end{array}
$$

It is very difficult to get a feeling for this. Most people will not bother to read the details, but will simply skip over them. So we need some way of summarizing data and making it easier to understand. The general term for this is ***data reduction***.

> **Data reduction** gives a simplified view of data. It shows the underlying patterns, but does not overwhelm us with details.

Data reduction has a number of advantages:

- it shows results in a compact form
- results are easy to understand
- it can use diagrams to present the results
- it emphasizes overall patterns
- it allows comparisons of different sets of data
- we can use quantitative measures

On the other hand, it has the disadvantages of:

- losing details of original data
- being irreversible – as the original data cannot be reconstructed

We can show the results of data reduction either in a diagram – perhaps using a graph, bar chart, histogram, or pictograph – or numerically. Diagrams are useful for giving a quick view, but they can be limiting. In this chapter we will concentrate on more useful numerical descriptions.

| *IN SUMMARY* |

Raw data must be processed to give useful information. Data reduction organizes and presents data to show the underlying patterns. Here, we concentrate on numerical descriptions.

Self-assessment questions

7.1 What is the difference between data and information?

7.2 Why do we need to reduce data?

7.3 How can you present statistical data?

7.2 Measures for average and spread

The most common way of summarizing data is to find the **_mean_**. For a set of n values, X_i, the mean – which is often called the average – is:

$$\text{mean} = \frac{\sum_{i=1}^{n} X_i}{n}$$

This gives a useful measure which has the advantages of:

- being easy to calculate
- being familiar and easy to understand
- using all the data
- being useful in other calculations

Sometimes the mean does not give an accurate view of the data. If 7 people enter a shop in 10 minutes, the average number entering is 0.7 a minute. But 0.7 people has no meaning, and it certainly is not a typical value. To get around this kind of problem we can use two other measures of the average.

- If observations are arranged in order of size, the middle observation is the *median*.
- The *mode* is the value that occurs most often.

WORKED EXAMPLE 7.1

In 5 consecutive days a hospital patient has 4, 2, 1, 7 and 1 visitors. What are the mean, median and mode of numbers visiting?

Solution

We can find the mean by adding the numbers and dividing by 5:

$$\text{mean} = (4 + 2 + 1 + 7 + 1)/5 = 15/5 = 3$$

If we arrange the numbers in order the median is the middle one – in this case the third number:

$$1, 1, \mathbf{2}, 4, 7 \qquad \text{median} = 2$$

The mode is the value that occurs most often, which is 1.

These three measures show the average or 'usual' values of a set of data, but they do not give a complete picture. Suppose two doctors and three receptionists work in a village health centre. Last year the gross annual pays earned by these five were £52 000, £48 000, £17 000, £9000 and £9000. The mean pay is £27 000 a year, the median is £17 000 and the mode is £9000. Each of these gives a view of the data, but none of them seem to describe the situation properly. The main problem is that these average values do not show the 'spread' of data.

Last year the mean number of people visiting the West Draycot Consumer Advice Centre was 105 a week. But this does not tell us how the numbers varied. They might have little variation from, say, 100 on quiet weeks to 110 on busy weeks; or they might a have lot of variation between 0 and 500. It would be much more difficult to organize the centre for a widely fluctuating demand than a steady one. So we need some measure for the variation in data.

The simplest measure of spread is the *range*:

$$\textbf{range} = \text{maximum value} - \text{minimum value}$$

But this does not give us much information, and a more useful measure is the **mean absolute deviation** (MAD) from the mean. We used this in the last chapter to measure the quality of forecasts:

$$\text{mean absolute deviation} = \frac{\sum\limits_{i=1}^{n} \text{ABS}[x_i - \mu]}{n}$$

where: x_i = the observations

μ = mean value of observations

n = number of observations

ABS $[x_i - \mu]$ = the absolute value of $x_i - \mu$

Unfortunately, the mean absolute deviation cannot be used for many other analyses. A better alternative is the mean squared error, which is called the *variance*:

$$\text{mean squared error} = \text{variance} = \frac{\sum\limits_{i=1}^{n} (x_i - \mu)^2}{n}$$

The units of variance are the square of the units of the original observations. If, for example, the original units of observations were tonnes, the variance would have the meaningless units of tonnes^2. To return the units to normal, we can take the square root of the variance, to get the *standard deviation*. This is the most widely used measure of spread:

$$\textbf{standard deviation} = \sqrt{\text{variance}}$$

WORKED EXAMPLE 7.2

Worked Example 7.1 described a hospital patient getting 4, 2, 1, 7 and 1 visitors on consecutive days. How can we measure the spread of this data?

Solution

The range is the difference between the largest and smallest values:

$$\text{range} = 7 - 1 = 6$$

The mean number of visitors is 3, so the mean absolute deviation is:

$$
\begin{aligned}
\text{MAD} &= \frac{\sum_{i=1}^{n} \text{ABS}[x_i - \mu]}{n} \\
&= \{\text{ABS}[4-3] + \text{ABS}[2-3] + \text{ABS}[1-3] + \text{ABS}[7-3] + \text{ABS}[1-3]\}/5 \\
&= 10/5 \\
&= 2
\end{aligned}
$$

The variance is:

$$
\begin{aligned}
\text{variance} &= \frac{\sum_{i=1}^{n} (x_i - \mu]^2}{n} \\
&= \{(4-3)^2 + (2-3)^2 + (1-3)^2 + (7-3)^2 + (1-3)^2\}/5 \\
&= 26/5 \\
&= 5.2
\end{aligned}
$$

Standard deviation is the square root of variance:

$$\text{standard deviation} = \sqrt{5.2} = 2.28$$

WORKED EXAMPLE 7.3

The Glendower Hotel is concerned about the number of people who book rooms by telephone but do not actually turn up. Over the past few weeks it has the following numbers of 'no-shows'. How can these data be summarized?

Day	1	2	3	4	5	6	7	8	9	10	11	12	13	14	15
No-shows	4	5	2	3	3	2	1	4	7	2	0	3	1	4	5

Day	16	17	18	19	20	21	22	23	24	25	26	27	28	29	30
No-shows	2	6	2	3	3	4	2	5	6	3	3	2	4	3	4

Day	31	32	33	34	35	36	37	38	39	40	41	42	43	44	45
No-shows	5	2	4	3	3	1	4	5	3	6	4	3	1	4	5

Solution

We can start by showing how often each number of no-shows occurs:

No-shows	0	1	2	3	4	5	6	7
No. of days	1	4	8	12	10	6	3	1

Now we can present these figures in various charts, such as a line graph, bar chart or pie chart (illustrated in Figure 7.2).

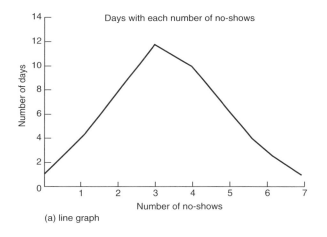

(a) line graph

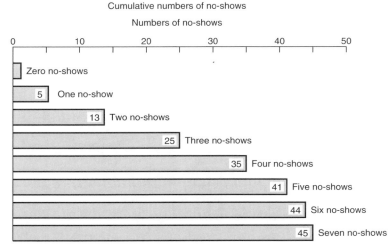

(b) horizontal bar chart

Figure 7.2 continued overleaf

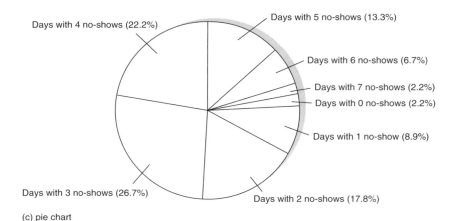

(c) pie chart

Figure 7.2 Graphical presentation of no-shows for Worked Example 7.3.

Alternatively, we could use numerical data. The mean, for example, is 151/45 = 3.3556. But there is no need to do all the calculations by hand. Figure 7.3 shows the result when we set a spreadsheet to describe the data. You can see that it gives the measures we have described, together with some other descriptions.

	A	B	C	D	E	F
1	**Data description**					
2						
3	**Data**				**Description**	
4	4	2	2			
5	5	6	2		Mean	3.355556
6	2	2	4		Median	3
7	3	3	3		Mode	3
8	3	3	3		Standard Deviation	1.53971
9	2	4	1		Variance	2.370707
10	1	2	4		Kurtosis	−0.22244
11	4	5	5		Skewness	0.14799
12	7	6	3		Range	7
13	2	3	6		Minimum	0
14	0	3	4		Maximum	7
15	3	2	3		Sum	151
16	1	4	1		Count	45
17	4	3	4			
18	5	4	5			

Figure 7.3 Spreadsheet showing description of data for Worked Example 7.3.

WORKED EXAMPLE 7.4

The mean weight and standard deviation of airline passengers are known to be 72 kg and 6 kg respectively. What are the mean weight and standard deviation of total passenger weight carried by a 200-seat aeroplane?

Solution

We can find the mean weight of 200 passengers by multiplying the mean weight of each passenger by the number of passengers:

$$\text{mean} = 200 * 72 = 14\,400 \text{ kg}$$

Standard deviations can never be added together, but variances can. So we can find the variance in weight of 200 passengers by multiplying the variance in weight of each passenger by the number of passengers:

$$\text{variance} = 200 * 6^2 = 7200 \text{ kg}^2$$

Then the standard deviation is $\sqrt{7200} = 84.85 \text{ kg}$

IN SUMMARY

We can describe the 'average' of a set of data by its mean, median or mode. This single value does not always describe data properly, and it is useful to have a measure for its 'spread'. For this, we can use the range, mean absolute deviation, variance or standard deviation.

Self-assessment questions

7.4   What three measures can you use for the average of a set of data?

7.5   Suggest four measures for the spread of a set of data.

7.6   Are there any other useful measures for data?

7.3 | Probability

So far in this book, we have assumed that the values of variables are known with certainty. When we looked at sales, we could say, '100 units will be sold to give a gross income of £10 000'. In reality, most situations are not so clear, and there is some uncertainty. Then we might say, 'we hope to sell 100 units, but might only sell about 80, and the income could be less than £9000'.

To deal with this kind of uncertainty, we can use *probabilities*. The probability of an event is a measure of its likelihood or relative frequency. When you toss a coin you know from experience that it will come down heads half the time and tails half the time. Then you can say, 'the probability of a coin coming down heads is 0.5'. So the probability of an event gives the proportion of times the event occurs.

There are 52 cards in a pack of cards and if you chose one at random there is a probability of 1/52 that it is the ace of hearts – or any other specified card. In the last 500 days the train to work has broken down 10 times, so the probability of it breaking down on any day is 10/500 or 0.02. For 200 of the last 240 trading days the Toronto Stock Exchange has had more advances than declines, so there is a probability of 200/240 or 0.83 that the stock exchange advances on a particular day. Because probabilities show relative frequencies, they are only defined in the range 0 to 1:

- probability = 0 means the event will **never** occur
- probability = 1 means the event will **always** occur
- probability between 0 and 1 gives the relative frequency
- probabilities outside the range 0 to 1 have no meaning

An event with a probability of 0.8 is quite likely (it will happen eight times out of ten); an event with a probability of 0.5 is equally likely to happen as not; an event with a probability of 0.2 is quite unlikely (it will happen two times out of ten).

WORKED EXAMPLE 7.5

A magazine advertised a prize draw with one first prize, five second prizes, 100 third prizes and 1000 fourth prizes. Winning entries are drawn at random, and after each draw the winning ticket is returned to the draw. By the closing date there were 10 000 entries and no ticket won more than one prize. What is the probability that a given ticket won first prize or that it won any prize?

Solution

There are 10 000 entries and one first prize, so the probability of a given ticket winning first prize is 1/10 000.

There are five second prizes, so the probability of winning one of these is 5/10 000. The probabilities of winning third or fourth prizes are 100/10 000 and 1000/10 000 respectively.

There are a total of 1106 prizes, so the probability of winning one of these is 1106/10 000. On the other hand, there are 8894 tickets that do not win a prize, so the probability of not winning is 8894/10 000.

There are two ways of finding probabilities:

- Theoretical arguments can lead to *a priori* probabilities. The probability that a husband and wife share the same birthday is 1/365 (ignoring leap years). This is an *a priori* probability, calculated by saying that there are 365 days on which the second partner can have a birthday and only one of these corresponds to the birthday of the first partner.

- Historical data can be used to give **empirical** values. The last 100 times a football team has played at home, it has attracted a crowd of more than 20 000 on 62 occasions. This gives an empirical probability of 62/100 = 0.62 that next week's game will have a crowd of more than 20 000 (all other things being equal).

IN SUMMARY

The probability of an event is the likelihood that the event will occur, or its relative frequency. This is measured on a scale of 0 to 1 with:

- **probabilities close to 0 meaning there is little chance of the event**
- **probabilities close to 1.0 meaning the event will probably happen**

7.4 | Calculating probabilities for independent events

An important idea for calculating probabilities is *mutually exclusive events*. Two events are mutually exclusive if one event's happening means that the other cannot happen. If a coin is tossed the event that it comes down heads is mutually exclusive with the event that it comes down tails. For mutually exclusive events, we can find the probabilities of one **or** another happening by adding the separate probabilities:

> For mutually exclusive events:
>
> OR means ADD probabilities

Then:

$$P(a \text{ OR } b) = P(a) + P(b)$$
$$P(a \text{ OR } b \text{ OR } c) = P(a) + P(b) + P(c)$$
$$P(a \text{ OR } b \text{ OR } c \text{ OR } d) = P(a) + P(b) + P(c) + P(d)$$

and so on.

You saw an illustration of this in Worked Example 7.5. The probability that a particular individual won a prize draw was calculated as 1106/10 000, while the probability that they did not win was 8894/10 000. Each ticket can either win or lose, and these two events are mutually exclusive, so:

$$P(\text{win OR lose}) = P(\text{win}) + P(\text{lose}) = 1$$

WORKED EXAMPLE 7.6

A company makes 40 000 washing machines a year. Of these 10 000 are for the home market, 8000 are exported to North America, 7000 to Europe, 5000 to South America, 4000 to the Far East, 3000 to Australasia and 3000 to other markets.

(a) What is the probability that a particular machine is sold on the home market?

(b) What is the probability that a machine is exported?

(c) What is the probability that a machine is exported to either North or South America?

(d) What is the probability that a machine is sold in either the home market or Europe?

Solution

(a) The probability that a machine is sold on the home market is:

$$P(\text{home}) = \frac{\text{number sold on home market}}{\text{number sold}} = \frac{10\,000}{40\,000} = 0.25$$

(b) The probability that a machine is exported is:

$$P(\text{exported}) = \frac{\text{number exported}}{\text{number sold}} = \frac{30\,000}{40\,000} = 0.75$$

Alternatively, we could say that all machines are sold somewhere, so the probability that a machine is sold is 1.0. It is either sold on the home market or exported so:

$$P(\text{sold}) = 1 = P(\text{exported}) + P(\text{home})$$

So: $P(\text{exported}) = 1 - P(\text{home}) = 1 - 0.25 = 0.75$

(c) $P(\text{North America OR South America}) = P(\text{North America}) + P(\text{South America})$
$$= 8000/40\,000 + 5000/40\,000$$
$$= 0.2 + 0.125 = 0.325$$

(d) $P(\text{home OR Europe}) = P(\text{home}) + P(\text{Europe})$
$$= 10\,000/40\,000 + 7000/40\,000$$
$$= 0.25 + 0.175 = 0.425$$

Another important idea for probabilities is independence. If the occurrence of one event does not affect the occurrence of a second event, they are said to be *independent events*. The fact that a person buys a particular newspaper, for example, is independent of the fact that they suffer from hay fever. Using the notation:

$P(a)$ = the probability of event a

$P(a/b)$ = the probability of event a given that b has already occurred

$P(a/\underline{b})$ = the probability of event a given that b has **not** occurred

two events, a and b, are independent if:

$$P(a) = P(a/b) = P(a/\underline{b})$$

and $P(b) = P(b/a) = P(b/\underline{a})$

So: $P(\text{buys Times}) = P(\text{buys Times / suffers from hay fever})$
$$= P(\text{buys Times / does not suffer from hay fever})$$

For independent events we can find the probability of one **and** another happening by multiplying the probabilities of the separate events:

> For independent events:
>
> AND means MULTIPLY probabilities

Then:

$$P(a \text{ AND } b) = P(a) * P(b)$$
$$P(a \text{ AND } b \text{ AND } c) = P(a) * P(b) * P(c)$$
$$P(a \text{ AND } b \text{ AND } c \text{ AND } d) = P(a) * P(b) * P(c) * P(d)$$

and so on.

WORKED EXAMPLE 7.7

A workshop combines two parts, X and Y, into a final assembly. This is tested and an average of 10% of X and 5% of Y are defective. If defects in X and Y are independent, what is the probability that a final assembly has both X and Y defective?

Solution

For independent events:

$$P(\text{X defective AND Y defective}) = P(\text{X defective}) * P(\text{Y defective})$$
$$= 0.1 * 0.05$$
$$= 0.005$$

Similarly: $P(\text{X not defective}) = 1 - P(\text{X defective}) = 1 - 0.1 = 0.9$

$P(\text{Y not defective}) = 1 - P(\text{Y defective}) = 1 - 0.05 = 0.95$

So: $P(\text{X defective AND Y defective}) = 0.1 * 0.05 = 0.005$

$P(\text{X defective AND Y not defective}) = 0.1 * 0.95 = 0.095$

$P(\text{X not defective AND Y defective}) = 0.9 * 0.05 = 0.045$

$P(\text{X not defective AND Y not defective}) = 0.9 * 0.95 = 0.855$

These are the only four possibilities, so it is not surprising that the probabilities add to 1.

WORKED EXAMPLE 7.8

A warehouse classifies its stock into three different categories: A, B and C. On all category A items it promises a service level of 97% (in other words, there is a probability of 0.97 that the warehouse can meet demand immediately from stock). On category B and C items it promises service levels of 94% and 90% respectively. If service levels are independent, what are the probabilities that the warehouse can immediately supply an order for:

(a) one item of category A and one item of category B

(b) one item from each category

(c) two different items from A, one from B and three from C

(d) three different items from each category?

Solution

(a) As the events are independent we can multiply the probabilities to give:

$$P(\text{one A AND one B}) = P(\text{one A}) * P(\text{one B}) = 0.97 * 0.94 = 0.912$$

(b) $P(\text{one A AND one B AND one C}) = P(\text{one A}) * P(\text{one B}) * P(\text{one C})$

$$= 0.97 * 0.94 * 0.90 = 0.821$$

(c) $P(\text{two A AND one B AND three C}) = P(\text{two A}) * P(\text{one B}) * P(\text{three C})$

We have to simplify this by saying that the probability of two items of category A is the probability the first is there AND the second is there. In other words:

$$P(\text{two A}) = P(\text{one A AND one A}) = P(\text{one A}) * P(\text{one A}) = P(\text{one A})^2$$

Similarly:

$$P(\text{three C}) = P(\text{one C})^3$$

Then the answer is:

$$P(\text{one A})^2 * P(\text{one B}) * P(\text{one C})^3 = 0.97^2 * 0.94 * 0.9^3 = 0.645$$

(d) $P(\text{three A AND three B AND three C}) = P(\text{one A})^3 * P(\text{one B})^3 * P(\text{one C})^3$

$$= 0.97^3 * 0.94^3 * 0.9^3 = 0.553$$

IN SUMMARY

For mutually exclusive events:

   OR means ADD probabilities, so $P(a \text{ OR } b) = P(a) + P(b)$

For independent events:

   AND means MULTIPLY probabilities, so $P(a \text{ AND } b) = P(a) * P(b)$

Self-assessment questions

7.7   What is the probability of an event?

7.8   What are independent events?

7.9 What are mutually exclusive events?

7.10 How can you find the probability that one of several mutually exclusive events occurs?

7.11 How can you find the probability that all of a set of independent events occur?

7.5 | Conditional probabilities for dependent events

The calculations described in the last section can only be done if events are independent. But sometimes events are not independent, and the occurrence of one event directly affects the occurrence of another. For example, the probability that a person is employed in one of the professions is not independent of their having higher education; the probability that a machine will break down this week is not independent of its age; the probability that there is a mistake on an invoice is not independent of the company sending the invoice.

The most important rule for *conditional probabilities* says that the probability of two dependent events occurring is the probability of the first, multiplied by the conditional probability that the second occurs given the first has already occurred. We can write this rather clumsy statement as:

$$P(a \text{ AND } b) = P(a) * P(b/a)$$

where: $P(a \text{ AND } b) =$ probability that both a and b occur

$P(a)$ = probability that a occurs

$P(b/a)$ = probability that b occurs given that a has already occurred

With a bit of thought, we can get the equivalent results:

$$P(a \text{ AND } b) = P(a) * P(b/a) = P(b) * P(a/b)$$

If we take the second two terms and rearrange them we get a result that is known as *Bayes' theorem*:

$$P(a/b) = \frac{P(b/a) * P(a)}{P(b)}$$

WORKED EXAMPLE 7.9

The following table describes the students in a class:

	Home	*Overseas*
Male	66	29
Female	102	3

(a) If a student is chosen at random from the class, what is the probability that they are from overseas?

(b) If the student chosen is female, what is the probability that she is from overseas?

(c) If the student chosen is male what is the probability that he is from overseas?

(d) If the student is from overseas, what is the probability that they are male?

(e) Check that $P(a \text{ AND } b) = P(a) * P(b/a)$ for several combinations of sex and origin.

Solution

(a) $P(\text{overseas})$ = number from overseas/number of students
$$= 32/200 = 0.16$$

(b) We can find this by considering only the 105 female students, to give:

$P(\text{overseas/female})$ = number overseas females/number females
$$= 3/105 = 0.029$$

We could get the same result using Bayes' theorem:

$$P(\text{overseas/female}) = P(\text{overseas AND female})/P(\text{female})$$

Now: $P(\text{overseas AND female}) = 3/200 = 0.015$
$P(\text{female}) = 105/200 = 0.525$

so: $P(\text{overseas/female}) = 0.015/0.525 = 0.029$

(c) $P(\text{overseas/male})$ = number overseas males/number males
$$= 29/95 = 0.305$$

Again, we could get the same result using Bayes' theorem:

$$P(\text{overseas/male}) = P(\text{overseas AND male})/P(\text{male})$$

Now: $P(\text{overseas AND female}) = 29/200 = 0.145$
$P(\text{male}) = 95/200 = 0.305$

so: $P(\text{overseas/male}) = 0.145/0.475 = 0.305$

(d) P(male/overseas) = number overseas males / number overseas
$$= 29/32 = 0.906$$

Again, we could find this from Bayes' theorem:

$$P(\text{male/overseas}) = P(\text{male AND overseas})/P(\text{overseas})$$

Now: P(male AND overseas) = 29/200 = 0.145
P(overseas) = 32/200 = 0.16

so: P(male/overseas) = 0.145/0.16 = 0.906

(e) We have already shown the relationship holds in parts (a) to (d), and can check some other combinations. For example:

$$P(\text{home AND male}) = P(\text{home}) * P(\text{male/home})$$
$$= 0.84 * 0.393 = 0.330$$

(compare this with 66/200 = 0.33)

$$P(\text{female AND overseas}) = P(\text{female}) * P(\text{overseas/female})$$
$$= 0.525 * 0.029 = 0.015$$

(compare this with 3/200 = 0.015)

WORKED EXAMPLE 7.10

Two machines make identical parts, which are combined on a production line. An old machine makes 40% of the units, of which 85% are of satisfactory quality. A new machine makes 60% of the units, of which 92% are of satisfactory quality. A random inspection further down the production line shows an unusual fault, and the machine that made the unit needs adjusting. What is the probability that the old machine made the unit?

Solution

This problem is summarized in Figure 7.4.

Using the abbreviations O for the old machine, N for the new machine, OK for good units and F for faulty ones, we want $P(\text{O/F})$. We can find this using Bayes' theorem:

$$P(a/b) = \frac{P(b/a) * P(a)}{P(b)} \quad \text{or} \quad P(\text{O/F}) = \frac{P(\text{F/O}) * P(\text{O})}{P(\text{F})}$$

We know that $P(\text{O}) = 0.4$ and $P(\text{F/O}) = 0.15$. Now we need to find $P(\text{F})$, the probability that a unit is faulty. A unit is either faulty or it is alright, so with a little thought, you can see that:

Probability that a unit is faulty = probability that it is faulty
from the old machine

OR that it is faulty from the new machine

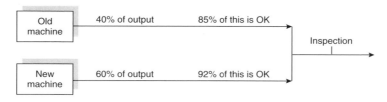

Figure 7.4   Production in Worked Example 7.10.

So: $P(F) = P(F \text{ AND } O) + P(F \text{ AND } N)$

$= P(F/O) * P(O) + P(F/N) * P(N) = 0.15 * 0.4 + 0.08 * 0.6 = 0.108$

Then: $P(O/F) = \dfrac{0.15 * 0.4}{0.15 * 0.4 + 0.08 * 0.6} = \dfrac{0.06}{0.108} = 0.556$

We can check this result by calculating:

$$P(N/F) = \frac{P(F/N) * P(N)}{P(F)} = \frac{0.08 * 0.6}{0.108} = 0.444$$

As the unit must have come from either the old or new machine, the fact that $P(O/F) + P(N/F) = 0.556 + 0.444 = 1.0$ confirms the result.

The arithmetic in this worked example was straightforward, but it can become tedious. An obvious answer is to use a computer, but there is a mechanical procedure that makes the arithmetic quite easy. This procedure starts by putting the probabilities in a table.

	Faulty	*OK*	
Old machine	0.15	0.85	0.4
New machine	0.08	0.92	0.6

The left-hand box gives the known conditional probabilities. So $0.15 = P(F/O)$, $0.08 = P(F/N)$, etc. The right-hand box gives the values of $P(O)$ and $P(N)$, which are called the prior probabilities. Now we can form a third box by multiplying each conditional probability in the left-hand box by the prior probability on the same line. So $0.15 * 0.4 = 0.060$, $0.08 * 0.06 = 0.048$, and so on. These results are called the **joint** probabilities.

	Faulty	OK		Faulty	OK
Old machine	0.15	0.85	0.4	0.060	0.340
New machine	0.08	0.92	0.6	0.048	0.552
				0.108	0.892

Adding the columns of joint probabilities gives a marginal probability. Then $0.060 + 0.048 = 0.108$, which is the probability that a unit is faulty: $0.340 + 0.552 = 0.892$, which is the probability that a unit is OK. Finally, dividing each joint probability by the marginal probability in the same column gives the element in a bottom box. Then $0.340/0.892 = 0.381$, $0.060/0.108 = 0.556$, and so on. This last result is the one we found above, and shows that we have found the conditional probabilities we are looking for, i.e. $P(O/F)$, $P(N/OK)$, etc.

	Faulty	OK		Faulty	OK
Old machine	0.15	0.85	0.4	0.060	0.340
New machine	0.08	0.92	0.6	0.048	0.552
				0.108	0.892
		Old machine		0.556	0.381
		New machine		0.444	0.619

This procedure may seem a bit strange, but if you look at the equation for Bayes' theorem, you can see that we are simply repeating the calculations. These probabilities are illustrated in Figure 7.5.

It is sometimes easier to visualize conditional probabilities on a **probability tree**. These diagrams are drawn from left to right with branches representing a sequence of possible events. Figure 7.6 shows a probability tree for the above example.

Each branch represents a possible event, and they emerge from nodes which are the circles. Node 1 is the starting point. From here there are two alternatives for a part:

● it comes from the new machine, with a probability of 0.6
● it comes from the old machine, with a probability of 0.4

At both nodes 2 and 3 there are two possibilities:

● the part is faulty
● the part is alright

Each branch is labelled with its probability, and as we include all possible events, the probabilities on branches leaving any node should add to 1. At the right of the tree you can see the probability of reaching the end point. We get these by

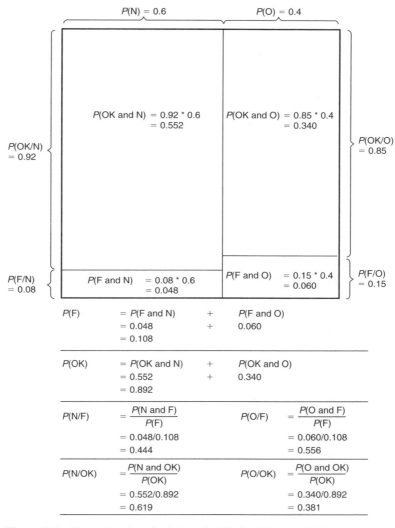

Figure 7.5 Illustrating the calculations for Worked Example 7.10.

multiplying the probabilities on all branches taken to reach that point. Then the first end node shows the probability that a part is faulty and it comes from the new machine, which is $0.6 * 0.08 = 0.048$. The second end node shows the probability that a part is alright and it comes from the new machine, which is $0.6 * 0.92 = 0.552$. Again, the sum of all end values should be 1.

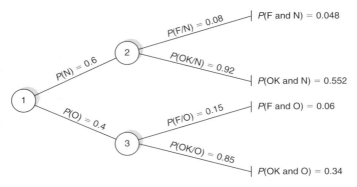

Figure 7.6 Probability trees for the original and updated probabilities in Worked Example 7.10.

WORKED EXAMPLE 7.11

Second-hand cars are either good buys or bad buys. Among good buys, 70% have low oil consumption and 20% have medium oil consumption. Among bad buys, 50% have high oil consumption and 30% have medium oil consumption. A test was done on a second-hand car and showed a low oil consumption. If 60% of second-hand cars are good buys, what is the probability that this particular car is a good buy?

Solution

We can start by defining the abbreviations GB and BB for good buy and bad buy; HOC, MOC and LOC for high, medium and low oil consumption. Then we can substitute the known values into Bayes' theorem. The results for this are shown in the spreadsheet in Figure 7.7.

	A	B	C	D	E	F	G	H
1	**Bayes' Theorem**							
2								
3		HOC	MOC	LOC		HOC	MOC	LOC
4	GB	0.1	0.2	0.7	0.6	0.060	0.120	0.420
5	BB	0.5	0.3	0.2	0.4	0.200	0.120	0.080
6						0.260	0.240	0.500
7					GB	0.231	0.500	0.840
8					BB	0.769	0.500	0.160

Figure 7.7 Spreadsheet showing calculations for Worked Example 7.11.

The probability that a car with a low oil consumption is a good buy is 0.84. The table also shows that the probability of a low oil consumption is 0.5 (compared with 0.26 for a high oil consumption). Figure 7.8 shows a probability tree for this problem.

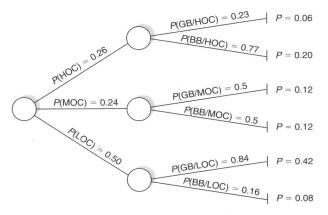

Figure 7.8 Probability tree for Worked Example 7.10.

IN SUMMARY

With dependent events we have to use conditional probabilities. Bayes' theorem gives an important calculation for these. The probabilities may be easier to visualize in a probability tree.

Self-assessment questions

7.12   What are dependent events?

7.13   What are conditional probabilities?

7.14   What is Bayes' theorem and when is it used?

7.6 | Probability distributions

A useful way of describing data is to draw a frequency distribution, which shows the numbers of observations in different classes. But we know that probabilities can be viewed as relative frequencies. So we can combine these two ideas and show how a set of data can be described by a ***probability distribution***.

In Worked Example 7.1, a hospital patient had 4, 2, 1, 7 and 1 visitors on consecutive days. So we can find the relative frequency – or probability – of each number of visitors by dividing the number in each class by the total number of observations (5):

Number of visitors	1	2	3	4	5	6	7
Frequency	2	1	0	1	0	0	1
Probability	0.4	0.2	0.0	0.2	0.0	0.0	0.2

We can draw a frequency distribution for this, as shown in Figure 7.9(a), or we can plot the probabilities, to get the probability distribution shown in Figure 7.9(b).

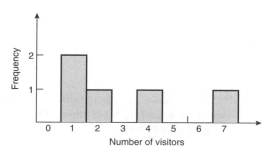

(a) frequency distribution

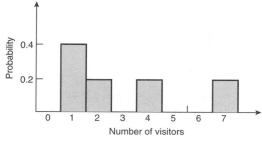

(b) probability distribution

Figure 7.9   Distributions for number of visitors.

WORKED EXAMPLE 7.12

Every day Glanford Mill restaurant has a number of people who book tables by telephone, but do not actually turn up. The number of no-shows was recorded over a typical period as follows:

2 4 6 7 1 3 3 5 4 1 2 3 4 3 5 6 2 4 3 2 5 5

0 3 3 2 1 4 4 4 3 1 3 6 3 4 2 5 3 2 4 2 5 3 4

Draw a probability distribution of this data. What is the probability that there are more than four no-shows?

Solution

Adding the number of days with various numbers of no-shows gives the frequency distribution of the data. Then dividing by the total number of observations (45) gives the following relative frequency or probability distribution:

No-shows	0	1	2	3	4	5	6	7
Frequency	1	4	8	12	10	6	3	1
Probability	0.02	0.09	0.18	0.27	0.22	0.13	0.07	0.02

We can now draw a histogram of the probability distribution, as shown in Figure 7.10. Remember that the **area** of each rectangle in this histogram represents the probability, so the total area under the histogram must equal 1. (Here each bar is one unit wide so you can read the probability directly from the height of the bars.)

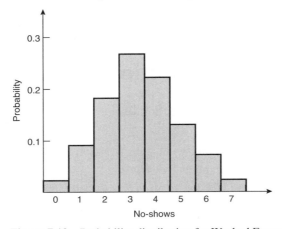

Figure 7.10 Probability distribution for Worked Example 7.12.

The probability of more than four no-shows is:

$$P(5) + P(6) + P(7) = 0.13 + 0.07 + 0.02 = 0.22$$

The probability distribution drawn above is empirical, which means that it was found from actual observations. You can draw an empirical distribution for any problem where observations are made, but the resulting distribution is specific to that particular problem. Fortunately, empirical distributions often follow standard patterns. So we can use some general probability distributions to describe a range of problems. Here we will look at the three most important:

- *binomial distribution*
- *Poisson distribution*
- *normal distribution*

IN SUMMARY

A probability distribution describes the relative frequency of events or observations. Empirical distributions describe specific situations, but several general distributions are widely used.

Self-assessment questions

7.15 What is the purpose of a probability distribution?

7.16 What is the difference between empirical and *a priori* probabilities?

7.17 What is the total area under a histogram of a probability distribution?

7.7 Binomial distribution

We can use the **binomial distribution** when a series of **trials** have the following characteristics:

- each trial has two possible outcomes, which are called success and failure
- the two outcomes are mutually exclusive
- there is a constant probability of success, p, and failure, $q = 1 - p$
- the outcomes of successive trials are independent

Tossing a coin is a standard example of a binomial process. Each toss is a trial – each head, say, is a success with a constant probability of 0.5, and each tail is a failure. Another example of a binomial process is the inspection of units of a product for defects. Each inspection is a trial. Then – using the conventional terms for binomial distributions – each fault is a success and each good unit is a failure.

The binomial distribution gives the probability of any number of faults in the batch.

In general, the binomial distribution gives the probability of r successes in n trials. It does this using the following argument. If the probability of a success in a trial is constant at p, and we want the probability of exactly r successes in n trials:

$$P(\text{exactly } r \text{ successes}) = P(r \text{ successes AND } n - r \text{ failures})$$

$$= P(r \text{ successes}) * P(n - r \text{ failures})$$

We know that for independent trials the probability of the first r being successes is p^r, and the probability of the next $n - r$ trials being failures is q^{n-r}. So the probability of the first r trials being successes **and** the next $n - r$ trials being failures is $p^r * q^{n-r}$.

But the sequence of r successes followed by $n - r$ failures is only one way of getting r successes in n trials. We have to find how many other possible sequences there are. In Chapter 5 we found that the number of ways of choosing r things from n, when the order of selection does not matter, is ${}^nC_r = n!/r!(n-r)!$. So there must be ${}^nC_r$ possible sequences of r successes and $n - r$ failures, each with probability $p^r * q^{n-r}$. The overall probability of r successes comes from multiplying the number of sequences with r successes by the probability of each sequence.

$$P(r \text{ successes in } n \text{ trials}) = {}^nC_r * p^r * q^{(n-r)}$$

$$= \frac{n!}{r! * (n-r)!} * p^r * q^{n-r}$$

WORKED EXAMPLE 7.13

A salesman knows that he has a 50% chance of making a sale when calling on a customer. One morning he arranges six calls.

(a) What is the probability of making exactly three sales?

(b) What are the probabilities of making other numbers of sales?

(c) What is the probability of making fewer than three sales?

Solution

The problem is a binomial process with the probability of success – that is, of making a sale – of $p = 0.5$. The probability of failure – not making a sale – is $q = 0.5$. The number of trials, n, is 6.

(a) The probability of making exactly three sales (so $r = 3$) is given by:

$$P(r \text{ successes in } n \text{ trials}) = {}^nC_r * p^r * q^{(n-r)}$$

$$P(3 \text{ successes in 6 trials}) = {}^6C_3 * 0.5^3 * 0.5^{(6-3)}$$

$$= \frac{6!}{3!3!} * 0.125 * 0.125 = 0.3125$$

(b) Substituting other values for r gives:

r	0	1	2	3	4	5	6
$P(r$ successes in 6 trials)	0.0156	0.0938	0.2344	0.3125	0.2344	0.0938	0.0156

These values are drawn in the probability distribution in Figure 7.11.

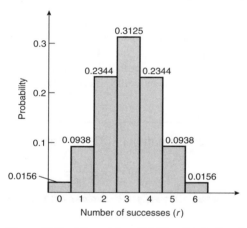

Figure 7.11 Binomial probability distribution for Worked Example 7.13.

(c) The probability of making fewer than three sales is the sum of the probabilities of making 0, 1 and 2 sales:

$$P(\text{fewer than 3 sales}) = P(0 \text{ sales}) + P(1 \text{ sale}) + P(2 \text{ sales})$$

$$= 0.0156 + 0.0938 + 0.2344 = 0.3438$$

The shape of the binomial distribution varies with p and n. For small values of p the distribution is asymmetrical with a peak to the left of centre. As p increases the peak moves towards the centre of the distribution, and with $p = 0.5$ the distribution is symmetrical. As p increases further the distribution again become asymmetrical but this time the peak is to the right. For larger values of n the distribution is flatter and broader. Some typical binomial distributions are shown in Figure 7.12.

The mean, variance and standard deviation of a binomial distribution are calculated from:

- mean $= \mu = n * p$
- variance $= \sigma^2 = n * p * q$
- standard deviation $= \sigma = \sqrt{n * p * q}$

The calculations of binomial probabilities are fairly simple, but you can also use standard tables – shown in Appendix B – or standard functions on a computer.

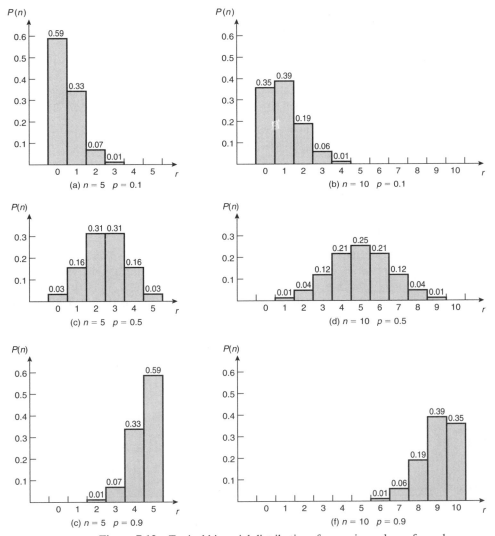

Figure 7.12 Typical binomial distributions for varying values of n and p.

WORKED EXAMPLE 7.14

A market researcher has to visit 12 houses in a given area. Previous calls suggest there will be someone at home in 85% of houses.

(a) Describe the probability distribution of the number of houses with people at home.

(b) What is the probability that the researcher will find someone at home in exactly 9 houses?

(c) What is the probability there will be someone at home in exactly 7 houses?

(d) What is the probability there will be someone at home in at least 10 houses?

Solution

(a) The process is binomial, with visiting a house as a trial and finding someone at home a success. Then $n = 12$, $p = 0.85$, $q = 0.15$, and:

mean number of houses with someone at home $= n * p = 12 * 0.85 = 10.2$

variance $= n * p * q = 12 * 0.85 * 0.15 = 1.53$

standard deviation $= \sqrt{1.53} = 1.24$

(b) Let $P(9)$ be the probability that there is someone at home in exactly 9 houses. Then:

$$P(9) = {}^{12}C_9 * 0.85^9 * 0.15^3 = 220 * 0.2316169 * 0.003375 = 0.172$$

You can check this in Appendix B. Values are only given for p up to 0.5, so to use the tables you have to redefine 'success' as finding a house with no-one at home. Then $p = 0.15$. Looking at the entry for $n = 12$, $p = 0.15$ and $r = 3$ (finding 9 houses with someone at home is the same as finding 3 houses with no-one at home) confirms the value 0.1720.

(c) The probability of finding exactly 7 people at home is:

$$P(7) = {}^{12}C_7 * 0.85^7 * 0.15^5 = 792 * 0.320577 * 0.000076 = 0.0193$$

(d) We want:

$$P(\text{at least } 10) = P(10) + P(11) + P(12)$$

You can either calculate these values or use tables to show that:

$$P(\text{at least } 10) = 0.2924 + 0.3012 + 0.1422 = 0.7358$$

We could, of course, use a statistical package for the calculations. Figure 7.13(a) shows a typical result when a statistics package is asked to calculate the binomial probabilities for $n = 20$ and $p = 0.3$. The first command in this MINITAB printout asks for the probability distribution function (pdf) and the subcommand gives the distribution. Figure 7.13(b) shows the same result from a spreadsheet.

```
MTB >        pdf;
SUBC>        binomial n = 20 p = 0.3.

   BINOMIAL WITH N = 20 P = 0.300000

   K        P(X = K)
   0        0.0008
   1        0.0068
   2        0.0278
   3        0.0716
   4        0.1304
   5        0.1789
   6        0.1916
   7        0.1643
   8        0.1144
   9        0.0654
  10        0.0308
  11        0.0120
  12        0.0039
  13        0.0010
  14        0.0002
  15        0.0000

MTB >        stop
```

(a) from a statistical package

	A	B	C
1	**Binomial probabilities**		
2			
3	**n**	**20**	
4			
5	**r**	**P[r]**	**Cum Prob**
6	1	0.0068	0.0068
7	2	0.0278	0.0347
8	3	0.0716	0.1063
9	4	0.1304	0.2367
10	5	0.1789	0.4156
11	6	0.1916	0.6072
12	7	0.1643	0.7715
13	8	0.1144	0.8859
14	9	0.0654	0.9512
15	10	0.0308	0.9821
16	11	0.0120	0.9941
17	12	0.0039	0.9979
18	13	0.0010	0.9989
19	14	0.0002	0.9992
20	15	0.0000	0.9992
21			

(b) from a spreadsheet

Figure 7.13 Calculating binomial probabilities.

Sometimes the arithmetic for binomial probabilities becomes rather difficult. Consider the following situation where n is very large. The accounts department of a company send out 10 000 invoices a month and on average five of these are returned with some error. What is the probability that exactly five invoices will be returned in a given month?

This is a typical application for the binomial distribution, where a trial is sending out an invoice, and a success is having an error. Unfortunately, as soon as we try to do the arithmetic we run into difficulties. Substituting known values gives:

$$n = 10\,000 \quad r = 5 \quad p = 5/10\,000 \quad q = 9995/10\,000$$

so:

$$P(r \text{ returns}) = \frac{n!}{r!(n-r)!} * p^r * q^{n-r} = \frac{10\,000!}{5! * 9995!} * (5/10\,000)^5 * (9995/10\,000)^{9995}$$

Although we could do this calculation, it does not seem reasonable to raise figures to the power of 9995 or to contemplate 10 000 factorial. Fortunately, there is an alternative. When the number of trials is large and the probability of success is small, we can approximate a binomial distribution by a Poisson distribution. This is described in the following section.

IN SUMMARY

We can use a binomial distribution when an event has two mutually exclusive, independent outcomes, called success and failure. It calculates the probability of r successes in n trials as:

$$P(r \text{ success in } n \text{ trials}) = {}^nC_r * p^r * q^{n-r}$$

Self-assessment questions

7.18   When can you use a binomial distribution?

7.19   How can you find the mean and standard deviation of a binomial distribution?

7.20   Find, from the tables in Appendix B, the probability of 2 successes from 7 trials, when the probability of success is 0.2.

7.8 Poisson distribution

The **Poisson distribution** is a close relative of the binomial distribution and can be used to approximate it when:

● the number of trials, n, is large (say, more than 20)

● the probability of success, p, is small (so that $n * p$ is less than 5)

As n gets larger and p gets smaller the approximation becomes better.

The Poisson distribution is also useful in its own right for solving problems where events occur at random. The number of accidents each month in a factory, the number of defects in a metre of cloth and the number of phone calls received each hour in an office follow Poisson distributions.

The binomial distribution uses both the number of successes and the number of failures, but the Poisson distribution only uses the number of successes; it assumes that there is a very large number of failures, so we are effectively looking for a few successes in a continuous background of failures. The number of spelling mistakes in a long report, the number of faults in a pipeline or the number of accidents in a month all look for the number of successes and do not bother with the large number of events that are conventionally called failures.

The Poisson distribution is described by the equation

$$P(r \text{ successes}) = \frac{e^{-\mu} * \mu^r}{r!}$$

where: e = exponential constant = 2.7183

μ = mean number of successes

Now we can finish the binomial example we looked at above. The accounts department send out 10 000 invoices a month and on average five of these are returned with some error. Here n is large and $\mu = n * p = 5$, so we can use the Poisson distribution to approximate the binomial distribution. Then the probability that there are exactly five errors is:

$$P(r \text{ successes}) = \frac{e^{-\mu} * \mu^r}{r!}$$

so

$$P(5 \text{ successes}) = \frac{e^{-5} * 5^5}{5!} = \frac{0.0067 * 3125}{120}$$

$$= 0.1755$$

WORKED EXAMPLE 7.15

Lasiter Construction has had 40 accidents in the past 50 weeks. In what proportion of weeks would you expect 0, 1, 2, 3 and more than 4 accidents?

Solution

A small number of accidents occur, presumably at random, over time. We are not interested in the number of accidents that did **not** occur, so we can describe the process by a Poisson distribution:

$$P(r \text{ successes}) = \frac{e^{-\mu} * \mu^r}{r!}$$

The mean number of accidents a week is 40/50 = 0.8, so substituting $\mu = 0.8$ and $r = 0$ gives:

$$P(0) = \frac{e^{-0.8} * 0.8^0}{0!} = 0.4493$$

Similarly, substituting $r = 1$ etc. gives:

$$P(1) = \frac{e^{-0.8} * 0.8^1}{1!} = 0.3595$$

$$P(2) = \frac{e^{-0.8} * 0.8^2}{2!} = 0.1438$$

$$P(3) = \frac{e^{-0.8} * 0.8^3}{3!} = 0.0383$$

$$P(4) = \frac{e^{-0.8} * 0.8^4}{4!} = 0.0077$$

There are standard tables of Poisson probabilities, and you can check these results in Appendix C.

Then:
$$\begin{aligned}
P(>4) &= 1 - P(\leq 4) \\
&= 1 - P(0) - P(1) - P(2) - P(3) - P(4) \\
&= 1 - 0.4493 - 0.3595 - 0.1438 - 0.0383 - 0.0077 \\
&= 0.0014
\end{aligned}$$

You can usually use a Poisson distribution for random events, but strictly speaking there are a number of other requirements. In particular, a Poisson process needs:

- events that are independent
- the probability of an event happening in an interval is proportional to the length of the interval
- in theory, an infinite number of events should be possible in an interval

The mean, standard deviation and variance of a Poisson distribution are calculated from:

- mean $= \mu = n * p$
- variance $= \sigma^2 = n * p$
- standard deviation $= \sigma = \sqrt{n * p}$

The shape and position of the Poisson distribution are set by the single parameter, μ. For small μ the distribution is asymmetrical with a peak to the left of centre. Then as μ gets bigger the distribution becomes more symmetrical. This is illustrated for some typical values in Figure 7.14.

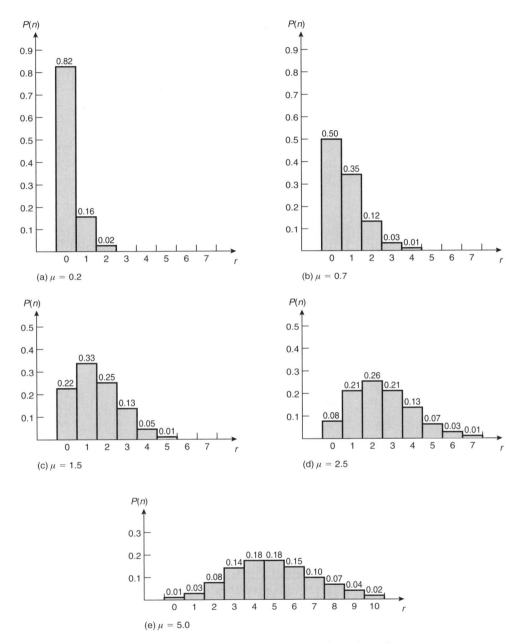

Figure 7.14 Typical Poisson distributions for varying values of μ.

We can, of course, use a statistics package for calculating Poisson probabilities, and Figure 7.15(a) shows a typical printout for $\mu = 6$. Figure 7.15(b) shows the same results from a spreadsheet.

```
MTB >       pdf;
SUBC>       poisson mu = 6.


     POISSON WITH MEAN = 6.000


     K          P(X = K)
     0          0.0025
     1          0.0149
     2          0.0446
     3          0.0892
     4          0.1339
     5          0.1606
     6          0.1606
     7          0.1377
     8          0.1033
     9          0.0688
    10          0.0413
    11          0.0225
    12          0.0113
    13          0.0052
    14          0.0022
    15          0.0009
    16          0.0003
    17          0.0001
    18          0.0000


MTB >          stop
```

(a) from a statistical package

	A	B	C
1	**Poisson distributions**		
2			
3	**mean**	**6**	
4			
5	**r**	**Prob[k]**	**Cum Prob**
6	0	0.0025	0.0025
7	1	0.0149	0.0174
8	2	0.0446	0.0620
9	3	0.0892	0.1512
10	4	0.1339	0.2851
11	5	0.1606	0.4457
12	6	0.1606	0.6063
13	7	0.1377	0.7440
14	8	0.1033	0.8472
15	9	0.0688	0.9161
16	10	0.0413	0.9574
17	11	0.0225	0.9799
18	12	0.0113	0.9912
19	13	0.0052	0.9964
20	14	0.0022	0.9986
21	15	0.0009	0.9995
22	16	0.0003	0.9998
23	17	0.0001	0.9999
24	18	0.0000	1.0000

(b) from a spreadsheet

Figure 7.15   Calculating Poisson probabilities.

WORKED EXAMPLE 7.16

A council was doing some tests at a road junction. During the tests cars arrived randomly at an average rate of 5 cars every 10 minutes.

(a) What is the probability that exactly 3 cars arrive during a 10-minute period?

(b) What is the probability that more than 5 cars arrive in a 10-minute period?

Solution

Random arrivals over time suggest a Poisson process. The mean number of successes (that is, cars arriving at the junction in 10 minutes) is $\mu = 5$.

(a) We can find the probability of exactly 3 cars arriving from:

$$P(r) = \frac{e^{-\mu} * \mu^r}{r!} \quad \text{so} \quad P(3) = \frac{e^{-5} * 5^3}{3!} = 0.1404$$

We can check this value in Appendix B by looking up the value for $\mu = 5$ and $r = 3$.

(b) To find the probability that more than 5 cars arrived at the junction in a 10-minute period we need to calculate:

$$P(>5) = 1 - P(5 \text{ or less})$$
$$= 1 - P(0) - P(1) - P(2) - P(3) - P(4) - P(5)$$

You can either calculate these values or look them up in tables to give:

$$P(>5) = 1 - 0.0067 - 0.0337 - 0.0842 - 0.1404 - 0.1755 - 0.1755$$
$$= 0.384$$

Figure 7.16 shows the probability distribution for this problem.

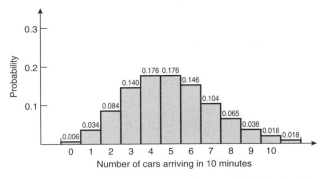

Figure 7.16 Probability distribution for arrivals in Worked Example 7.16.

Sometimes the calculations for Poisson distributions are difficult. This happens particularly when p is high and r is large. Consider the following example. A motor insurance policy is only available to drivers with low risk of accidents. One hundred drivers holding the policy in a certain area would expect an average of 0.2 accidents each a year. What is the probability that less than 15 drivers will have accidents in one year?

This is a binomial process with mean $= n*p = 100*0.2 = 20$. The probability that exactly r drivers will have accidents in the year is given by:

$$P(r \text{ drivers have accidents}) = {}^{20}C_r * 0.2^r * 0.8^{100-r}$$

Then we can find the probability that less than 15 drivers will have accidents in the year by adding this calculation for all values of r from 0 to 14:

$$P(\text{less than 15 drivers have accidents}) = \sum_{r=0}^{14} {}^{20}C_r * 0.2^r * 0.8^{100-r}$$

This is a bit messy to calculate, so we should look for a Poisson approximation. Unfortunately $n*p = 100*0.2 = 20$ which does not meet the requirement that $n*p$ be less than 5. So we have to use another approach. This time we will use the most common probability distribution of all. When n is large and $n*p$ is greater than 5, the binomial distribution can be approximated by the normal distribution. This is described in the following section.

IN SUMMARY

The Poisson distribution can be used as an approximation to the binomial distribution when the probability of success is small. It also describes infrequent, random events:

$$P(r \text{ successes}) = \frac{e^{-\mu} * \mu^r}{r!}$$

Self-assessment questions

7.21   When can you use a Poisson distribution?

7.22   How can you find the mean and standard deviation of a Poisson distribution?

7.23   The average number of defects per square yard of material is 0.8. Use the tables in Appendix D to find the probability that a square yard has exactly two defects.

7.24   When can you use a Poisson distribution as an approximation to a binomial distribution?

7.9 | Normal distribution

Both the binomial and Poisson distributions describe discrete data – so there is always a whole number of successes. But we often want a probability distribution for continuous data, which can take non-integer values, such as lengths of material, weights, times or profits. Although these two are very similar in principle, there is one fundamental difference. With discrete probabilities we can find the probability of exactly 5 successes in 10 trials – but with continuous data we cannot find the probability that a person weighs exactly 80.456456456 kg. If we make the measurement precise enough, the probability of this happening is always zero. So with continuous data we really want the probability that a value is within a specified range, e.g. the probability that a person weighs between 80.4 kg and 80.5 kg.

The most widely used distribution for continuous data is the **normal distribution**. This bell-shaped curve – shown in Figure 7.17 – is used in many different circumstances. Many natural phenomena, such as the heights of trees, harvest from an acre of land, weight of horses and daily temperature, follow this distribution. It also describes many business functions, such as daily takings in a shop, weight of raw materials used each week, number of customers a week, production in a factory, and so on. The distribution is so common that we can use a rule of thumb, 'for large numbers of observations use the normal distribution'.

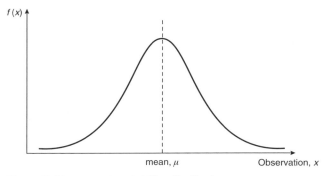

Figure 7.17   Normal probability distribution.

The **normal distribution**:

- is continuous
- is symmetrical about the mean value, μ
- has mean, median and mode all equal
- has the total area under the curve equal to 1
- in theory the curve extends to plus and minus infinity on the x-axis

The equation for the normal distribution gives the height of the curve at any point:

$$f(x) = \frac{1}{\sigma * \sqrt{2 * \pi}} \, e^{-(x - \mu)^2 / 2\sigma^2}$$

where: x = value of interest

                μ = mean value

                σ = standard deviation

                π, e = constants taking their usual values of 3.14159
                     and 2.71828 respectively

Fortunately we do not have to worry about this equation as it is hardly ever used. With continuous data the height of the curve at any point does not have much meaning. We are more interested in finding probabilities from the area under the curve.

Suppose a factory makes boxes of chocolates with a mean weight of 1000 g. There will be small variations in the weight of each box, and with a large number of boxes these weights will follow a normal distribution. Managers in the factory will not be interested in the number of boxes that weigh exactly 1005.0000 g, but they may be interested in the number of boxes that weigh more than 1005 g. They can find this from the area under the right-hand tail of the distribution, shown in Figure 7.18.

There are three ways of finding the area under the tail of the distribution:

- We can use the definite integral to find the area under the curve between 1005.0 and infinity (which is rather tedious).
- We can get a computer to do the calculation.
- We can look up values in standard tables (shown in Appendix D).

Normal distribution tables use a value, Z, which is the number of standard deviations a point is away from the mean. Then the tables show the probability that a value greater than this will occur. With the boxes of chocolates mentioned

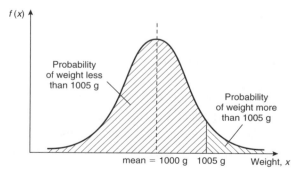

Figure 7.18   Distribution of weights of chocolate boxes.

above, the mean weight is 1000 g and we want to find the probability that a box weighs more than 1005 g. If the standard deviation is 3 g, we have:

$$Z = \text{number of standard deviations from the mean}$$

$$= \frac{\text{value} - \text{mean}}{\text{standard deviation}} = \frac{x - \mu}{\sigma}$$

$$= \frac{1005 - 1000}{3} = 1.67$$

Looking up 1.67 in Appendix D gives a value of 0.0475. This is the probability that a box weighs more than 1005 g. (Tables of normal probabilities have slight differences so you must be careful when using them.)

Because the normal distribution curve is symmetrical about the mean, the probability that a box of chocolates weighs less than 995 g is the same as the probability that it weighs more than 1005 g. We have found that this is 0.0548 (as shown in Figure 7.19).

The mean and standard deviation affect the position and shape of the normal curve. The curve is wider for larger standard deviations, and its position on the x-axis is set by the mean (as shown in Figure 7.20).

In a normal distribution about 68% of observations are within one standard deviation of the mean, 95% are within two standard deviations and 99.7% are within three standard deviations (shown in Figure 7.21).

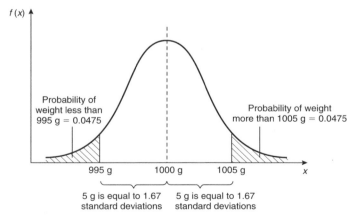

Figure 7.19 Symmetrical distribution of weights of chocolate boxes.

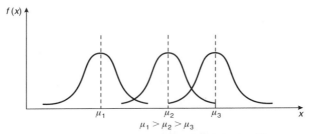

(a) distributions with same standard deviation but different means

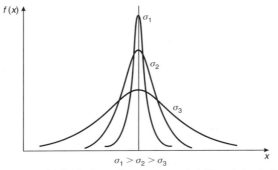

(b) distributions with same means but different standard deviations

Figure 7.20   Different shapes of normal distribution.

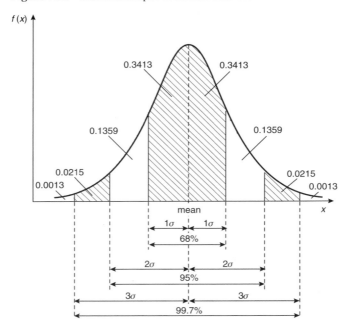

Figure 7.21   Areas under the normal curve.

WORKED EXAMPLE 7.17

An auctioneer has kept records of the weight of horses sold at his market. This has a mean of 950 kg and a standard deviation of 150 kg. What proportion of horses have weights:

(a) more than 1250 kg

(b) less than 850 kg

(c) between 1100 kg and 1250 kg

(d) between 800 kg and 1300 kg?

Solution

We can assume that the auctioneer sold a large number of horses, so we can use a normal distribution with $\mu = 950$ and $\sigma = 150$.

(a) We can find the probability of weight greater than 1250 kg as follows:

$$Z = \text{number of standard deviations from the mean}$$
$$= (1250 - 950)/150 = 2.0$$

Looking this up in Appendix D gives a value of 0.0228, which is the required probability (see Figure 7.22).

(b) The probability of weight less than 850 kg is found in the same way:

$$Z = (850 - 950)/150 = -0.67$$

The table only shows positive values, but as the distribution is symmetrical we can use the value for $+0.67$, which is 0.2514. This is the area under the tail of the curve and is the required probability.

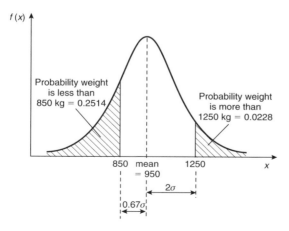

Figure 7.22   Calculations for Worked Example 7.17 parts (a) and (b).

Because the tables only show probabilities under the tail of the distribution we often have to do some juggling of the values. There are several different ways of doing the following calculations, all of which give the same results.

(c) The calculation that the weight is between 1100 kg and 1250 kg relies on the relationship (see Figure 7.23):

$$P(\text{between } 1100\,\text{kg and } 1250\,\text{kg})$$
$$= P(\text{greater than } 1100\,\text{kg}) - P(\text{greater than } 1250\,\text{kg})$$

For weight above 1100 kg:

$$Z = (1100 - 950)/150 = 1 \quad \text{probability} = 0.1587$$

For weight above 1250 kg:

$$Z = (1250 - 950)/150 = 2 \quad \text{probability} = 0.0228$$

So the probability that the weight is between these two is

$$0.1587 - 0.0228 = 0.1359$$

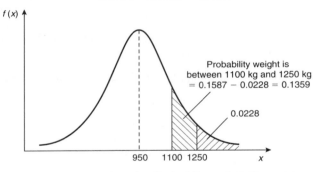

Figure 7.23   Calculations for Worked Example 7.17 part (c).

(d) The calculation that the weight is between 800 kg and 1300 kg relies on the relationship (see Figure 7.24):

$$P(\text{between } 800\,\text{kg and } 1300\,\text{kg})$$
$$= 1 - P(\text{less than } 800\,\text{kg}) - P(\text{greater than } 1300\,\text{kg})$$

For weight below 800 kg:

$$Z = (800 - 950)/150 = -1 \quad \text{probability} = 0.1587$$

For weight above 1300 kg:

$$Z = (1300 - 950)/150 = 2.33 \quad \text{probability} = 0.0099$$

So the probability that the weight is between these two is

$$1 - 0.1587 - 0.0099 = 0.8314$$

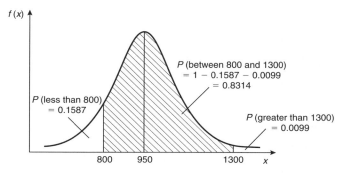

Figure 7.24 Calculations for Worked Example 7.17 part (d).

We can use a statistical package to check these results. Figure 7.25 shows typical results for parts (a) and (c). For part (a) MINITAB has calculated the cumulative probability of weight up to 1250 kg as 0.9772, so the probability that a horse weighs less than this is $1 - 0.9772 = 0.0228$. For part (c) it calculated the cumulative probabilities of weights up to 1250 kg and 1100 kg, and subtracting these gives the result of 0.1359. We could check the other results in the same way, but you can see that for small problems it is often easier to use normal tables.

```
MTB    >       # solutions to worked example 7.17
MTB    >       # solution to part (a)
MTB    >       cdf 1250;
SUBC   >       normal mu=950,sigma=150.
   1.25E + 03  0.9772
MTB    >       # solution to part (c)
MTB    >       set c1
DATA   >       1250,1100
DATA   >       end
MTB    >       cdf values in c1 put results in c2;
SUBC   >       normal mu=950, sigma=150.
MTB    >       let k1=c2(1)-c2(2)
MTB    >       print k1
K1        0.135905

MTB    >       stop
```

Figure 7.25 Using a statistical package to check results.

WORKED EXAMPLE 7.18

We could not use a Poisson distribution for the example of motor insurance described earlier, where policies are only available to drivers with low risk of accidents. One hundred drivers holding the policy would expect an average of 0.2 accidents each a year. Use a normal distribution to find the probability that less than 15 drivers will have accidents in a year. How could you take into account the integer number of accidents?

Solution

This is a binomial process with $n = 100$ and $p = 0.2$, so the mean $= n*p = 100*0.2 = 20$. The standard deviation of a binomial distribution is $\sqrt{n*p*q} = \sqrt{100*0.2*0.8} = \sqrt{16} = 4$. To find the probability of less than 15 drivers having an accident

$$Z = (15 - 20)/4 = -1.25 \quad \text{so probability} = 0.1056$$

Because the number of accidents is discrete we can use a 'continuity correction'. We are looking for the probability of less than 15 accidents but it is clearly impossible to have **between** 14 and 15 accidents. So we can add an allowance to interpret 'less than 15' as 'less than 14.5' (see Figure 7.26).

This continuity correction gives:

$$Z = (14.5 - 20)/4 = -1.375 \quad \text{and probability} = 0.0846$$

If the question had asked for '15 or less' accidents, we could have used the continuity correction to interpret this as 'less than 15.5'. Then:

$$Z = (15.5 - 20)/4 = -1.125 \quad \text{and probability} = 0.1303$$

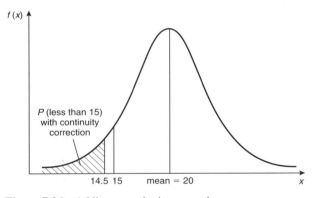

Figure 7.26 Adding a continuity correction.

WORKED EXAMPLE 7.19

On average a supermarket sells 500 pints of milk a day with a standard deviation of 50 pints.

(a) If the supermarket has 600 pints in stock at the beginning of a day, what is the probability that it will run out of milk?

(b) What is the probability that demand is between 450 and 600 pints in a day?

(c) How many pints should the supermarket stock if it wants the probability of running out to be 0.05?

(d) How many should it stock if it wants the probability of running out to be 0.01?

Solution

(a) To find the probability that demand is more than 600 pints we have:

$$Z = (600 - 500)/50 = 2.0 \quad \text{probability} = 0.0228$$

Although pints of milk are really discrete, the numbers here are so large that a continuity correction will make almost no difference (see Figure 7.27).

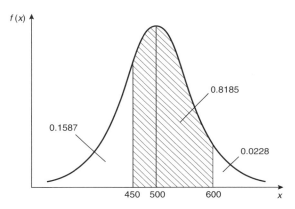

Figure 7.27 Probabilities for Worked Example 7.19.

(b) The probability of demand greater than 600 is 0.0228. For demand less than 450 pints

$$Z = (450 - 500)/50 = -1.0 \quad \text{probability} = 0.1587$$

So the probability of demand between 450 and 600 is:

$$1 - 0.0228 - 0.1587 = 0.8185$$

(c) Here we know the probability and want to see how far this is from the mean. So we look up the probability $= 0.05$ in the body of the normal tables, and this is midway between 1.64 and 1.65. So we can take $Z = 1.645$. The point we are interested in is 1.645 standard deviations from the mean, or $1.645 * 50 = 82.25$ pints from the mean. So the supermarket needs $500 + 83 = 583$ pints at the beginning of the day (rounding up to make sure the probability of stock-outs is less than 0.05).

(d) For probability 0.01, $Z = 2.33$. This is $2.33 * 50 = 116.5$ pints from the mean. So the supermarket needs $500 + 117 = 617$ pints at the beginning of the day (shown in Figure 7.28).

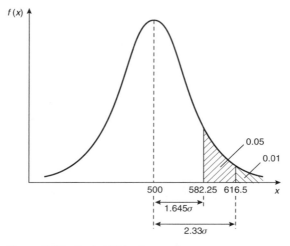

Figure 7.28   Probabilities for stock-outs.

IN SUMMARY

Large numbers of observations often follow a normal distribution. This is a continuous distribution, which gives the probability that observations are within specified ranges. These probabilities can easily be found from standard tables.

Self-assessment questions

7.25   When can you use a normal distribution?

7.26   What is the most obvious difference between a normal distribution and a binomial or Poisson distribution?

7.27   What two factors affect the location and shape of a normal distribution?

7.28   If the mean of a set of observations is 100 and the standard deviation is 10, what proportion of observations will be between 90 and 110?

7.29   What is a 'continuity correction' for discrete data?

CHAPTER REVIEW

This chapter gave an overview of some important statistical ideas. In particular it:

- discussed the need for data reduction
- described how information can be summarized in diagrams or figures
- described measures for averages and spread
- discussed the idea of probabilities
- calculated probabilities for independent events
- described Bayes' theorem for conditional probabilities
- developed probability distributions to describe relative frequencies
- showed how to use the binomial distribution
- described the Poisson distribution
- described the normal distribution

KEY TERMS

Bayes' theorem	mutually exclusive events
binomial distribution	normal distribution
conditional probabilities	Poisson distribution
data reduction	probabilities
independent events	probability distribution
mean	range
median	standard deviation
mode	variance

Case study

The Gamblers' Press

The Gamblers' Press is a weekly paper that publishes information for gamblers. It has detailed sections on horse racing, greyhound racing, football, and other major sporting events. It also runs regular features on card games, casinos and any topic that gamblers may find interesting.

The Gamblers' Press was founded in 1897 and now has a regular circulation of around 50 000 copies. It is a highly respected paper and has a strict policy of only giving factual information. It never gives tips or advice.

Last year *The Gamblers' Press* decided to run a special feature on misleading or dishonest practices. This idea was suggested when four unconnected reports were passed to the editors.

The first of these reports concerned an 'infallible' way of winning at roulette. Customers were charged £250 for the details of the method. This involved recording all the numbers that won during an evening. Then the customers were advised to bet on two sets of numbers:

- those that had come up more often, because the wheel might be biased in their favour
- those that had come up least often, because the laws of probability say that numbers which appear less often on one night, must appear more often on another night

The second report showed that a number of illegal chain letters were circulating in the South East. These letters contained a list of eight names. Individuals were asked to send a pound to the name at the top of the list. Then they should delete the name at the top, insert their own name at the bottom, and send a copy of the letter to eight of their friends. As each name moved to the top of the list they would get money from people who joined the chain later. The advertising that came with these letters guaranteed to make respondents millionaires, with frequent claims of 'you cannot lose!!!'. It also said that people not responding would be letting down their friends and would inevitably be plagued by bad luck.

The third report was from 'a horse racing consultant'. This person sent a letter saying which horse would win a race the following week. A week later he sent a second letter saying that the chosen horse had won, and giving another tip for the following week. This was repeated for a third week. Then after three wins the consultant said he would send the name of another horse which was guaranteed to win next week, but this time there would be a cost of £1000. This seemed a reasonable price as the horse was certain to win, and bets of any size could be placed. Unfortunately, this scheme had a drawback. *The Gamblers' Press* thought that the consultant sent out about 10 000 of the original letters, and randomly tipped each horse in a five-horse race. He only sent the second letter to those people who had been given the winning horse. The next two letters followed the same pattern, with follow-up letters only sent to those who had been given the winning horse.

The fourth report concerned a North American lottery. For this people chose six numbers in the range 00 to 99, and bought a lottery ticket for $1 containing these numbers. At the end of a week a computer would randomly generate a set of six numbers. Anyone with the same six numbers would win the major prize (typically around five million dollars), and people with four or five matching numbers would win smaller prizes. A magazine reported a way of dramatically increasing the chances of winning. This suggested taking your eight favourite numbers and then betting on all possible combinations of six numbers from these eight. The advertisement explained the benefit of this by saying: 'Suppose there is a chance of one in a million of winning the first prize. If one of your lucky numbers is chosen by the computer, you will have this number in over a hundred entries, so your chances of winning are raised by 100 to only one in 10 000'.

Question

The Gamblers' Press knew of many schemes like these four, and they decided to write a major article on them. Your job is to write this article. You should start by explaining why the four schemes mentioned do not work, and then give other examples of bogus advice for gamblers.

Problems

7.1 How can you represent the following data in diagrams?

14 21 35 24 18 40 18 22 15 31 40 33 21 29 42 22 32 17 23 19
16 19 23 15 23 17 22 30 24 20 17 20 28 41 27 27 28 22 25 25
24 18 38 20 25 21 25 23 17 19 22 34 35 22 24 16 33 19 28 21
23 35 23 37 26 30 19 24 25 23 23 18 20 21 26 20 26 18 31 20
38 16 20 24 23 26 22 15 27 22 39 19 36 29 17 26 32 23 22 16
24 37 23 25 19 23 24 23 28 24 16 14 21 24 29 21 27 31 25 23

Calculate the mean, median and mode for the data. What are the range, variance and standard deviation?

7.2 There are five equally likely outcomes to a trial, A, B, C, D and E. What is the probability of C occurring? What is the probability of A or B or C occurring? What is the probability that neither A nor B occur?

7.3 Four mutually exclusive, independent events A, B, C and D have probabilities of 0.1, 0.2, 0.3 and 0.4 respectively. What are the probabilities of:

- A and B occurring?
- A or B?
- neither A nor B?
- A and B and C
- A or B or C
- none of A, B or C

7.4 If $P(a) = 0.4$ and $P(b/a) = 0.3$, what is $P(a$ AND $b)$? If $P(b) = 0.6$ what is $P(a/b)$?

7.5 The probabilities of two events X and Y are 0.4 and 0.6 respectively. The conditional probabilities of three other events A, B and C occurring, given that X or Y has already occurred, are given in the following table:

	A	B	C
X	0.2	0.5	0.3
Y	0.6	0.1	0.3

What are the conditional probabilities of X and Y occurring given that A, B or C has already occurred?

7.6 A manufacturer uses three suppliers for a component. X supplies 35% of the component, Y supplies 25% and Z supplies the rest. The quality of each component is described as 'good', 'acceptable' or 'poor', with the proportions from each supplier given below.

	Good	Acceptable	Poor
X	0.2	0.7	0.1
Y	0.3	0.65	0.05
Y	0.1	0.8	0.1

What information can you find using Bayes' theorem on these figures? Draw probability trees for the problem.

7.7 Describe the probability distribution of the following set of observations:

10 14 13 15 16 12 14 15 11 13 17 15 16 14 12 13 11 15 15 14
12 16 14 13 13 14 13 12 14 15 16 14 11 14 12 15 14 16 13 14

7.8 A company calculates its likely profit for next year with the following probabilities:

Profit (£)	−100 000	−50 000	0	50 000	100 000	150 000
Probability	0.05	0.15	0.3	0.3	0.15	0.05

What is the probability the company will make a profit next year? What is the probability the profit will be at least £100 000?

7.9 A binomial process has a probability of success of 0.15. If eight trials are run, what is the mean number of successes and the standard deviation? What is the probability of (a) exactly two successes in the eight trials, (b) seven successes, (c) at least six successes?

7.10 In a town, 60% of families are known to drive British cars. If a sample of 10 families is chosen, what is the probability that at least eight will drive British cars? If a sample of 1000 families is chosen, what is the probability that at least 800 will drive British cars?

7.11 An oil company is drilling some exploratory wells on the mainland of Scotland. The results are described as either a 'dry well' or a 'producer well'. Past experience suggests that 10% of such exploratory wells can be classified as producer wells. If 12 wells are drilled, what is the probability that all 12 wells will be producer wells? What is the probability that all 12 wells will be dry wells? What is the probability that exactly 1 well will be a producer? What is the probability that at least 3 wells will be producers?

7.12 One hundred trials are run for a Poisson process. If the probability of a success is 0.02, what is the mean number of successes and the standard deviation? What is the probability of: (a) exactly 2 successes, (b) exactly seven successes, (c) at least six successes?

7.13 A machine makes a product, with 5% of units having faults. If a sample of 20 units is taken, what is the probability at least 1 is defective? If a sample of 200 units is taken, what is the probability at least 10 are defective?

7.14 Some observations follow a normal distribution with mean 40 and standard deviation 4. What proportion of observations have values: (a) greater than 46, (b) less than 34, (c) between 34 and 46, (d) between 30 and 44, (e) between 43 and 47?

7.15 A large number of observations are found to have a mean of 120 and variance of 100. What proportion of observations is: (a) below 100, (b) above 130, (c) between 100 and 130, (d) between 130 and 140, (e) between 115 and 135?

7.16 A fast-food restaurant finds the number of meals it serves in a week is normally distributed with a mean of 6000 and a standard deviation of 600. What is the probability that in a given week the number of meals served will be less than 5000? What is the probability that more than 7500 will be served? What is the probability that between 5500 and 6500 will be served? There is a 90% chance that the number of meals served in a week will exceed what value?

Discussion questions

7.1 Probabilities do not really help with decision-making. Managers need to know with certainty what is going to happen, and probabilities do not give this information. Do you think this is true?

7.2 Last year Jim Petterson bought a company whose accountants claimed it 'had a 99% chance of winning a contract and making £100 000 profit next year'. In fact the company did not win the contract and made a loss of £35 000. Jim approached the accountants for an explanation. What do you think they would say?

7.3 It is difficult to find events that are really independent. It is safer to use conditional probabilities. Do you think this is true?

7.4 Two difficulties with statistical analyses are getting enough reliable data and persuading managers that the results are valid. What can be done to overcome these difficulties?

7.5 People often guess, or use 'subjective' probabilities. Then they use these figures in misleading descriptions and wrong calculations. The use of statistics is so poor that you cannot trust any results. What can you do about this?

Statistical sampling and testing

CHAPTER OUTLINE

The last chapter introduced the ideas of statistics. This chapter describes some ways of using statistics. It talks about reliability, sampling and hypothesis testing. After reading the chapter you should be able to:

- calculate the reliability of a system of components
- understand the need for planned maintenance
- discuss the use of samples
- use sampling distributions
- understand the approach of hypothesis testing
- test hypotheses about population values found from samples

| 8.1 | Reliability and replacement

8.1.1 Reliability of equipment

When you buy a car, computer, or any other piece of equipment, you want it to be as reliable as possible. You do not want the inconvenience of a breakdown, or the expense of a repair. Organizations spend a lot of money on equipment, and they also want it to be reliable. If the production line in a factory breaks down there can be very high costs. But there are even more important problems with reliability in, for example, heart pacemakers, aeroplane parts, nuclear power stations, helicopter rotors and space capsules.

Unfortunately, all equipment can fail. The failures are generally random and occur at inconvenient times – usually when the equipment is actually working. By studying reliability, we want to increase the probability that equipment will continue to work normally.

> **Reliability** is the probability that a piece of equipment continues to work normally during a specified period.

If we define:

R = the reliability of a piece of equipment

= the probability that the equipment continues to work normally during a specified period

F = the probability the equipment will fail within the period

then: $R + F = 1$

We can use these definitions, together with the probability distributions described in the last chapter, to look at some problems with reliability.

WORKED EXAMPLE 8.1

A railway goods yard has 10 elderly shunting engines. These are used on weekdays, and at weekends a maintenance crew does routine maintenance and repairs. Over the past 12 weeks there have been 12 occasions when an engine has broken down and had to stop working. The goods yard needs at least 8 engines working in a week.

(a) What is the reliability of the engines measured on a weekly basis?

(b) What is the probability that at least 8 engines will continue to work throughout a week?

Solution

(a) The probability that an engine breaks down during a week is:

$$F = \text{number of breakdowns} / \text{number of operating weeks}$$
$$= 12/12 * 10 = 0.1$$

Then the reliability is:

$$R = 1 - F = 1 - 0.1 = 0.9$$

(b) This is a binomial process. An engine continuing to work is a 'success' which has a probability of 0.9, and an engine breaking down is a 'failure' which has a probability of 0.1. The probability that at least 8 engines work throughout a week is:

$$P(\geq 8 \text{ work}) = P(8 \text{ work}) + P(9 \text{ work}) + P(10 \text{ work})$$

We can find these probabilities from tables, statistical packages, or by calculating:

$$P(r) = p^r * q^{n-r} * {}^nC_r$$

It is easy to find that:

$$P(8) = (0.9^8 * 0.1^2 * 10!) / (8! * 2!) = 0.1937$$
$$P(9) = (0.9^9 * 0.1^1 * 10!) / (9! * 1!) = 0.3874$$
$$P(10) = (0.9^{10} * 0.1^0 * 10!) / (10! * 0!) = 0.3487$$

So the probability that at least 8 engines will continue working is:

$$0.1937 + 0.3874 + 0.3487 = 0.9298$$

WORKED EXAMPLE 8.2

In the last 100 working days a dragline in an opencast coal mine has had 160 faults.

(a) What is the expected distribution of days with each number of faults?

(b) It takes an average of 4 hours and costs £200 in parts to make each repair. How would you estimate the annual maintenance cost of the excavator?

Solution

(a) Random events, such as these faults, follow a Poisson distribution. The mean number of faults in a working day is $160/100 = 1.6$. We can find the probabilities of r faults in a day from Poisson tables, a statistical package or by calculating:

$$P(r) = e^{-\mu} * \mu^r / r!$$

Multiplying these probabilities by 365 gives the expected number of days in a year with each number of breakdowns. Then multiplying the number of days by the number of faults in each day gives the total number of faults (with some allowance for rounding errors).

Number of faults	Probability	Number of days in year with this number	Total number of faults
0	0.2019	73.69	0.00
1	0.3230	117.90	117.90
2	0.2584	94.32	188.64
3	0.1378	50.30	150.90
4	0.0551	20.11	80.44
5	0.0176	6.42	32.10
6	0.0047	1.72	10.32
7	0.0011	0.40	2.80
8	0.0002	0.07	0.56
9	0.0000	0.00	0.00
Totals	0.9998	364.93	583.66

(b) The mean number of breakdowns in a year is $1.6 * 365 = 584$, which you can check from the last column of the table above. Each of these takes 4 hours, to give a total of 2336 hours a year. This is around 1.5 full-time employees. In addition there are material costs of $£200 * 584 = £116\,800$.

WORKED EXAMPLE 8.3

A small steam turbine has three sets of blades. Each of these has a working life which is normally distributed with mean 15 000 hours and standard deviation 3000 hours. If one set of blades fails, they must all be replaced.

(a) How often should the blades be replaced to give a reliability of more than 90%?

(b) What is the annual cost of maintaining the turbine if it is run for 7000 hours a year and new blades for the turbine cost £10 000?

(c) What is the cost of improving the reliability of the turbine to 99%?

Solution

(a) If R is the probability that one set of blades does not fail between replacements, the probability that none of the three sets of blades fails is R^3. We want this reliability to be 90%, so:

$$R^3 = 0.9 \quad \text{or} \quad R = 0.9655$$

Normal tables in Appendix D show that this corresponds to $Z = 1.82$ standard deviations from the mean. Then you can see from Figure 8.1 that the age of replacement, x, comes from:

$$Z = (\mu - x)/\sigma \quad \text{or} \quad 1.82 = (15\,000 - x)/3000$$

to give $\quad x = 9540$ hours.

(b) If the blades are replaced after 9540 hours, the number of replacements a year is $7000/9540 = 0.7338$. Each of these costs £10 000 so the maintenance cost is £7338 a year. We have to add to this the cost of repairing the turbine on the 10% of occasions when it fails while working.

(c) Raising the reliability to 99% has $R^3 = 0.99$, or $R = 0.9967$. This corresponds to $Z = 2.72$ and the time for replacement, x, comes from:

$$Z = (\mu - x)/\sigma \quad \text{or} \quad 2.72 = (15\,000 - x)/3000$$

or $\quad x = 6840$ hours.

Then blades are replaced $7000/6840 = 1.0234$ times a year, so the annual maintenance cost goes up to £10 234. But there will now be fewer failures while the turbine is working.

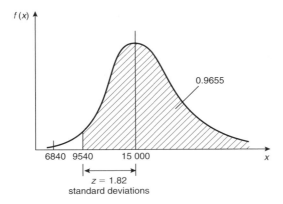

Figure 8.1 Distribution of working life of turbine blades (Worked Example 8.3).

IN SUMMARY

The reliability of equipment measures the probability that it will continue to work normally during a specified period. We can use standard probability distributions to do a number of related calculations.

8.1.2 Reliability of components

We can often view a piece of equipment as a system of connected components. To increase the reliability of the equipment, we can add some backup components. These backups are not usually used, but when a normal component fails they start working and allow the equipment to continue. Examples of such backups are the spare wheel in a car, an emergency generator and a reserve fuel tank.

The reliability of a system of components depends on both the reliability of individual components, and on the way the components are arranged. If we put two components in parallel, we increase reliability – assuming that the second component can start to work when the first component fails. Adding more components in parallel increases reliability, as the system only fails if **all** the individual components fail.

Suppose we have two identical components in parallel, with the reliability of each component R, as shown in Figure 8.2. The probability that both components fail is $F^2 = (1 - R)^2$. The reliability of the system, which is the probability that at least one of the components is working, is $1 - (1 - R)^2$. If we have n identical components in parallel, the probability that they all fail is $F^n = (1 - R)^n$. Then the reliability of the system is $1 - (1 - R)^n$. It follows that any system of parallel components is more reliable than the individual components.

Putting components in series reduces the reliability of the system. This is because a system of components in series only works if **all** the separate components are working. Suppose we have two components in series, as shown in Figure 8.3. If the reliability of each is R, the reliability of the two is the probability that both are working, which is R^2. If there are n components in series their

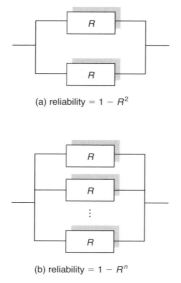

(a) reliability $= 1 - R^2$

(b) reliability $= 1 - R^n$

Figure 8.2   Reliability of components in parallel.

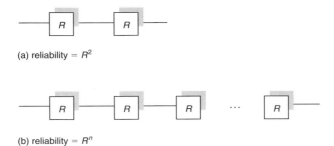

(a) reliability $= R^2$

(b) reliability $= R^n$

Figure 8.3 Reliability of components in series.

reliability is R^n. So a system of components in series is less reliable than the individual components.

To find the reliability of complex systems of components, we have to reduce them to simpler forms.

WORKED EXAMPLE 8.4

Six pieces of equipment work as the components of a system shown in Figure 8.4, where the figures on each component show their reliability. What is the overall reliability of the system?

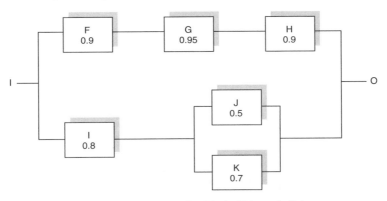

Figure 8.4 System of components for Worked Example 8.4.

Solution

To solve this problem we have to divide the system into smaller parts. To start with, we can take components J and K which are in parallel. For this part of the system to fail, both J and K must fail. The probability of this, with $R_i = 1 - F_i$ as the reliability of component i, is:

$$F = F_J * F_K = (1 - R_J) * (1 - R_K) = (1 - 0.5) * (1 - 0.7) = 0.15$$

So the reliability of this part of the system is $1 - 0.15 = 0.85$.

Now we can take the three components F, G and H which are in series. The reliability of this part of the system is:

$$R = R_F * R_G * R_H = 0.9 * 0.95 * 0.9 = 0.77$$

We have now simplified the system to:

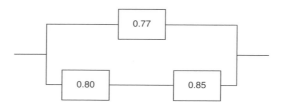

Taking the bottom two elements, which are in series, the reliability is the probability that they both continue to work. This is $0.8 * 0.85 = 0.68$. Now we have simplified the system to:

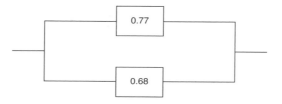

The probability that these two components in parallel both fail is $(1 - 0.77) * (1 - 0.68) = 0.07$. So the overall reliability of the system is $1 - 0.07 = 0.93$.

WORKED EXAMPLE 8.5

Figure 8.5 shows the layout of a shop floor in Kaiser Winter Garments. This has three parallel production lines A, B and C, whose outputs are 10 000, 12 000 and 20 000 units a week respectively. The diagram shows the reliability of each machine, and if a line fails during the week all its production during the week is lost.

(a) Find the reliability of each line.

(b) Find the possible outputs from the process and the probability of each.

(c) What is the expected output of the process?

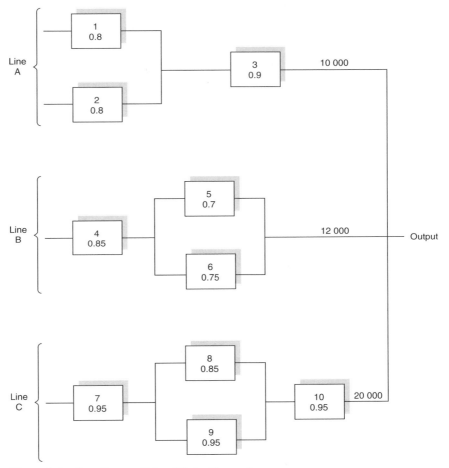

Figure 8.5 Shop floor at Kaiser Winter Garments.

Solution

(a) The first step is to find the reliability of each line.

With R_i as the probability that machine i continues to work during a week, the reliability of line A is:

$$R_A = [1 - (1 - R_1) * (1 - R_2)] * R_3 = [1 - (0.2 * 0.2)] * 0.9 = 0.864$$

The reliability of line B is:

$$R_B = R_4 * [1 - (1 - R_5) * (1 - R_6)] = 0.85 * [1 - (0.3 * 0.25)] = 0.786$$

The reliability of line C is:

$$R_C = R_7 * [1 - (1 - R_8) * (1 - R_9)] * R_{10}$$
$$= 0.95 * [1 - (0.15 * 0.1)] * 0.95 = 0.889$$

(b) We can find the total output by taking various combinations of lines failing. If lines A and B fail while line C continues to work, the output will be 20 000. This has a probability of:

$$(1 - R_A) * (1 - R_B) * R_C = 0.136 * 0.214 * 0.889 = 0.026$$

The other possible outputs can be calculated as shown in the following table:

Output	Probability	
0	$(1 - R_A) * (1 - R_B) * (1 - R_C)$	$= 0.003$
10 000	$R_A * (1 - R_B) * (1 - R_C)$	$= 0.021$
12 000	$(1 - R_A) * R_B * (1 - R_C)$	$= 0.012$
20 000	$(1 - R_A) * (1 - R_B) * R_C$	$= 0.026$
22 000	$R_A * R_B * (1 - R_C)$	$= 0.075$
30 000	$R_A * (1 - R_B) * R_C$	$= 0.164$
32 000	$(1 - R_A) * R_B * R_C$	$= 0.095$
42 000	$R_A * R_B * R_C$	$= 0.604$

(c) The expected output is the sum of (probability * output), so:

$$\text{expected output} = (0 * 0.003) + (10\,000 * 0.021) + (12\,000 * 0.012) + \dots \text{ etc.}$$
$$= 35\,852$$

Case example

Maintenance of cranes

Maintenance of equipment can have a major effect on its reliability – and the cost of operations. An organization that saves money on maintenance can have high bills for breakdowns and disruptions. Each organization can set the best level of maintenance for its own operations, but sometimes there are agreed standards. Cranes, for example, have international agreements for maintenance.

ISO TC 96/SC 5 is the international standard for the maintenance of cranes. Case studies at paper mills in Canada, Finland, Sweden and America show that this standard can reduce annual maintenance costs by 33 – 64%, the number of defects by 46 – 60% and production failures by 33 – 97%.

Similar studies in steel mills in Sweden, Canada and America reduced annual maintenance costs by 28 – 56%, the number of defects by 50 – 83% and the number of production failures by 63 – 95%.

The maintenance programmes also provide wider benefits of:

- giving operators safer working conditions
- saving owners money with fewer repairs, production failures, injuries, insurance, etc.
- giving manufacturers higher quality

IN SUMMARY

The reliability of a system of components depends on both the reliability of individual components and their layout.

- **Putting components in parallel increases the reliability of the system.**
- **Putting components in series decreases the reliability of the system.**

Self-assessment questions

8.1 What is 'reliability'?

8.2 If a number of components are put in parallel, is the reliability of the system increased or decreased?

8.3 Do you think it likely that the maintenance costs for a machine will decrease over time?

8.1.3 Replacement of items that deteriorate over time

In the last section we assumed that components either fail or continue to work normally. But the performance of a lot of equipment declines with age. A machine, for example, might make poorer quality product or cost more to run as it gets older. Then we want to find the best age to replace the machine. The easiest way of tackling such problems is to compare a number of alternatives and find the cheapest.

WORKED EXAMPLE 8.6

An office block has 100 identical smoke detectors. A signal light shows when a detector stops working and a maintenance team is sent to replace it at an average cost of £100. The probability that a detector is working properly at the end of a year declines over time as shown in the following table:

Age (years)	0	1	2	3	4
Probability of detector working	1.0	0.8	0.4	0.1	0.0

The company is now considering a replacement policy where all 100 detectors are replaced in a block at regular intervals. This would lower the costs of each replacement to £50. There would be no more special calls to replace failed units, but an annual inspection would replace any units that fail between block replacements at a cost of £100. How often should the company replace the detectors?

Solution

The table shows the probability that detectors continue to work at various ages. We can redraw this as a table of probabilities that detectors fail in any year:

Year	0	1	2	3	4
Probability of working at year end	1.0	0.8	0.4	0.1	0.0
Probability of failing in year		0.2	0.4	0.3	0.1

If the company continues its current ad hoc replacement of detectors, 20% fail within one year, 40% within two years, 30% within three years and the remaining 10% within four years. Assuming detectors fail, on average, halfway through the year, the expected life is:

$$0.2*0.5 + 0.4*1.5 + 0.3*2.5 + 0.1*3.5 = 1.8 \text{ years}$$

As there are 100 detectors the average number of replacements each year is $100/1.8 = 55.56$. Each of these costs £100 so the average annual cost is £5556.

Using a block replacement, the number to be replaced each year can be shown in a kind of probability tree, which is called a **failure tree**. The failure tree for this example is given in Figure 8.6.

In this diagram the horizontal lines show the number of units that are still working, and the diagonal lines show the numbers failing in the year. With 100 units starting, 20 will fail within the first year, 20% of these replacements will fail within the second year and so on. The number of detectors failing or working in any year must obviously add up to 100, and we can find the number of failures in any year by adding the numbers on all sloping lines.

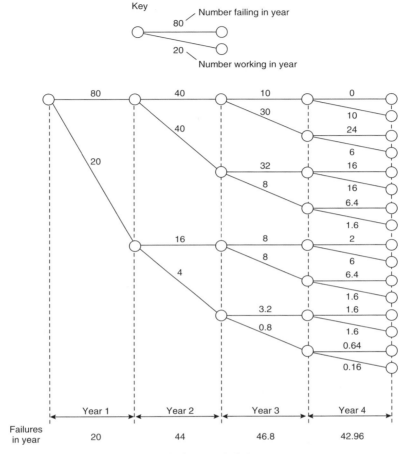

Figure 8.6 Failure tree for Worked Example 8.6.

If a block replacement is done every year there are no annual inspections. If the block replacement is done every 2 years, 20 detectors are replaced at the intermediate annual inspection. If the block replacement is done every 3 years, 20 detectors are replaced at the first annual inspection and 44 at the second. These figures are summarized in the following table:

Block replacement at end of year	Cost of block replacement	Cost of annual inspections	Total cost	Average cost per year
1	5000	0	5000	5000
2	5000	2000	7000	3500 **
3	5000	6400	11400	3800
4	5000	11080	16080	4020

You can see that the best policy is to replace the detectors in a block every 2 years, with an annual inspection at the end of alternate years to replace the expected 20 defective units. This has a cost of £3500 a year compared with £5556 for the current arrangements. If the company did a block replacement less frequently than every 4 years, the costs would continue to rise – so we need not draw any more of the table.

WORKED EXAMPLE 8.7

A grinder is set to finish a cylindrical shaft to a size of 10.00 cm. Any shaft outside the range 9.99 cm to 10.01 cm is rejected, at a cost of £10. When the grinder is set to a size μ it actually produces shafts that are normally distributed with mean μ and standard deviation 0.004 cm. The grinder produces 1000 units a shift but at the end of the shift its diameter has been reduced by an average of 0.001 cm. Any subsequent production has its mean size increased by this amount, but the standard deviation does not change. A new grinding wheel costs £800, and fitting costs £200. How often should the grinding wheel be replaced?

Solution

The cost of wear of the grinding wheel is in two parts: the direct cost of replacement and the cost of units rejected. A wheel should be replaced at the age that minimizes the total cost per good unit produced. The calculations for this are shown in the following table. The probability of rejection because shafts are outside the acceptable range come from normal tables.

No. of shifts since last replacement	Mean size of production	Prob. of rejection		Expected no. rejects per shift
		too large	too small	
0	10.000	0.0062	0.0062	12.4
1	10.001	0.0122	0.0030	15.2
2	10.002	0.0228	0.0013	24.1
3	10.003	0.0401	0.0006	40.7
4	10.004	0.0668	0.0002	67.0

The expected cost of rejects is added to the cost of replacing the wheel and dividing this total by the number of good units produced gives a cost per unit. With replacement every shift the cost of rejects (12.4 * 10) is added to the cost of a new wheel (800 + 200) and divided by the number of good units (1000 − 12.4) to give a cost of 1.14 per unit produced. The alternatives are summarized in the following table.

Replace after shift	Average cost of replacement per unit produced	Average cost of rejects per unit produced	Total cost per unit produced
1	1.01	0.13	1.14
2	0.51	0.14	0.65
3	0.34	0.18	0.52
4	0.26	0.24	0.50*
5	0.21	0.33	0.54

The best policy is to replace the grinding wheel every four shifts, with a total maintenance cost of £0.50 per good unit produced.

Case example

Trident submarines

For many years Britain had a fleet of nuclear submarines which carried Polaris missiles. By the 1980s these were getting old and the government decided to replace them with larger submarines that carried Trident missiles. These were introduced during the 1990s.

An important question was, how many of the new submarines should the government buy? Each new submarine had considerably more power than the older ones, so the navy would need fewer of them. At the same time, there had been significant political changes, particularly in Eastern Europe, which reduced the need for massive defence expenditure. Most countries were significantly reducing their arms budgets.

The government chose a base of four Trident submarines. But at any time only one of these would be on active duty. A second would be getting ready to go on active duty, a third would be in dock for a refit (equivalent to a minor service) and the fourth would be in dock for an overhaul (equivalent to a major service).

This means that one active Trident submarine can provide Britain's perceived capacity for nuclear defence. Making sure this capacity is always available actually takes four submarines, as routine maintenance puts three of the fleet out of action at any time. Initial estimates for the cost of this fleet were £10 billion.

| *IN SUMMARY* |

The performance of almost everything deteriorates with age. We can build models which include an increasing probability of failure or increasing cost with age. The simplest models compare the costs of operating over specified periods.

Self-assessment questions

8.4   How might the performance of equipment deteriorate over time?

8.5   It is always cheaper to use regular block replacement of units that fail, such as light bulbs. Do you think this is true?

8.2 Sampling

8.2.1 Introduction

All models need reliable data, and *sampling* can reduce the effort needed to collect this information.

> The aim of **sampling** is to get reliable data by looking at a few observations rather than every possible observation.

Suppose you want to measure the quality of products leaving a factory. You might reduce costs, and still get a reliable view of the overall quality, by sampling 10% of the output. This approach is used in opinion polls when a political party wants to know how many votes it can expect at an election. There are two ways of finding this:

- it can ask every person eligible to vote in the constituency what their intentions are (this is a *census*)

- it can take a sample of eligible people, ask them their intentions and use these to estimate the voting intentions of the population as a whole.

The second approach has a number of advantages:

- **cost and time.** Data is expensive to collect, so the more people who are surveyed the more it costs. Using a sample will reduce the cost and time needed to get results.

- **reliability.** Even if an entire population of people is surveyed – for a census – it is unlikely that they will all answer the questions, or that they will tell the truth, or that their views will stay the same over time. Even a complete survey can be unreliable, so a sample can give results that are just as good with far less effort.

- **point.** Sometimes there would be no point in testing all of a population. It would, for example, be senseless to find the mean life of light bulbs made in a factory by testing the entire output until they failed. A sample is the only realistic way of getting results.

- **feasibility.** There may be an infinite number of tests to perform. A new drug may claim to cure some disease. But to test the drug on everybody who might take it, in all possible circumstances, would give a virtually infinite number of combinations.

Despite these obvious advantages, sampling has a number of drawbacks. Perhaps the most important is the need to find a reliable sample that fairly represents the whole population. Notice that we are using the term ***population*** to refer to all things that could be examined rather than its more general use for populations of people.

> A **population** is all the things that could be tested.
>
> A **sample** is the things that actually are tested.

The purpose of sampling is to take a sample of units from the population, measure the desired property (numbers, quality, opinions, weight, length, etc.) and use this to estimate the value of the property for the population as a whole. This process is called ***statistical inference***.

Statistical inference only works if the sample fairly represents the whole population. One way of ensuring this is to take samples at random. There are many ways of getting a ***random sample***, and a popular method uses random numbers. Suppose we are interested in the number of people travelling in each car on a particular stretch of road. The cars might be travelling too quickly to count the number of people in each, so we should choose a sample of cars. For this we can get a computer to generate a string of random digits – or use a set of random number tables. We might get a set of numbers like 836351847101, and then we could look at the eighth car, then the third after that, the sixth after that and so on. We will return to the idea of random sampling with simulation in Chapter 12.

With random sampling each member of the population has an equal probability of being chosen. This is an important point for statistical analysis. The models we are going to look at assume that a sample is randomly drawn from a population. If this is not true, then the analyses are no longer valid.

IN SUMMARY

Sampling is used to collect data. This allows us to find some characteristic of a population by looking at the characteristic in a sample.

8.2.2 Sampling distributions

If we have any population and take a series of samples from it, we would expect some variation between samples. Suppose that apples are delivered to a jam factory in boxes with a nominal weight of 10 kg. If we take a sample of 10 boxes we would expect the mean weight to be about 10 kg, but would not be surprised by small variations around this. Samples of 10 boxes taken over consecutive days might have mean weights of 10.2 kg, 9.8 kg, 10.9 kg, 10.1 kg, 9.7 kg, and so on. If we continued this sampling over some period we could build a distribution of sample means.

Any distribution that is found from samples is called a *sampling distribution*. When we build a distribution of sample means it is called the sampling distribution of the mean (see Figure 8.7).

Now we can relate the properties of the sampling distribution of the mean back to the original population. To do this we use a result of the central limit theorem. This says that if we take large random samples from a population, the sample means are normally distributed. This is true regardless of the distribution of the original population. Suppose we have:

- a population with size of N, mean of μ and standard deviation of σ
- a sample with size n, mean $\bar{x}$ and standard deviation s

The central limit theorem tells us:

- If a population is normally distributed, the sampling distribution of the mean is also normally distributed.
- If the sample size is large (say more than 30) the sampling distribution of the mean is normally distributed regardless of the population distribution.
- The sampling distribution of the mean has a mean μ and a standard deviation of $\sigma/\sqrt{n}$.

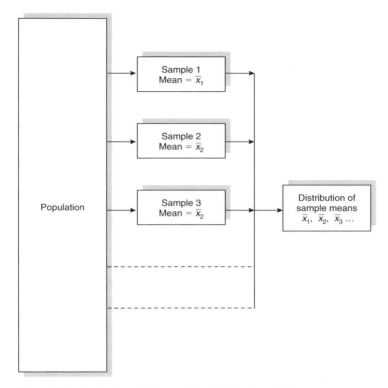

Figure 8.7   Derivation of the sampling distribution of the mean.

So with a reasonable-sized sample, the sampling distribution of the mean is normally distributed, with the same mean as the population and a smaller standard deviation. As the sample size increases, the standard deviation of the sampling distribution of the mean – which is often called the ***standard error*** – decreases (see Figure 8.8).

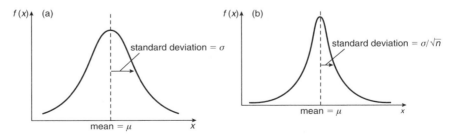

Figure 8.8   Comparing the distribution of (a) the population (b) sampling distribution of the mean.

One problem with talking about statistical inference is the clumsy descriptions we have to use, such as 'the mean of the sampling distribution of the mean'. The ideas behind these phrases are fairly simple, but you have to think clearly about what they describe. Remember the basic distribution is the distribution of sample means. This is the sampling distribution of the mean, which has its own mean and standard deviation.

WORKED EXAMPLE 8.8

A production line makes units with a mean length of 60 cm and standard deviation of 1 cm. What is the probability that a sample of 36 units taken from a large population has a mean length of less than 59.7 cm?

Solution

With samples of 36 units, the sampling distribution of the mean is:

- normally distributed
- has mean length $= \mu = 60$ cm
- has standard deviation $= \sigma/\sqrt{n} = 1/\sqrt{36} = 0.167$ cm

We can find the probability that one sample has a mean length less than 59.7 cm from the area in the tail of this sampling distribution of the mean. To find this area we need the number of standard deviations the point of interest (59.7) is away from the mean:

$$Z = (60 - 59.7)/0.167 = 1.80$$

Looking this up in normal tables gives the probability of 0.0359, so we would expect 3.59% of samples to have a mean length of less than 59.7 cm (as shown in Figure 8.9).

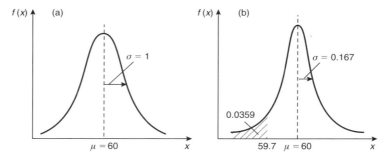

Figure 8.9 (a) Population distribution and (b) sampling distribution of the mean for Worked Example 8.8.

WORKED EXAMPLE 8.9

Soft drinks are put into cans which hold a nominal 200 ml, but the filling machine introduces a standard deviation of 10 ml. These cans are packed into cartons of 25 and exported to a market where the mean weight of a carton must be at least the amount specified by the manufacturer. To make sure this happens, the canner sets the machine to fill cans to 205 ml. What is the probability that a carton chosen at random will not pass the quantity test?

Solution

The mean volume per can is set at 205 ml and has a standard deviation of 10 ml. Taking a random sample of 25 cans gives a sampling distribution of the mean which has a mean of 205 ml and standard deviation of $10/\sqrt{25} = 2$ ml. The case will fail the quantity test if the average quantity per can is less than 200 ml. That is:

$$Z = (205 - 200)/2 = 2.5$$
$$\text{probability} = 0.0062$$

About six cases in a thousand will fail the test.

IN SUMMARY

If samples of size n are taken from a large population with mean μ and standard deviation σ:

- **the mean of sample means equals μ**
- **the standard deviation of the sample means equals $\sigma/\sqrt{n}$**
- **if the sample size is large the distribution of sample means is normal**

8.2.3 Confidence interval

The last two worked examples found the characteristics of a sample from the known characteristics of the population. But we are usually working the other way around, and want to find the characteristics of a population from a sample.

Suppose we take a sample of 100 parts and find that the mean length is 30 cm. How can we estimate the mean length of the population of parts? An obvious starting point is to suggest the sample gives a fair representation of the population, in which case we can estimate the population mean at 30 cm. This single value is a ***point estimate***. Unfortunately, we know that any point estimate comes from a sample and is unlikely to be exactly right. It should be close to the population mean, but is likely to contain some error.

To overcome the problem with point estimates, we can define a range which the population mean is likely to be within. This gives an ***interval estimate***. But for an interval estimate we need two measures:

- the width of the interval
- a level of confidence that the mean is within the interval

As the limits of the interval get narrower, we would expect the confidence that the mean is within the limits to get smaller. If we have a sample of 100 parts with mean length of 30 cm we might be 99% confident that the population mean is in the interval 20 to 40 cm; we might be 95% confident that the mean is between 25 and 35 cm and we might be 90% confident that the mean is between 27 and 33 cm. This kind of range is called a ***confidence interval***, and we will typically make a statement such as, 'We are 95% confident that the population mean lies within the range …'.

We can calculate the 95% confidence interval using the following argument. The sample mean, $\bar{x}$, is the best point estimate for the population mean, μ. But this point estimate is one observation from the sampling distribution of the mean. This sampling distribution is normal, so 95% of observations lie within 1.96 standard deviations of the mean. Now the standard deviation of the sampling distribution of the mean is $\sigma/\sqrt{n}$. So 95% of samples will be in the range:

$$\mu - 1.96 * \sigma/\sqrt{n} \quad \text{to} \quad \mu + 1.96 * \sigma/\sqrt{n}$$

In other words, the probability that the sample mean is within this range is:

$$P(\bar{x} - 1.96 * \sigma/\sqrt{n} \leq \bar{x} \geq \mu + 1.96 * \sigma/\sqrt{n}) = 0.95$$

But we can rearrange this to give the confidence interval for the population:

$$P(\bar{x} - 1.96 * \sigma/\sqrt{n} \leq \mu \geq \bar{x} + 1.96 * \sigma/\sqrt{n}) = 0.95$$

The 95% confidence interval for the population mean is:

$$\bar{x} - 1.96 * \sigma/\sqrt{n} \quad \text{to} \quad \bar{x} + 1.96 * \sigma/\sqrt{n}$$

Similarly the 90% confidence interval for the population mean is:

$$\bar{x} - 1.645 * \sigma/\sqrt{n} \quad \text{to} \quad \bar{x} + 1.645 * \sigma/\sqrt{n}$$

and the 99% confidence interval is:

$$\bar{x} - 2.58 * \sigma/\sqrt{n} \quad \text{to} \quad \bar{x} + 2.58 * \sigma/\sqrt{n}$$

WORKED EXAMPLE 8.10

A machine produces parts that have a standard deviation in length of 1.4 cm. A random sample of 100 parts has a mean length of 80 cm. What is the 95% confidence interval for the true mean length of the parts?

Solution

A sample of size 100 is taken from a population with a standard deviation of 1.4 cm. The mean length of parts is 80 cm. So the point estimate for the population mean is 80 cm (shown in Figure 8.10).

The sampling distribution of the mean has a mean of 80 cm and standard deviation of $\sigma/\sqrt{n} = 1.4/\sqrt{100} = 0.14$ cm. 95% of observations are within 1.96 standard deviations of the mean, so we expect 95% of observations to be within the range:

$$\bar{x} - 1.96 * \sigma/\sqrt{n} \quad \text{to} \quad \bar{x} + 1.96 * \sigma/\sqrt{n}$$
$$80 - 1.96 * 0.14 \quad \text{to} \quad 80 + 1.96 * 0.14$$

i.e. $\qquad$ 79.73 cm $\quad$ to $\quad$ 80.27 cm

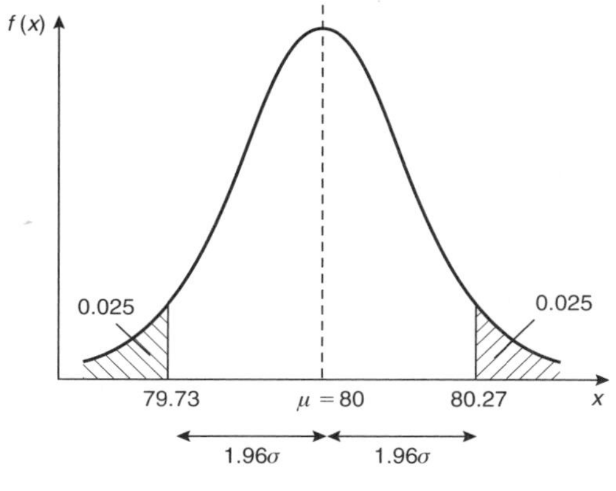

Figure 8.10 Confidence limits for Worked Example 8.10.

In this last worked example we estimated the population mean from a sample mean – but we assumed the standard deviation of the population was known. Although possible, it seems unlikely that we would know the standard deviation of a population, but not its mean. It is much more likely that we will only have information from the sample and will use this to estimate both the population mean and standard deviation.

The obvious estimator of the population standard deviation is the sample standard deviation, s. Then the 95% confidence interval becomes:

$$\bar{x} - 1.96 * s/\sqrt{n} \quad \text{to} \quad \bar{x} + 1.96 * s/\sqrt{n}$$

WORKED EXAMPLE 8.11

Cantor Security employs night watchmen to patrol warehouses. They want to find the time needed to patrol a certain type of warehouse, and on a typical night they find the time to patrol 40 similar warehouses has a mean of 76.4 minutes, and standard deviation of 17.2 minutes. What are the 95% and 99% confidence intervals on the true mean?

Solution

The point estimate for the population mean is 76.4 minutes.

The standard deviation of the sample is 17.2 minutes, so if we use this as an approximation for the standard deviation of the population, we get a standard error of $\sigma/\sqrt{n} = 17.2/\sqrt{40} = 2.72$ minutes. Then:

- 95% confidence interval:

$$76.4 - 1.96 * 2.72 \quad \text{to} \quad 76.4 + 1.96 * 2.72$$
$$= 71.07 \quad \text{to} \quad 81.73$$

- 99% confidence interval:

$$76.4 - 2.58 * 2.72 \quad \text{to} \quad 76.4 + 2.58 * 2.72$$
$$= 69.38 \quad \text{to} \quad 83.42$$

Obviously, the more confident we want to be that the true mean lies within a given range, the wider the range must be.

Case example

Total Quality Management

Traditionally, a lot of sampling has been related to quality control. In recent years, many organizations have radically changed the way they view quality. They no longer set acceptable levels of defects, and assume that operations are working well if they achieve this level. Instead, they are aiming at 'zero-defects'. Their approach uses Total Quality Management (TQM) which has the whole organization working together to systematically improve product quality.

One of the 'quality gurus' who started work on TQM is Edward Deming. He summarized his findings in a list of 14 key points:

1 Create constancy of purpose towards product quality.
2 Refuse to accept customary levels of mistakes, delays, defects and errors.

3 Stop depending on mass inspections, but build quality into products in the first place.

4 Stop awarding business on the basis of price alone – reduce the number of suppliers and insist on meaningful measures of quality.

5 Develop programmes for continuous improvement of costs, quality, productivity and service.

6 Institute training for all employees.

7 Focus supervision on helping employees to do a better job.

8 Drive out fear by encouraging two-way communications.

9 Break down barriers between departments and encourage problem solving through teamwork.

10 Eliminate numerical goals, posters and slogans that demand improvements without saying how these can be achieved.

11 Eliminate arbitrary quotas that interfere with quality.

12 Remove barriers that stop people having pride in their work.

13 Institute vigorous programmes of lifelong education, training and self-improvement.

14 Put everyone to work on implementing these 14 points.

There are many stories of success after implementing TQM. Japan Steel Works in Hiroshima, for example, increased production by 50% while reducing the number of employees by 20% – and the costs of defects fell from 1.57% of sales to 0.4%. Ford of America reduced the number of warranty repairs by 45%, and the faults reported by new owners by 50%. Hewlett-Packard increased labour productivity by 40% while reducing faults in integrated circuits by 89%, faults with soldering by 98% and faults in final assembly by 93%.

IN SUMMARY

We can use the sampling distribution of the mean to give point estimates and confidence intervals for a population mean.

Self-assessment questions

8.6 What is the purpose of sampling?

8.7 What is the sampling distribution of the mean?

8.8 Describe the shape of the sampling distribution of the mean.

8.9 What is the 95% confidence interval for a value?

▌ 8.3 ▐ Hypothesis testing

8.3.1 Approach to hypothesis testing

In the last section we saw how statistical inference used data from a sample to estimate values for a population. Now we can extend this idea by testing whether a belief about a population is supported by the evidence from a sample. This is the basis of *hypothesis testing*.

Suppose we have some preconceived idea about the value taken by a population variable. We might, for example, believe that domestic electricity bills have risen by 15% in the past year. This is a hypothesis we want to test. For this test we take a sample from the population and see if the results support our hypothesis or do not support it. The formal procedure for this is as follows:

- define a simple, precise statement about the situation (the hypothesis)
- take a sample from the population
- test this sample to see if it supports the hypothesis, or if it makes the hypothesis highly unlikely
- if the hypothesis is highly unlikely reject it, otherwise accept it

In practice statisticians are rather more cautious than this, and they do not often talk about 'accepting' a hypothesis. Instead they say that a hypothesis 'can be rejected' if it is highly unlikely, or it 'cannot be rejected' if it is more likely.

WORKED EXAMPLE 8.12

Boxes are filled with a nominal 400 g of ingredients. There are small deviations from this nominal amount and the actual weights are normally distributed with a standard deviation of 20 g. Periodic samples are taken to make sure the mean weight is still 400 g. One sample box contains 446 g. Are the boxes now being overfilled?

Solution

An initial hypothesis is that the mean weight of boxes is still 400 g. We have a limited sample which gives data for testing this hypothesis. The distribution of box weights should be normal with mean 400 g and standard deviation 20 g.

Assuming this is still true, we can find the probability of getting a sample containing 446 g. The number of standard deviations from the mean is:

$$Z = (446 - 400)/20 = 2.3$$

Normal tables show this has probability $= 0.01$.

If our hypothesis about the population is true, finding a box weighing 446 g is highly unlikely (1% of occasions). We can, therefore, reject the initial hypothesis that the mean content is 400 g, as we now believe the boxes are being overfilled.

The original statement is called the **null hypothesis**, which is usually called H_0. The name 'null' suggests that there has been no change in the value being tested since the hypothesis was formulated. If we reject the null hypothesis then we implicitly accept an alternative. In the worked example above we rejected the hypothesis that the mean weight of boxes is 400 g, so we accepted the **alternative hypothesis** that the mean weight is not 400 g. For each null hypothesis there is always an alternative hypothesis, which is usually called H_1. If the null hypothesis, H_0, is that electricity bills have risen by 15% in the last year, the alternative hypothesis, H_1, is that they have not risen by 15%; if the null hypothesis, H_0, is that first-class letters take 2 days to deliver, the alternative hypothesis, H_1, is that they do not take 2 days to deliver, and so on.

Notice that the null hypothesis must be a simple, specific statement, while the alternative hypothesis is more vague and simply suggests that some statement other than the null hypothesis is true. In practice, this invariably means that the null hypothesis is phrased in terms of one thing equalling another. We might have a null hypothesis that the mean weight is 1.5 kg and an alternative hypothesis that the mean weight is not 1.5 kg; a null hypothesis might be that the average salary in an office is £20 000, while the alternative hypothesis is that the average salary is lower than this.

IN SUMMARY

A null hypothesis is a precise statement about a situation. Hypothesis testing uses a sample to see if the evidence supports this statement, or if we should reject the hypothesis.

8.3.2 Errors in hypothesis testing

When we use a sample, we cannot be certain that it accurately represents an entire population, so there is always some uncertainty. When we use a sample to test a null hypothesis, we can never be certain of the result. In Worked Example 8.12 we said the result was unlikely and therefore rejected the null hypothesis, but in 1%

of samples the result found would occur by chance, and we would be rejecting a perfectly true hypothesis. In general, there are two ways of getting the wrong answer with hypothesis testing:

- we may reject a null hypothesis which is true (this is a **Type I error**)
- we may not reject a null hypothesis which is false (this is a **Type II error**)

Decision	Null hypothesis is actually	
	True	*False*
Not reject	Correct decision	Type II error
Reject	Type I error	Correct decision

Ideally, we would like the probability of both Type I and Type II errors to be close to zero. The only way of doing this is to use a large sample. If we try any other adjustments to reduce the probability of Type I errors, the probability of Type II errors increases, and vice versa. With a limited sample size, we have to accept a compromise between the two errors.

WORKED EXAMPLE 8.13

The mean wage in a certain industry is said to be £300 a week with a standard deviation of £60. There is a feeling that this is no longer true and a random sample of 36 wages is checked. It is decided to reject the null hypothesis if the sample of wages has a mean less than £270 or greater than £330. What are the probabilities of making a Type I error?

Solution

We can start by defining a null hypothesis, H_0, that the mean wage is £300, and the alternative hypothesis, H_1, that the mean wage is not £300.

Hypothesis tests assume that the null hypothesis is true while the tests are being done. So we assume the population has a mean of £300 and a standard deviation of £60. With a sample of 36, the standard error (which is the standard deviation of the sampling distribution of the mean) is $s/\sqrt{n} = 60/\sqrt{36} = 10$.

We can find the probability that a sample of 36 wages is greater than £330 from normal tables with $Z = (330 - 300)/10 = 3$. The probability of this is 0.0013. By symmetry the probability that a sample has a mean of less than £270 is also 0.0013. The null hypothesis is rejected if the sample value is outside the range £270 to £330, so there is a probability of $2 * 0.0013 = 0.0026$ that the hypothesis is rejected even though it is actually true. This is the probability of a Type I error.

WORKED EXAMPLE 8.14

A city takes a survey of monthly food and shelter costs for a particular type of family. It is suggested that the mean cost is £160 with a standard deviation of £48.90. A sample of 100 families was taken and found to have an average expenditure of £171.25. Is the suggested value of £160 true?

Solution

The null hypothesis, H_0, is that the monthly cost of food and shelter equals £160 while the alternative hypothesis, H_1, is that it does not equal £160.

With a sample of 100 the standard error is $48.90/\sqrt{100} = 4.89$. Then $Z = (171.25 - 160)/4.89 = 2.3$, which corresponds to a probability of 0.0107.

There is a probability of 0.0107 that the monthly cost of food and shelter is £171.25, so this outcome is very unlikely. So we should reject the null hypothesis and accept the alternative hypothesis.

IN SUMMARY

Results from samples always contain uncertainty. In hypothesis testing this means there are two types of error:

- **Type I error, of rejecting a null hypothesis that is true**
- **Type II error, of not rejecting a null hypothesis that is false**

8.3.3 Significance levels

In the last section we rejected the null hypothesis when we thought the results were unlikely. But we only used an opinion to say a result was 'unlikely', and did not use a precise measure. Now we can formalize these judgements into a *significance level*:

> The **significance level** is the minimum acceptable probability that an observation is a random sample from the hypothesized population.

If we set a 5% significance level, we will not reject a null hypothesis if there is a probability greater than 5% that an observation comes from a population with the specified value. On the other hand, if there is a probability of less than 5% that the observation came from such a population we reject the null hypothesis.

If we take a large sample, the value we are testing will be normally distributed. If we are working with a 5% significance level, we are concerned with the range that is within 1.96 standard deviations of the mean. In other words, we will not reject the null hypothesis if the sample result is within 1.96 standard deviations of the mean, and reject it if it is outside this range (see Figure 8.11).

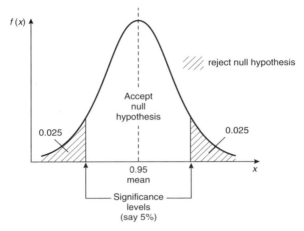

Figure 8.11 Acceptance and rejection regions for hypothesis tests with 5% significance level.

With a 5% significance level we reject the null hypothesis when an observation falls outside the 95% acceptance range. But if the null hypothesis is true, 5% of observations will fall outside this range anyway. In other words there is a 5% chance of rejecting a true null hypothesis, which is a Type I error. So the significance level is the probability of a Type I error.

Although we can use any reasonable significance level, the one used most often in business is 5%, followed by 1% and occasionally 0.1%. If a 1% significance level is used, the null hypothesis is not rejected if the observation is within 2.58 standard deviations of the mean. This is a less stringent test, and shows how smaller significance levels need stronger evidence to reject the null hypothesis. With lower significance levels the probability of a Type I error is reduced, but the probability of a Type II error is increased.

WORKED EXAMPLE 8.15

The mean value of accounts received by a firm is thought to be £260. An auditor checks this by taking a sample of 36 accounts which have a mean of £243 and a standard deviation of £45. Use a 5% significance level to test whether the original view is supported by the evidence from the sample. What happens with a 1% significance level?

Solution

The null hypothesis is that the mean value of all accounts is £260, while the alternative hypothesis is that the mean is not £260:

$$H_0: \quad \mu = 260 \quad H_1: \quad \mu \neq 260$$

With a sample of 36, the sampling distribution of the mean is normal with mean 260 and standard deviation $45/\sqrt{36} = 7.5$. For a 5% significance level we look at the points that are within 1.96 standard deviations of the mean. The acceptance range is then:

$$260 - 1.96 * 7.5 \quad \text{to} \quad 260 + 1.96 * 7.5$$

or
$$245.3 \quad \text{to} \quad 274.7$$

The actual observation is outside this range, so we reject the null hypothesis and accept the alternative hypothesis that the mean value of accounts does not equal £260.

With a 1% significance level the acceptance range is:

$$260 - 2.58 * 7.5 \quad \text{to} \quad 260 + 2.58 * 7.5$$

or
$$240.65 \quad \text{to} \quad 279.35$$

The actual observation is within this range, so we cannot reject the null hypothesis that the mean value of accounts equals £260 (see Figure 8.12).

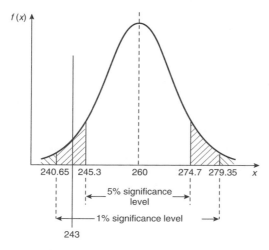

Figure 8.12 Acceptance regions and significance levels for Worked Example 8.15.

Now we have described all the steps in hypothesis testing as:

- state the null and alternative hypotheses
- specify the level of significance to be used
- calculate the acceptance range for the variable tested
- find the actual value for the variable tested
- decide whether or not to reject the null hypothesis
- state the conclusion reached

WORKED EXAMPLE 8.16

The average income per capita in an area is claimed to be £15 000. A sample of 45 people found their mean income to be £14 300 with a standard deviation of £2000. Use a 5% significance level to check the original claim. What is the effect of using a 1% significance level?

Solution

To solve this problem we use the procedure described above.

- State the null and alternative hypotheses
$$H_0: \quad \mu = 15\,000 \quad H_1: \quad \mu \neq 15\,000$$

- Specify the level of significance to be used
This is given as 5%

- Calculate the acceptance range for the variable tested
With a sample of 45, the sampling distribution of the mean is normal with mean 15 000 and standard deviation $2000/\sqrt{45} = 298.14$. For a 5% significance level we look at the points that are within 1.96 standard deviations of the mean. The acceptance range is then:
$$15\,000 - 1.96 * 298.14 \quad \text{to} \quad 15\,000 + 1.96 * 298.14$$
or $\qquad 14\,416 \quad$ to $\quad 15\,584$

- Find the actual value for the variable tested
This is £14 300.

- Decide whether to accept or reject the null hypothesis
The actual value is outside the acceptance range, so we must reject the null hypothesis.

- State the conclusion reached

  The evidence from the sample does not support the original claim that the average income per capita in the area is £15 000.

With a 1% significance level, the acceptance range is within 2.58 standard deviations of the mean, or:

$$15\,000 - 2.58 * 298.14 \quad \text{to} \quad 15\,000 + 2.58 * 298.14$$
$$14\,231 \quad \text{to} \quad 15\,769$$

The actual observation of £14 300 is within this range, and we cannot reject the null hypothesis.

IN SUMMARY

A significance level is the minimum acceptable probability that an observation is a random sample from the hypothesized population. It is the probability of a Type I error.

8.3.4 One-sided tests

So far we have used a null hypothesis with the form:

$$H_0: \quad \mu = 10$$

and an alternative hypothesis with the form:

$$H_1: \quad \mu \neq 10$$

In practice we may only want to know that a value is above (or maybe below) the claimed value. If we buy a box of chocolates, we only want to know that the weight is not below the specified value; on the other hand, if we are delivering parcels, we only want to know that the weight is not above the claimed value. We can tackle these problems using the standard procedure, but with an adjustment to the wording of the alternative hypothesis.

If we are buying boxes of chocolates with a claimed weight of 500 g, we want to make sure the actual weight is not below this, so we can use:

Null hypothesis, H_0:	$\mu = 500\,\text{g}$
Alternative hypothesis, H_1:	$\mu < 500\,\text{g}$

If we are delivering parcels with a claimed weight of 25 kg, we want to make sure the actual weight is not above this, so we can use:

Null hypothesis, H_0:	$\mu = 25\,\text{kg}$
Alternative hypothesis, H_1:	$\mu > 25\,\text{kg}$

For this kind of test we only use one tail of the sampling distribution, so the acceptance range is altered. A 5% significance level has the 5% area of rejection in one tail of the distribution. In a normal distribution this point is 1.645 standard deviations from the mean, as shown in Figure 8.13.

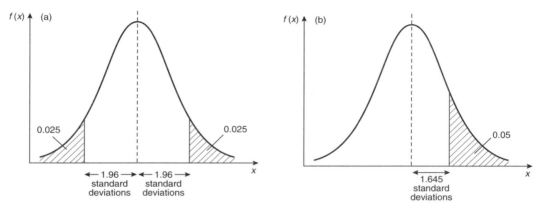

Figure 8.13 Acceptance ranges with 5% significance level for (a) two-tailed test and (b) one-tailed test.

You can think of **one-sided tests** as measuring consumers' risk or producers' risk. If a packet of soap powder has a stated weight of 1 kg, consumers will only be concerned if the actual quantity is less than this. So consumer groups will sample packets using a null hypothesis that the mean weight is 1 kg and an alternative hypothesis that the weight is less than 1 kg. Producers are concerned if the quantity is much more than 1 kg. They will sample packets using a null hypothesis that the mean weight is 1 kg and an alternative hypothesis that the mean weight is above 1 kg. (In practice, of course, their testing is much more complicated than this.)

WORKED EXAMPLE 8.17

A mail-order company charges a customer a flat rate for delivery based on a mean weight for packages of 1.75 kg with a standard deviation of 0.5 kg. Postal charges now seem high and it is suggested that the mean weight is greater than 1.75 kg. A random sample of 100 packages has a mean weight of 1.86 kg. Does this support the view that the mean weight is more than 1.75 kg?

Solution

We can again use the standard procedure.

- State the null and alternative hypotheses

  We want to make sure the mean weight is not above 1.75 kg, so we have:

  $$H_0: \quad \mu = 1.75 \, \text{kg} \quad H_1: \quad \mu > 1.75 \, \text{kg}$$

- Specify the level of significance to be used

  This is not given, so we will assume 5%

- Calculate the acceptance range for the variable tested

  With a sample of 100, the sampling distribution of the mean is normal with mean of 1.75 kg and standard deviation $0.5/\sqrt{100} = 0.05$ kg. For a 5% significance level and a one-sided test, we look at points that are more than 1.645 standard deviations above the mean. The acceptance range is then below $1.75 + 1.645 * 0.05 = 1.83$ kg

- Find the actual value for the variable tested

  The actual weight of parcels is 1.86 kg.

- Decide whether to accept or reject the null hypothesis

  The actual value is outside the acceptance range, so we must reject the null hypothesis.

- State the conclusion reached

  The evidence from the sample does not support the view that the mean weight of packages is 1.75 kg. The evidence suggests the mean weight is more than this (shown in Figure 8.14).

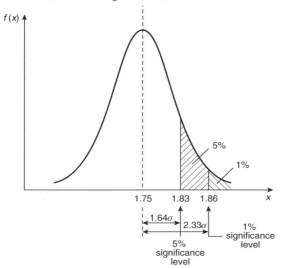

Figure 8.14 Acceptance range for Worked Example 8.17.

WORKED EXAMPLE 8.18

A management consultant claims that a receptionist should not do more than 10 minutes of paperwork in each hour, with a standard deviation of 3 minutes. A check is made on 40 random hours of operation and the mean time spent on paperwork is 11.05 minutes. Use a 1% significance level to test the management consultant's claim.

Solution

- State the null and alternative hypotheses

  We want to check that the time spent on paperwork is not above 10 minutes in an hour. So we have:

  $$H_0: \quad \mu = 10 \text{ minutes} \quad H_1: \quad \mu > 10 \text{ minutes}$$

- Specify the level of significance to be used

  This is given as 1%.

- Calculate the acceptance range for the variable tested

  With a sample of 40, the sampling distribution of the mean is normal with mean of 10 minutes and standard deviation $3/\sqrt{40} = 0.47$ minutes. For a 1% significance level and a one-sided test, we look at the points that are more than 2.33 standard deviations above the mean. Then the acceptance range is below $10 + 2.33 * 0.47 = 11.10$ minutes.

- Find the actual value for the variable tested

  The actual number of minutes spent on paperwork in each hour is 11.05.

- Decide whether to accept or reject the null hypothesis

  The actual value is inside the acceptance range, so the null hypothesis cannot be rejected.

- State the conclusion reached

  The evidence from the sample supports the view that the mean time spent on paperwork is 10 minutes an hour.

IN SUMMARY

The standard two-sided analysis can be extended to a one-sided analysis when we are only interested in means that are above or below specified levels.

Self-assessment questions

8.10 What are the steps in testing a hypothesis?

8.11 What are Type I and Type II errors?

8.12 What is a significance level?

8.13 If an observation is in the acceptance range, does this prove that the null hypothesis is true?

CHAPTER REVIEW

The last chapter introduced some ideas of statistics. This chapter developed these ideas and described some uses of statistics. In particular it:

● looked at the reliability of equipment and used probability distributions in models of different situations

● discussed the reliability of systems made up of components

● outlined an approach to problems where the performance of equipment declines with age

● discussed the aims of sampling

● described the sampling distribution of the mean

● found point estimates and confidence intervals for population values

● used hypothesis testing to see if a statement about a population – a null hypothesis – is supported by the evidence from a sample

KEY TERMS

alternative hypothesis	*population*
census	*random sample*
confidence interval	*reliability*
hypothesis testing	*sampling*
interval estimate	*sampling distribution*
null hypothesis	*significance level*
one-sided tests	*standard error*
point estimate	*statistical inference*

Case study

Willingham Consumer Protection Department

Willingham Consumer Protection Department (WCPD) are responsible for administering all weights and measures legislation in their area. A large part of their work responds to customer complaints against specific companies, but they also do precautionary tests to stop problems developing. For example, they inspect food preparation areas to make sure they are clean and will cause no health problems.

In the past WCPD did a wide range of tests on consumer products, but restrictions on their budget now force them to concentrate on the priority areas of food and drink. They take large numbers of samples, to make sure the actual contents correspond to the advertised contents.

One week, WCPD decided to test containers of milk. Historically this was an important function as small dairies and farmers had difficulty meeting strict regulations. Nowadays most milk products are sold through large dairies, and there are very few problems with either the quantity or quality. WCPD visited a large dairy in the area, did some random tests and looked through historical records. They also visited local shops and milk roundsmen to buy some more random samples.

On two consecutive days they bought 50 containers with a nominal content of 4 pints or 2.27 litres. The actual contents of these, in litres, are as follows:

Day 1:

2.274	2.275	2.276	2.270	2.269	2.271	2.265	2.275	2.263	2.278
2.260	2.278	2.280	2.275	2.261	2.280	2.279	2.270	2.275	2.263
2.275	2.781	2.266	2.277	2.271	2.273	2.283	2.260	2.259	2.276
2.286	2.275	2.271	2.273	2.291	2.271	2.269	2.265	2.258	2.283
2.274	2.278	2.276	2.281	2.269	2.259	2.291	2.289	2.276	2.283

Day 2:

2.270	2.276	2.258	2.259	2.281	2.265	2.278	2.270	2.294	2.255
2.271	2.284	2.276	2.293	2.261	2.270	2.271	2.276	2.269	2.268
2.272	2.272	2.273	2.280	2.281	2.276	2.263	2.260	2.295	2.257
2.248	2.276	2.284	2.276	2.270	2.271	2.269	2.278	2.276	2.274
2.291	2.257	2.281	2.276	2.274	2.273	2.273	2.270	2.272	2.278

When they were collecting these figures, WCPD inspectors were convinced that there were no problems with the large dairy, but they were not so sure of the small operators. The large dairy could afford modern, well-designed equipment and employed special quality assurance staff. Smaller operators used older, less reliable equipment, and could not afford a quality assurance department.

WCPD identified two companies they thought needed some further checks. Random samples of 15 containers were taken from each of these dairies, with the following results.

Company 1: 2.261 2.273 2.250 2.268 2.268 2.262 2.272 2.269 2.268 2.257
2.260 2.270 2.254 2.249 2.267

Company 2: 2.291 2.265 2.283 2.275 2.248 2.286 2.268 2.271 2.284 2.256
2.284 2.255 2.283 2.275 2.276

WCPD was facing continued pressure to reduce costs. Each test involved a considerable cost, especially if it involved laboratory analyses of contents. The council was suggesting that these routine tests were a waste of money. Why bother to test the big dairies if their results were always satisfactory? And they could do so few tests in smaller dairies that they were unlikely to find any real problems. The results they were worried about only seemed to have differences in the third or fourth decimal place.

Question

What kind of report would you write about the milk inspections?

Problems

8.1 A shop floor has 10 machines of which an average of 2 break down a week. What are the probabilities of 0, 1, 2 and 3 breaking down in a given week?

8.2 A manufacturer of electric cable has an average of 1.5 faults in each 100 m of a low-quality cable. What are the probabilities of 0, 1, 2 and 3 faults in a 100 m length?

8.3 The following diagram shows the reliability of each component in a network. What is the reliability of the network as a whole?

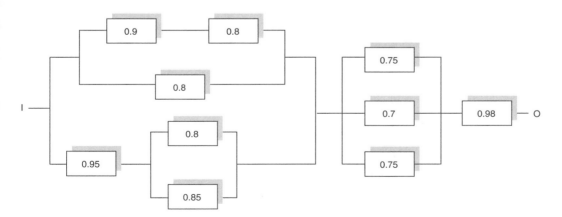

8.4   The probability that a piece of equipment fails in each year of operation is given below. A factory has 100 pieces of equipment of this type and they are currently replaced as soon as they fail at a cost of £150 a unit. A block replacement program is suggested, where all units are replaced after a fixed number of years of operation – with any units failing replaced at the end of the year. Block replacement would cost £100 a unit. What is the cheapest replacement policy?

Year of operation	1	2	3	4
Probability of failing in year	0.1	0.3	0.4	0.2

8.5   A production line makes units with a mean weight of 80 g and standard deviation of 5 g. What is the probability that a sample of 100 units has a mean weight of less than 79 g?

8.6   A machine produces parts with a variance of 14.5 cm in length. A random sample of 50 parts is taken and has a mean length of 106.5 cm. What are the 95% and 99% confidence limits for the length of parts?

8.7   During an audit, a random sample of 60 invoices is taken from a large population. The mean value of invoices in this sample was £125.50 and the standard deviation was £10.20. Find the 90% and 95% confidence intervals for the mean value of all invoices.

8.8   A management consultant times 60 people doing a job. The mean time is 6.4 minutes, with a standard deviation of 0.5 minutes. How long would it take the population to do this job?

8.9   A food processor specifies the mean weight of a product as 200 g. The output is normally distributed with a standard deviation of 15 g. A random sample of 20 has a mean of 195 g. Does this evidence suggest the mean weight is too low?

8.10   A bus company says that its long-distance coaches take 5 hours for a particular journey. Last week a consumer group tested these figures by timing a sample of 30 journeys. These had a mean time of 5 hours 10 minutes with a standard deviation of 20 minutes. What report can the consumer group make?

Discussion questions

8.1   Customers will no longer accept poor quality goods. This means that all units produced must be tested – or some defects are bound to get through to customers. So when does sampling give results that are good enough?

8.2 Because customers and producers tend to look at different measures of performance, there must always be some conflict between the two. Do you think that this is true?

8.3 Opinion polls often say things like, '19 times out of 20 this result is within 2% of actual values'. This kind of statement is so cautious and confusing that it is of little practical value. Do you think this is true?

8.4 If a result is obvious, we do not need statistics to show it. If a result is not obvious, no amount of statistical testing is convincing. So why do we use statistics?

8.5 Saying, 'we cannot reject the null hypothesis' is exactly the same as saying 'the null hypothesis is true'. To say anything else is just playing around with words. Do you think this is true?

Decision analysis

CHAPTER OUTLINE

This chapter introduces decision analysis. It shows a rational approach to decision-making, and develops methods for improving decisions in different circumstances. After reading the chapter you should be able to:

- draw maps of decision-making situations
- use payoff matrices
- make decisions under certainty
- describe situations of uncertainty and use decision criteria to suggest the best alternatives
- describe situations of risk and use expected values to suggest the best alternatives
- use Bayes' theorem to update conditional probabilities for decisions under risk
- appreciate the use of utilities
- draw decision trees for sequential decisions

9.1 | Giving structure to decisions

Everybody has to make decisions: which car should we buy; where should we live; can we afford a holiday; where should we eat; should we drive to work or go by train; which film should we go to; should we make tea or coffee, and so on. Most of these decisions are unimportant, and we choose the best alternative using experience and intuition. But in business, managers have to make decisions that are both important and difficult. These need a more formal approach to decision-making.

Suppose a company makes a product, but thinks its profit is too low. There are two obvious remedies – reduce costs or increase the price. But if the price is increased the demand may fall. On the other hand, reducing the costs may allow the price to go down, and demand will rise. If demand changes, the factory will have to reschedule production and change its marketing strategies. But changing production schedules affects the production of other items, number of people employed, shifts worked, raw materials needed, sales efforts, and so on.

We could go on with these more or less random thoughts for some time, but would soon lose track of the main arguments. It is useful to have a simple diagram to show the main points of the argument, and their interactions. We can use a ***problem map*** for this, and Figure 9.1 shows part of a map for the discussion above.

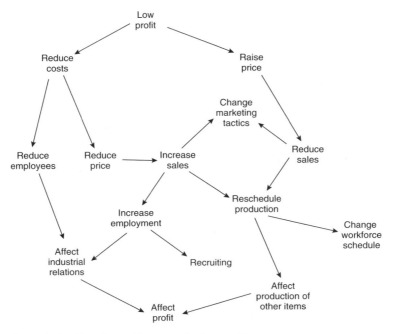

Figure 9.1 Part of a problem map for low profit.

As you can see, maps give an informal way of representing a stream of connected thoughts. They are useful for sorting out ideas and clearly showing the interactions. But they do not help directly in decision-making – they do not say which decisions are best. For this, we need to look more closely at the problems tackled. We can start by listing the components of a decision.

- A decision needs a decision maker who is responsible for making decisions.
- The decision maker has a number of alternatives, and must choose one of them.
- The object of the decision maker is to choose the best alternative.
- When the decision has been made, events occur over which the decision maker has no control.
- Each combination of an alternative chosen, followed by an event happening, leads to an outcome that has some measurable value.

Consider a house owner who is offered fire insurance at a cost of £200 a year. The decision maker is the person who owns the house. They have an objective of minimizing costs and must choose the best alternative from:

1   insure the house, or

2   do not insure the house

Then an event happens, but the decision maker has no control over whether it is:

1   the house burns down, or

2   the house does not burn down

This is obviously a simplified model – in reality there are many different insurance companies and policies, the house may be damaged but not destroyed, the costs may vary, and so on. If the value of the house is £70 000 and the insurance company pays for all costs and inconvenience if the house burns down, we can summarize the combinations of alternatives, events and outcomes in the following table:

		Events	
		House burns down	House does not burn down
Alternatives	Insure house	£200	£200
	Do not insure house	£70 000	£0

This is a *payoff matrix*, and the entries show the cost to the house owner of every combination of alternative and event. The house owner has to choose the best alternative, then an event occurs, and the outcomes are in consistent units which may be either costs or gains.

We have now used two distinct formats to describe the circumstances around a decision: maps and payoff matrices. Both of these are useful in adding a structure to a complex situation.

| *IN SUMMARY* |

Managers make decisions in complex situations. Maps and payoff matrices describe these situations and add structure to problems.

Self-assessment questions

9.1   'Problem maps show the best decisions in any situation.' Is this true?

9.2   Why are problem maps and payoff matrices used?

9.3   What are the five main components of a decision?

9.2 | Decision-making under certainty

The main characteristic of decision-making under *certainty* is that we know, with certainty, which event will occur. We need only consider one event and the method of solution is obvious – we can look at the outcome for each alternative, and choose the alternative with the best outcome.

Suppose we have £1000 to invest for a year. We could list all the alternatives we want to consider and get the following payoff matrix. This is obviously a simplified view, listing only a few alternatives and forecasts of returns:

		Event Get interest to give at year end
	Bank	£1065
	Building society	£1075
Alternatives	Government stock	£1085
	Stock market	£1100
	Others	£1060

There is only one event 'get interest', and by looking down the list of outcomes we can see the best. The highest value comes from investing in the stock market – so this is the best alternative.

In reality, even decisions under certainty can be difficult, particularly in complex situations or where subjective views are important. Would it be better, for example, for the Health Service to invest money in buying more kidney dialysis machines, giving nurses higher wages, reducing doctors' working hours, doing open-heart surgery, screening for prostate cancer, funding fertility clinics, or providing more parking spaces at hospitals?

WORKED EXAMPLE 9.1

A restaurant manager has a booking for a wedding banquet. He has a number of ways of getting staff, each with a different cost. His most convenient alternatives are to pay full-time staff to work overtime (costing £800), hire current part-time staff for the day (£600), hire new temporary staff (£700), or use an agency (£1100). Draw a payoff matrix for this decision and find the best alternative.

Solution

The payoff matrix for this decision under certainty is shown below.

		Event pay staff
	Pay full-time staff for overtime	800
Alternatives	Hire current part-time staff	600
	Hire new temporary staff	700
	Use an agency	1100

The entries in this payoff matrix are costs, so we want to find the lowest. This is £600 for hiring current part-time staff for the day.

Self-assessment questions

9.4 What is meant by 'decision-making under certainty'?

9.5 'With only one event it is always easy to make decisions.' Do you think this is true?

9.3 | Decision-making under uncertainty

Usually, more than one event can occur. Sometimes it is impossible to say which one actually will occur, or even give reliable probabilities. When you take a new job, a number of events may happen; you may not like the new job and quickly start looking for another, you may get the sack, you may like the job and stay, you might be moved by the company. You do not really have any control over these events, and cannot give reliable probabilities.

When we cannot put probabilities to events we are dealing with strict *uncertainty*. Then we can use simple rules called *decision criteria* to recommend a solution. There are many different criteria, and we will illustrate these by three common ones.

9.3.1 Laplace decision criterion

As we cannot give probabilities to the events, *Laplace* suggests that we treat them as equally likely, and give no more weight to one event than to others. Then we can find the best alternative by:

1 For each alternative find the mean value of the outcomes (that is, the average of each row in the payoff matrix).

2 Choose the alternative with the best average outcome (that is, the lowest cost or highest gain).

WORKED EXAMPLE 9.2

Use the Laplace decision criterion on the example of house insurance described above.

		Events	
		House burns down	House does not burn down
	Insure house	£200	£200
Alternatives			
	Do not insure house	£70 000	£0

Solution

Following the steps described:

1 Find the average of outcome for each alternative.

- insure house has an average cost of $(200 + 200)/2 = £200$.
- do not insure house has an average cost of $(70\,000 + 0)/2 = £35\,000$.

2 Choose the alternative with the best average outcome. As the figures are costs, the best is the lower, which is to insure the house.

WORKED EXAMPLE 9.3

Some fruit retailers are going to set up a stall at a local gala. On the morning of the gala they visit the wholesale market and must buy a large, medium or small quantity of seasonal fruit. Their profit is found by subtracting the costs of buying fruit and the cost of unsold fruit, from the gross income. This depends on the number of people attending the gala, and this in turn depends on the weather. The matrix of profits (in thousands of pounds) for different weather conditions is given below. What quantity of fruit should the retailers buy?

		Events		
		Weather good	Weather average	Weather poor
	Large quantity	10	4	−2
Alternatives	Medium quantity	7	6	2
	Small quantity	4	1	4

Solution

1 Take the average outcomes for each alternative:

- large quantity $(10 + 4 - 2)/3 = 4$
- medium quantity $(7 + 6 + 2)/3 = 5$
- small quantity $(4 + 1 + 4)/3 = 3$

2 Choose the best average outcome. As these figures are profits the best is the highest, which is to buy a medium quantity.

$\boxed{\textit{IN SUMMARY}}$

Situations of uncertainty have a number of events, but we cannot give reliable probabilities to these. Decision criteria can suggest the best alternative. The Laplace criterion finds the average outcome for each alternative and chooses the alternative with the best average outcome.

9.3.2 Wald decision criterion

Most organizations have limited resources and cannot afford to risk a big loss. This is the basis of the **Wald** decision criterion, which assumes that decision makers are cautious – or even pessimistic – and want to avoid large potential losses. The steps are:

1 For each alternative find the worst outcome.

2 Choose the alternative with the best of these worst outcomes.

With payoff matrices showing costs, this is sometimes called the 'minimax cost' criterion. It looks at the maximum cost of each alternative and then chooses the alternative with the minimum of these – which is the minimum [maximum] cost or minimax cost. With payoff matrices showing gains it is known as the 'maximin gain' criterion, as it looks at the minimum gain for each alternative and chooses the alternative with the highest of these.

WORKED EXAMPLE 9.4

Use the Wald decision criterion for the example of house insurance described above.

		Events	
		House burns down	House does not burn down
Alternatives	Insure house	**£200**	**£200**
	Do not insure house	**£70 000**	£0

Solution

Following the procedure described above:

1 Take the worst outcomes for each alternative;

- insure house = worst of 200 and 200 = MAX [200, 200] = £200
- do not insure house = worst of 70 000 and 0 = MAX [70 000, 0] = £70 000

2 Choose the better of these to give the lower, worst cost = MIN [200, 70 000] = £200. So we should insure the house.

WORKED EXAMPLE 9.5

Use the Wald decision criterion for the example of a fruit stall at a local gala described by the following gains matrix:

		Events		
		Weather good	Weather average	Weather poor
	Large quantity	10	4	−2
Alternatives	Medium quantity	7	6	2
	Small quantity	4	1	4

1 Taking the worst value of outcomes for each alternative:

- large quantity = MIN [10, 4, −2] = −2
- medium quantity = MIN [7, 6, 2] = 2
- small quantity = MIN [4, 1, 4] = 1

2 Choose the best of these worst outcomes. As the figures are profits the best is the highest, which comes from buying a medium quantity.

IN SUMMARY

The Wald decision criterion is pessimistic and assumes that the worst outcome will occur. Then it chooses the alternative that gives the best of these worst outcomes.

9.3.3 Savage decision criterion

Sometimes we are judged not by how well we actually do, but how well we could possibly have done. Students who get 70% in an exam might be judged by the fact that they did not get 100%. An investment broker who suggested a client should invest in platinum may be judged not by the fact that platinum rose 15% in value, but by the fact that gold rose 25%. This happens particularly when performance is judged by someone other than the decision maker.

In such cases there is a ***regret***, which is the difference between actual outcome and best possible outcome. A student who gets 70% in an exam has a regret of $100 - 70 = 30\%$. An investor who gains 15% when they could have gained 25% has a regret of $25 - 15 = 10\%$. The ***Savage*** criterion is based on these regrets. It is essentially pessimistic and minimizes the maximum regret. The steps are:

1   For each event find the best possible outcome (that is, find the best entry in each column of the payoff matrix).

2   Find the regret for every other entry in the column, which is the difference between the best in the column and the entry.

3   Put the regrets found in Step 2 into a 'regret matrix'. There is at least one zero in each column and regrets are always positive.

4   For each alternative find the highest regret (that is, the largest number in each row).

5   Choose the alternative with the lowest value of these highest regrets.

As you can see, steps 4 and 5 apply the Wald criterion to the regret matrix.

WORKED EXAMPLE 9.6

Use the Savage decision criterion on the example of house insurance described above.

		Events	
		House burns down	House does not burn down
	Insure house	**£200**	£200
Alternatives			
	Do not insure house	£70 000	**£0**

Solution

Following the steps described above:

1   The best outcomes for each event are:

- house burns down: best of 200 and 70 000 = MIN [200, 70 000] = 200
- house does not burn down: best of 200 and 0 = MIN [200, 0] = 0

2   Now we can find the regret for not getting the best outcome for an event. For every other entry in a column this is the difference between the best value and the actual value.

- House burns down. The best alternative is to insure the house with a cost of 200. If we had done this there is zero regret. If we had chosen the other alternative of not insuring the house the cost is £70 000 – to give a regret of 70 000 − 200 = £69 800.

- House does not burn down. The best alternative is to not insure the house with a cost of zero. If we had done this there is no regret. If we had chosen the other alternative of insuring the house the cost is £200 – to give a regret of £200 − 0 = £200.

3   Put these values into a regret matrix – replacing the original values in the cost matrix by the regrets.

		Events	
		House burns down	House does not burn down
Alternatives	Insure house	£0	**£200**
	Do not insure house	**£69 800**	£0

4   Find the maximum regret for each alternative:

- insure house = MAX [0, 200] = 200
- do not insure house = MAX [69 800, 0] = 69 800

5   Choose the alternative with the lowest of these maximum regrets, which is to insure the house.

WORKED EXAMPLE 9.7

Use the Savage criterion for the example of a fruit stall at a local gala described by the following gains matrix:

		Events		
		Weather good	Weather average	Weather poor
Alternatives	Large quantity	**10**	4	−2
	Medium quantity	7	**6**	2
	Small quantity	4	1	**4**

Solution

1   The best outcome for each event is underlined (that is, with good weather a large quantity, with average weather a medium quantity, and with poor weather a small quantity).

2   The regret for every other entry in the column is the difference between this underlined value and the actual entry. If the weather is good and a medium quantity is bought the regret is $10 - 7 = 3$; if the weather is good and a small quantity is bought the regret is $10 - 4 = 6$, and so on.

3   Form these regret figures into a regret matrix, replacing the original profit figures.

		Events		
		Weather good	Weather average	Weather poor
Alternatives	Large quantity	0	2	**6**
	Medium quantity	**3**	0	2
	Small quantity	**6**	5	0

4   For each alternative find the highest regret:

- large quantity = MAX [0, 2, 6] = 6
- medium quantity = MAX [3, 0, 2] = 3
- small quantity = MAX [6, 5, 0] = 6

5   Choose the alternative with the lowest of these maximum regrets. This is the medium quantity.

IN SUMMARY

The Savage criterion calculates a regret as the difference between the best outcome for each event and the actual outcome. Then it uses the Wald criterion on the regret matrix.

9.3.4 Choosing the criterion to use

Different criteria often recommend the same alternative, but there is no guarantee of this. When criteria recommend different alternatives, we should use the most relevant criterion. Suppose the decision makers are working as consultants and the quality of their decisions is judged by other people. Then we could suggest the Savage criterion. If the decision is made for a small company which cannot afford to risk high losses, then Wald may be best. If there is really nothing to choose between the different events, Laplace may be useful.

Although it is difficult to go beyond these general guidelines you can notice one other point; both the Wald and Savage criteria effectively use one outcome – the worst for Wald and the one which leads to the highest regret for Savage. This means the choice might be dominated by a few atypical results. The Laplace criterion is the only one to use all the outcomes.

Of course, a manager may feel that none of the criteria we have described is suitable. We only chose these as illustrations, and there are many others. An ambitious organization might aim for the highest profit and use a criterion which chooses the highest return (a 'maximax profit' criterion). Alternatively it may try to balance the best and worst outcomes for each event and use a criterion based on the value for:

$$\alpha * \text{best outcome} + (1-\alpha) * \text{worst outcome}$$

where α has a value between zero and one.

Ultimately, of course, criteria make suggestions, managers have to make the decisions. A major strength of decision criteria is that they describe the structure of a problem and allow informed discussion.

WORKED EXAMPLE 9.8

The following payoff matrix shows the gains from a decision. Use the Laplace, Wald and Savage decision criteria to choose the best alternatives.

	1	2	3
1	14	23	6
2	11	17	14
3	12	16	15

Solution

Figure 9.2 shows the printout from a simple package for decision analysis. It shows the results as:

● Laplace chooses either of alternatives 1 or 3

● Wald chooses alternative 3

● Savage chooses alternative 2

Then it looks at two other criteria which choose alternatives 1 and 3.

```
Program: Decision-Making Under Uncertainty
Problem Title: Worked Example 9.8

***** Input Data *****

Type of Problem: Gains
-----------------------------------------------
                     Event 1     Event 2     Event 3
-----------------------------------------------
Alternative 1        14.000      23.000       6.000
Alternative 2        11.000      17.000      14.000
Alternative 3        12.000      16.000      15.000
-----------------------------------------------
Hurwicz Alpha Coefficient:       0.300
                ***** Program Output *****
<= shows the best alternative(s)

Laplace (best mean)
------------------------------
   Alternative    Expected Value
------------------------------
        1            14.333 <=
        2            14.000
        3            14.333 <=
------------------------------

Wald (maximin)
------------------------------
   Alternative    Expected Value
------------------------------
        1             6.000
        2            11.000
        3            12.000 <=
------------------------------

Savage (Minimax regret)
------------------------------
   Alternative    Maximum Regret
------------------------------
        1             9.000
        2             6.000 <=
        3             7.000
------------------------------

Maximax (best best)
------------------------------
   Alternative    Maximax Payoff
------------------------------
        1            23.000 <=
        2            17.000
        3            16.000
------------------------------

Hurwicz (α*best + [1-α]*worst)
------------------------------
   Alternative    Hurwicz Payoff
------------------------------
        1            11.000
        2            12.800
        3            13.200 <=
------------------------------
                ***** End of Output *****
```

Figure 9.2   Computer printout for Worked Example 9.8.

As you can see, there is some disagreement about the best alternative – but these figures have been specially chosen, and the difference is not usually so great.

9.3.5 Maximum fee worth paying for perfect information

Sometimes we can buy more information about a problem from a consultant or some other expert. This extra information should allow better decisions. But how much is it worth paying to get the extra information?

Suppose a company is about to launch a new product, whose success depends on the economic climate. The product can be made in three styles – deluxe, standard and basic – and the company must decide which style to launch. A payoff matrix showing the gains, in thousands of pounds a year, is shown below:

	Economy stagnant	Economy medium	Economy buoyant
Launch deluxe version	10	15	30
Launch standard version	5	20	10
Launch basic version	15	10	−5

If the company has no further information, it could use decision criteria to suggest the best alternative. But it might hire economic forecasters to give more detailed information on the state of the economy. How much should the company pay for this extra information?

Assuming the information given by the economic forecasters is correct – so they give *perfect information* – the company will know in advance which event is going to occur. Then it can choose the alternative that gives the highest gains for this event. If the economic forecasters say the economy will be stagnant, the company will launch the cheap product and gain £15 000 a year. If the forecasters say the economy will be medium, the company will launch the standard product and gain £20 000 a year. If the forecasters say the economy will be buoyant, the company will launch the deluxe version and gain £30 000 a year. From these profits the company has to subtract the forecasters' fee, F. So it has effectively added a fourth alternative of 'Pay a fee of F for perfect information' which we can add to the original gains matrix.

	Economy stagnant	Economy medium	Economy buoyant
Launch deluxe version	10	15	30
Launch standard version	5	20	10
Launch basic version	15	10	−5
Pay fee of F for information	$15 - F$	$20 - F$	$30 - F$

Now we can tackle this revised problem in the usual way, but with the solution phrased in terms of F.

Using the Laplace criterion, average values for alternatives are:

- deluxe version gives average gains of $(10 + 15 + 30)/3 = 18.3$

- standard version gives average gains of $(5 + 20 + 10)/3 = 11.7$

- cheap version gives average gains of $(15 + 10 - 5)/3 = 6.7$

- paying fee of F gives average gains of $(15 - F + 20 - F + 30 - F)/3 = 21.7\text{-}F$

The highest of these depends on the value of F, and is either 18.3 or $21.7 - F$. Then it is worth paying a fee when:

$$21.7 - F \geq 18.3$$

$$F \leq 3.4$$

The maximum fee worth paying for perfect information is £3400. This gives a final decision to pay for information if the fee is less than £3400, and otherwise launch the deluxe product.

Other decision criteria will give different suggestions. Wald would calculate the worst outcomes as:

- deluxe version worst outcome is   MIN [10, 15, 30] = 10

- standard version worst outcome is   MIN [5, 20, 10] = 5

- basic version worst outcome is   MIN [15, 10, −5] = −5

- paying fee of F worst outcome is   MIN [15 − F, 20 − F, 30 − F] = 15 − F

The best of these depends on the value of F, and is either 10 or $15 - F$. The Wald criterion suggests paying the fee when:

$$15 - F \geq 10$$

$$F \leq 5$$

The maximum fee worth paying for perfect information is £5000. So the final decision is to get the information if the fee is less than £5000 and otherwise launch the deluxe version.

Finally, we can look at the Savage criterion which forms the regret matrix as follows:

	Economy stagnant	Economy medium	Economy buoyant
Launch deluxe version	5	5	0
Launch standard version	10	0	20
Launch basic version	0	10	32
Pay fee of F for information	F	F	F

The highest regret for each alternative is:

- deluxe version gives highest regret of   MAX [5, 5, 0] = 5
- standard version gives highest regret of   MAX [10, 0, 20] = 20
- basic version gives highest regret of   MAX [0, 10, 32] = 32
- paying fee of F gives highest regret of   MAX $[F, F, F] = F$

The lowest of these depends on the value of F, and is either 5 or F. So the final decision is to get the information if the fee is less than £5000 and otherwise launch the deluxe version.

WORKED EXAMPLE 9.9

Calculate the cost of perfect information for the following matrix of gains:

		Events		
		1	2	3
	a	142	150	119
Alternatives	b	124	161	135
	c	102	147	150

Solution

Adding a fourth alternative (d) of paying a fee of F for perfect information gives the revised matrix of gains:

		Events		
		1	2	3
	a	142	150	119
	b	124	161	135
Alternatives	c	102	147	150
	d	$142 - F$	$161 - F$	$150 - F$

- The Laplace criterion suggests the alternative with the highest of:

  a. $411/3 = 137$

  b. $420/3 = 140$

  c. $399/3 = 133$

  d. $453/3 - F = 151 - F$

The highest is alternative d when $151 - F \geq 140$, or $F \leq 11$. Otherwise it is alternative b.

- The Wald criterion suggests the alternative with the highest of:

  a. 119

  b. 124

  c. 102

  d. $142 - F$

The highest is alternative d if $142 - F \geq 124$, or $F \leq 18$. Otherwise it is alternative b.

- The Savage criterion forms the regret matrix:

		Events		
		1	2	3
	a	0	11	31
	b	18	0	15
Alternatives	c	40	14	0
	d	F	F	F

Then it suggests the alternative with the lowest of:

  a. 31

  b. 18

  c. 40

  d. F

This is alternative d if $F \leq 8$. Otherwise it is alternative b.

$\boxed{\textit{IN SUMMARY}}$

Sometimes we can buy additional information. This adds another alternative, which we can use to calculate the maximum fee worth paying.

Self-assessment questions

9.6 What is meant by 'decision-making under uncertainty'?

9.7 List three useful decision criteria.

9.8 How many of these criteria use *all* the outcomes for an alternative?

9.9 What is 'the maximum fee worth paying for perfect information'?

9.4 | Decision-making under risk

The last section looked at decision-making under uncertainty. This had a number of events that could occur, but no way of showing the relative likelihood of each. With decision-making under *risk* there is again a number of events that might occur, but now we can put probabilities to each of them. As we should include every event, these probabilities should add to one. A simple example of decision-making under risk is betting on the outcome of spinning a coin. The events are the coin coming down heads or tails and the probability of each of these is 0.5.

9.4.1 Expected values

The usual way of solving problems with risk is to calculate the *expected value* for each alternative, and choose the alternative with the best expected value. The expected value is defined as the sum of the probabilities multiplied by the outcomes:

$$\text{expected value} = \sum (\text{probability} * \text{outcome})$$

The expected value for an alternative is the average gain or cost if the decision is repeated a large number of times. It is not the value we would get **every** time – but the average value for a large number of repetitions.

Then for decision under risk there are two steps:

1 Calculate the expected value for each alternative.

2 Choose the alternative with the best expected value (highest value for gains and lowest value for costs).

WORKED EXAMPLE 9.10

Which is the best alternative for the following matrix of gains?

		Events			
		1 $P = 0.1$	2 $P = 0.2$	3 $P = 0.6$	4 $P = 0.1$
Alternatives	A	10	7	5	9
	B	3	20	2	10
	C	3	4	11	1
	D	8	4	2	16

Solution

The expected value for each alternative is the sum of the probability times the value of the outcome, giving:

- alternative A $0.1*10 + 0.2*7 + 0.6*5 + 0.1*9 = 6.3$
- alternative B $0.1*3 + 0.2*20 + 0.6*2 + 0.1*10 = 6.5$
- alternative C $0.1*3 + 0.2*4 + 0.6*11 + 0.1*1 = 7.8$
- alternative D $0.1*8 + 0.2*4 + 0.6*2 + 0.1*16 = 4.4$

As these are gains, the best alternative is C with an expected value of 7.8. If this decision is made repeatedly, the average return in the long run is 7.8: if the decision is made only once the gain could be any of the four values 3, 4, 11 or 1.

WORKED EXAMPLE 9.11

A transport firms bids for a long-term contract to move newspapers from a printing works to wholesalers. It can submit one of three tenders: a low one which assumes that newspaper sales will increase to give lower unit transport costs; a medium one which gives a reasonable return if newspaper sales stay the same; or a high one which assumes that newspaper sales will decline to give higher unit transport costs. The probabilities of newspaper sales and profits (in thousands of pounds) for the transport firm are shown in the following table. Which tender should the firm submit?

	Newspaper sales		
	decrease $P = 0.4$	stay same $P = 0.3$	increase $P = 0.3$
Low tender	10	15	16
Medium tender	5	20	10
High tender	18	10	−5

Solution

Calculating the expected value for each alternative:

- low tender $0.4*10 + 0.3*15 + 0.3*16 = 13.3$
- medium tender $0.4*5 + 0.3*20 + 0.3*10 = 11.0$
- high tender $0.4*18 + 0.3*10 - 0.3*5 = 8.7$

As these are profits, the best alternative is the one with highest expected value, which is the low tender.

The expected value gives a balanced view of returns. Managers could, of course, decide not to take such a balanced view, and they might want to use some other criterion. They might, for example, put more weight on a large potential gain, even if there is a small chance that it will occur.

With decisions under uncertainty we calculated the value of additional, perfect information. Now we can do the same thing for risk. Suppose market researchers can run a test to say, with certainty, whether the sales of newspapers in the last example will increase, stay the same or decrease. Then, if the market researchers say that newspaper sales will decrease, the transport firm will put in a high tender and make a profit of £18 000; if the researchers said that sales will stay the same, the firm will put in a medium tender for profits of £20 000; and if the researchers say that sales will increase the firm will put in a low tender for profits of £16 000. From each of these the company has to subtract the fee, F, charged by the market researchers. So we can add the extra alternative 'pay a fee of F for perfect information' to give the following payoff matrix:

	Newspaper sales		
	decrease $P = 0.4$	stay same $P = 0.3$	increase $P = 0.3$
Low tender	10	15	16
Medium tender	5	20	10
High tender	18	10	−5
Pay fee F for info.	$18 - F$	$20 - F$	$16 - F$

Calculating the expected values as before:

- low tender = 13.3
- medium tender = 11.0
- high tender = 8.7
- pay fee F for info. $= 0.4*(18 - F) + 0.3*(20 - F) + 0.3*(16 - F) = 18.0 - F$

The highest of these depends on the value of F, and is either 13.3 or $18.0 - F$. Paying for the market research is better if:

$$18 - F \geq 13.3$$
$$F \leq 4.7$$

So the final decision is to pay for the extra information if the fee is less that £4700, and otherwise submit a low tender.

IN SUMMARY

With situations of risk we can give probabilities to each event. The expected value is the most common way of finding the best alternative. We can calculate a fee worth paying for perfect information.

9.4.2 Using Bayes' theorem to update probabilities

Chapter 7 showed how **Bayes' theorem** can update conditional probabilities:

$$\textbf{Bayes' theorem:} \quad P(a/b) = \frac{P(b/a)*P(a)}{P(b)}$$

where: $P(a/b)$ = probability of a happening given that b has already happened

$P(b/a)$ = probability of b given that a has already happened

$P(a)$, $P(b)$ = probabilities of a and b respectively

WORKED EXAMPLE 9.12

The crowd for a sports event might be small (with a probability of 0.4) or large. To help with final arrangements, advance sales of tickets can be analysed a week before the event takes place. Advanced sales can be high, average or low, with the probability of advanced sales conditional on crowd size given by the following table:

		Advance sales		
		High	Average	Low
Crowd size	Large	0	2	6
	Small	3	0	2

The organizers must choose one of two plans for running the event and the table below gives the net profit in thousands of pounds for each combination of plan and crowd size:

		Plan 1	Plan 2
Crowd size	Large	10	14
	Small	9	5

If the organizers use the information on advance sales, how can they maximize their expected profits? How much should the organizers pay for the information on advanced sales? How much would perfect information be worth?

Solution

We can use the abbreviations:

- CL and CS for crowd size large and crowd size small
- ASH, ASA and ASL for advance sales high, average and low

If the organizers do not use the information on advance sales, the best they can do is to use the probabilities of large and small crowd (0.6 and 0.4 respectively) to calculate expected values for the two plans:

- Plan 1: $0.6*10 + 0.4*9 = 9.6$
- Plan 2: $0.6*14 + 0.4*5 = \mathbf{10.4}$ better plan

The organizers should use plan 2 with an expected value of £10 400.

But the organizers can make better decisions if they use the information on advance ticket sales. This information gives the conditional probabilities $P(ASH/CL)$, $P(ASH/CS)$, etc., but they need these the other way around, $P(CL/ASH)$, $P(CS/ASH)$, etc., and must use Bayes' theorem. The calculations for this are shown in the following table:

	ASH	ASA	ASL		ASH	ASA	ASL
CL	0.7	0.3	0.0	0.6	0.42	0.18	0.00
CS	0.2	0.2	0.6	0.4	0.08	0.08	0.24
					0.50	0.26	0.24
				CL	0.84	0.69	0.00
				CS	0.16	0.31	1.00

The probability of advance sales being high is 0.5. If this happens, the probability of a large crowd is 0.84 and of a small crowd is 0.16. Then, if the organizers choose plan 1 the expected value is $0.84*10 + 0.16*9 = 9.84$; if the organizers choose plan 2 their expected value is $0.84*14 + 0.16*5 = 12.56$. So if the advance sales are high, they should choose plan 2.

We can calculate the values for other results in the same way.

ASH: Plan 1 $0.84*10 + 0.16*9 = 9.84$
          Plan 2 $0.84*14 + 0.16*5 = \mathbf{12.56}$

ASA: Plan 1 $0.69*10 + 0.31*9 = 9.69$
          Plan 2 $0.69*14 + 0.31*5 = \mathbf{11.21}$

ASL: Plan 1 $0.00*10 + 1.00*9 = \mathbf{9.00}$
          Plan 2 $0.00*14 + 1.00*5 = 5.00$

As you can see, the decisions which maximise the organizers' expected profit are:

- if the advance sales are high choose plan 2 and gain 12.56
- if advance sales are medium choose plan 2 and gain 11.21
- if they are low choose plan 1 and gain 9.00

We can go a little further with this analysis, as we know the probability of high, average and low advance sales are respectively 0.5, 0.26 and 0.24. So we can calculate the overall expected value of making these decisions:

$$0.5*12.56 + 0.26*11.21 + 0.24*9 = 11.35$$

This compares with an expected profit of £10 400 when the advance sales information is not used. So using the additional information raises expected profits by 11 350 − 10 400 = £950, or over 9%.

Finally, we can calculate a value of **perfect** information on advance ticket sales. If we know with certainty that crowd size will be large we would use plan 2 with an expected profit of £14 000: if we know that crowd size will be small we will use plan 1 with a profit of £9000. The probability of large and small crowd is 0.6 and 0.4 respectively so the profit with perfect information is   0.6*14 + 0.4*9 = 12.

To summarize these results, the expected value:

- with perfect information   = £12 000
- using advance sales information   = £11 350
- not using advance sales information = £10 400

WORKED EXAMPLE 9.13

An oil company drills an exploration well in deep water off the Irish coast. The company is uncertain of the amount of recoverable oil it will find, but experience suggests it will be minor (with a probability of 0.3), significant (with probability 0.5) or major. The company now has to decide how to develop the find and has a choice of either moving quickly to minimize the cost of long-term debt, or moving slowly to maintain income. The profits for every combination of size of find and development speed are given in the following table, where entries are in millions of pounds:

	Size of find		
	Minor	Significant	Major
Develop quickly	100	130	180
Develop slowly	80	150	210

Some further geological tests could give a more accurate picture of the size of the find, but these cost £2.5 million and are not entirely accurate. The tests give results A, B or C, with conditional probabilities of results given size of find shown in the following table:

		Test results		
		A	B	C
	Minor	0.3	0.4	0.3
Size of find	Significant	0.5	0.0	0.5
	Major	0.25	0.25	0.5

If the oil company wants to maximize its profits, should it do the geological tests? What is the value of perfect information?

Solution

We can start by defining the abbreviations:

- MIN, SIG and MAJ for minor, significant and major finds
- QUICK and SLOW for the quick and slow development

Without using the further geological test, the expected values with each speed of development are:

- QUICK 0.3*100 + 0.5*130 + 0.2*180 = 131
- SLOW 0.3*80 + 0.5*150 + 0.2*210 = **141**

The company should develop the find slowly with an expected value of £141 million.

The oil company wants information from geological tests in the form $P(MIN/A)$, etc. It actually gets information in the form $P(A/MIN)$, etc., so it must use Bayes' theorem:

	A	B	C		A	B	C
MIN	0.3	0.4	0.3	0.3	0.09	0.12	0.09
SIG	0.5	0.0	0.5	0.5	0.25	0.00	0.25
CS	0.25	0.25	0.5	0.2	0.05	0.05	0.10
					0.39	0.17	0.44
		MIN			0.23	0.71	0.20
		SIG			0.64	0.00	0.57
		MAJ			0.13	0.29	0.23

If the test result is A, the probabilities of minor, significant and major finds are 0.23, 0.64 and 0.13 respectively. Developing the well quickly will give an expected profit of:

$$0.23*100 + 0.64*130 + 0.13*180 = 129.6$$

Repeating this calculation for other results gives:

Result A: QUICK 0.23*100 + 0.64*130 + 0.13*180 = 129.6
           SLOW   0.23*80 + 0.64*150 + 0.13*210 = **141.7**

Result B: QUICK 0.71*100 + 0.00*130 + 0.29*180 = **123.2**
           SLOW   0.71*80 + 0.00*150 + 0.29*210 = 117.7

Result C: QUICK 0.20*100 + 0.57*130 + 0.23*180 = 135.5
           SLOW   0.20*80 + 0.57*150 + 0.23*210 = **149.8**

The best choices are to develop slowly with test results A or C, and quickly with test results B. This gives an expected profit of:

$$0.39*141.7 + 0.17*123.2 + 0.44*149.8 = 142.12$$

The profit without doing the tests is £141 million, and with the test this rises to £142.12 million minus the cost of £2.5 million. In these circumstances it is not worth doing the tests, and would not be worth doing them unless their cost was less than £1.12 million.

With perfect information the expected value is:

$$0.3*100 + 0.5*150 + 0.2*210 = 147$$

So this information is worth $147 - 141 = £6$ million.

9.4.3 Utilities

Expected values are easy to use but they do not always show real preferences. Consider an investment with the payoff matrix shown below:

		Events	
		Gain $P = 0.1$	Lose $P = 0.9$
Alternatives	Invest	£500 000	−£50 000
	Do not invest	£0	£0

You can see that this has a 90% chance of making a loss. But the expected values are:

- invest $0.1*500\,000 - 0.9*50\,000 = £5000$

- do not invest $0.1*0 + 0.9*0 = £0$

Faced with this decision, most people would not want to invest. We could, of course, say that most people are wrong – but it is more likely that something is wrong with the expected values. Remember that expected values give the average return in the long run when the decision is repeated a large number of times. If a decision is made only once, they give misleading advice. They also assume a strict linear relationship between the amount of money and its value. Then £100 has a value a hundred times greater than £1, and £1 000 000 has a value ten thousand times greater than £100. In practice, this strict linear relationship is not accurate.

To overcome these problems, we can use **utilities**. These are measures that show more accurately the real value of money. Figure 9.3 shows the graph of a typical utility function. As you can see, the value of money does not rise linearly with the amount.

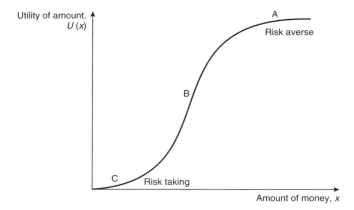

Figure 9.3 A typical utility function relating amounts of money to their value.

There are three distinct regions in Figure 9.3. At the top, near point A, the utility is rising slowly with the amount of money. A decision maker in this region already has a lot of money and does not put a high value on even more. But the decision maker would certainly not want to lose money and move nearer to point B where the utility falls quickly. Gaining some money is not very attractive, but losing some is very unattractive, so this leads to a conservative decision maker who does not like to take risks.

In region B of the graph the utility function is almost linear, which is the assumption of expected values. A decision maker at the bottom, near point C, does not have much money, so losing some hardly affects the utility. But the decision maker would be keen to gain money and move nearer to B where the utility rises very quickly. Gaining money is very attractive, but losing some is not important, so this leads to a decision maker who is willing to take risks.

Utilities are useful in principle, but it is very difficult to find a reasonable utility function. Each individual and organization values money differently, and has a different utility function. As circumstances change, these curves vary over time. But when we can find a convincing function, the way to choose the best alternative is to calculate expected utilities, instead of expected values.

WORKED EXAMPLE 9.14

Martha Jones has noticed that her utility curve is a reasonable approximation to $\sqrt{x}$. What is her best decision when faced by the following matrix of gains?

			Events	
		A $P = 0.7$	B $P = 0.2$	C $P = 0.6$
Alternatives	1	14	24	12
	2	6	40	90
	3	1	70	30
	4	12	12	6

Solution

For interest, we can calculate the expected value of each alternative:

- alternative 1 $0.7*14 + 0.2*24 + 0.1*12 = 15.8$
- alternative 2 $0.7*6 + 0.2*40 + 0.1*90 = \textbf{21.2}$
- alternative 3 $0.7*1 + 0.2*70 + 0.1*30 = 17.7$
- alternative 4 $0.7*12 + 0.2*12 + 0.1*6 = 11.4$

Using expected values, Martha's best alternative is number 2. Now we can repeat the calculations but replacing the amount of money, x, by its utility, $U(x)$, which in this case is the square root of the amount.

- alternative 1 $0.7*\sqrt{14} + 0.2*\sqrt{24} + 0.1*\sqrt{12} = \textbf{3.95}$
- alternative 2 $0.7*\sqrt{6} + 0.2*\sqrt{40} + 0.1*\sqrt{90} = 3.93$
- alternative 3 $0.7*\sqrt{1} + 0.2*\sqrt{70} + 0.1*\sqrt{30} = 2.92$
- alternative 4 $0.7*\sqrt{12} + 0.2*\sqrt{12} + 0.1*\sqrt{6} = 3.36$

Although the difference is small, Martha's best alternative has shifted to 1. This is because the value of money has changed, and the relative attractiveness of the gain of 90 in alternative 2 has declined.

IN SUMMARY

Utilities show the value of different amounts of money. Expected utilities can help with decisions in situations of risk, provided we can find a realistic utility function.

Self-assessment questions

9.10   What is meant by 'decision-making under risk'?

9.11   What is an 'expected value'?

9.12   Could a 'subjective probability' be used for problems with risk?

9.13   When is Bayes' theorem used to calculate expected values?

9.14   Why might expected utilities be a better measure than expected values?

9.5 | Sequential decisions and decision trees

So far we have looked at single decisions. In other words, the problem is solved when we have looked at a set of alternatives and found the best. But there are many situations where one decision leads to a series of other decisions. If you decide to buy a car, your first decision might be to choose a new one or a second-hand one. If you choose a new car, this opens the choice of cars built in Britain, Japan, France, Germany, Italy, or somewhere else. If you choose a car built in Britain the choice is Rover, Jaguar, Ford, Rolls Royce, Vauxhall, Nissan, Toyota, and so on. Then if you choose a Rover you have to make some more decisions about the model, colour, and extras. At each stage in the decision process, choosing one alternative opens up a series of other choices or events. We can show this kind of problem in a **decision tree**, where the alternatives and events are represented by the branches of a horizontal tree.

WORKED EXAMPLE 9.15

A company wants to expand, and it asks a bank manager for a loan. The bank manager has to decide whether or not to grant the loan. If the bank manager grants the loan, the company expansion may be successful or it may not. If the bank manager does not grant the loan, the company may continue banking as before, or it may move its account to another bank. Draw a decision tree of this situation.

Solution

A decision tree shows the sequence of alternatives and events. There is a notional time-scale going from left to right with early decisions or events on the left followed by later ones towards the right. There is only one decision in this example followed by events over which the bank manager has no control, so the sequence is:

- the manager makes a decision
- one of several possible events happens.

These are shown in the decision tree in Figure 9.4.

In the decision tree the alternatives and events are represented by branches, so each branch represents a different path (decision or event) that may be followed through the tree. There are three distinct types of nodes, which are the points that branches come from:

○ **random node**. These show points where things happen, so all branches leaving random nodes are events with known probabilities.

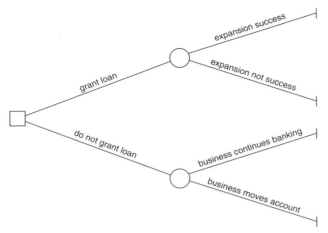

expansion success

expansion not success

grant loan

do not grant loan

business continues banking

business moves account

Figure 9.4   Decision tree for Worked Example 9.15.

☐   **decision node**. These show points where decisions are made, so all branches leaving a decision node are alternatives, and we choose the best.

| **terminal node**. These are at the right-hand side of the tree and show the ends of all sequences of decisions and events.

This gives the basic structure of the tree, but we still have to add probabilities and values. Suppose the bank currently values its business with the company at £2000 a year. If the manager grants the loan and the expansion succeeds the value to the bank will increase to £3000 a year. If the expansion does not succeed the bank will still have business valued at £1000 a year – reduced because of the allowance for bad debt. There is a probability of 0.7 that the expansion plan will succeed. If the manager does not grant the loan there is a probability of 0.6 that the company will transfer its account to another bank.

We can put the probabilities on event branches, remembering to include all events so that the sum of probabilities from each random node equals one. We can also put the values on terminal nodes, which show the total value of moving through the tree and reaching the end-points. In this case, these values are the annual business expected by the bank. This gives the tree shown in Figure 9.5.

The next stage of the analysis moves from right to left through the tree and assigns a value to each node in turn. To do this we find the best decision at each decision node, and the expected value at each random node.

● At each decision node the alternative branches leaving are connected to following nodes. We compare the values on these following nodes, choose the best branch, and add the node value.

● At each random node the value is the expected value of the leaving event branches. This is the sum, for all branches, of the probability of leaving by a branch times the value of the node at the end of the branch.

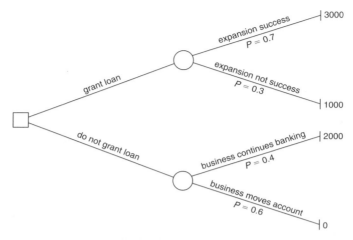

Figure 9.5   Decision tree with added probabilities and terminal values.

The value at the left-hand, originating node is the overall expected value of following the best policies.

Using this procedure on the tree in Figure 9.5 gives the results shown in Figure 9.6. The calculations for nodes are as follows:

- at random node A calculate expected value: $0.7 * 3000 + 0.3 * 1000 = 2400$
- at random node B calculate expected value: $0.4 * 2000 + 0.6 * 0 = 800$
- at decision node C choose the best alternative: Maximum of $[2400, 800] = 2400$

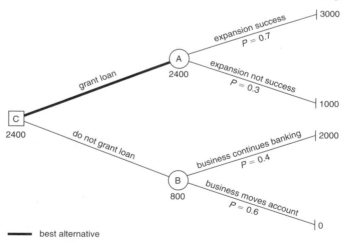

Figure 9.6   Analysing the decision tree.

The best policy is to grant the loan, and this has an expected value of £2400.

WORKED EXAMPLE 9.16

Williamson Workshop is about to buy a new machine for stamping and pressing parts for domestic appliances. Three suppliers have made bids to supply the machine. The first supplier offers the Basicor machine which automatically produces parts of acceptable, but not outstanding, quality. The output from the machine is variable and could be 1000 a week (with probability 0.1), 2000 a week (with probability 0.7) or 3000 a week. The notional profit for this machine is £4 a unit made. The second supplier offers a Superstamp machine which makes higher quality parts. The output from this can be 700 a week (with probability 0.4) or 1000 a week, with a notional profit of £10 a unit. The third supplier offers the Switchover machine which can be set to make either 1300 high-quality parts a week at a profit of £6 a unit, or 1600 medium-quality parts a week with a profit of £5 a unit.

If the machine makes 2000 or more units a week, it is possible to export all production as a single bulk order. Then there is a 60% chance of selling for 50% more profit, and a 40% chance of selling for 50% less profit.

What should Williamson Workshop do to maximize its expected profits?

Solution

The tree for this decision is shown in Figure 9.7. The terminal node values are the weekly profit, which is found by multiplying the number made by the profit per unit. If 1000 are made on the Basicor machine the value is £4000, and so on. If the output from Basicor is exported, profit may be increased by 50% (i.e. to £6 a unit) or reduced by 50% (i.e to £2 a unit).

The calculations at each node are as follows:

A. expected value at random node $= 0.6 * 12\,000 + 0.4 * 4000 = 8800$

B. expected value at random node $= 0.6 * 18\,000 + 0.4 * 6000 = 13\,200$

C. best alternative at decision node $= \text{MAX} \, [8800, 8000] = 8800$

D. best alternative at decision node $= \text{MAX} \, [13\,200, 12\,000] = 13\,200$

E. expected value at random node $= 0.1 * 4000 + 0.7 * 8800 + 0.2 * 13\,200 = 9200$

F. expected value at random node $= 0.4 * 7000 + 0.6 * 10\,000 = 8800$

G. best alternative at decision node $= \text{MAX} \, [7800, 8000] = 8000$

H. best alternative at decision node $= \text{MAX} \, [9200, 8800, 8000] = 9200$

Overall, the best decision is to buy the Basicor machine and if it produces more than 2000 units, export all production. The expected profit from this policy is £9200 a week.

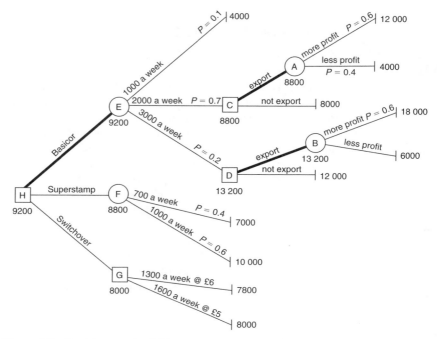

Figure 9.7   Decision tree for Williamson Workshop in Worked Example 9.16.

WORKED EXAMPLE 9.17

A new reservoir has been built by damming a river. This gives a nearby city a reliable supply of water, but a farmer lower down the river valley now finds that the supply to his cattle has dried up. He has the options of either connecting to the local mains water supply, at a cost of £22 000, or drilling a new well. The cost of the well is not known with certainty but could be £16 000 (with a probability of 0.3), £22 000 (with a probability of 0.3) or £28 000, depending on the underground rock structure and depth of water.

The farmer can hire a local water survey company to do on-site tests. For a cost of £300 they will give either a favourable or an unfavourable report on the chances of easily finding water. The reliability of this report, phrased in terms of the probability of a favourable report given the drilling cost will be low, etc., is given in the following table:

	Drilling well costs		
	£16 000	£22 000	£28 000
Favourable report	0.8	0.6	0.2
Unfavourable report	0.2	0.4	0.8

Use a decision tree to find the farmer's best decisions.

Solution

We know the conditional probabilities one way around, but need them the other way around for the decision tree. So we have to use Bayes' theorem.

		Favourable	Unfavourable		Favourable	Unfavourable
	16 000	0.8	0.2	0.3	0.24	0.06
Cost	22 000	0.6	0.4	0.3	0.18	0.12
	28 000	0.2	0.8	0.4	0.08	0.32
					0.50	0.50
			16 000		0.48	0.12
			22 000		0.36	0.24
			28 000		0.16	0.64

We can add these probabilities and other values, to give the farmer's decision tree shown in Figure 9.8.

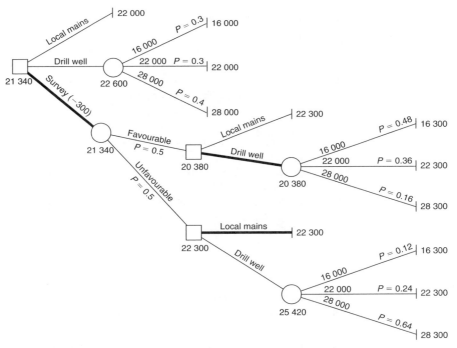

Figure 9.8 Farmer's decision tree for Worked Example 9.17.

Completing the analysis shows the farmer's best option is to use the survey and follow its advice, with an expected cost of £21 340.

Case example

IN SUMMARY

We can use decision trees to analyse sequential decisions. These show the series of alternatives and events as the branches of a tree. The procedure for analysing a tree is:

- find all the alternatives, events and their probabilities, outcomes, etc.
- draw a tree (moving from left to right) showing the sequences of events and alternatives, and setting the values at terminal nodes
- analyse the tree (moving from right to left) choosing the best alternative at each decision node and calculating the expected value at each random node

Self-assessment questions

9.15 Why should sequential decisions be considered differently from a series of separate decisions?

9.16 List the three types of node in a decision tree.

9.17 How is the node value calculated at a terminal node, a decision node and a random node?

9.18 How can you identify the best decisions in a decision tree?

CHAPTER REVIEW

This chapter has described some aspects of decision analysis. In particular it:

- talked about complicated decisions and the benefits of giving them some structure using maps, payoff matrices or decision trees
- described the standard features of decisions
- looked at decision-making under certainty
- described decision criteria for making decisions with uncertainty
- used expected values for decisions with risk
- found the value of information in different circumstances
- used utilities to describe the value of money
- used decision trees to deal with sequential decisions

KEY TERMS

Bayes' theorem
certainty
decision criteria
decision tree
expected value
Laplace
payoff matrix
perfect information

problem map
regret
risk
Savage
uncertainty
utilities
Wald

Case study

John Sparrow's petrol additive

Two years ago John Sparrow was a postgraduate student of chemistry. He was doing research into the combustive properties of analhydric benzoprophyline acyclic-polymentaphosphodine, when he found an additive for petrol that could marginally reduce the fuel consumption of cars. He published a report of this in a technical journal and a fuller account was given in his PhD thesis.

Since John left university he has been working for a small plastics company, but this is now closing down and he will soon be unemployed. His most straightforward option is to find a new job. Although he enjoyed working for the plastics company, John feels that this may be the time to start a business of his own. In particular, he could look at the commercial development of his petrol additive.

John was not sure that there would be any interest in his additive. To gauge reactions, he approached an established company to see if they would be willing to manufacture and market it. His first talks were with the New Developments section of Bonded Chemicals who owned the plastics company John worked for. Bonded Chemicals had read John's technical reports on the additive – it was this work that persuaded them to employ him in the first place. They knew his abilities, and were confident that they could do something with his ideas.

A quick reply from the company said that they would be interested in making a conditional offer for the additive. This would be based on a cash payment of £50 000 to John and further royalties based on the success of the product. In effect Bonded Chemicals would manufacture and market the additive; if they considered it a commercial success they would give John royalties of 2% of profit; if they considered it a failure they would give him no royalties at all. Unfortunately, there is no means of saying, in advance, if the additive will be a commercial success or not. The experiences of other people offered similar contracts suggest there is a 50% chance of the company considering the product successful and royalty payments then average £25 000 a year. If the additive proves successful in the first year the company often (on 60% of occasions) offer a cash payment of £60 000 to the developers instead of paying any further royalties.

Another option open to John would be to set up his own company and start making and marketing the additive himself. Unfortunately, he is still young and has no business experience or proven skills. He has talked to the local Development Agency Small Business Encouragement Division who could offer a limited amount of advice. They were encouraging in some respects, but said that only 20% of small businesses were successful in the first 3 years of operation. 40% ceased trading and the remaining 40% continued to operate but were only just covering costs. They also recommended a marketing firm that could prepare a market evaluation to see if the additive is likely to sell. This marketing firm specializes in assessing the potential demand for new products and for a fee of £15 000 will run a series of interviews, surveys and trials. At the end of these they make one of three reports: either the product has potential for good sales, or it does not have potential for good sales, or it is too new and not enough information is available to judge its likely sales.

John went home and analysed the information he had been given and did some calculations. Firstly, it seemed unrealistic to plan beyond 3 years, so he decided only to consider his income and costs over this period. Then, if his company is a success he could expect to take a salary and profits of £30 000 a year. If the company just covers costs he could take a salary of £15 000 a year. If the company closes down he could expect to have a net loss over 3 years of £10 000. Secondly, he looked at the reliability of the marketing firm and found that they said a new product had potential for good sales 30% of times, it did not have potential for good sales 45% of times, and they could not say 25% of times. Their reliability could also be described by the following table of conditional probabilities. This shows the probability that the marketing company said that a product had potential for good sales given that it eventually sold well and the new company was successful, etc.

	Company successful	Company covered costs	Company ceased trading
Potential for good sales	0.6	0.3	0.1
No potential for good sales	0.2	0.4	0.4
Not enough information	0.3	0.4	0.3

After receiving results from the marketing firm, John could still decide to simply find another job, or go into business on his own, or sell the additive to Bonded Chemicals. But Bonded Chemicals would certainly hear about the survey, and if they were now offered the product would understand that the survey was not optimistic. Then they would exactly halve all payments made in their offer without the survey. Because they are a large company with considerable experience in the area, the probabilities that Bonded Chemicals could make a success of the product are not affected by the marketing firm's report, which is based on a small company environment.

There is one final course that John could take. If he starts his own company and finds it is a success, he could consider expansion or selling out to a larger company. He talked about these options to his bank manager who said that if he expands and the business really takes off there is no reason why his pay and profits should not reach £40 000 a year, but the probability of this is only about 0.3. It is more likely that an expansion so soon will not cover costs and leave John with a total income of £25 000 a year. On the other hand, if John develops a successful business, a buyer could be found to pay John a total of about £100 000 over 3 years.

Question

John must decide what to do fairly quickly. At the moment he is rather confused by the details of his problem. The only decision he has made so far is that he should aim to maximise his own expected income over the next 3 years. What can you suggest to help him?

Problems

9.1 A pub on the seafront at Blackpool notices that its profits are declining. The landlord has a number of alternatives for increasing his profits (attracting more customers, increasing prices, getting customers to spend more, etc.) but each of these has follow-on effects. Draw a map to show the interactions for this situation.

9.2 Find the best alternatives in the situation of certainty described by the following matrix of gains:

		Event
	a	100
	b	950
	c	−250
Alternatives	d	0
	e	950
	f	500

9.3 Use the Laplace, Wald and Savage decision criteria to suggest alternatives in the following matrices:

(a) matrix of costs

		Events				
		1	2	3	4	5
	a	100	70	115	95	60
	b	95	120	120	90	150
Alternatives	c	180	130	60	160	120
	d	80	75	50	100	95
	e	60	140	100	170	160

(b)   matrix of gains

		Events			
		1	2	3	4
	a	1	6	3	7
	b	2	5	1	4
Alternatives	c	8	1	4	2
	d	5	2	7	8

9.4 What is the highest fee worth paying for perfect information in the payoff matrices of Problem 9.3?

9.5 (a) What is the best alternative in the situation of risk described by the following matrix of gains:

		Events		
		1	2	3
		$P = 0.4$	$P = 0.3$	$P = 0.3$
	a	100	90	120
Alternatives	b	80	102	110

(b) Will this decision change if a utility function $U(x) = \sqrt{x}$ is used?

9.6 A company can launch one of three versions of a new product, X, Y or Z. The profit depends on market reaction and there is a 30% chance that this will be good, a 40% chance it will be medium and a 30% chance it will be poor. Which version should the company launch if profits are given in the following table?

		Market reaction		
		Good	Medium	Poor
	X	100	110	80
Version	Y	70	90	120
	Z	130	100	70

A market survey can be done to give more information on market reaction. Experience suggests these surveys give results A, B or C with probabilities $P(A/Good)$, etc. shown in the following table:

		Results		
		A	B	C
	Good	0.2	0.2	0.6
Market reaction	Medium	0.2	0.5	0.3
	Poor	0.4	0.3	0.3

How much should the company pay for this information? What is the value of perfect information?

9.7 A road haulage contractor owns a lorry with a one-year-old engine. He has to decide now, and again in a year's time, whether to replace the engine. If he decides to replace it, the cost is £500. If he does not replace it, there is an increased chance it will break down during the year and the cost of replacing an engine then is £800. If an engine is replaced during the year the replacement engine is assumed to be one year old at the time when the next decision is taken. The probability of breakdown of an engine during a year is as follows:

	Age of engine in years		
	0	1	2
Probability of breakdown	0.0	0.2	0.7

Draw a decision tree for this problem and find the decisions that minimize costs over the next 2 years.

9.8 An organization is considering launching an entirely new service. If the market reaction to this service is good (which has a probability of 0.2) the organization will make £3000 a week; if market reaction is medium (with probability 0.5) it will make £1000 a week, but if reaction is poor (with probability 0.3) it will lose £1500 a week. The organization could run a survey to test market reaction with results A, B or C. Experience suggests that the reliability of such surveys is described by the following matrix of $P(A/good)$, etc. How much should the organization be willing to pay for this survey?

		Result		
		A	B	C
	Good	0.7	0.2	0.1
Market reaction	Medium	0.2	0.6	0.2
	Poor	0.1	0.4	0.5

9.9 A television company has an option on a new six-part series. They could sell the rights to this series to the network for £100 000, or they could make the series themselves. If they make the series themselves, advertising profit from each episode is not known exactly but could be £15 000 (with a probability of 0.25), £24 000 (with a probability of 0.45) or £29 000, depending on the success of the series.

A local production company can be hired to run a pilot for the series. For a cost of £30 000 they will give either a favourable or an unfavourable report on the chances of the series being a success. The reliability of their report (phrased in terms of the probability of a favourable report given the likely advertising profit, etc.) is given in the following table:

Advertising profit (£)	15 000	24 000	29 000
Unfavourable report	0.85	0.65	0.3
Favourable report	0.15	0.35	0.7

Draw a decision tree of this problem and identify the best course of action and expected profit.

Discussion questions

9.1 One of the main benefits of decision analysis is not the analysis itself, but the benefits gained from describing the structure of the problem. Why do you think this is?

9.2 Decision criteria use so many simplifications that they can only be used for very simple problems. Do you think this is true?

9.3 What types of decision criteria would be useful for complicated problems?

9.4 How could you find a company's utility curve? What would your result actually show? Is utility a real measure or a theoretical concept?

Project management | 10 |

CHAPTER OUTLINE

This chapter describes projects, and shows how network analysis can help with their planning, scheduling and control. After reading the chapter you should be able to:

- understand why complex projects need careful planning
- list the aims of project managers
- represent projects by networks of connected activities and events
- analyse the timing of projects
- find critical activities and overall project duration
- extend these analyses to PERT networks
- change the times of activities to achieve different objectives
- draw Gantt charts
- schedule the resources for a project

10.1 | **Background to project management**

> A ***project*** is a unique, self-contained job that makes a one-off product. It has a distinct start and finish, and all operations must be coordinated within this time.

You can see from this definition that we all do a number of projects every day. We might prepare a meal, write a report, build a fence, organize a party, or investigate some problem at work. We do these small projects with almost no formal planning – and with a little thought they generally run smoothly. But some projects are very big and expensive – such as the installation of a new computer system, building a nuclear power station, organizing the Olympic Games, introducing new car models, or building the Channel tunnel. These large projects will only be successful if they are very carefully planned. This planning is the function of ***project management***.

> **Project management** deals with all aspects of planning, organizing, staffing and controlling a project.

All projects have two phases:

- a **planning phase** – during which the project is defined, its feasibility tested, goals are set, detailed design work done, resources allocated, times agreed, management and work organized, etc.

- an **execution phase** – during which materials are purchased and delivered, the work is done, finished products are handed over to customers, initial operations are tested, etc.

You can imagine these phases with building a house. In the planning phase an architect draws plans, a site is found, local authorities give planning approval, a building society arranges finance, and all arrangements are finalized. In the execution phase, the site and foundations are prepared, walls are built, electrical and plumbing work is done, and the house is actually built.

The people in charge of projects are called **project managers**. Their aim is to complete the project successfully – giving the customer the product they want, keeping within the specified time, and within the budget. But they often have to compromise between costs, time and resources. If a project gets behind schedule, the project managers must decide whether to accept the delay, or to increase costs by using more resources. Then they have to decide how many extra resources to use, where to find them, and how to use them. Decisions like these form a part of every project manager's job. In more detail, they can be responsible for:

1 identifying all the activities in the project

2 setting the order in which these activities have to be done

3 estimating the time for each activity, the total length of the project, and the time when each activity must be finished

4 finding how much flexibility there is in the times of activities, and which activities are most critical to the completion time

5 estimating costs and keeping within the budget

6 allocating and scheduling resources

7 monitoring progress on the project, reacting quickly to any deviations from plans, and adjusting schedules as necessary

8 anticipating problems and taking any actions needed to avoid them

9 giving regular reports on progress.

The first six of these deal with scheduling the project in the planning phase; the last three deal with control of the project in the execution phase.

Case example

Major construction projects

In December 1990 Transmanche Link, a consortium of ten British and French companies, finished the first continuous tunnel under the English Channel. The main tunnels were opened in 1994, and handed over to Eurotunnel to start operations. This was a significant step in a huge project.

The Channel tunnel was the world's biggest privately funded construction project. It was funded by the largest banking syndicate ever put together. By 1996 the cost of the tunnel was estimated at £10000 million, British Rail was investing £1400 million in rolling stock and infrastructure and French Rail had made a similar investment. At its peak, the project employed 14500 people and cost over £3 million a day.

In 1802 Albert Mathieu, one of Napoleon's engineers, drew a crude plan for a tunnel underneath the Channel. So the idea of a tunnel under the Channel was not new, and several trial tunnels have been dug at different times. This project had clearly been developing for a very long time, and it was carried out by some very successful and experienced companies. By all accounts, the tunnel was a triumph of construction and the project was voted a great success. Nonetheless, it cost several times the original estimates of £4500 million, the consortium was continually looking for additional funding, the opening date was delayed so much that extra interest charges, bankers' and lawyers' fees amounted to £1000 million, and the legal battles between participants are likely to last for many years.

By definition, each project is unique so there is little prior experience. There is also a lot of uncertainty, as inflation raises costs, difficult conditions are met in construction, activities take longer than expected, specifications change, and so on. Because of this, major projects often overrun their schedule and budget. There are many examples of this, including the development of the RB-211 jet engine, building Canary Wharf, Nimrod early warning system, the M25, health service computerization, almost any project in the nuclear electricity industry, and the Space Shuttle. In 1994 the British Library was half built after 12 years, the cost had tripled to £450 million and a House of Commons Committee reported, 'no-one – ministers, library staff, building contractors, anyone at all – has more than the faintest idea when the building will be completed, when it will be open for use, or how much it will cost'. By 1995 Denver International Airport had cost $4.9 billion rather than $2 billion and it was still not finished 18 months behind schedule.

There are, of course, many examples of projects that go very well. But the failures show how important it is to have good project management. In a study of 1449 projects by the Association of Project Managers, twelve came in on time and under budget.

IN SUMMARY

Projects are self-contained pieces of work that make a unique product. Projects of any size need careful planning. There are many opportunities for mistakes in project management.

Self-assessment questions

10.1 What is a project?

10.2 What is the purpose of project management?

10.3 'Project management is only concerned with major capital projects.' Do you think this is true?

10.4 What are the two main phases of a project?

10.2 Project networks

10.2.1 Introduction

The management of a project starts with a *statement of work*. This is a description of the goals of the projects, the work to be done, a proposed start and finish date, budget, and a list of milestones to check progress. With building a house the statement of work could give the aim of the project (which is the completion of a house); the work involved (which is designing the house, clearing the ground, building the foundations, etc.); the proposed time (starting on January 1st and finishing by September 1st); the budget (£100 000); a list of milestones (prepare plans by February 1st, clear ground by July 1st, finish roof by August 1st), and so on.

If the project is very large, it can be broken down into smaller parts. This is done in a *work breakdown structure* which shows the different parts of a project that must be finished by different times. The next level of detail describes the whole project as a series of *activities*. These activities are the basic elements in a project, and are used for all the detailed planning. To help with this, project managers use project *network analysis*.

Project network analysis was developed independently by two groups working in the late 1950s. The first group worked on the Polaris missile project for the United States Department of Defence. They developed a technique called *PERT (project evaluation and review technique)* to help control the work done by 3000 contractors. This reduced the length of the project by 2 years.

The second group worked for Du Pont, and they developed *CPM (critical path method)* for planning maintenance programmes in chemical plants. PERT and CPM were always very similar, and any differences in the original ideas have disappeared over time. The only difference now is that CPM assumes the durations of activities are fixed while PERT uses probabilistic durations.

> ## IN SUMMARY

Project network analysis has played a major role in project management since the 1950s.

10.2.2 Drawing networks

To draw a project network we start with a list of **activities** that make up the project. Then we can represent the project by a network of these activities. The network consists of a series of circles, or nodes, connected by arrows. Each activity is represented by an arrow and each node represents the point when activities start and finish. The nodes are called *events* and a network consists of alternating activities and events.

Figure 10.1 shows part of a project network. This has two activities A and B, and three events. Event 1 is the start of activity A, event 2 is the finish of activity A and the start of activity B, and event 3 is the finish of activity B.

These networks are called **activity on arrow** networks. There is another format which has nodes representing activities and the arrows showing the relationships. The choice between these is largely a matter of personal preference. Because some of the calculations are easier with activity on arrow networks, we will stick to this notation.

Figure 10.1 Part of a project network.

WORKED EXAMPLE 10.1

A gardener is building a greenhouse from a kit. The instructions show that this is a project with three parts:

- A, preparing the base, which will take 3 days
- B, building the frame, which will take 2 days
- C, fixing the glass, which will take 1 day.

Draw a network for the project.

Solution

The project has three activities which must be done in a fixed order – building the frame must be done after preparing the base and before fixing the glass. We can describe this order in a *dependence table*. This lists, for each activity, the other activities that must be finished before it can start.

Activity	Duration (days)	Description	Immediate predecessor
A	3	prepare base	–
B	2	build frame	A
C	1	fix glass	B

Labelling the activities A, B and C is a convenient shorthand that allows us to say that activity B has activity A as its immediate predecessor. This is normally stated as 'B depends on A'. This table only shows the **immediate** predecessors. We do not have to say that C depends on A as well as B – this is obvious from the other dependencies. Activity A has no immediate predecessors and can start at any convenient time.

Now we can draw a network from the dependence table, as shown in Figure 10.2.

Figure 10.2 Project network for building a greenhouse in Worked Example 10.1.

The directions of the arrows in a project network show precedence – each preceding activity must be finished before the following one is started – and following activities can start as soon as preceding ones are finished. In the worked example above, preparing the base must be done first, and as soon as this is finished, the frame can be built. The glass can then be fixed as soon as the frame is built.

After drawing the basic network for the project we can look at its timing. If we take a notional starting time of zero for the project, we can find the start and finish times of each activity.

WORKED EXAMPLE 10.2

Find the times for each activity in the last example. What happens if the base takes more than 3 days, or the glass is delayed, or the frame takes less than 2 days?

Solution

If we take a starting time of 0, preparing the base can be finished by the end of day 3. Then we can start building the frame. This takes 2 days, so we can finish by the end of day 5. Then we can start fixing the glass. This takes 1 day, so we can finish the whole project by the end of day 6.

If the concrete of the base takes more than 3 days to set, or the glass is not delivered by day 5, the project will be delayed. If building the frame takes less than 2 days the project will be finished early.

Now we have a timetable for the project showing when each activity starts and finishes, and we can use this to schedule resources. So a list of the important steps in project network analysis is:

- define all the separate activities
- find the dependence and duration of each activity
- draw a network
- analyse the timing of the project
- schedule resources

This approach can be used for almost any type of project, but it is most useful for those which are:

- fairly large, so there is a reasonable amount of money involved and it is worth collecting the data and analysing it
- complex, so there are enough opportunities for things go wrong

Typical projects include construction (roads, bridges and buildings), organization of large events, launching new products, planning equipment maintenance and manufacture of one-off items.

IN SUMMARY

Project network analysis divides a project into a number of activities, and represents these by a network of alternating activities and events. This network can be used for timing and resource allocations.

10.2.3 Drawing larger networks

We can draw larger networks in exactly the same way as the small example above. This becomes easy with practice, but a useful approach is to start on the left-hand side with the activities that do not depend on any others. Then we can add the activities that only depend on these first activities; then we can add activities that only depend on the latest activities added, and so on. This systematically expands the network, working from left to right, until we have added all the activities and the network is complete. During this, there are two main rules:

- before an activity can begin, all preceding activities must be finished
- the arrows representing activities only show precedence and neither the length nor orientation is important

There are also, by convention, two other rules:

- a network has only one starting and finishing event
- any two events can only be connected by one activity

This last rule is only for convenience, so we can refer to 'the activity between events i and j' and know exactly which one we are talking about. Using these rules we can draw networks of almost any size.

WORKED EXAMPLE 10.3

Allied Commercial is opening a new office. This gives a project with the following activities and dependencies:

Activity	Description	Depends on
A	find office location	–
B	recruit new staff	–
C	make office alterations	A
D	buy new equipment	A
E	install equipment	D
F	train staff	B
G	start operations	C, E, F

Draw a network of this project.

Solution

Activities A and B have no predecessors and can start at any convenient time. As soon as activity A is finished both C and D can start; E can start as soon as D is finished and F can start as soon as B is finished. G can only start when C, E and F have all finished. Figure 10.3 shows these dependencies in a network.

You can see from this network that the project starts with activities A and B. But this does not mean that these must start at the same time – only that they can start as soon as convenient and must be finished before any following activity can start. On the other hand, event 5 is the point where C, E and F are finished. But this does not mean that they must finish at the same time – only that they must all be finished before G can start.

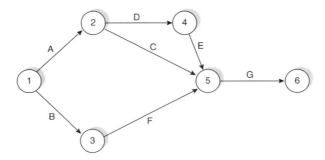

Figure 10.3 Project network for Allied Commercial in Worked Example 10.3.

Now we can draw networks of almost any size, but there are two situations that cause difficulties. You can see the first in the following dependence table:

Activity	Depends on
A	–
B	A
C	A
D	B, C

You may be tempted to draw this as shown in Figure 10.4(a). But this breaks one of the rules above which says, 'any two events can only be connected by one activity'. The way around this is to define a ***dummy activity*** which is not a part of the project, has zero duration and uses no resources – it is simply added to give a proper network. In this case the dummy makes sure that only one activity goes between two events and is called a ***uniqueness dummy***. Figure 10.4(b) shows the dummy activity as the broken line, X.

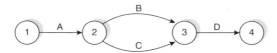

(a) incorrect network

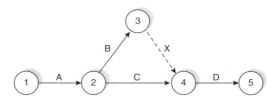

(b) correct network using dummy activity X.

Figure 10.4   Networks showing a uniqueness dummy.

You can see a second situation that needs a dummy activity in the part of a dependence table shown below:

Activity	Depends on
D	not given
E	not given
F	D, E
G	D

You might be tempted to draw this part of the network as shown in Figure 10.5(a), but the dependence is clearly wrong. Activity F is shown as depending on D and

E, which is correct, but G is shown as having the same dependence. The dependence table shows that G can start as soon as D is finished, but the network says it has to wait for E to finish as well. The way around this is to separate the dependencies by introducing a dummy activity, as shown in Figure 10.5(b). Now the dependence of F on D is shown through the dummy activity X. In effect the dummy cannot start until D has finished and then F cannot start until the dummy and E are finished: as the dummy activity has zero duration this does not add any time to the project. This kind of dummy is called a *logical dummy*.

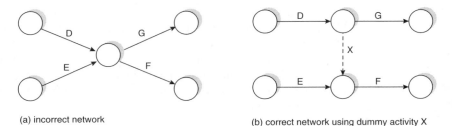

(a) incorrect network

(b) correct network using dummy activity X

Figure 10.5   Parts of networks showing a logical dummy.

These are the only two circumstances – making sure that only one activity goes between any two nodes, and giving the correct logic – where we need dummy activities.

WORKED EXAMPLE 10.4

A project has the activities described by the following dependence table. Draw the network for this project.

Activity	Depends on
A	–
B	–
C	A
D	A
E	C
F	D
G	B
H	G
I	E, F
J	H, I

Solution

We can start with activities A and B which have no immediate predecessors. Then we can add activities C, D and G, which only depend on A and B. Then we can add E, F and H. Activity I cannot start until both activities E and F are finished, while J must wait until both H and I are finished. Figure 10.6 shows the final network for this project.

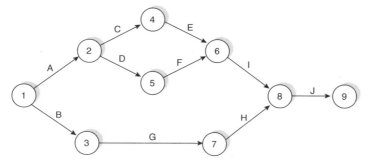

Figure 10.6 Project network for Worked Example 10.4.

WORKED EXAMPLE 10.5

Draw a network of the project described by the following dependence table:

Activity	Depends on	Activity	Depends on
A	J	I	J
B	C, G	J	–
C	A	K	B
D	F, K, N	L	I
E	J	M	I
F	B, H, L	N	M
G	A, E, I	O	M
H	G	P	O

Solution

This may seem a difficult network, but the steps are fairly straightforward. Activity J is the only one that does not depend on anything else, so this starts the network. Then we can add activities A, E and I, which only depend on J. Then we can add the activities that only depend on A, E and I. Continuing to add activities in this systematic way leads to the network shown in Figure 10.7. As you can see, this includes four dummy activities.

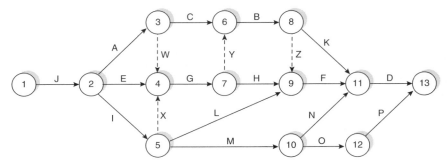

Figure 10.7 Project network for Worked Example 10.5.

If you remember our initial example of building a greenhouse, we divided the project into three activities. But we could have divided it into a lot more – such as choose a location, clear vegetation, level and prepare the ground, dig the foundations, lay hardcore, mix concrete and lay concrete base. This would give a more complex network, where each activity is less important. With project networks, we always have to have this balance between using too few activities – which will not be much use for planning – and using too many activities – which will increase the complexity.

If there are a lot of activities, it is obviously best to use a computer package. But the quality of these is variable. The networks can be difficult to follow, especially if they are printed over several pages. For large projects it is best to start with a general, master network that shows the major activities of the project. Then we can expand each of these major activities into a separate, more detailed network. For very large projects we can go further and break down the more detailed networks into even smaller parts. This approach is particularly useful when several contractors and subcontractors work on a single project. Then the owner of the project can have a master network, each contractor can have a network covering their own work, and any major subcontractors can have separate networks of their parts of the work. At each stage the networks cover less of the overall project, but show more detail.

Case example

Loch Moraigh distillery

In 1996 the managers of Loch Moraigh whisky distillery started to update their inventory control system, so that future stock levels would match forecast demand. They expanded their main computer system to analyse past demand and set appropriate stock levels. These stock levels are then passed to a production control module that varies the amounts bottled.

The first part of this system is called DFS (Demand Forecasting System) while the second part is ICS (Inventory Control System). It took 18 months to introduce these systems, including links to the production control module that was already working. The introduction of DFS and ICS was a self-contained project with the following activities:

Activity	Description
A	examine existing system and environment of ICS
B	collect costs and other data relevant to ICS
C	construct and test models for ICS
D	write and test computer programs for ICS models
E	design and print data input forms for ICS data
F	document ICS programs and monitoring procedures
G	examine sources of demand data and its collection
H	construct and test models for DFS
I	organize past demand data
J	write and test computer programs for DFS models
K	design and print data input forms for DFS data
L	document DFS programs and monitoring procedures
M	train staff in the use of DFS and ICS
N	initialize data for ICS programs (ICS staff)
P	initialize data for DFS programs (DFS staff)
Q	create base files for DFS
R	run system for trial period
S	implement final system

One set of results from a typical package gave the results in Figure 10.8.

```
PROBLEM: DISTILLERY                                Date: 09-09-1996
------------------------------------------------------------------
                       ORIGINAL NETWORK DATA

                                      Letter Code for Immediately
     Letter                               Preceding Activities
     No.  Code      Name        Completion Time  1   2   3   4   5   6   7
------------------------------------------------------------------
      1    A     Examine system      2.00
      2    B     Collect ICS data    1.00         A
      3    C     Test ICS models     2.00         A
      4    D     Program ICS         4.00         C
      5    E     Design ICS forms    1.00         C
      6    F     Document ICS        2.00         D   E
      7    G     Examine demand      2.00
```

Figure 10.8 continued overleaf

8	H	Test DFS models	4.00	A	G
9	I	Organise data	2.00	G	
10	J	Program DFS	6.00	H	K
11	K	Design DFS forms	2.00	A	G
12	L	Document DFS	3.00	J	
13	M	Train staff	2.00	F	L
14	N	Initialise ICS	1.00	B	M
15	P	Initialise DFS	1.00	I	M
16	Q	Create DFS files	1.00	P	
17	R	Trial period	4.00	N	Q
18	S	Implement	2.00	R	
19	D*1	Dummy–1	0.00		
20	D*2	Dummy–2	0.00		
21	D*3	Dummy–3	0.00		
22	D*4	Dummy–4	0.00		
23	D*5	Dummy–5	0.00		
24	D*6	Dummy–6	0.00		

ACTIVITY REPORT

Activity			Events		Planning Times				
No.	Code	Name	Beg.	End	Exp.t	ES	LS	EF	LF	Slack
1	A	Examine sys	1	2	2.0	0.0	0.0	2.0	2.0	0.0
2	B	Collect ICS	2	12	1.0	2.0	17.0	3.0	18.0	15.0
3	C	Test ICS mo	2	4	2.0	2.0	7.0	4.0	9.0	5.0
4	D	Program ICS	4	5	4.0	4.0	9.0	8.0	13.0	5.0
5	E	Design ICS	4	5	1.0	4.0	12.0	5.0	13.0	8.0
6	F	Document IC	5	10	2.0	8.0	13.0	10.0	15.0	5.0
7	G	Examine dem	1	3	2.0	0.0	0.0	2.0	2.0	0.0
8	H	Test DFS mo	6	8	4.0	2.0	2.0	6.0	6.0	0.0
9	I	Organise da	3	13	2.0	2.0	15.0	4.0	17.0	13.0
10	J	Program DFS	8	9	6.0	6.0	6.0	12.0	12.0	0.0
11	K	Design DFS	7	8	2.0	2.0	4.0	4.0	6.0	2.0
12	L	Document DF	9	10	3.0	12.0	12.0	15.0	15.0	0.0
13	M	Train staff	10	11	2.0	15.0	15.0	17.0	17.0	0.0
14	N	Initialise	12	15	1.0	17.0	18.0	18.0	19.0	1.0
15	P	Initialise	13	14	1.0	17.0	17.0	18.0	18.0	0.0
16	Q	Create DFS	14	15	1.0	18.0	18.0	19.0	19.0	0.0
17	R	Trial perio	15	16	4.0	19.0	19.0	23.0	23.0	0.0
18	S	Implement	16	17	2.0	23.0	23.0	25.0	25.0	0.0
19	D*1	Dummy–1	3	6	0.0	2.0	2.0	2.0	2.0	0.0
20	D*2	Dummy–2	2	6	0.0	2.0	2.0	2.0	2.0	0.0
21	D*3	Dummy–3	2	7	0.0	2.0	4.0	2.0	4.0	2.0
22	D*4	Dummy–4	3	7	0.0	2.0	4.0	2.0	4.0	2.0
23	D*5	Dummy–5	11	13	0.0	17.0	17.0	17.0	17.0	0.0
24	D*6	Dummy–6	11	12	0.0	17.0	18.0	17.0	18.0	1.0

Expected Project Duration: 25

The following path(s) are critical.

A	D*2	H	J	L	M	D*5	P	Q	R	S
G	D*1	H	J	L	M	D*5	P	Q	R	S

Figure 10.8 continued opposite

NETWORK EVENT MILESTONE REPORT

	Event Connections			Times			Activitiy Connections		
Event	Predecessors	Successors		TE	TL	Slack	Ending		Starting
1	:none	: 2 3 —	:	0.0	0.0	0.0	: none		: A G
2	: 1 — —	: 12 4 6	:	2.0	2.0	0.0	: A	—	: B C
	:	: 7 — —	:				:		: D*2 D*3
3	: 1 — —	: 13 6 7	:	2.0	2.0	0.0	: G	—	: I D*1
	:	:	:				:		: D*4 —
4	: 2 — —	: 5 5 —	:	4.0	9.0	5.0	: C	—	: D E
5	: 4 4 —	: 10 — —	:	8.0	13.0	5.0	: D	E	: F —
6	: 3 2 —	: 8 — —	:	2.0	2.0	0.0	: D*1	D*2	: H —
7	: 2 3 —	: 8 — —	:	2.0	4.0	2.0	: D*3	D*4	: K —
8	: 6 7 —	: 9 — —	:	6.0	6.0	0.0	: H	K	: J —
9	: 8 — —	: 10 — —	:	12.0	12.0	0.0	: J	—	: L —
10	: 5 9 —	: 11 — —	:	15.0	15.0	0.0	: F	L	: M —
11	: 10 — —	: 13 12 —	:	17.0	17.0	0.0	: M	—	: D*5 D*6
12	: 2 11 —	: 15 — —	:	17.0	18.0	1.0	: B	D*6	: N —
13	: 3 11 —	: 14 — —	:	17.0	17.0	0.0	: I	D*5	: P —
14	: 13 — —	: 15 — —	:	18.0	18.0	0.0	: P	—	: Q —
15	: 12 14 —	: 16 — —	:	19.0	19.0	0.0	: N	Q	: R —
16	: 15 — —	: 17 — —	:	23.0	23.0	0.0	: R	—	: S —
17	: 16 — —	: none	:	25.0	25.0	0.0	: S	—	: none

Expected Project Duration: 25

The following path(s) are critical.

```
1   2   6   8   9   10   11   13   14   15   16   17
1   3   6   8   9   10   11   13   14   15   16   17
```

Figure 10.8 Computer printout for distillery example.

IN SUMMARY

We can use a systematic approach to draw networks for projects of any size. These networks may need dummy activities – either uniqueness or logical. We always have to balance the amount of detail in a network with the benefit from using it.

Self-assessment questions

10.5 In the networks we have drawn, what are represented by the nodes and arrows?

10.6 What information do you need to draw a project network?

10.7 What are the two main rules of drawing a project network?

10.8 When are dummy activities used?

10.3 Timing of projects

CPM (critical path method) assumes that each activity has a fixed duration; **PERT** (project evaluation and review technique) assumes that there is some uncertainty in the duration. Apart from this, the two methods are identical. So we will illustrate the methods by CPM, and then move on to look at PERT.

10.3.1 Event analysis

We can start by finding the earliest and latest times that events can occur. It is easiest to show these calculations for an example. Suppose a project has the following dependence table, including activity durations (in weeks):

Activity	Duration	Depends on
A	3	–
B	2	–
C	2	A
D	4	A
E	1	C
F	3	D
G	3	B
H	4	G
I	5	E, F

Figure 10.9 shows the network for this project, with durations noted under the activities.

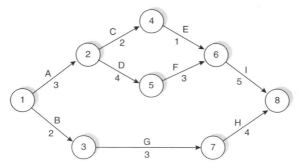

Figure 10.9   Basic network for text example.

If we assume a notional start time of zero for the project as a whole, we can find the earliest possible time for each event. The earliest time for event 1 is clearly 0. The earliest time for event 2 is when activity A finishes, which is 3 weeks after its earliest start at 0: the earliest time for event 4 is the time when C finishes, which is 2 weeks after its earliest start at 3 (i.e. week 5). Similarly, the earliest time for event 5 is $4 + 3 = 7$, for event 3 is 2 and for event 7 is $2 + 3 = 5$.

When several activities have to finish before an event, the earliest time for the event is the earliest time by which **all** preceding activities can be finished. The earliest time for event 6 is when both E and F finish. E can finish 1 week after its earliest start at 5 (i.e. week 6); F can finish 3 weeks after its earliest start at 7 (i.e. week 10). So the earliest time when both of these can finish is week 10. Similarly, event 8 must wait until both activities H and I finish. Activity H can finish by week $5 + 4 = 9$ while activity I can finish by week $10 + 5 = 15$. So the earliest time for event 8 is the later of these, which is week 15. This gives the overall duration of the project as 15 weeks. Figure 10.10 shows the earliest times for each event added to the network.

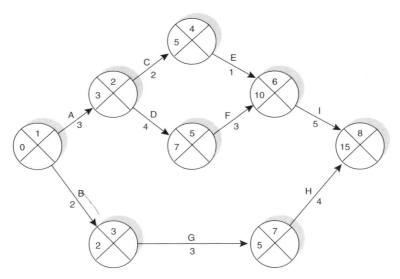

Figure 10.10   Network with earliest event times added.

The **earliest time** of an event is the earliest time that all preceding activities can be finished by.

The formal statement of the calculations for earliest event time is:

$$ET(l) = 0$$
$$ET(j) = \text{MAX}[ET(i) + D(i, j)]$$

where: $ET(i)$ = the earliest time of event i

              $D(i, j)$ = duration of activity linking events i and j

Having gone through the network and found the earliest time for each event we can do a similar analysis to find the latest time for each. The procedure for this is almost the reverse of the procedure for finding the earliest times. Starting at the end of the project with event 8, this has a latest time for completion of week 15. To allow activity I to finish by week 15 it must start 5 weeks before this, so the latest time for event 6 is week $15 - 5 = 10$. The latest H can finish is week 15, so the latest time it can start is 4 weeks before this and the latest time for event 7 is week $15 - 4 = 11$. Similarly the latest time for event 3 is $11 - 3 = 8$, for event 5 is $10 - 3 = 7$ and for event 4 is $10 - 1 = 9$.

For events that have more than one following activity, the latest time must allow all following activities to finish on time. Event 2 is followed by activities C and D; C must finish by week 9 so it must be started 2 weeks before this (i.e. week 7), while D must finish by week 7 so it must start 4 weeks before this (i.e. week 3). The latest time for event 2 that allows both C and D to start on time is the earlier of these, which is week 3.

The latest time for event 1 must allow both A and B to finish on time. The latest start time for B is $8 - 2 = 6$ and the latest start time for A is $3 - 3 = 0$. The latest time for event 1 must allow both of these to start on time and this means a latest time of 0. Figure 10.11 shows the network with latest times added for each event.

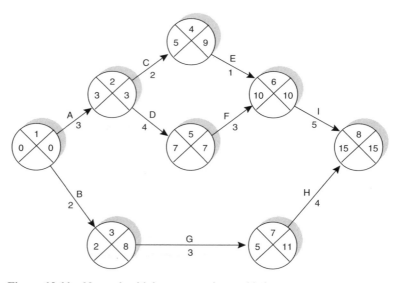

Figure 10.11 Network with latest event times added.

The **latest time** for an event is the latest time that allows **all** following activities to be started on time.

The formal statement of the calculation of latest event time is:

$$LT(n) = ET(n)$$
$$LT(i) = \text{MIN } [LT(j) - D(i, j)]$$

where: $LT(i)$ = latest time of event i

n = number of events (with the terminal event numbered n)

You can see that some of the events have a certain amount of flexibility in timing. Event 3, for example, can occur any time between week 2 and week 8, while event 7 can occur any time between weeks 5 and 11. Other events are fixed at specific times. Events 1, 2 and 5, for example, are fixed at times 0, 3 and 7 respectively. The amount an event can move is called the **slack**. This is defined as the difference between the latest and earliest times:

> Slack for = latest time − earliest time
> event i for i for i
>
> $$S(i) = LT(i) - ET(i)$$

Events with more slack have more flexibility in their timing, and less chance of causing problems. If there is no slack, an event must occur at the specified time and any delay will delay the whole project. Slack values for the example above are shown in Figure 10.12.

> ## IN SUMMARY

After drawing a network, we can analyse the project's timing. The first part of this finds the earliest and latest times for each event. The difference between these two is the slack.

10.3.2 Activity analysis

We can extend the analysis of project times to activities. Then we can find earliest and latest start times for each activity, and the corresponding earliest and latest finish times.

The earliest start time for an activity is the earliest time of the preceding event. The earliest finish time is the earliest start time plus the duration (see Figure 10.13). Looking at one specific activity in Figure 10.12, say G, the earliest start

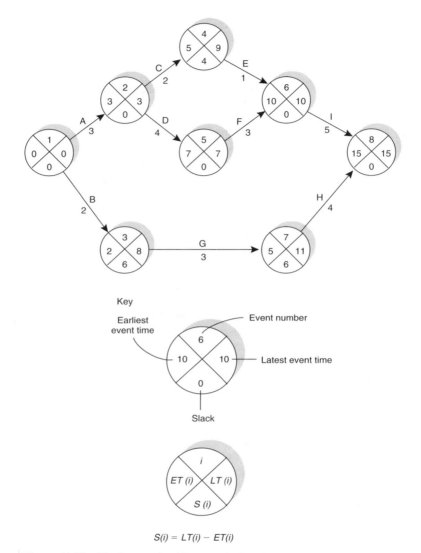

Figure 10.12 Final network with event slacks added.

time is week 2, so the earliest finish time is week $2 + 3 = 5$. In general for an activity k:

$$ES(k) = ET(i)$$
$$EF(k) = ES(k) + D(i, j)$$

where:
$ES(k)$ = earliest start time of activity k which is between events i and j

$EF(k)$ = earliest finish time of activity k

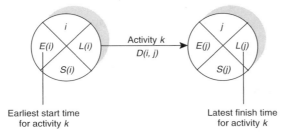

Figure 10.13 Earliest and latest times for activities.

We can find the latest start and finish time for an activity using similar reasoning, but working backwards. The latest finish time for each activity is the latest time of the following event; the latest start time is the latest finish time minus the duration. For activity G the latest finish is week 11 and the latest start is week $11 - 3 = 8$. In general for activity k:

$$LF(k) = LT(j)$$
$$LS(k) = LF(k) - D(i, j)$$

where $LF(k) =$ latest finish of activity k which is between events i and j

               $LS(k) =$ latest start time of activity k

Repeating these calculations for all activities in the project gives the following results:

Activity	Duration	Earliest start	Earliest finish	Latest start	Latest finish
A	3	0	3	0	3
B	2	0	2	6	8
C	2	3	5	7	9
D	4	3	7	3	7
E	1	5	6	9	10
F	3	7	10	7	10
G	3	2	5	8	11
H	4	5	9	11	15
I	5	10	15	10	15

In this table you can see that some activities have flexibility in time: activity G can start as early as week 2 or as late as week 8, while activity C can start as early as week 3 or as late as week 7. On the other hand, some activities have no flexibility at all: activities A, D, F, and I have no freedom and their latest start time is the same as their earliest start time. The activities that must be done at a fixed time are called the ***critical activities***.

> Activities that must be done at a fixed time are the **critical activities**. They form a continuous path through the network, called the **critical path**. This path sets the overall duration of the project.

The length of the critical path sets the overall project duration. If one of the critical activities is extended by a certain amount, the overall project duration is extended by this amount; if one of the critical activities is delayed, the overall project duration is extended by the time of the delay. On the other hand, if one of the critical activities is made shorter the overall project duration may be reduced by this amount.

The activities that have some flexibility in timing are the ***non-critical activities*** and these may be delayed or extended without necessarily affecting the overall project duration. But there is a limit to the amount they can expand and this is measured by the **float**.

In the same way that slack defines the amount an event can move, float defines the amount an activity can move. There are three important kinds of float for an activity: total, free and independent.

The **total float** is the difference between the maximum amount of time available for an activity and the time it actually needs:

> **Total float** = latest finish − earliest start − duration
>
> $$TF(k) = LT(j) - ET(i) - D(i,j)$$

The total float is the maximum amount an activity can expand without affecting the completion date of the project (see Figure 10.14). It follows that the total float of critical activities is zero, and it has some positive value for non-critical activities.

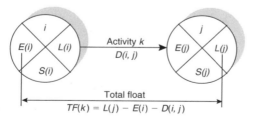

$$TF(k) = L(j) - E(i) - D(i, j)$$

Figure 10.14 Calculating the total float.

If all activities start at their earliest times, we can define a **free float** as the maximum amount an activity can expand without affecting any following activity (this is shown in Figure 10.15):

Free float = earliest time − earliest time − duration
of following of preceding
event event

$$FF(k) = ET(j) - ET(i) - D(i,j)$$

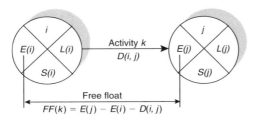

Free float
$$FF(k) = E(j) - E(i) - D(i, j)$$

Figure 10.15 Calculating the free float.

Finally, if every activity preceding an activity finishes as late as possible and every activity following starts as early as possible, there may still be some **independent float**:

Independent float = earliest time − latest time − duration
of following of preceding
event event

$$IF(k) = ET(j) - LT(i) - D(i,j)$$

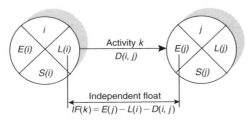

Independent float
$$IF(k) = E(j) - L(i) - D(i, j)$$

Figure 10.16 Calculating the independent float.

This is the maximum amount an activity can expand without affecting either preceding or following activities (see Figure 10.16).

Calculating the floats for activity G in our example has $ET(i) = 2$, $LT(i) = 8$, $ET(j) = 5$, $LT(j) = 11$ and $D(i, j) = 3$. Then:

$$TF(k) = LT(j) - ET(i) - D(i, j) = 11 - 2 - 3 = 6$$
$$FF(k) = ET(j) - ET(i) - D(i, j) = 5 - 2 - 3 = 0$$
$$IF(k) = ET(j) - LT(i) - D(i, j) = 5 - 8 - 3 = -6 \text{ (which is taken as zero)}$$

The total float of G is 6 weeks, which shows that it can expand by up to 6 weeks without affecting the overall duration of the project. Activities only have independent float if there is still spare time when preceding activities finish as late as possible and following activities start as early as possible. Activities that are squeezed for time will have zero independent float and in some cases it will go negative – when it is usually recorded as zero.

Repeating the calculations for other activities in the example gives the results shown in the spreadsheet in Figure 10.17.

	A	B	C	D	E	F	G	H	I	J
1	**Analysis of Activity Times**									
2										
3										
4	**Activity**	**Duration**	**Earliest**		**Latest**		**Float**			
5			**Start**	**Finish**	**Start**	**Finish**	**Total**	**Free**	**Independent**	**Critical**
6	A	3	0	3	0	3	0	0	0	****
7	B	2	0	2	6	8	6	0	0	
8	C	2	3	5	7	9	4	0	0	
9	D	4	3	7	3	7	0	0	0	****
10	E	1	5	6	9	10	4	4	0	
11	F	3	7	10	7	10	0	0	0	****
12	G	3	2	5	8	11	6	0	0(−6)	
13	H	4	5	9	11	15	6	6	0	
14	I	5	10	15	10	15	0	0	0	****

Figure 10.17   Spreadsheet of activity times and floats.

WORKED EXAMPLE 10.6

Building a small telephone exchange is a project with ten major activities. Estimated durations (in days) and dependencies are shown in the following table. Draw the network for this project, find its duration and calculate the floats of each activity.

Activity	Description	Duration	Depends on
A	design internal equipment	10	–
B	design exchange building	5	A
C	order parts for equipment	3	A
D	order material for building	2	B
E	wait for equipment parts	15	C
F	wait for building material	10	D
G	employ equipment assemblers	5	A
H	employ building workers	4	B
I	install equipment	20	E, G, J
J	complete building	30	F, H

Solution

The network for this is shown in Figure 10.18. Calculating the times and floats for activities gives the results shown in Figure 10.19.

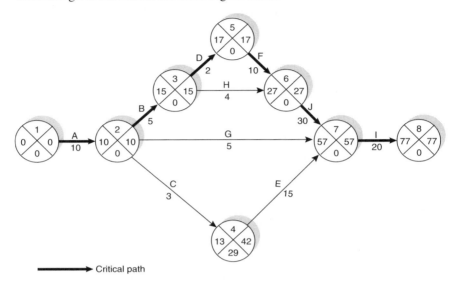

Figure 10.18   Project network for Worked Example 10.6.

	A	B	C	D	E	F	G	H	I	J
1	**Analysis of Activity Times**									
2										
3										
4	**Activity**	**Duration**	**Earliest**		**Latest**		**Float**			
5			**Start**	**Finish**	**Start**	**Finish**	**Total**	**Free**	**Independent**	**Critical**
6	A	10	0	10	0	10	0	0	0	★★★★
7	B	5	10	15	10	15	0	0	0	★★★★
8	C	3	10	13	39	42	29	0	0	
9	D	2	15	17	15	17	0	0	0	★★★★
10	E	15	13	28	42	57	29	29	0	
11	F	.10	17	27	17	27	0	0	0	★★★★
12	G	5	10	15	52	57	42	42	42	
13	H	4	15	19	23	27	8	8	8	
14	I	20	57	77	57	77	0	0	0	★★★★
15	J	30	27	57	27	57	0	0	0	★★★★

Figure 10.19   Spreadsheet of activity times for Worked Example 10.6.

The duration of the project is 77 days, defined by the critical path A, B, D, F, I and J.

We can find the earliest and latest start and finish time for each activity. The amount of movement in these times is measured by the floats – total, free and independent. Critical activities are at fixed times and have zero float. The critical activities form a critical path through the network.

Self-assessment questions

10.9   What are the earliest and latest times for an event?

10.10 What is the 'slack' of an event?

10.11 What do the 'floats' of an activity measure?

10.12 What is a 'critical path'?

10.4 Programme evaluation and review technique

In the last section we assumed that the duration of each activity is known exactly. This approach is called the critical path method (CPM). But often we do not know exactly how long an activity will take. There may be unexpected problems and the activity takes longer than expected – or things may go well and the activity is finished early. It would be useful to add this kind of uncertainty to our analyses. This is done using PERT (project evaluation and review technique).

Experience shows that the duration of an activity can often be described by a beta distribution. This looks something like a skewed normal distribution and has one very useful property – the mean and variance can be found from three estimates of duration. In particular it needs:

- an optimistic duration (O), which is the shortest time an activity will take if everything goes smoothly and without any difficulties

- a most likely duration (M), which is the duration of the activity under normal conditions

- a pessimistic duration (P), which is the time needed if there are significant problems and delays

The expected activity duration and variance are then calculated from the *rule of sixths*:

$$\text{expected duration} = \frac{O + 4 * M + P}{6}$$

$$\text{variance} = \frac{(O - P)^2}{36}$$

Suppose an activity has an optimistic duration of 4 days, a most likely duration of 5 days and a pessimistic duration of 12 days. Assuming a beta distribution for the duration:

$$\text{expected duration} = (O + 4 * M + P)/6 = (4 + 4 * 5 + 12)/6 = 6$$

$$\text{variance} \qquad = (P - O)^2/36 \qquad = (12 - 4)^2/36 \qquad = 1.78$$

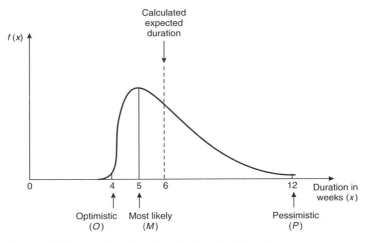

Figure 10.20 A typical beta distribution of activity durations.

Expected durations can be used in the network for analysis of timings in the same way as the single estimate of CPM.

WORKED EXAMPLE 10.7

A network has nine activities with dependencies and estimated activity durations shown in the following table. Draw the network, find the critical path and estimate the overall duration of the project.

			Duration	
Activity	*Depends on*	*Optimistic*	*Most likely*	*Pessimistic*
A	–	2	3	10
B	–	4	5	12
C	–	8	10	12
D	A, G	4	4	4
E	B	3	6	15
F	B	2	5	8
G	B	6	6	6
H	C, F	5	7	15
I	D, E	6	8	10

Solution

Using the rule of sixths for the duration of activity A:

$$\text{expected duration} = (O + 4*M + P)/6 = (2 + 4*3 + 10)/6 = 4$$
$$\text{variance} \quad = (P - O)^2/36 \quad = (10 - 2)^2/36 \quad = 1.78$$

Then repeating these calculations for the other activities gives the following results:

Activity	Expected duration	Variance
A	4	1.78
B	6	1.78
C	10	0.44
D	4	0
E	7	4.00
F	5	1.00
G	6	0
H	8	2.78
I	8	0.44

Figure 10.21 shows the network for this problem. The critical path for the project is B, G, D and I which has an expected duration of 24.

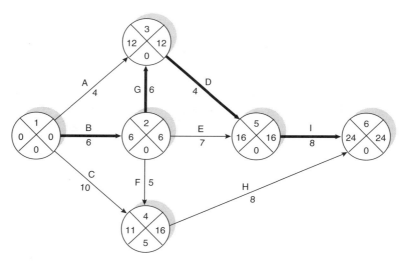

Figure 10.21   Project network for Worked Example 10.7.

The analysis of activity times gives:

Activity	Expected duration	ES	EF	LS	LF	Total	Float Free	Independent	
A	4	0	4	8	12	8	8	8	
B	6	0	6	0	6	0	0	0	*
C	10	0	10	6	16	6	1	1	
D	4	12	16	12	16	0	0	0	*
E	7	6	13	9	16	3	3	3	
F	5	6	11	11	16	5	0	0	
G	6	6	12	6	12	0	0	0	*
H	8	11	19	16	24	5	5	0	
I	8	16	24	16	24	0	0	0	*

The length of the critical path is the sum of the durations of activities making up that path. If there is a large number of activities on the path, and if the duration of each activity is independent of the others, the overall duration of the project is normally distributed. This distribution has:

● a mean equal to the sum of the expected durations of activities on the critical path

● a variance equal to the sum of the variances of activities on the critical path

WORKED EXAMPLE 10.8

What are the probabilities that the project described in the last worked example will be finished before (a) day 26 (b) day 20?

Solution

The critical path has activities B, G, D and I, with expected durations of 6, 6, 4 and 8 respectively and variances of 1.78, 0, 0 and 0.44 respectively. Although the number of activities on the critical path is small, we can still assume the overall duration of the project is normally distributed (shown in Figure 10.22). Then the expected duration has a mean of $6 + 6 + 4 + 8 = 24$. The variance is $1.78 + 0 + 0 + 0.44 = 2.22$, so the standard deviation is $\sqrt{2.22} = 1.49$.

(a) We can find the probability that it will not be finished before day 26 using normal distribution tables. Z is the number of standard deviations the point of interest is away from the mean:

$$Z = (26 - 24)/1.49 = 1.34 \text{ standard deviations}$$

Normal tables show that this corresponds to a probability of 0.0901. So the probability that the project will be finished is $1 - 0.0901 = 0.9099$ or almost 91%.

(b) Similarly, to finish the project by day 20 we have:

$$Z = (24 - 20)/1.49 = 2.68 \text{ standard deviations}$$

Normal tables show this corresponds to a probability of 0.0037.

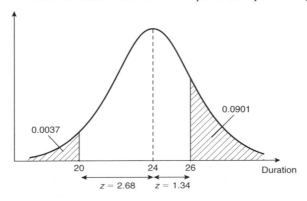

Figure 10.22 Normal duration of project in Worked Example 10.8.

WORKED EXAMPLE 10.9

The following table shows the dependency of activities and three estimates of durations for a project.

(a) What is the probability that the project will be completed before 17?

(b) By what time is there a probability of 0.95 that the project will be finished?

Activity	Depends on	Duration		
		Optimistic	Most likely	Pessimistic
A	–	1	2	3
B	A	1	3	6
C	B	4	6	10
D	A	1	1	1
E	D	1	2	2
F	E	3	4	8
G	F	2	3	5
H	D	7	9	11
I	A	0	1	4
J	I	2	3	4
K	H, J	3	4	7
L	C, G, K	1	2	7

Solution

The rule of sixths finds the expected duration and variance for each activity as follows:

Activity	Expected duration	Variance
A	2.00	0.11
B	3.17	0.69
C	6.33	1.00
D	1.00	0.00
E	1.83	0.03
F	4.50	0.69
G	3.17	0.25
H	9.00	0.44
I	1.33	0.44
J	3.00	0.11
K	4.33	0.44
L	2.67	1.00

The network for this project is shown in Figure 10.23.

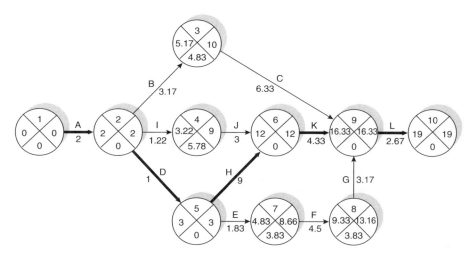

Figure 10.23 Project network for Worked Example 10.9.

The critical path is A, D, H, K and L. Adding the expected durations and variances for these activities shows the overall duration of the project has a mean of 19 with variance of 1.99 and standard deviation of 1.41.

(a) The probability that the project is finished before 17 is:

$$Z = (19 - 17)/1.41 = 1.42 \text{ standard deviations}$$

so $\qquad$ probability $= 0.0778$

(b) To get a 95% chance of completion Z must be 1.64 and the point of interest is $1.64 * 1.41 = 2.31$ from the mean. There is a 95% chance that the project will be finished by time $19 + 2.31 = 21.31$.

IN SUMMARY

PERT is an extension to CPM which allows for uncertain activity durations. We can find expected activity durations and variances using the rule of sixths. The overall project duration is normally distributed with mean and variance found by adding values for activities on the critical path.

Self-assessment questions

10.13 What is the main difference between CPM and PERT?

10.14 What is the 'rule of sixths'?

10.15 How would you calculate the expected duration of a project and its variance?

10.5 | Changing project times

After analysing the times of a project, we may want to make some changes. We might find, for example, that the project takes too long; or during the execution an activity takes longer than originally planned. Here we will see what happens when we adjust the times of activities.

10.5.1 Delays in a project

Increasing the duration of a critical activity will extend the project by the same amount. If a critical activity takes 2 weeks longer than expected, the finish of the whole project is delayed by 2 weeks. But what happens if a non-critical activity is extended? We can find the answer from the floats, as shown in the following example.

WORKED EXAMPLE 10.10

Draw the network for the following dependence table and calculate the total, free and independent float of each activity:

Activity	Duration	Depends on
A	4	–
B	14	–
C	10	A
D	6	A
E	4	C
F	6	D, E
G	12	B

Solution

Figure 10.24 shows the network for this project, with times and floats given in the following table:

Activity	Duration	ES	EF	LS	LF	Total	Free	Independent	
A	4	0	4	2	6	2	0	0	
B	14	0	14	0	14	0	0	0	*
C	10	4	14	6	16	2	0	0	(−2)
D	6	4	10	14	20	10	8	6	
E	4	14	18	16	20	2	0	0	(−2)
F	6	18	24	20	26	2	2	0	
G	12	14	26	14	26	0	0	0	*

The column heading over Total, Free and Independent is *Float*.

The critical path is B and G and the project duration is 26.

If you look at activity D, you can see how delays in a non-critical activity affect the project duration. D has an independent float of 6 so any extension up to this has no effect on any other activity in the project. If the duration increases above 6 other activities are affected. Increasing the duration of D by 7 to 13 makes no difference to the event times on the network, but other activities are now affected. Originally A could finish as late as 6 and F could start as early as 18. This is still true provided only one of them occurs – it is no longer possible for **both** A to finish at 6 and F to start at 18 as D does not fit into the gap.

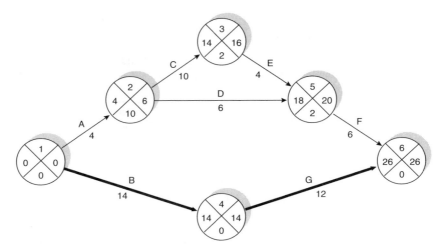

Figure 10.24 Project network for Worked Example 10.10.

If the duration of D is raised by 9 to 15 all its free float is used and following activities are affected (see Figure 10.25). In particular the early start time for F is delayed from 18 to 19.

Finally, if D is expanded by 11 to 17, all the total float is used and the project is delayed. Originally there was a total float of 10 and, as the activity has been expanded by 11, the project will be delayed by 1. This is shown in Figure 10.26 where the critical path has switched from B and G to A, D and F.

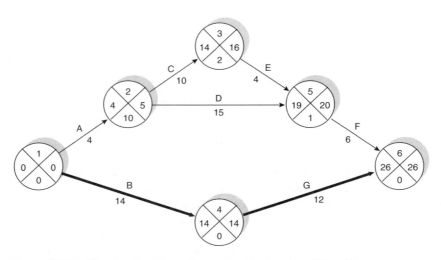

Figure 10.25 Showing the effect of increasing the duration of D to 15.

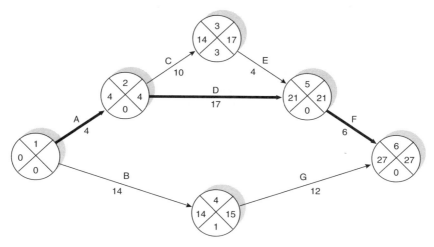

Figure 10.26 Showing the effect of increasing the duration of D to 17.

IN SUMMARY

When the duration of an activity expands beyond the independent float it begins to interfere with other activities. When it expands beyond the free float it affects following activities and when it expands by more than the total float the critical path changes and the project is delayed by:

delay = expansion of activity − total float of activity

10.5.2 Reducing the length of a project

Suppose we analyse the times of a project and realize that it takes too long. How can we adjust the duration? We can start by saying that we can only reduce the duration of a project by reducing the durations of critical activities; reducing non-critical activities has no effect on the overall project duration. But if we keep reducing critical activities, there must come a point when some other path through the network becomes critical. We can find this point from the total float on paths parallel to the critical path. When the critical path is reduced by more than the total float of a parallel path, the parallel path becomes critical.

WORKED EXAMPLE 10.11

Figure 10.27 shows a project network with duration of 14, through the critical path A, B and C.

If each activity can be reduced by up to 50% of the original duration, how would you reduce the overall duration to: (a) 13 weeks, (b) 11 weeks, (c) 9 weeks?

If reductions cost an average of £1000 a week what is the cost of finishing the project by week 9?

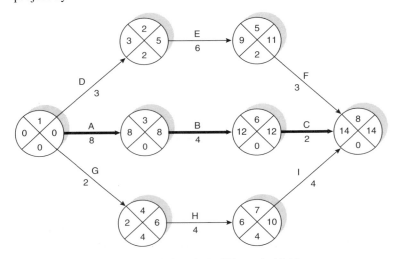

Figure 10.27 Project network for Worked Example 10.11.

Solution

Analysing the activity times for this project gives the following results:

Activity	Duration	Earliest		Latest		Total float
		start	finish	start	finish	
A	8	0	8	0	8	0*
B	4	8	12	8	12	0*
C	2	12	14	12	14	0*
D	3	0	3	2	5	2
E	6	3	9	5	11	2
F	3	9	12	11	14	2
G	2	0	2	4	6	4
H	4	2	6	6	10	4
I	4	6	10	10	14	4

To see how much the critical path can be reduced without affecting any parallel path, we have to look at the total float of the parallel paths. In this network there are three parallel paths, A–B–C, D–E–F and G–H–I. The total float of activities on these paths are 0, 2 and 4 respectively. This means that we can reduce the critical path A–B–C by up to 2, but if we reduce it any more the path D–E–F becomes critical. If we reduce the critical path by more than 4, the path G–H–I also becomes critical.

(a) To finish in 13 weeks we need a reduction of 1 week in the critical path. Reducing the longest activity – as it is usually easier to find savings in longer activities – gives A a duration of 7 weeks and the project is finished by week 13.

(b) To finish in 11 weeks needs a further reduction of 2 weeks in the critical path. We can also remove this from A. Unfortunately the path D–E–F has now become critical with a duration of 12 weeks. We can remove the extra week from E – again chosen as the longest activity in the critical path.

(c) To finish in 9 weeks we need a reduction of 5 weeks from the path A–B–C (say 4 from A and 1 from B), 3 weeks from the path D–E–F (say from E) and 1 week from the path G–H–I (say from H).

To get a 5 week reduction in the project duration we have reduced individual activities by a total of $5 + 3 + 1 = 9$ weeks. This costs $9 * 1000 = £9000$.

IN SUMMARY

We can only reduce the duration of a critical path by a certain amount before another path becomes critical. This amount is given by the total float of a parallel path.

10.5.3 Minimizing costs

The total cost of a project is made up of **direct costs** such as labour and materials, **indirect costs** such as management and financing, and **penalty costs** if the project is not finished by a specified date:

total cost = direct costs + indirect costs + penalty costs

All of these are affected by the duration of the project. There are no penalty costs if the project is finished on time, but this might need more resources and increase the direct costs. Sometimes a bonus is paid if a project is finished early – but this again might need extra resources and increase direct costs. Overall, we usually have to make some kind of balance between project duration and total cost. We can find this balance using two figures:

- *Normal time* is the expected time to complete the activity – and this has associated *normal costs*.
- *Crashed time* is the shortest possible time to complete the activity – and this has the higher *crashed costs*.

To simplify the analysis, we shall assume that the cost of completing an activity in any particular time is a linear combination of these costs. Then the cost of crashing an activity by a unit of time is:

$$\text{cost of crashing by one time unit} = \frac{\text{crashed cost} - \text{normal cost}}{\text{normal time} - \text{crashed time}}$$

This suggests an approach to minimizing the total cost of a project. We can start by assuming that all activities are done at their normal time and cost. Then we can systematically reduce the duration of critical activities. Initially the cost of the project may decline, but if we reduce the duration any further there will come a point when the cost begins to rise. When this happens we have found the minimum cost of the project. The formal procedure for this is as follows:

Step 1 Draw a project network – then analyse the cost and timings assuming all activities take their normal times.

Step 2 Find the critical activity with the lowest cost of crashing a unit time. If there is more than one critical path they must all be considered at the same time.

Step 3 Reduce the time for this activity until either:
- it cannot be reduced any further
- another path becomes critical, or
- the cost of the project begins to rise.

Step 4 Repeat steps 2 and 3 until the cost of the project begins to rise.

WORKED EXAMPLE 10.12

The following table shows some details of a project. The times are in weeks and costs are in thousands of pounds.

There is a penalty cost of £3500 for every week the project finishes after week 18. When should the project finish to minimize costs?

Activity	Depends on	Normal time	Normal cost	Crashed time	Crashed cost
A	–	3	13	2	15
B	A	7	25	4	28
C	B	5	16	4	19
D	C	5	12	3	24
E	–	8	32	5	38
F	E	6	20	4	30
G	F	8	30	6	35
H	–	12	41	7	45
I	H	6	25	3	30
J	D, G, I	2	7	1	14

Solution

Using the procedure described above:

Step 1. Figure 10.28 shows the network for this project, with times based on normal durations.

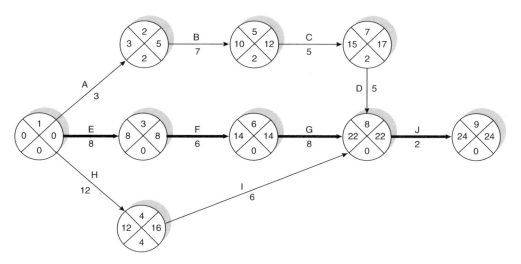

Figure 10.28 Initial times for Worked Example 10.12.

The critical path is E–F–G–J which has a duration of 24 weeks. We can find the total cost by adding the normal costs of each activity (£221 000) to the 24 – 18 = 6 days of penalty costs (£21 000), giving a total of £242 000.

The following table shows the cost of crashing each activity (in £'000 a week):

Activity	A	B	C	D	E	F	G	H	I	J
Normal time	3	7	5	5	8	6	8	12	6	2
Crashed time	2	4	4	3	5	4	6	7	3	1
Reduction in weeks	1	3	1	2	3	2	2	5	3	1
Crashed cost	15	28	19	24	38	30	35	45	30	14
Normal cost	13	25	16	12	32	20	30	41	25	7
Cost of reduction	2	3	3	12	6	10	5	4	5	7
Cost per week	2	1	3	6	2	5	2.5	0.8	1.7	7

The total float of activities on the parallel path A–B–C–D is 2, so this is the amount we can reduce E–F–G–J before another path becomes critical.

Step 2 finds the activity on the critical path E–F–G–J with the lowest cost of crashing. This is E at £2000 a week.

Step 3 reduces the time for activity E by 2 weeks, as beyond this the path A–B–C–D–J becomes critical.

> Total cost of crashing by 2 weeks = 2 * 2000 = £4000
>
> Total savings = 2 * 3500 = £7000

This step has reduced the penalty cost by more than the crashing cost, so we look for more savings.

Step 2 finds the lowest costs in the critical paths as E in E–F–G–J and B in A–B–C–D–J.

Step 3 reduces the time of these activities by 1 week, as E is then reduced by the maximum allowed.

> Total cost of crashing by 1 week = 2000 + 1000 = £3000
>
> Total savings = £3500

Again the overall cost has been reduced, so we look for more savings.

Step 2 finds the lowest costs in the critical paths as B in A–B–C–D–J and G in E–F–G–J.

> Total cost of crashing by 1 week = 1000 + 2500 = £3500
>
> Total savings = £3500

At this point the savings exactly match the cost. This shows that we have found the minimum total cost, and if we crash any more activities the cost will be more than the savings from reduced penalties.

The duration of the project is now 20 days, with cost of £221 000 for normal activities, £10 500 for crashing and £7000 for penalties to give a total of £238 500. This is a saving of £3500 or 1.5%.

Projects often need a compromise between costs and times. We can find the duration that gives a minimum cost, by using a combination of crashed and normal times and costs.

Self-assessment questions

10.16 Which activities must be shortened to reduce the overall duration of a project?

10.17 By how much can a critical path usefully be shortened?

10.18 By how much can a non-critical activity be expanded without affecting the project duration?

10.19 What is the crashed time of an activity?

10.20 'Penalty costs, labour costs, financing costs, etc. all decline with project duration, so the total cost of a project must decline with its duration.' Do you think this is true?

10.6 Gantt charts and resource levelling

When a project is in the execution phase – and work is being done – managers have to check progress to make sure the activities are actually done at the right times. But it can be quite difficult to see these times on a network. It is much easier to monitor progress using a *Gantt chart*.

A Gantt chart is another way of presenting a project, which emphasizes the timing of activities. The chart has a time scale across the bottom, activities are listed down the left-hand side, and times when activities should be done are blocked off in the body of the chart.

WORKED EXAMPLE 10.13

Draw a Gantt chart for the original data in the last example, assuming each activity starts as early as possible.

Solution

The activity times for this example were as follows:

Activity	Duration	Earliest		Latest		Total float
		start	finish	start	finish	
A	8	0	8	0	8	0 *
B	4	8	12	8	12	0 *
C	2	12	14	12	14	0 *
D	3	0	3	2	5	2
E	6	3	9	5	11	2
F	3	9	12	11	14	2
G	2	0	2	4	6	4
H	4	2	6	6	10	4
I	4	6	10	10	14	4

If each activity starts as early as possible, we can show the time needed by the blocked off areas in Figure 10.29. The total float of each activity is added afterwards as a broken line. Provided an activity is finished before the end of the broken line it is keeping within the schedule. But if an activity has not been finished by the end of the broken line the project may be delayed.

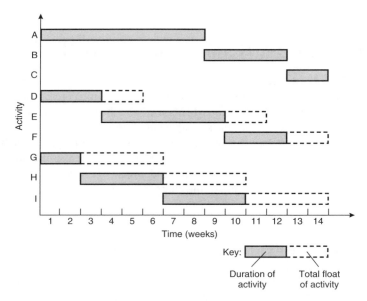

Figure 10.29 Gantt chart for Worked Example 10.13.

Gantt charts show where each activity should be at any time. They show the activities that are about to start, those that should already have started, and those that should have finished. Gantt charts are also useful for planning and allocating resources. Consider the chart shown in Figure 10.29 and assume, for simplicity, that each activity uses one unit of a particular resource – perhaps one team of workers. If all activities start as soon as possible, we can draw a vertical bar chart to show the resources it needs. The project starts with activities A, D and G so it needs three teams. At the end of week 2 one team can move from G to H, but it still needs three teams. If we continue to allocate the teams in this way, we get the graph of resources shown in Figure 10.30.

As you can see, the use of resources is steady for most of the project and only begins to fall near the end. This is the kind of pattern that allows resources to be used most efficiently. Unfortunately, in practice there is usually a series of peaks and troughs, and we need some way of smoothing these. Critical activities are at fixed times so any levelling must be done by rescheduling non-critical activities, and in particular by delaying those activities with large total floats.

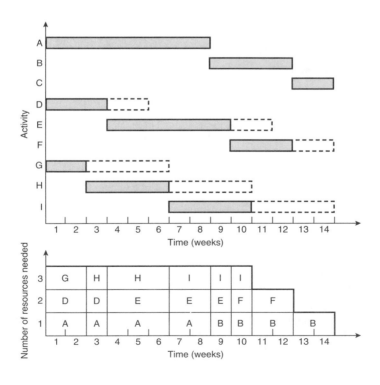

Figure 10.30 Resources used during Worked Example 10.13.

WORKED EXAMPLE 10.14

Figure 10.31 shows a project network with 11 activities over a period of 19 months. If each activity uses one work team, how many teams are needed at each stage of the project? Could we schedule the activities so that a maximum of three work teams are used at any time?

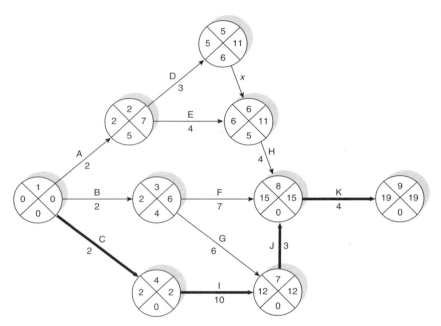

Figure 10.31 Project network for Worked Example 10.14.

Solution

Figure 10.32 shows a Gantt chart for this project, when all activities start as early as possible. This uses a maximum of five work teams during months 3 to 5.

To smooth the number of work teams, we have to delay activities with large floats. One schedule would delay the start of D until month 7, the start of F until 9 and the start of H until 10. This reduces the maximum number of work teams to 3 and gives a smoother workload, as shown in Figure 10.33.

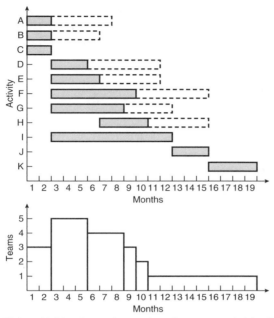

Figure 10.32   Gantt chart and work teams needed for Worked Example 10.14.

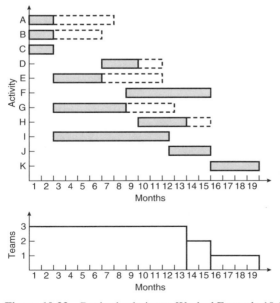

Figure 10.33   Revised solution to Worked Example 10.14.

Rescheduling a project can be done easily by computer. However, the quality of software is variable. The output from one simple package is shown in Figure 10.34. This package does not actually draw a network, but simply analyses the times.

Program: CPM With Crashing
Problem Title: Simple Example

***** Input Data *****

| | | | TIME | | COST | |
| | Start | End | | | | |
Activity	Node	Node	Normal	Crash	Normal	Crash
1	1	2	4.00	3.50	100.00	150.00
2	1	3	5.00	4.50	200.00	250.00
3	2	4	2.00	2.00	150.00	150.00
4	3	5	6.00	5.50	800.00	1200.00
5	4	6	4.00	3.50	450.00	800.00
6	5	6	7.00	6.50	1200.00	1500.00

***** Program Output *****

| | | Crashing | Extra | New | |
Activity	Nodes	Crash by	Cost	Time	Cost
1	1 –> 2	0.00	0.00	4.00	100.00
2*	1 –> 3	0.50	50.00	4.50	250.00
3	2 –> 4	0.00	0.00	2.00	150.00
4*	3 –> 5	0.00	0.00	6.00	800.00
5	4 –> 6	0.00	0.00	4.00	450.00
6*	5 –> 6	0.50	300.00	6.50	1500.00
(* : Critical Path Activities)			350.00		3250.00

Expected Normal Completion Time : 18.00
Expected Crashed Completion Time : 17.00

***** End of Output *****

Figure 10.34   Example of a simple computer printout for crashing a project.

A lot of programmes use an 'activity on node' format, where nodes are activities and arrows are events. This is somewhat easier to programme, but it can be a little more difficult to analyse. The ideas and analyses behind these two formats are exactly the same.

IN SUMMARY

Gantt charts give a different view of projects to emphasize timing. These charts can help with scheduling resources, and particularly smoothing the demands over time.

Self-assessment questions

10.21 What are the main benefits of Gantt charts?

10.22 How can you smooth the use of resources during a project?

CHAPTER REVIEW

This chapter described some aspects of project management. It emphasized the use of networks and Gantt charts. In particular it:

- outlined the needs of project managers
- showed how to represent projects as networks
- described 'activity on arrow' networks
- analysed the timing of events and the use of slacks
- analysed the timing of activities and the use of floats
- showed how the critical path sets the overall duration of a project
- considered crashing activities to reduce costs
- used Gantt charts to follow the progress of projects
- rescheduled activities to smooth the use of resources

KEY TERMS

activities	*network analysis*
CPM	*non-critical activities*
crashed costs	*normal costs*
crashed time	*normal time*
critical activities	*PERT*
critical path	*project*
critical path method	*project evaluation and review technique*
dependence table	*project management*
dummy activity	*rule of sixths*
events	*statement of work*
Gantt chart	*uniqueness dummy*
logical dummy	*work breakdown structure*

Case study

Accime Products

Background

Accime Products is a small manufacturing company based in the north of Italy. It designs and makes cheap gadgets for the home, usually for use in kitchens or cars. Their gadgets are always simple, contain few parts, are cheap, include a new gimmick of some kind, and have a short life cycle. Accime makes the initial designs for its gadgets, manufactures them, and markets them vigorously for a short time. Then when sales decline, they withdraw old products and introduce new ones. Recent products include a slicer for vegetables, a pocket coin holder, a windscreen de-icer that plugs into car cigarette lighters, a window cleaning brush that is attached to a hosepipe, a door chime that plays tunes, and a sensor that stops saucepans from boiling over. The company markets about 20 products at any time.

Accime's survival depends on a frequent change of products, with a typical product made for only 6 months. All the development between initial design and final marketing usually takes a few weeks. There is strong competition from other companies, mainly based in the Far East. If Accime price a product too highly or do not withdraw it quickly from the market, competitors introduce very similar designs, usually with lower quality and considerably cheaper.

Accime is always looking at ways of reducing the time needed to introduce new products. In 1997, they wanted to see if project network analysis could provide any benefits, and ran a test with their next product.

The company held a meeting to discuss the new product (a plastic shelf that allows several dishes of varying size to go into a microwave at the same time). At this meeting each area put forward their views on the times necessary for various activities. The following is an agreed summary of the meeting.

Design

The new product was slightly more complicated than usual, but quite a lot of work had already been done and initial designs could be ready in 14 days. These initial designs are passed to Production who make a set of prototypes which are passed to Sales and Marketing for trials.

When the results from a market survey are returned, the design team make any necessary changes (taking 6 days) and again pass details to Production.

The design team also works on packaging for the product, which takes 5 days, and uses some of the artwork supplied by Advertising. The ideas on packaging are then sent to specialist manufacturers, who tender for the work

(18 days). When the best tender is accepted, discussions may alter the design somewhat to reduce costs (3 days) and the packaging is then available 14 days later.

Production

Preparations for manufacturing the product are in several stages. Initially a single machine is set up (5 days) to make prototypes (which takes 8 days). This machine is then available for training production staff (for 2 days) so they are familiar with the new product.

With their experience of setting up the single machine the final production is planned (taking 4 days) and when designs for the product are finalized the remaining production machines are set up (10 days) and production starts on samples. With usual teething problems, the first production samples should be ready 5 days after the start of production. The machines then have any necessary fine-tuning (2 days) and are ready to start final production in earnest.

Sales and Marketing

The Sales and Marketing department makes initial plans for the campaign to launch the product (5 days), but their effort really starts with a market survey using the prototypes (10 days). The results of this survey are passed back to Design with suggested modifications.

Later, when the sample of final products is ready, Sales and Marketing arrange a series of demonstrations of the product in various department stores and shows. This campaign needs some planning (3 days), followed by the recruitment of sufficient demonstrators (8 days) and their training (1 day).

When the sample of products is available, company salesmen take them around shops and obtain orders, usually taking 5 days for first orders to arrive at the company.

Sales and Marketing arrange delivery of the finished product to shops. Tenders are requested from transport companies (18 days) and the cheapest bid is accepted, with deliveries then made within 2 days of manufacture.

Advertising

Accime always run an intensive advertising campaign, which must be planned (6 days) and run (10 days). This starts at least 2 days after products are available in shops. The artwork for this campaign takes 10 days to prepare and is based on pictures of the initial sample of products. This artwork is also used in brochures (which take 8 days to write and 7 days to print) and for the packaging (which is worked on by Design).

Timing

Generally, each department is so small that it can only work on one activity at a time, but if there is enough pressure, they might work over the weekends. If the timing is still not good enough, Accime can hire extra staff. As always, Accime want to introduce the new product as soon as possible, but do not want to spend too much on overtime or temporary staff. How do you think they could use project network analysis for their product planning?

Problems

10.1 A project has the activities shown in the following dependence table. Draw the network for this project.

Activity	Depends on		Activity	Depends on
A	–		G	B
B	–		H	G
C	A		I	E, F
D	A		J	H, I
E	C		K	E, F
F	B, D		L	K

10.2 (a) An amateur dramatic society is planning its annual production and is interested in using a network to coordinate the various activities. What activities do you think should be included in the network?

(b) If discussions lead to the following activities, what would the network look like?

- assess resources and select play
- prepare scripts
- select actors and cast parts
- rehearse
- design and organize advertisements
- prepare stage, lights and sound
- build scenery
- sell tickets
- make final arrangements for opening

10.3   Draw a network for the following dependence table:

Activity	Depends on	Activity	Depends on
A	H	I	F
B	H	J	I
C	K	K	L
D	I, M, N	L	F
E	F	M	O
F	–	N	H
G	E, L	O	A, B
H	E	P	N

10.4   If each activity in Problem 10.3 has a duration of 1 week, find the earliest and latest times for each event. Calculate the earliest and latest start and finish times for each activity and the corresponding floats.

10.5   Draw the network for the following dependence table and calculate the floats for each activity.

Activity	Duration (weeks)	Depends on
A	5	–
B	3	–
C	3	B
D	7	A
E	10	B
F	14	A, C
G	7	D, E
H	4	E
I	5	D

If each activity can be reduced by up to 2 weeks, what is the shortest duration of the project and which activities are reduced?

10.6   Do a complete analysis of times for the project described by the following dependence table:

Activity	Depends on	Duration	Activity	Depends on	Duration
A	B, E	3	J	K, L, Q	7
B	M	5	K	C, N	1
C	P	4	L	O	4
D	G, H, J	8	M	–	6
E	I	4	N	O	2
F	–	6	O	F	5
G	A	5	P	–	8
H	B, C, E, L	7	Q	O	2
I	–	2			

If each activity can be reduced by up to 2, what is the shortest duration of the project and which activities are reduced?

10.7 Draw a Gantt chart for the project described in Problem 10.6. If each activity uses one team of men, draw a graph of the teams needed assuming each activity starts as soon as possible. How could you smooth these demands?

10.8 A project is represented by the following table which shows the dependency of activities and three estimates of durations.

- What is the probability that the project will be finished before 17?

- By what time is there a probability of 0.95 that the project will be finished?

Activity	Depends on	Duration		
		Optimistic	Most likely	Pessimistic
A	–	1	2	3
B	A	1	3	6
C	B	4	6	10
D	A	1	1	1
E	D	1	2	2
F	E	3	4	8
G	F	2	3	5
H	D	7	9	11
I	A	0	1	4
J	I	2	3	4
K	H, J	3	4	7
L	C, G, K	1	2	7

10.9 A project has the following dependence table:
- Draw the network for this project.
- For each activity calculate the expected duration and its variance.
- Find the earliest and latest start and finish for each activity.
- Calculate the total, free and independent floats.
- What is the critical path?
- What is the expected duration of the project?
- What are the probabilities that the project will finish by days 36, 40 and 43?
- By what days would you be 80%, 90% and 95% sure that the project will be finished?

Activity	Depends on	Duration (in days)		
		Optimistic	Most likely	Pessimistic
A	–	4	6	8
B	A	1	2	2
C	B	2	4	10
D	B	3	3	3
E	A	6	10	16
F	C, D	5	6	8
G	C, D	4	4	5
H	D	3	5	7
I	D, E	2	3	4
J	D, E	4	6	8
K	F	10	12	14
L	G, H	14	15	18
M	I, J	8	12	18
N	K, L, M	5	6	6

10.10 Analyse the times and resource requirements of the project described by the following data:

Activity	Depends on	Duration	Resources
A	–	4	1
B	A	4	2
C	A	3	4
D	B	5	4
E	C	2	2
F	D, E	6	3
G	–	3	3
H	G	7	1
I	G	6	5
J	H	2	3
K	I	4	4
L	J, K	8	2

10.11 In the project described in Problem 10.12 it costs £1000 to reduce the duration of an activity by 1. If there is £12 000 available to reduce the overall duration of the project how should this be allocated and what is the shortest time in which the project can be completed? What are the minimum resources needed by the revised schedule?

Discussion questions

10.1 Recently, managers have been realizing that many of their jobs are really projects and not continuous processes, so project management has become increasingly important. What changes do you think this will make?

10.2 Network analysis – and other methods of project management – are only really useful for major construction projects. Do you think this is true?

10.3 If project management is so good, why do most projects still finish late and cost more than expected?

10.4 If a project is really unique, there is no relevant past experience. So any planning is little more than guesswork. Do you think this is true?

Inventory control

CHAPTER OUTLINE

Every organization holds stocks. These are the stores of items that are not needed when they become available. Stocks are expensive, and this chapter looks at ways of controlling the costs. After reading the chapter you should be able to:

- understand why organizations hold stocks
- define the costs of holding stock
- find an economic order quantity and do related calculations
- find the effects of finite production rates
- use service levels to deal with uncertain demand
- describe periodic review systems
- use a single period model
- do ABC analyses
- use materials requirement planning to schedule orders
- understand the aims of just-in-time systems

‖ 11.1 ‖ Background to stock control

11.1.1 Reasons for holding stocks

You probably imagine stocks being held by organizations like wholesalers, supermarkets or factories. In fact, every organization holds stocks of some kind.

> **Stocks** are supplies of goods and materials that are stored by an organization. They are formed whenever the organization's inputs or outputs are not used at the time they become available.

When a filling station gets a delivery of petrol from a tanker, it is held as stock until sold to customers; when a factory moves finished goods to a warehouse, they are put into stock; when a restaurant buys vegetables, they are put into stock until delivered with a meal. As there are always costs of holding stocks – to cover warehouse operations, tied-up capital, deterioration, insurance, etc. – an obvious question is, 'Why do organizations hold stock?'. There are several answers to this, but the usual one is, 'To give a buffer between supply and demand'. Stocks allow a supermarket, for example, to get large deliveries from suppliers, and then sell small quantities to customers.

> The main **purpose of stocks** is to act as a buffer between supply and demand.

Other reasons for holding stocks include:

* to act as a buffer between different operations
* to allow for demands that are bigger than expected, or at unexpected times
* to allow for deliveries that are delayed or too small
* to take advantage of price discounts on large orders
* to buy items when the price is low and expected to rise
* to buy items that are going out of production or are difficult to find
* to make full loads and reduce transport costs
* to provide cover for emergencies.

Just about everything is held as stock somewhere, whether it is raw materials in a factory, finished goods in a shop, or tins of baked beans in a pantry. We can classify these stocks as:

* **Raw materials** – the materials, parts and components that have been delivered to an organization, but are not yet being used.

- **Work in progress** – materials that have started, but not yet finished, their journey through a process.

- **Finished goods** – products that have finished their process and are waiting to be shipped out to customers.

This is a fairly arbitrary classification, as one company's finished goods are another company's raw materials. Some organizations (such as retailers and wholesalers) only have stocks of finished goods; other organizations (such as manufacturers) have all three types. Nationally, around 30% of stocks are raw materials, 40% work in progress and 30% finished goods. But some items held in stock do not fall easily into these categories, and we can define two other types (see Figure 11.1):

- **Spare parts** for machinery, equipment, etc.

- **Consumables** such as oil, fuel, paper, etc.

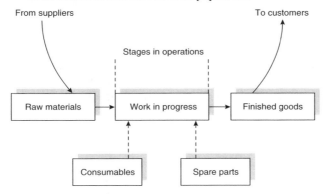

Figure 11.1 Types of stock holding.

Case example

Stock holdings

Tesco

Tesco is the largest food retailer in Britain, where it has over 14% of the market. It also has stores in France, Hungary, Poland, the Czech Republic and Slovakia. Their 1997 annual report gave the following figures for UK operations:

Total sales	£13 118 million
Fixed assets	£5849 million
Number of stores	568
Total sales area	14 million square feet
Employees	89 649
Annual growth of sales	14.8%
Stocks	£550 million

ICI

In 1996 ICI had total assets of £9 billion, a turnover of £10.5 billion and a trading profit of £340 million. It is one of the world's leading chemical companies, with five divisions for paints, materials, explosives, industrial chemicals and regional businesses. ICI holds huge stocks around the world. These were estimated at £1.4 billion, including £450 million of raw materials and consumables, £100 million of work in progress and £850 million of finished goods.

L.T. Francis

L.T. Francis is a manufacturer of pre-cast concrete fittings for the building trade. Their 1997 annual report gave the following figures:

Sales	£17 million
Total assets	£4.2 million
Stock	£3.2 million

You can see from these three examples that organizations hold large stocks. In Tesco the stock is around 4% of sales, in ICI it is 13%, and in L.T. Francis it is 19%. Many organizations have even higher stocks, and it is not unusual for manufacturers to hold over 25% of annual sales.

IN SUMMARY

Stocks are the store of goods that are held until they are needed. Every organization holds stocks of some kind. These allow for variations in supply and demand.

11.1.2 Costs of carrying stock

The total cost of holding stock is typically around 25% of its value a year. Not surprisingly, organizations look for ways of reducing these costs. At first sight you may think that minimizing costs is the same as minimizing stocks, but it is not. If a shop holds no stock at all, it certainly has no inventory costs, but it also has no sales. If we take a slightly broader view, we can define four separate costs – unit, reorder, holding and shortage.

Unit cost

The *unit cost* is the price of the item charged by the supplier, or the cost to the organization of getting one unit of the item. It may be fairly easy to find values by looking at quotations or recent invoices from suppliers. But it is more difficult when there are several suppliers offering slightly different products, or different conditions. If a company makes the item itself, it may be difficult to set a reliable production cost or a transfer price.

Reorder cost

The *reorder cost* is the cost of placing a repeat order for an item. It might include costs for setting up and agreeing the order, correspondence and telephone, receiving goods, moving them to stores, and any follow-up. Sometimes, the reorder cost also includes quality control, transport and sorting.

The reorder cost is for repeat orders and not first orders – which have extra costs for finding suitable suppliers, checking reliability and quality, and negotiations. In practice, you might get a reasonable estimate for a reorder cost by dividing the total annual cost of the purchasing department by the number of orders it sends out.

There is a special case of the reorder cost when the company makes the item itself. Then the reorder cost is a batch set-up cost and might include production planning costs, allowance for production lost while resetting machines, idle time of operators, material spoilt in test runs, time of specialist tool setters, and so on.

Holding cost

The *holding cost* is the cost of holding one unit of an item in stock for a period of time. It might, for example, be the cost of holding a spare engine in stock for a year. The obvious cost is tied-up money. This money is either borrowed – in which case there are interest charges – or it is cash that the organization could put to other use – in which case there are opportunity costs. Other holding costs come from storage space (for a warehouse, rent, rates, heat, light, etc.), loss (due to damage, deterioration, obsolescence and pilferage), handling (including special packaging, refrigeration, putting on pallets, etc.), administration (stock checks, computer updates, etc.) and insurance. Typical annual values for these, as percentages of unit cost, are:

	% of unit cost
cost of money	10–20
storage space	2–5
loss	4–6
handling	1–2
administration	1–2
insurance	1–5
Total	19–40

Shortage cost

The *shortage cost* occurs when an item is needed but it cannot be supplied from stock. In the simplest case a retailer may lose direct profit from a sale. But the effects of shortages are usually much more widespread and include loss of goodwill, reputation and potential future sales. If an assembly line runs out of raw materials, there can be serious disruptions. Shortage costs might also include payments for positive action to get around the shortage, such as expediting orders, sending out emergency orders, paying for special deliveries, storing partly finished goods, or using alternative, more expensive suppliers.

Because of the uncertain effects, shortage costs are always difficult to find – but we know that they can be very high. So organizations are willing to hold stocks because the holding costs are less than shortage costs.

WORKED EXAMPLE 11.1

Overton Travel Group employ a purchasing clerk who earns £12 000 a year. He places an average of 100 orders a month and has a budget of £4800 for the telephone, stationery and postage. Inspections of supplies arriving cost £30 an order. The cost of borrowing money is 15%, the obsolescence rate is 5% and insurance and other costs average 3%. What are the reorder and holding costs for Overton?

Solution

The total number of orders a year is $12 * 100 = 1200$ orders. Now we can find the reorder cost, by adding all the costs that occur for an order:

$$\text{salary} = £12\,000/1200 = £10 \text{ an order}$$
$$\text{expenses} = £4800/1200 = £4 \text{ an order}$$
$$\text{inspection} = £15 \text{ an order}$$

So the reorder cost is $10 + 4 + 15 = £29$ an order.

Holding costs include all costs that occur for holding stock:

$$\text{borrowing} = 15\%$$
$$\text{obsolescence} = 5\%$$
$$\text{insurance and taxes} = 3\%$$

So the holding cost is $15 + 5 + 3 = 23\%$ of inventory value a year.

IN SUMMARY

There are always costs with holding stock, and these can be quite high. We have classified these costs as unit, reorder, holding and shortage.

11.1.3 Approaches to inventory control

Sometimes a retailer, for example, does not carry stocks itself, but guarantees to get an item within a specified time. This approach works when someone else holds stocks – perhaps a manufacturer, wholesaler, importer or main distributor. This centralized stock may reduce overall costs, but the service – measured by delivery time – is inevitably worse.

When an organization holds stock itself, there are two distinct approaches to *inventory control*:

- **independent demand models** – which use quantitative models to forecast demand and find the order patterns that minimize costs.
- **dependent demand models** – which start with a production plan and 'explode' this to give a list of the materials needed.

Both of these approaches are looking for solutions to three basic questions.

What items should be stocked?

No item, however cheap, should be stocked without considering the costs and benefits.

When should an order be placed?

This depends on the inventory control system used, type of demand (high or low, steady or erratic, known exactly or estimated), value of the item, lead time between placing an order and receiving it into stock, supplier reliability, and a number of other factors. Two different ordering policies are common:

- **fixed order quantity** – where an order of fixed size is placed whenever stock falls to a certain level. A central heating plant, for example, may order 25 000 litres of oil whenever the amount in the tank falls to 2500 litres.
- **periodic review system** – where orders of varying size are placed at regular intervals to raise the stock level to a specified value. Goods on supermarket shelves, for example, may be refilled every evening to replace whatever was sold during the day.

Variations in the stock levels over time for these two approaches are illustrated in Figure 11.2.

How much should be ordered?

If an organization places large, infrequent orders, the average stock level is high but the costs of placing and administering orders is low. On the other hand, if it places small, frequent orders, the average stock level is low but the costs of placing and administering orders is high – as shown in Figure 11.3.

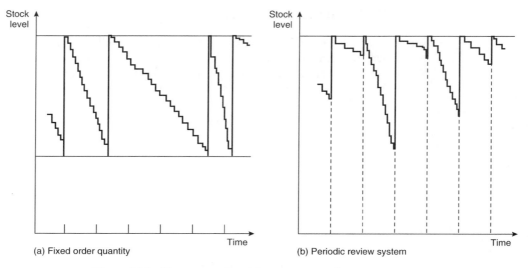

Figure 11.2 Two approaches to inventory control.

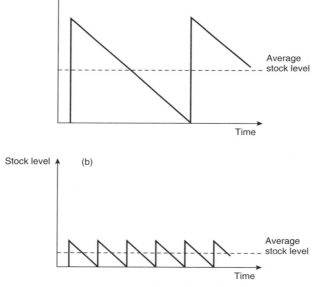

Figure 11.3 Comparing (a) large, infrequent orders with (b) small, frequent orders to meet the same demand.

In the rest of this chapter we will look for answers to these three questions.

Self-assessment questions

11.1   What is the main reason for holding stock?

11.2   How could you classify stock holdings?

11.3   List four types of cost associated with holding stock.

11.4   What are the basic questions for inventory control systems?

‖ 11.2 ‖ Fixed order quantities

11.2.1 The economic order quantity

We will start by looking at a fixed order quantity system – so we want to find the order quantity, Q, that minimizes costs. Suppose there is a constant demand, D, per unit time for the item, and that the lead time between placing an order and having it arrive is known. Then we can arrange orders so that the next order arrives exactly as existing stock runs out. We will also assume that we know the unit cost (UC), reorder cost (RC) and holding cost (HC), but that the shortage cost (SC) is so high that no shortages are allowed. Now the stock level follows the saw-tooth pattern shown in Figure 11.4.

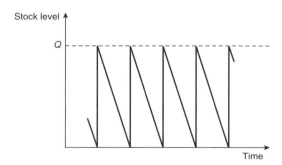

Figure 11.4   Changes in stock level over time.

Have a look at one cycle of this saw-tooth pattern shown in Figure 11.5.

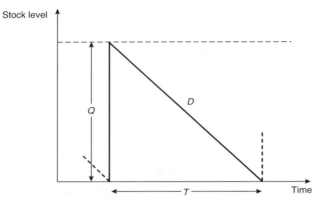

Figure 11.5   A single stock cycle.

At some point an order of size Q arrives. This is used at a constant rate, D, until no stock is left. The resulting stock cycle has length T and we know:

amount entering stock in the cycle = amount leaving stock in the cycle

so: $Q = D * T$

We also know that the stock level varies between Q and 0, so the average level is $(Q + 0)/2 = Q/2$.

We can find the total cost for the cycle by adding the four components of cost – unit, reorder, holding and shortage. But we know that no shortages are allowed so we can ignore these. We also know that the cost of buying the item is fixed regardless of the ordering policy – so we can also leave this out of the calculations.

Then the variable cost for the cycle is:

$$\text{total reorder cost} = \text{number of orders } (1) * \text{reorder cost } (RC)$$
$$= RC$$

$$\text{total holding cost} = \text{average stock level } (Q/2) * \text{time held } (T)$$
$$* \text{holding cost } (HC)$$

$$= \frac{HC * Q * T}{2}$$

Adding these two gives the total cost for the cycle, and if we divide this by the cycle length, T, we get the variable cost per unit time, VC, as:

$$VC = \frac{RC + HC * Q * T/2}{T} = \frac{RC}{T} + \frac{HC * Q}{2}$$

But we know that $Q = DT$, and substituting this gives:

$$VC = \frac{RC * D}{Q} + \frac{HC * Q}{2}$$

We can plot the two parts on the right-hand side of this equation separately against Q, as shown in Figure 11.6.

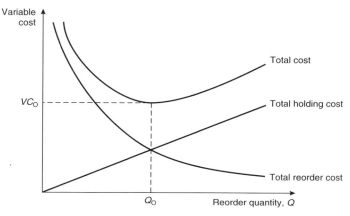

Figure 11.6   Variable cost and reorder quantity.

From this graph you can see that:

- the total holding cost, $HC * Q/2$, rises linearly with Q
- the total reorder cost, $RC * D/Q$, falls as Q increases
- large infrequent orders (to the right of the graph) give high total holding costs and low total reorder costs; small frequent orders (to the left of the graph) give low total holding costs and high total reorder costs
- adding the two costs gives a total cost curve that is an asymmetric U shape with a distinct minimum. This minimum cost shows the optimal order size

The optimal order quantity, Q_o, is called the ***economic order quantity, EOQ***. We can find a value for this by differentiating the equation for variable cost with respect to Q, and setting the result to equal zero:

$$0 = - \frac{RC * D}{Q_o^2} + \frac{HC}{2}$$

or

$$\text{Economic order quantity, } Q_o = \sqrt{\frac{2 * RC * D}{HC}}$$

WORKED EXAMPLE 11.2

John Pritchard buys stationery for Penwynn Motors. The demand for printed forms is constant at 20 boxes a month. Each box of forms costs £50, the cost of processing an order and arranging delivery is £60, and the holding cost is £18 a box a year. What are the economic order quantity, cycle length and costs?

Solution

Listing the values we know in consistent units:

$$D = 20 * 12 = 240 \text{ units a year}$$
$$UC = £50 \text{ a unit}$$
$$RC = £60 \text{ an order}$$
$$HC = £18 \text{ a unit a year.}$$

We can substitute these values to find the economic order quantity:

$$Q_o = \sqrt{\frac{2 * RC * D}{HC}} = \sqrt{\frac{2 * 60 * 240}{18}} = 40 \text{ units}$$

Now we can find the variable cost from:

$$VC = \frac{RC * D}{Q} + \frac{HC * Q}{2} = \frac{60 * 240}{40} + \frac{18 * 40}{2} = £720 \text{ a year}$$

There is also the fixed cost of buying the boxes. This is the number of boxes bought a year, D, times the cost of each box, UC. Adding this to the variable cost gives the total stock cost:

$$\text{total cost} = UC * D + VC = 50 * 240 + 720 = £12\,720 \text{ a year}$$

The cycle length comes from $Q = D * T$, or $T = Q/D$:

$$T = \frac{Q}{D} = \frac{40}{240} = 1/6 \text{ years or 2 months}$$

The best policy – with total costs of £12 720 a year – is to order 40 boxes of paper every 2 months.

You can see another useful point in this worked example. The calculation for the variable cost was:

$$VC = \frac{RC * D}{Q} + \frac{HC * Q}{2} = \frac{60 * 240}{40} + \frac{18 * 40}{2} = £720 \text{ a year}$$

But if you check the arithmetic:

$$\frac{RC * D}{Q} = \frac{60 * 240}{40} = 360$$

and
$$\frac{HC * Q}{2} = \frac{18 * 40}{2} = 360$$

It is not a coincidence that these two are the same – for the optimal solution, they are always equal. So you could save a little time by calculating the variable cost as:

$$\frac{2 * HC * Q}{2} = HC * Q$$

WORKED EXAMPLE 11.3

A company works 50 weeks a year and has demand for an item that is constant at 100 units a week. The cost of each unit is £20 and the company aims for a return of 20% on capital invested. Annual warehouse costs are 5% of the value of goods stored. The purchasing department of the company costs £45 000 a year and sends out an average of 2000 orders. Find the optimal order quantity for the item, the time between orders and the annual inventory costs.

Solution

Listing the values we know and making sure the units are consistent:

$$D = 100 * 50 = 5000 \text{ units a year}$$

$$UC = £20 \text{ a unit}$$

$$RC = \frac{\text{annual cost of purchasing department}}{\text{number of orders sent a year}} = \frac{45\,000}{2000}$$
$$= £22.50 \text{ an order}$$

$$HC = (20\% + 5\%) \text{ of unit cost a year} = (0.2 + 0.5) * UC$$
$$= £5 \text{ a unit a year}$$

Then substitution gives:

$$Q_o = \sqrt{2 * RC * D/HC} = \sqrt{2 * 22.5 * 100/5} = 212.13 \text{ units}$$

The cycle length comes from $Q = D * T$:

$$T = \frac{Q}{D} = \frac{212.13}{5000} = 0.042 \text{ years} = 2.21 \text{ weeks}$$

The variable cost comes from:

$$HC * Q = 5 * 212.13 = £1060.65$$

We can check this variable cost using:

$$VC = \frac{RC * D}{Q} + \frac{HC * Q}{2} = \frac{22.5 * 5000}{212.13} + \frac{5 * 212.13}{2}$$

$$= £1060.65 \text{ a year (allowing for rounding)}$$

To find the total cost we add the fixed cost of buying the item:

$$\text{total cost} = UC * D + VC = 20 * 5000 + 1060.66$$

$$= £101\,060.65 \text{ a year}$$

So the best policy – with variable costs around a £1060 a year – is to order 212 units every 2 weeks or so.

IN SUMMARY

The economic order quantity balances costs to find the best order quantity. This equals $\sqrt{2 * RC * D / HC}$. We can do a number of related calculations for costs and cycle lengths.

11.2.2 Moving away from the economic order quantity

In the worked example above, the **economic order quantity** was 212.13 units. This is clearly an awkward order size, so it would be useful to see what happens to the costs if we order, say, 200 or 250 units. For this we can use the cost curve shown in Figure 11.6. We know that at any point on this curve the variable cost is:

$$VC = \frac{RC * D}{Q} + \frac{HC * Q}{2}$$

But we also know that the lowest point has $Q_o = \sqrt{2 * RC * D / HC}$. If we substitute this value for Q_o into the equation for VC, we can get the lowest variable cost as:

$$VC_o = \sqrt{2 * RC * HC * D}$$

So if we order Q instead of Q_o, the variable cost rises from VC_o to VC. We can take the ratio of these, and do some more arithmetic to find:

$$\frac{VC}{VC_o} = \frac{1}{2} * \left(\frac{Q}{Q_o} + \frac{Q_o}{Q} \right)$$

Using an order quantity of 200 instead of 212.13 in Worked Example 11.3 gives:

$$\frac{VC}{VC_o} = \frac{1}{2} * \left(\frac{Q}{Q_o} + \frac{Q_o}{Q} \right)$$

$$\frac{VC}{1060.65} = \frac{1}{2} * \left(\frac{200}{212.13} + \frac{212.13}{200} \right)$$

$$VC = 1060.65 * 1.0017 = £1062.50 \text{ a year}$$

A reduction of almost 6% in order size increases the variable cost by only 0.17%. Repeating this calculation for an order size of 250 shows that an increase of almost 18% in order size increases variable cost by 1.4% to £1075.03. Now you can see why the economic order quantity is so useful: the calculation is based on a series of assumptions, but the total cost rises very slowly around the optimal (see Figure 11.7). So the EOQ usually gives a very good guideline for order size.

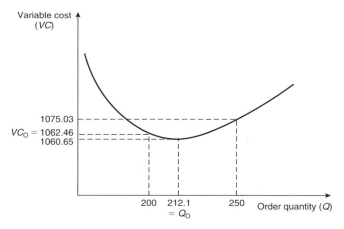

Figure 11.7   Changes in the variable cost with order size.

If we take the equation above, we can substitute specific values. For example, costs will rise by 10% when:

$$\frac{VC}{VC_o} = \frac{1.1}{1} = \frac{1}{2} * \left(\frac{Q}{Q_o} + \frac{Q_o}{Q} \right)$$

Setting Q as a proportion of Q_o, so that $Q = f * Q_o$ gives:

$$2.2 = f/1 + 1/f$$

or $\qquad f^2 - 2.2 * f + 1 = 0$

Solving this quadratic equation gives either $f = 0.64$ or $f = 1.56$. In other words, Q_o can increase to 156% of the optimal value or decline to 64% and only raise variable costs by 10%. In the last worked example the economic order quantity was 212.13 units, so any order size between 135.8 and 330.9 gives a variable cost within 10% of optimal. Extending the analysis shows that any order quantity between 114.6 ($= 0.54*Q_o$) and 394.6 ($= 1.86*Q_o$) has variable costs within 20% of optimal (as shown in Figure 11.8).

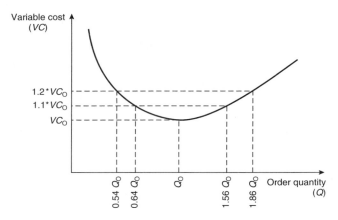

Figure 11.8   Changes in the variable cost with moves away from Q_o.

IN SUMMARY

The cost curve is very shallow around the economic order quantity. Provided we use an order size that is reasonably close to the EOQ, the costs will be very close to optimal.

11.2.3 Adding a finite lead time

When an organization buys something, there is a ***lead time*** between placing the order and having the goods arrive in stock. This is the time taken to prepare an order, send it to the supplier, allow the supplier to assemble the goods and get them ready for shipment, ship the goods back to the customer, allow the customer to receive and check the goods and put them into stock. Depending on circumstances, this lead time can vary between a few minutes and months or even years.

Suppose the lead time, LT, is constant. To make sure a delivery arrives just as stock is running out, we have to place an order a time LT before. The easiest way of finding this point is to look at the current stock and place an order when there is just enough left to last the lead time. With constant demand, D, we have to place an order when the stock level falls to $LT*D$. This point is called the ***reorder level*** (see Figure 11.9).

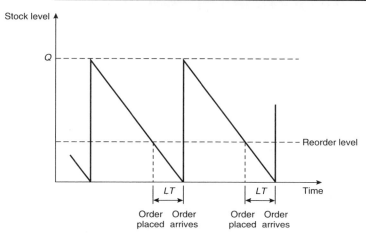

Reorder level = lead time demand
$ROL = LT * D$

Figure 11.9 Reorder level with a fixed lead time.

Inventories are almost always computerised. So a computer simply keeps a record of all transactions and sends a message when it is time to place an order. Sometimes it is easier to use a **two-bin system**. This keeps stock in two bins – the first bin holds the reorder level and the second bin holds all the rest of the stock. Demand is met from the second bin until it is empty. At this point the stock level has fallen to the reorder level and it is time to place an order. When the order arrives, the first bin is filled to the reorder level, and all the rest of the delivery is put in the second bin.

WORKED EXAMPLE 11.4

Demand for an item is constant at 20 units a week, the reorder cost is £125 an order and holding cost is £2 a unit a week. If suppliers guarantee delivery within 2 weeks, what is the best ordering policy for the item?

Solution

Listing the variables in consistent units:

$$D = 20 \text{ units a week}$$
$$RC = £125 \text{ an order}$$
$$HC = £2 \text{ a unit a week}$$
$$LT = 2 \text{ weeks}$$

Substituting these gives the economic order quantity:

$$Q_o = \sqrt{\frac{2 * RC * D}{HC}} = \sqrt{\frac{2 * 125 * 20}{2}} = 50 \text{ units}$$

The reorder level $= LT * D = 2 * 20 = 40$ units

So the best policy is to place an order for 50 units whenever stock falls to 40 units.

This calculation only works when the lead time is shorter than a stock cycle. In the last example the lead time was 2 weeks and the stock cycle was 2.5 weeks. But suppose the lead time is 3 weeks. The calculation for reorder level then becomes:

$$\text{Reorder level} = LT * D = 3 * 20 = 60 \text{ units}$$

The problem is that the stock level never actually rises to 60 units – it varies between 0 and 50 units. To get around this, we have to recognize that the calculated reorder level refers to both stock on hand and stock on order. Then the reorder level equals lead time demand minus any stock that is already on order:

$$\text{Reorder level} = \text{lead time demand} - \text{stock on order}$$

In the example, the order quantity is 50 units, so a lead time of 3 weeks would have one order of 50 units outstanding when it is time to place another order. Then:

$$\text{Reorder level} = 3 * 20 - 50 = 10 \text{ units}$$

We should place an order for 50 units whenever actual stock falls to 10 units. Then there will always be at least one order outstanding, as shown in Figure 11.10.

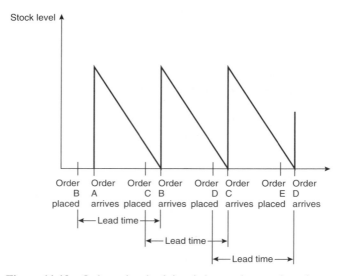

Figure 11.10   Orders when lead time is longer than stock cycle.

WORKED EXAMPLE 11.5

Demand for an item is constant at 500 units a month. Unit cost is £100 and shortage costs are known to be very high. The purchasing department sends out an average of 3000 orders a year, and their total operating costs are £180 000. Any stocks have financing charges of 15%, warehouse charges of 7% and other overheads of 8% a year. The lead time is constant at 1 week.

(a) What is the best ordering policy for the item?

(b) What is the reorder level if the lead time increases to 3 weeks?

(c) What range of order size keeps variable costs within 10% of optimal?

(d) What is the variable cost if orders are placed for 200 units at a time?

Solution

Listing the values we know and making sure the units are consistent:

$$D = 500 * 12 = 6000 \text{ units a year}$$

$$UC = £100 \text{ a unit}$$

$$RC = \frac{\text{annual cost of purchasing department}}{\text{number of orders a year}} = \frac{180\,000}{3000}$$

$$= £60 \text{ an order}$$

$$HC = (15\% + 7\% + 8\%) \text{ of unit cost a year} = 0.3 * UC$$

$$= £30 \text{ a unit a year}$$

$$LT = 1 \text{ week}$$

(a) We can find the best ordering policy by substituting these values into the equations:

- order quantity,

$$Q_o = \sqrt{\frac{2 * RC * D}{HC}} = \sqrt{\frac{2 * 60 * 6000}{30}} = 154.9 \text{ units}$$

- cycle length, $T = Q/D = 154.9/6000 = 0.026$ years or 1.3 weeks
- variable cost a year, $VC = HC * Q = 30 * 154.9 = £4647$ a year
- total cost a year $= UC * D + VC = 100 * 6000 + 4647 = £604\,647$ a year
- The lead time is less than the stock cycle, so:

$$\text{Reorder level} = LT * D = 1 * 6000/52 = 115.4 \text{ units}$$

The optimal policy is to order 154.9 units whenever stock declines to 115.4 units.

(b) If the lead time increases to 3 weeks, there will be 2 orders outstanding when it is time to place another. Then:

$$\text{Reorder level} = LT*D - 2*Q_o = 3*6000/52 - 2*154.9$$
$$= 36.4 \text{ units}$$

(c) To keep variable costs within 10% of optimal, the quantity ordered can vary between 64% of Q_o, which is 99.1 units, and 156% of Q_o, which is 241.6 units.

(d) With fixed order sizes of 200 units the variable costs are:

$$VC = \frac{RC*D}{Q} + \frac{HC*Q}{2} = \frac{60*6000}{200} + \frac{30*200}{2} = £4800 \text{ a year}$$

IN SUMMARY

Orders should be placed when stock on hand – plus stock in any outstanding order – falls to the reorder level. This equals the demand during the lead time.

Self-assessment questions

11.5 What are the main assumptions of the EOQ analysis?

11.6 What exactly is the economic order quantity?

11.7 How does placing small, frequent orders – rather than large infrequent ones – affect inventory costs?

11.8 What exactly is the reorder level?

11.3 Production systems

If an organization makes a product, it will move into the stock of finished goods at a steady rate, rather than in batches. Products coming off an assembly line at a rate of 100 an hour, will go into stocks of finished goods steadily at 100 an hour. The actual stocks will not rise by this amount, as there is also a steady demand that is removing items (see Figure 11.11). In these circumstances we can again find a batch size that minimizes inventory costs.

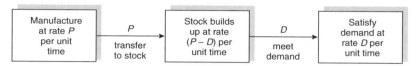

Figure 11.11 A manufacturer producing for stock.

If the rate of production is less than the rate of demand – so *P* is less than *D* – there is no problem with stock holding. Supply does not keep up with demand, and as soon as a unit is made it is sent straight out to a customer. There are only inventory problems when the rate of production is higher than demand – so *P* is greater than *D*. Then stock builds up at a rate (*P* − *D*) for as long as production continues. Production must be stopped at some point – or stocks will keep on rising. Suppose that production stops after some time *TP*. Then demand continues at a rate *D* and is met from the accumulated stock. At some further time, *TD*, all the stock is used and production must restart. The resulting stock level is shown in Figure 11.12.

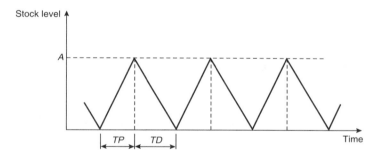

Figure 11.12 Varying stock level with finite production rate.

Consider one **stock cycle** with this pattern, shown in Figure 11.13. Batches of size *Q* are made and fed into stock at a finite rate. These are continuously being removed to meet demand, so the maximum stock level is lower than *Q* and occurs at the point where production stops.

We can start by finding the value for *A*, the highest actual stock level. Looking at the productive part of the cycle, *TP*, we have:

$$A = (P - D) * TP$$

We also know that total production during the period is:

$$Q = P * TP \quad \text{or} \quad TP = Q/P$$

Substituting this value for TP into the equation for *A* gives:

$$A = Q * (P - D)/P$$

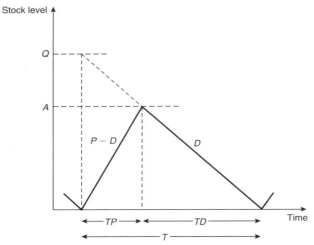

Figure 11.13   One stock cycle with a finite production rate.

We can now continue the analysis, remembering that in this case RC, the reorder cost, is really a production set-up cost.

Variable cost for cycle:

- total set-up cost = number of production set-up (1) * set-up cost (RC) = RC
- total holding cost = average stock level $(A/2)$ * time held (T)
  * holding cost (HC)

$$= (HC*A*T)/2 = (HC*Q*T)/2 * (P-D)/P$$

Adding these two gives the variable cost per cycle as:

$$= RC + (HC*Q*T)/2 * (P-D)/P$$

Dividing this by the cycle length, T, gives a cost per unit time, VC:

$$VC = RC/T + (HC*Q)/2 * (P-D)/P$$

Then substituting $Q = D*T$ gives:

$$VC = (RC*D)/Q + (HC*Q)/2 * (P-D)/P$$

If you compare this with the result for the EOQ, you can see that the only difference is the factor $(P-D)/P$. We could continue to do the arithmetic, plotting the variable cost against the batch size, finding an asymmetric U-shaped curve with a distinct minimum, and differentiating to find the optimal batch size, Q_o. But we do not need to repeat the arithmetic, as the result only differs from the EOQ by the factor $(P-D)/P$. In particular:

$$\text{With finite production} \quad Q_o = \sqrt{\frac{2*RC*D}{HC}} * \sqrt{\frac{P}{P-D}}$$

WORKED EXAMPLE 11.6

There is a steady demand for an item of 100 units a year. Unit cost is £50, the cost of processing an order is £20 and holding cost is £10 a unit a year. If the item is made at a rate of 10 units a week, what is the best production policy?

Solution

Listing the values we know:

$$D = 100 \text{ units a year}$$
$$P = 10 * 52 = 520 \text{ units a year}$$
$$UC = £50 \text{ a unit}$$
$$RC = £20 \text{ an order}$$
$$HC = £10 \text{ a unit a year}$$

With a finite production rate we get:

$$Q_o = \sqrt{\frac{2 * RC * D}{HC}} * \sqrt{\frac{P}{P - D}} = \sqrt{\frac{2 * 20 * 100}{10}} * \sqrt{\frac{520}{520 - 100}} = 22.25$$

WORKED EXAMPLE 11.7

Demand for an item is 1200 units a month and relevant costs are:

- production set-up cost of £3.20 an order
- shop order preparation of £2.50 an order
- scheduling of shop order at £5.90 an order
- insurance of 0.5% of unit cost a year
- obsolescence, deterioration and depreciation allowance of 2% of unit cost a year
- capital costs of 20% of unit cost a year
- storage space at £3.50 per unit per annum
- handling costs of £0.60 per unit per annum.

Each unit costs the company £10 and the rate of production is 2500 units a month. Find the best batch size and the minimum variable cost a year.

Solution

In this example we have to be careful with the definitions of costs. Every cost must be classified as unit, reorder or holding (as there are no shortage costs). Then:

$$D = 1200*12 = 14\,400 \text{ units a year}$$
$$P = 2500*12 = 30\,000 \text{ units a year}$$
$$UC = £10 \text{ a unit}$$

Collecting together all the costs per order gives:

$$RC = 3.2 + 2.5 + 5.9 = £11.60 \text{ per order}$$

There are two parts to the holding cost, a percentage (0.5%, 2% and 20%) of unit costs and a fixed amount (£3.50 + £0.60) a unit a year:

$$HC = (3.5 + 0.6) + (0.005 + 0.02 + 0.2)*10 = £6.35 \text{ a unit a year}$$

Then we can substitute these values to get:

$$Q_o = \sqrt{\frac{2*RC*D}{HC}} * \sqrt{\frac{P}{P-D}}$$
$$= \sqrt{\frac{2*11.6*14\,400}{6.35}} * \sqrt{\frac{30\,000}{30\,000 - 14\,400}} = 318 \text{ units}$$

We can find the cycle length from $Q = D*T$:

$$T = Q/D = 318/14\,400 = 0.022 \text{ years}$$

The variable cost per unit time is:

$$VC = RC*D/Q + (HC*Q)/2 * (P-D)/P$$

so with $Q = 318$ we get:

$$\dot{VC} = (11.6*14\,400)/318 + (6.35*318)/2 * (30\,000 - 14\,400)/30\,000$$
$$= £1050 \text{ a year}$$

IN SUMMARY

In production systems, units go into stock at a finite rate. We can find the batch size that minimizes total inventory costs. This gives an extension to the basic EOQ model.

Self-assessment questions

11.9 'Finite production rates are only important for stock control when the production rate is greater than demand.' Is this true?

11.10 If a batch of size Q is produced at a finite production rate of P units per unit time, is the highest actual stock level higher or lower than Q?

11.11 When compared with instantaneous replenishment, does a finite production rate lead to larger or smaller batches?

| 11.4 | Uncertain demand

11.4.1 Safety stock and service level

So far we have assumed that demand is constant and known exactly. In practice, demand can vary widely, and may not be known in advance. A company producing a new CD, for example, does not know how many copies will sell, or how sales will vary over time. When the variation is small, the basic EOQ model still gives useful results. But results are not so good when the demand varies more widely.

Imagine that we do not know the demand for an item exactly, but we know that it is normally distributed. You can easily see why the EOQ will not give good results. The reorder level is the lead time demand, $LT*D$, where D is the mean demand. But if the demand is normally distributed, it will be above D in 50% of cycles and stock will run out (see Figure 11.14). In most circumstances, a system that gives shortages in 50% of cycles is not acceptable.

In principle, we should be able to find the costs of running out of stock, and balance them against the costs of holding stock. Unfortunately, it is difficult to find reliable shortage costs. One thing we can say is that shortage costs are usually much higher than holding costs. This means that organizations are willing to hold extra stocks – above their expected needs – to add a margin of safety. These *safety stocks* are used when the normal working stock runs out.

Suppose a shop sells an average of 10 computers a week, and deliveries arrive in batches of 20. So far we have assumed that the shop will have its stock of computers fall to zero at the end of the second week, and at this point a new delivery arrives. But if the demand varies, the shop will not want to risk running out of stock before the next delivery. So it might keep an extra five units as a safety stock. The shop can then use this safety stock if there is suddenly a higher than usual demand.

The safety stock has no effect on the reorder quantity, which is still set by the EOQ. But it does affect the time when an order is placed (see Figure 11.15). In particular, the reorder level is raised by the amount of the safety stock to give:

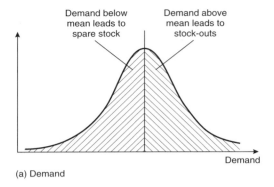

(a) Demand

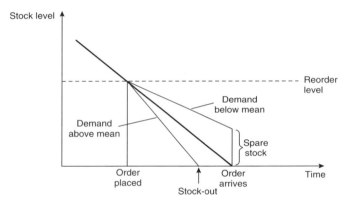

(b) Stock levels

Figure 11.14 Effects of normally distributed demand in lead time on (a) demand, (b) stock levels.

> reorder level $=$ lead time demand $+$ safety stock
>
> reorder level $= LT * D +$ safety stock

The larger the safety stock, the greater the cushion against unexpectedly high demand, and the higher the customer service. But the inventory costs are also higher. So we want to find the amount of safety stock that gives the best compromise between costs and service. This is largely a matter of management judgement. They must decide – based on their experience, objectives and knowledge of customer expectations – how much it is worth paying to get a particular level of service.

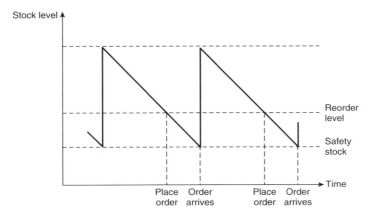

Figure 11.15 Stock levels with safety stock added.

We can define a ***service level*** as the probability that a demand is met directly from stock. An organization will typically give a service level of 95%. Then it can meet 95% of orders from stock, while shortages mean the remaining 5% of orders are not met from stock. There are really several ways of defining service level, including percentage of orders met from stock, percentage of units met from stock, percentage of periods without stock-outs, percentage of stock cycles without stock-outs, and percentage of time there is stock available. Here we will use the probability of not running out of stock in a stock cycle. This is sometimes called the ***cycle service level***.

Suppose that demand for an item is normally distributed with a mean of D per unit time and standard deviation of σ. If the lead time is constant at LT, the lead time demand is normally distributed with mean of $LT*D$, variance of σ^2*LT and standard deviation of $\sigma*\sqrt{LT}$. This result comes from the fact that variances can be added, but standard deviations cannot.

If   • demand in a single period has mean D and variance σ^2,

then   • demand in two periods has mean $2*D$ and variance $2*\sigma^2$,

        • demand in three periods has mean $3*D$ and variance $3*\sigma^2$,

and   • demand in LT periods has mean $LT*D$ and variance $LT*\sigma^2$

The service level sets the probability of a shortage. If the lead time demand is normally distributed, we can turn this probability into a number of standard deviations from the mean. This is the value of Z. Then we can find the safety stock from:

$$\textbf{safety stock} = Z*\text{ standard deviation of lead time demand}$$
$$= Z*\sigma*\sqrt{LT}$$

You can look up some probabilities in normal tables (see Appendix D) and see that:

- $Z = 1$ corresponds to a probability of 0.1587, which gives a stock-out in 15.87% of stock cycles,
- $Z = 2$ corresponds to a probability of 0.0228, which gives a stock-out in 2.3% of stock cycles,
- $Z = 3$ corresponds to a probability of 0.0013, which gives a stock-out in 0.1% of stock cycles.

If demand varies widely, the standard deviation of lead time demand is high – so very high safety stocks are needed to give a service level near to 100%. This is usually too expensive and organizations set a lower level, typically around 95%. Sometimes it is better to give items different service levels depending on their importance. Then very important items have service levels close to 100%, while less important ones are around 85%.

WORKED EXAMPLE 11.8

A company advertises a 95% service level for all items it stocks. They buy stock from a single supplier who guarantees a lead time of 4 weeks. What reorder level should the company use for an item that has a normally distributed demand with mean 1000 units a week and standard deviation of 100 units? What is the reorder level if they advertise a 98% service level?

Solution

The reorder level is given by:

$$ROL = LT * D + \text{safety stock} = 4 * 1000 + \text{safety stock}$$
$$= 4000 + \text{safety stock}$$

- For a service level of 95%, the number of standard deviations from the mean, Z, is 1.64. Then

$$\text{safety stock} = Z * \sigma * \sqrt{LT} = 1.64 * 100 * \sqrt{4} = 328$$

So the reorder level is 4328 units.

- If the service level is raised to 98%, $Z = 2.05$ and

$$\text{safety stock} = Z * \sigma * \sqrt{LT} = 2.05 * 100 * \sqrt{4} = 410$$

So the reorder level is 4410 units.

WORKED EXAMPLE 11.9

Associated Kitchen Furnishings run a retail shop to sell kitchen cabinets. Their demand for cabinets is normally distributed with a mean of 200 units a week and a standard deviation of 40 units. The reorder cost, including delivery, is £200, holding cost is £6 a unit a year and lead time is fixed at 3 weeks. How could the shop get a 95% cycle service level? What is the cost of holding the safety stock in this case? How much would the costs rise if they raise the service level to 97%?

Solution

Listing the values we know:

$$D \ = 200 \text{ units a week} = 10\,400 \text{ units a year}$$
$$\sigma \ = 40 \text{ units}$$
$$RC = £200 \text{ an order}$$
$$HC = £6 \text{ a unit a year}$$
$$LT \ = 3 \text{ weeks}$$

Substituting these gives:

$$Q_{\mathrm{o}} = \sqrt{2 * RC * D/HC} = \sqrt{2 * 200 * 200 * 52/6}$$
$$= 833 \text{ (to the nearest integer)}$$
$$\text{Reorder level} = LT * D + \text{safety stock} = 3 * 200 + \text{safety stock}$$
$$= 600 + \text{safety stock}$$

For a 95% service level $Z = 1.64$ standard deviations from the mean. Then:

$$\text{safety stock} = Z * \sigma * \sqrt{LT} = 1.64 * 40 * \sqrt{3}$$
$$= 114 \text{ (to the nearest integer)}$$

The best policy is to order 833 units whenever stock falls to $600 + 114 = 714$ units. On average orders will arrive when there are 114 units left.

- The cost of holding the safety stock is simply:

$$= \text{safety stock} * \text{holding cost} = 114 * 6 = £684 \text{ a year}$$

- If the service level is raised to 97%, Z becomes 1.88 and:

$$\text{safety stock} = Z * \sigma * \sqrt{LT} = 1.88 * 40 * \sqrt{3} = 130$$

The cost of holding this is:

$$= \text{safety stock} * \text{holding cost} = 130 * 6 = £780 \text{ a year}$$

:

When the demand varies, the normal EOQ model does not give good results. To improve performance, we have to add a safety stock. The size of safety stock sets the reorder level, and hence the service level. For normally distributed demand during lead time the reorder level is:

$$\text{ROL} = \text{lead time demand} + \text{safety stock} = LT*D + Z*\sigma*\sqrt{LT}$$

11.4.2 Periodic review systems

The models we have described so far all use a **fixed order quantity**. We have calculated this as the EOQ. But there is an alternative **periodic review system**. This is the method that supermarkets use when at the end of each day they replace whatever was sold from the shelves during the day.

If the demand is constant these two systems are the same. Differences only appear when demand varies. So we can extend the last analysis, and look at a periodic review system where demand is normally distributed. Now we are looking for answers to two questions:

● How long should the interval between orders be?

● What should the target stock level be?

The order interval, *T*, can be any convenient period. It might be easiest to place an order at the end of every week, or every morning, or at the end of a month. If there is no obvious cycle we might aim for a certain number of orders a year, or some average order size. One useful approach is to calculate an economic order quantity, and then find the period that gives orders of about this size. The final decision is largely a matter for management judgement.

Whatever interval is chosen we need to find a *target stock level*. The system works by looking at the amount of stock on hand when an order is placed, and ordering the amount that brings this up to the target stock level, *TSL*.

For a periodic review system:

order quantity = target stock level − stock on hand

Suppose the lead time is constant at *LT*. When an order is placed, the stock on hand plus this order must be enough to last until the next order arrives, which is $T + LT$ away (as shown in Figure 11.16).

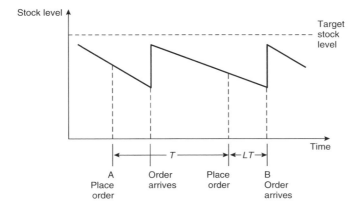

Figure 11.16 An order placed at A must cover all demand until B.

The mean demand over this period is $D*(T + LT)$. As demand is normally distributed, we need some safety stock to allow for the 50% of cycles when demand is higher than average. Assuming both the cycle length and lead time are constant, the demand over $T + LT$ is normally distributed with mean of $D*(T + LT)$, variance of $\sigma^2*(T + LT)$ and standard deviation of $\sigma^2*\sqrt{T + LT}$. Then we can define the safety stock as:

$$\text{safety stock} = Z*\text{standard deviation of demand over }(T + LT)$$
$$= Z*\sigma*\sqrt{T + LT}$$

So:

$$\boxed{\begin{aligned}\textbf{target stock level} &= \text{demand over }(T + LT) + \text{safety stock} \\ &= D*\sqrt{T + LT} + Z*\sigma*\sqrt{T + LT}\end{aligned}}$$

WORKED EXAMPLE 11.10

Demand for an item has a mean of 200 units a week and standard deviation of 40 units. Stock is checked every 4 weeks and lead time is constant at 2 weeks. Describe an inventory policy that gives a 95% service level. If the holding cost is £2 a unit a week, what is the cost of the safety stock? What is the effect of a 98% service level?

Solution

The variables are:

$$D = 200 \text{ units}$$
$$\sigma = 40 \text{ units}$$
$$HC = £2 \text{ a unit a week}$$
$$T = 4 \text{ weeks}$$
$$LT = 2 \text{ weeks}$$

- For a 95% safety stock we can find Z from normal distribution tables to be 1.64. Then:

  safety stock $= Z*\sigma*\sqrt{T+LT} = 1.64*40*\sqrt{4+2} = 161$ (to the nearest integer)

  $$\text{target stock level} = D*(T+LT) + \text{safety stock}$$
  $$= 200*6 + 161 = 1361$$

When it is time to place an order, the policy is to find the stock on hand, and place an order for:

$$\text{order size} = 1361 - \text{stock on hand}$$

If, for example, there are 200 units in stock, we will order $1361 - 200 = 1161$ units.

- The cost of holding the safety stock is $161*2 = £322$ a week.
- If the service level is increased to 98%, $Z = 2.05$ and

  $$\text{safety stock} = 2.05*40*\sqrt{6} = 201$$

The target stock level is then 1401 units and the cost of the safety stock is $201*2 = £402$ a week.

IN SUMMARY

Periodic review systems place orders at regular intervals. The order size is enough to raise stocks to a target stock level. For normally distributed demand this is equal to $D*(T+LT) + Z*\sigma*\sqrt{T+LT}$.

Self-assessment questions

11.12 What is a service level?

11.13 What is safety stock?

11.14 How can the service level be increased?

11.15 How is the order size calculated for a periodic review system?

11.16 Will the safety stock be higher for a fixed order quantity system or a periodic review system?

11.5 | **Single period models**

Sometimes managers have to make decisions about stocks over a very limited period. This often happens with seasonal goods. A stock of Christmas cards, for example, should satisfy all demand in December, but any cards left in January have almost no value. There are many problems of this kind, where managers effectively set stock levels over a single cycle. A classic example of these *single period models* is phrased in terms of a newsboy who sells papers on a street corner. The demand is uncertain, and the newsboy must decide how many papers to buy from his supplier. If he buys too many papers he is left with unsold stock that has no value at the end of the day; if he buys too few papers he has unsatisfied demand that could have given a higher profit.

To solve this *newsboy problem,* we assume that demand follows a known probability distribution – so we know the probability of selling each number of newspapers. Then we can use the profit on each paper sold, S, and the loss on each paper bought but not sold, N, to suggest an optimal policy.

Suppose the newsboy buys n newspapers. His expected profit on the nth is $S * P_n$ where P_n is the probability he sells the nth paper. Alternatively, we could say that the expected loss on the nth paper is $N * (1 - P_n)$, where $(1 - P_n)$ is the probability he does not sell the nth paper. As P_n is the probability that the nth paper is sold, it is really the cumulative probability that the demand is greater than or equal to n. The newsboy will only buy n papers if his expected profit is greater than his expected loss. In other words:

$$S * P_n \geq N * (1 - P_n)$$

or $$P_n \geq \frac{N}{(S + N)}$$

The newsboy's profit continues to rise with n while the inequality remains valid, but at some point the inequality will become invalid and his profit begins to fall. This point identifies the best policy – he should buy the largest value of n for which the inequality is still valid.

WORKED EXAMPLE 11.11

In mid-December the owner of a conifer plantation hires a contractor to cut enough trees to meet the expected demand for Christmas trees. She supplies these to a local wholesaler in batches of 100. Over the past few years the demand has been as follows:

Batches	0	1	2	3	4	5	6	7	8	9
Probability	0.0	0.05	0.1	0.15	0.2	0.2	0.15	0.1	0.05	0

If it costs £8 to cut and trim a tree that sells for £12, how many trees should she cut?

Solution

S is the profit on a batch of 100 trees sold, which is $100 * (12 - 8) = £400$.

N is the loss on a batch of trees not sold, which is $100 * 8 = £800$.

So we want the highest value of n for which the inequality is still valid:

$$P_n \geq \frac{N}{S + N} \geq \frac{800}{400 + 800} \geq 0.67$$

The cumulative probabilities of selling at least n batches of trees are:

n	1	2	3	4	5	6	7	8	9
P_n	1.0	0.95	0.85	0.70	0.5	0.3	0.15	0.05	0

So the largest value of n for which the inequality is valid is 4. The plantation owner should cut 400 trees.

WORKED EXAMPLE 11.12

Polmain Coach Tours want to book a number of hotel rooms for anticipated holiday bookings. The number of bookings they get is equally likely to be any number between 0 and 99 (for convenience rather than reality). Each hotel room booked costs Polmain £150, and they charge holiday-makers £250. How many rooms should they book?

Solution

Here $N = 150$ and $S = 250 - 150 = 100$.

We want $P_n \geq N/(S + N) \geq 150/(100 + 150) \geq 0.6$.

As each number of bookings is equally likely, the probability of each number, n, is 0.01 for all values of n from 0 to 99. So the cumulative probabilities are:

n	0	1	2	3	4		39	40	41...
P_n	1.0	0.99	0.98	0.97	0.96...		0.61	0.60	0.61...

The largest value of n for which the inequality is valid is 40.

| *IN SUMMARY* |

Managers often have to make decisions for a single stock cycle. To solve such 'newsboy problems' we find the largest value of n that still has $P_n \geq N/(S + N)$.

Self-assessment questions

11.17 What is a single period model?

11.18 What is P_n in the newsboy problem?

| 11.6 | ABC analysis of inventories

Inventory control systems require a lot of effort. Most systems are computerized, but they still need some effort to input data, check values, update supplier details, confirm orders, analyse reports, and do other routine jobs. For some items – especially very cheap ones – this effort may not be worthwhile. Very few organizations, for example, include routine stationery or nuts and bolts in their computerised stock system. At the other end of the scale are very expensive items that need special care above the routine calculations. An aircraft engine, for example, can cost several million pounds, and airlines will look very carefully at their stocks of engines.

An **ABC analysis** shows the amount of effort worth spending on inventory control. This kind of analysis is sometimes called a Pareto analysis or the 'rule of 80/20'. This suggests that 20% of inventory items need 80% of the attention, while the remaining 80% of items need only 20% of the attention. To be specific, ABC analyses define:

- A items as expensive and needing special care
- B items as ordinary ones needing standard care
- C items as cheap and needing little care.

Typically an organization might use an automated system to deal with all B items. The computer system might make some suggestions for A items, but managers make these decisions after reviewing the situation. Some C items might be in the automatic system, but the very cheap ones can be left out and dealt with using *ad hoc* procedures.

An ABC analysis starts by calculating the total annual use of items in terms of value. We find this by multiplying the number of units used in a year by the unit cost. Usually, a few expensive items account for a lot of use, while many cheap ones account for little use. If we list the items in order of decreasing annual use by value, A items are at the top of the list, B items are in the middle and C items are at the bottom. We might typically find:

Category	% of items	Cumulative % of items	% of use by value	Cumulative % of use by value
A	10	10	70	70
B	30	40	20	90
C	60	100	10	100

Plotting the cumulative percentage of annual use against the cumulative percentage of items gives the graph shown in Figure 11.17.

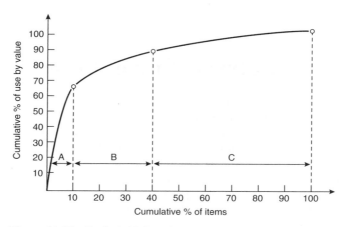

Figure 11.17   Typical ABC analysis of inventories.

WORKED EXAMPLE 11.13

A small store has ten types of product with the following costs and annual demands:

Product	X1	X2	X3	Y1	Y2	Y3	Z1	Z2	Z3	Z4
Cost (£)	20	25	30	1	4	6	10	15	20	22
Annual demand ('00s)	3	2	2	10	8	7	30	20	6	4

Do an ABC analysis of these items. If resources for inventory control are limited, which items should be given least attention?

Solution

The annual use of X1 in terms of value is $300 * 20 = £6000$. Repeating this calculation for the other items, and sorting the results into decreasing order gives:

Product	Z1	Z2	Z3	Z4	X1	X3	X2	Y3	Y2	Y1
Cumulative % of items	10	20	30	40	50	60	70	80	90	100
Annual use by value (£'00)	300	300	120	88	60	60	50	42	32	10
Cumulative annual use	300	600	720	808	868	928	978	1020	1052	1062
Cumulative % annual use	28	56	68	76	82	87	92	96	99	100
Category	←— A —→		←———— B ————→				←———— C ————→			

The boundaries between categories of items is often unclear, but here Z1 and Z2 are clearly A items and the Y group are clearly C items (shown in Figure 11.18).

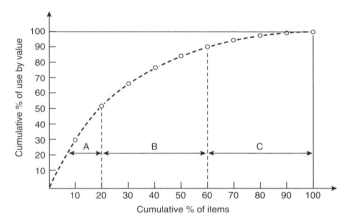

Figure 11.18 ABC analysis for Worked Example 11.13.

The C items account for only 8% of annual use by value and these should be given least attention if resources are limited.

IN SUMMARY

Controlling inventories can take a lot of effort. For some products this effort is not worthwhile – while others products need more attention. ABC analyses show which products fall into each category.

Self-assessment questions

11.19 What is the purpose of an ABC analysis of inventories?

11.20 Which items can best be dealt with by routine, automated control procedures?

|| 11.7 || Dependent demand inventory systems

11.7.1 Material requirements planning

The models we have described so far have 'independent demand', which means that the demand for a product is usually forecast from past demand figures. But there is another approach to inventory control, which does not use these forecasts. These **dependent demand inventory systems** were developed for manufacturing industry, and they find the demand for parts directly from planned production. If a company is going to make ten tables next month, it will need ten table tops and 40 legs. So it can minimize stocks by having these parts delivered just before they are needed. This is the basis of *material requirements planning (MRP)*.

MRP starts with a detailed production plan, and 'explodes' this using a **bill of materials** – which is simply a list of all the parts needed to make a product – to give detailed requirements for components and raw materials. These are ordered to arrive just before they are needed. We can show how this works using an example.

WORKED EXAMPLE 11.14

Johnson's Furniture assembles tables using bought-in parts of a top and four legs. These have lead times of 1 week and 3 weeks respectively, and assembly takes 1 week. The company wants to make 20 tables in week 5 of a production period and 40 tables in week 7, but has stocks of only two complete tables, 22 tops and 40 legs. When should it order parts?

Solution

We can represent the process by Figure 11.19, where 'level 0' refers to final products and 'level 1' to the parts.

Starting at the lowest level, we can draw a production plan for tables as shown below. Here 'Gross requirements' shows what the company needs, while 'Opening stock' show what it currently has; the difference between the two forms 'Net requirements'. So the opening stock of two tables is carried through to week

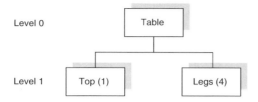

Figure 11.19 Bill of materials for a table in Worked Example 11.14.

5 where it is used to meet the first order and still leaves a net requirement of 18. There is an assembly time of 1 week so production for these 18 must start in week 4. Similarly assembly of 40 units must start in week 6.

Week	1	2	3	4	5	6	7
Tables							
Gross requirements					20		40
Opening stock	2	2	2	2	2		
Net requirements					18		40
Start assembly				18		40	

Now we can repeat this analysis for level 1 items, where the gross requirements are set by the planned assembly for level 0 items. Eighteen table tops are needed in week 4, and 40 in week 6; 72 legs are needed in week 4 and 160 in week 6. If there is not enough stock on hand to meet gross requirements, subtracting stock on hand gives net requirements. To make sure the parts arrive on time, they must be ordered the lead time in advance (i.e. 1 week for tops and 3 weeks for legs).

Week	1	2	3	4	5	6	7
Tops							
Gross requirements				18		40	
Opening stock	22	22	22	22	4	4	
Net requirements						36	
Place order					36		
Legs							
Gross requirements				72		160	
Stock on hand	40	40	40	40			
Net requirements				32		160	
Place order	32		160				

Now we can summarize these results in a weekly schedule with:

- week 1 order 32 legs
- week 3 order 160 legs
- week 4 assemble 18 tables
- week 5 order 36 tops
- week 6 assemble 40 tables

As you can see, the main advantages of MRP are that it gives a clear timetable for activities and stock is set to exactly meet production need.

WORKED EXAMPLE 11.15

A production schedule needs 45 units of a product in week 9 of a cycle, 60 units in week 10 and 40 units in week 13. There are currently 10 units of the product in stock, but the company always keeps 5 units in reserve to cover emergency orders. Each unit of the product takes 2 weeks to assemble from 2 units of part B and 3 units of part C. Each unit of part B is made in 1 week from 1 unit of material D and 3 units of material E. Part C is assembled in 2 weeks from 2 units of component F. Lead times for D, E and F are 1, 2 and 3 weeks respectively. Current stocks are 50 units of B, 100 of C, 40 of D, 360 of E and 100 of F. The company keeps minimum stocks of 20 units of D, 100 of E and 50 of F. The minimum order size for E is 300 units, while F can only be ordered in discrete batches of 100 units. Orders already placed for 10 units of D will arrive in week 6, 300 units of E will arrive in week 7, 200 units of F will arrive in week 6, and 20 units of C will arrive in week 8. Design a timetable of activities for the company.

Solution

As you can see, even a simple MRP problem needs a lot of calculations and gets very complicated. In practice a computer is always used. The printout from a simple program (Figure 11.20) shows the results for this problem.

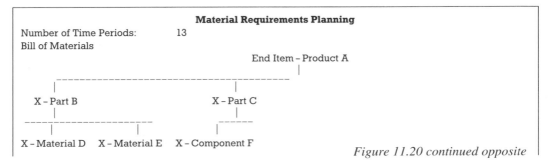

Figure 11.20 continued opposite

Level 0 – End Item
  Item Number: Part–0
  Description: Product A

Beginning Inventory: 10
Lead Time: 2
Safety Stock: 5
Lot Size: 1

	Week 6	Week 7	Week 8	Week 9	Week 10	Week 11	Week 12	Week 13
Gross Requirements :	0	0	0	45	60	0	0	40
Available :	10	10	10	10	5	5	5	5
Net Requirements :	0	0	0	40	60	0	0	40
Receipts :	0	0	0	40	60	0	0	40
Requests :	0	40	60	0	0	40	0	0

Level 1 – Comp 1
  Item Number: Part–1
  Description: Part–B
  Bill of Materials: 2

Beginning Inventory: 50
Lead Time: 1
Safety Stock: 0
Lot Size: 1

	Week 6	Week 7	Week 8	Week 9	Week 10	Week 11	Week 12	Week 13
Gross Requirements :	0	80	120	0	0	80	0	0
Available :	50	50	0	0	0	0	0	0
Net Requirements :	0	30	120	0	0	80	0	0
Receipts :	0	30	120	0	0	80	0	0
Requests :	30	120	0	0	80	0	0	0

Level 2 – Comp 1–1
  Item Number: Part–2
  Description: Material–D
  Bill of Materials: 1

Beginning Inventory: 40
Lead Time: 1
Safety Stock: 20
Lot Size: 1

	Week 6	Week 7	Week 8	Week 9	Week 10	Week 11	Week 12	Week 13
Gross Requirements :	30	120	0	0	80	0	0	0
Available :	40	20	20	20	20	20	20	20
Net Requirements :	10	120	0	0	80	0	0	0
Receipts :	10	120	0	0	80	0	0	0
Requests :	120	0	0	80	0	0	0	0

Level 2 – Comp 1–2
  Item Number: Part–3
  Description: Material–E
  Bill of Materials: 3

Beginning Inventory: 360
Lead Time: 2
Safety Stock: 100
Lot Size: 300

	Week 6	Week 7	Week 8	Week 9	Week 10	Week 11	Week 12	Week 13
Gross Requirements :	90	360	0	0	240	0	0	0
Available :	360	270	210	210	210	270	270	270
Net Requirements :	0	190	0	0	130	0	0	0
Receipts :	0	300	0	0	300	0	0	0
Requests :	0	0	300	0	0	0	0	0

Figure 11.20 continued overleaf

Level 1 – Comp 2

Item Number: Part–4				Beginning Inventory:		100		
Description: Part–C				Lead Time:		2		
Bill of Materials: 3				Safety Stock:		0		
				Lot Size:		1		

	Week 6	Week 7	Week 8	Week 9	Week 10	Week 11	Week 12	Week 13
Gross Requirements :	0	120	180	0	0	120	0	0
Available :	100	100	0	0	0	0	0	0
Net Requirements :	0	20	180	0	0	120	0	0
Receipts :	0	20	180	0	0	120	0	0
Requests :	180	0	0	120	0	0	0	0

Level 1 – Comp 2-1

Item Number: Part–5				Beginning Inventory:		100		
Description: Component–F				Lead Time:		3		
Bill of Materials: 2				Safety Stock:		50		
				Lot Size:		100		

	Week 6	Week 7	Week 8	Week 9	Week 10	Week 11	Week 12	Week 13
Gross Requirements :	360	0	0	240	0	0	0	0
Available :	100	140	140	140	100	100	100	100
Net Requirements :	310	0	0	150	0	0	0	0
Receipts :	400	0	0	200	0	0	0	0
Requests :	200	0	0	0	0	0	0	0

Figure 11.20   Computer printout for Worked Example 11.15.

The program starts at level 0, with production of the final product, A. The company keeps a minimum stock of 5 units of A, so we must remember this reserved stock when calculating the net requirements. Then it moves on to level 1 materials and expands the assembly plan for A into gross requirements for components B and C. The 40 units of A assembled in week 7 is expanded into gross requirements of 80 units of part B and 120 units of part C. The 60 units of A assembled in week 8 is expanded into gross requirements of 120 units of B and 180 units of C, and so on.

Gross requirements for B and C can be partly met from opening stocks, with the shortfall shown as net requirements. We must also remember the planned delivery of 20 units of part C in week 7. This schedule for level 1 parts can now be expanded to give the timetable for level 2 items.

The gross requirements for materials D and E are found from the assembly plans for part B. Thirty units of B are started in week 6 and this expands into gross requirements for 30 units of D and 90 units of E, and so on. One complication here is the minimum order size of 300 units of E. In week 7 there is a gross requirement of 360 for material E, 170 of which can be met from free stock (keeping the reserve stock of 100). The net requirement is 190, but 300 have to be ordered with the spare 110 added to stock.

Finally, the gross requirements for component F can be found from the assembly plan for part C. 180 units of C are started in week 6 so this expands into a gross requirement of 360 units of F, and so on. Orders must be in discrete batches of 100 units, so they are rounded to the nearest hundred above net requirements.

The timetable of activities now becomes:

- week 6: start making 30 of B and 180 of C
  place orders for 120 units of D and 200 units of F
  orders arrive for 10 units of D and 400 units of F

- week 7: start making 40 of A and 120 of B
  finish 30 units of B
  orders arrive for 20 units of C, 120 units of D and 300 units of E

- week 8: start making 60 units of A
  finish 120 units of B and 180 units of C
  place order for 300 units of E

- week 9: finish making 40 units of A
  start making 120 of C
  place order for 80 units of D
  order arrives for 200 units of F

- week 10: finish 60 units of A
  start making 80 units of B
  orders arrive for 80 units of D and 300 units of E

- week 11: start making 40 units of A
  finish 80 units of B and 120 units of C

- week 13: finish 40 units of A

Case example

Alco Office Supplies

Alco Office Supplies make a range of desks, filing cabinets and other office furniture. In 1979 they introduced MRP for the manufacture of standard filing cabinets. The manufacturing process was simple, and with the help of a consultant, a new system was working in slightly less than a year, with a cost of £80 000. By the end of the second year the system was judged a success and was extended to other products.

Alco's move to MRP illustrates the amount of information needed. Although they had integrated computer systems, these had to be thoroughly checked and overhauled before they were reliable enough for MRP. The biggest single job was getting data in a suitable form. Some of the old systems updated data records overnight. These had to be replaced with real-time systems, with all data files consolidated into a company-wide database.

Alco's experience also shows the complexity of real MRP systems. Their standard four-drawer filing cabinet is assembled from 162 different parts. Many of these are small and duplicated, but exploding the master production schedule required a lot of calculations. They make 24 variations on this basic filing cabinet, and a total of 3500 different products. Each of these needed a separate MRP run, and then common parts were combined into larger orders.

On their first trial run of the MRP system, the weekly report was over 8000 pages long. Needless to say, when the system became operational this was trimmed to 200 pages. You can get a feel for this report from the simplified printout in Figure 11.21.

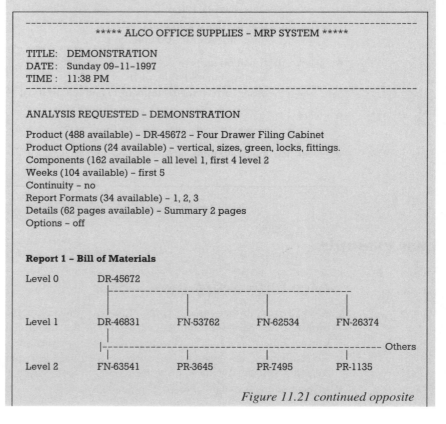

```
-------------------------------------------------------------------------
              ***** ALCO OFFICE SUPPLIES – MRP SYSTEM *****

  TITLE:  DEMONSTRATION
  DATE:   Sunday 09–11–1997
  TIME :  11:38 PM
-------------------------------------------------------------------------

  ANALYSIS REQUESTED – DEMONSTRATION

  Product (488 available) – DR-45672 – Four Drawer Filing Cabinet
  Product Options (24 available) – vertical, sizes, green, locks, fittings.
  Components (162 available – all level 1, first 4 level 2
  Weeks (104 available) – first 5
  Continuity – no
  Report Formats (34 available) – 1, 2, 3
  Details (62 pages available) – Summary 2 pages
  Options – off
```

Report 1 – Bill of Materials

Level 0	DR-45672			
Level 1	DR-46831	FN-53762	FN-62534	FN-26374
Level 2	FN-63541	PR-3645	PR-7495	PR-1135

Others

Figure 11.21 continued opposite

Report 2 – Inventory

NAME	# OF SUBCOMP	# PER PARENT	INVENTORY ON HAND	LEAD TIME	LOT SIZE
DR-45672	4	–	125	1	50
DR-46831	8	4	487	2	1250
FN-53762	16	4	257	2	1200
FN-62534	16	4	1253	2	2000
FN-26374	16	4	566	3	2000
FN-63541	8	4	124	4	1000
PR-3645	4	2	255	1	1500
PR-7495	4	2	458	1	1500
PR-1135	4	2	1087	1	2500

Report 3 – Master production Schedule

The Master Production Schedule

PRODUCT NAME : DR-45672
NUMBER OF SUBCOMPONENTS : 4
ON HAND INVENTORY : 125
LEAD TIME (WEEKS) : 1

WEEK	REQUIRED QUANTITY
1	175
2	250
3	250
4	175
5	175

Item: DR-45672   Level: 0
Parent: NONE   Lead Time: 1

Week	Gross Required	On hand Inventory	Net Required	Planned Receipts	Planned Releases
1	175	125	50	50	250
2	250	_____	250	250	250
3	250	_____	250	250	175
4	175	_____	175	175	175
5	175	_____	175	175	_____

Item: DR-46831   Level: 1
Parent: DR-45672   Lead Time: 2

Week	Gross Required	On hand Inventory	Net Required	Planned Receipts	Planned Releases
1	1000	487	513	1250	_____
2	1000	737	263	1250	_____
3	700	987	_____	_____	1250
4	700	287	413	1250	1250
5	_____	837	_____	_____	_____

Figure 11.21 continued overleaf

| Item: FN-53762 | | | | Level: 1 | |
| Parent: DR-45672 | | | | Lead Time: 2 | |
Week	Gross Required	On hand Inventory	Net Required	Planned Receipts	Planned Releases
1	1000	257	743	1200	-------
2	1000	457	543	1200	-------
3	700	657	43	1200	1200
4	700	1157	-------	-------	1200
5	-------	257	-------	-------	1200

Figure 11.21 Example of a simplified MRP printout for ALCO Office Supplies.

MRP has become very popular in recent years and has been extended in many ways. The first extensions allowed for variable lead times, variations in deliveries, wastage, defective quality, and so on. Figure 11.22 shows a summary of the overall MRP process.

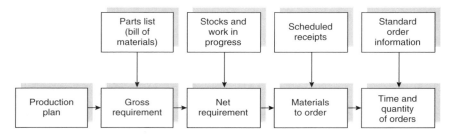

Figure 11.22 The MRP process.

Later extensions to MRP looked at broader aspects of planning. The production plan can also be used to find the machinery and equipment needed in each period. This in turn gives manning levels, and transport needs. Eventually the MRP process can be used to plan most of the resources of a factory. This approach is called Manufacturing Resource Planning, or MRP II.

IN SUMMARY

MRP is an example of dependent demand inventory systems. Demand for parts is found directly from the production schedule. This has the advantages of keeping inventories low, emphasizing the importance of the production schedule, giving early warning of shortages or problems, and assigning priorities to certain jobs. There are several extensions to the basic MRP process.

11.7.2 Just-in-time systems

In recent years many organizations have started to use *just-in-time* or *JIT*. The basis of JIT is that all operations occur just at the time they are needed. This means, for example, that if materials are needed for production, they are not bought some time in advance and kept in stock, but are delivered directly to the production process just as they are needed. In its simplest form, JIT gives a dependent demand inventory systems that tries to eliminate stocks. By 1988 an estimated 25% of European manufacturers used some form of JIT, and this had risen to over 50% by the early 1990s.

> **Just-in-time** systems organize operations to occur just as they are needed.

The main purpose of stock is to allow for short-term mismatches between supply and demand. Independent demand inventory systems allow for this mismatch by keeping stocks that are high enough to cover expected demand. Sometimes, particularly with widely varying demand, independent demand systems can give very high stocks. MRP overcomes this problem by using a production schedule to match the supply of materials more closely to demand. The more closely we can match supply to demand, the smaller are the stocks we need to cover any differences. Then if the mismatch can be completely eliminated, so can stocks (see Figure 11.23).

You see an example of this when you mow a lawn. If your lawnmower has a petrol engine there is a mismatch between the fuel supply which you buy from a garage, and demand when you actually mow the lawn. So you have to keep stocks of fuel in the petrol tank and spare can. If you have an electric motor the supply of electricity exactly matches demand and you do not keep any stocks. The petrol engine uses an independent demand inventory system, while the electric motor uses a JIT system.

You can imagine JIT in practice by thinking of a car assembly line. Just as the chassis moves down the line to a work station, an engine arrives at the same point and is fitted. This is repeated for all parts. As the car body arrives at another work station, four doors also arrive and are added. All the way down the line materials arrive just at the time they are needed, so the car is assembled in one smooth process.

JIT is really a simple idea, and we can summarize its main argument about inventories as follows:

- Stocks are held in an organization to cover short-term variation and uncertainty in supply and demand.

- JIT assumes these stocks serve no useful purpose – they only exist because poor co-ordination does not match the supply of materials to demand.

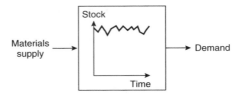

(a) Independent demand system needs high stocks to cover mismatch between supply and demand

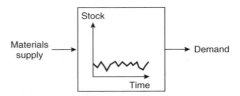

(b) MRP gives lower stocks as mismatch is reduced

(c) JIT eliminates stock as supply exactly matches demand

Figure 11.23 Variation of costs with number of units processed.

- As long as stocks are held, managers will not try to improve their coordination.
- This means that operations will continue to be poorly managed, with many problems hidden by the stocks.
- The proper thing for an organization to do is improve its management, find the reasons why there are differences between supply and demand, and then take whatever action is needed to overcome them.

Now you can begin to see the wider role of JIT. Although we have introduced JIT as a way of reducing stock levels, it is much more than this. JIT really involves a change in the way an organization looks at its operations. Its supporters described it as 'a way of eliminating waste', or, 'a way of enforced problem solving'.

$\boxed{\textit{IN SUMMARY}}$

Just-in-time systems organize operations so they occur just as they are needed. For inventory control this means that materials are delivered just-in-time for their use, and stocks are eliminated. But inventory control is only one aspect of JIT, which changes the way that organizations work.

Self-assessment questions

11.21 What is MRP?

11.22 What are the advantages of MRP over independent inventory systems?

11.23 'Just-in-time systems are only concerned with inventory control.' Do you think this is true?

CHAPTER REVIEW

This chapter described some approaches to inventory control. In particular it:

- discussed the reasons for holding stocks
- described the costs of stocks
- looked at independent demand inventory control systems
- derived an economic order quantity
- extended the basic EOQ model to include finite production rates
- calculated safety stocks for uncertain demand
- looked at periodic review systems
- described a model for single periods
- did ABC analyses of inventories
- illustrated dependent demand systems by material requirements planning
- outlined the approach of JIT.

KEY TERMS

ABC analysis
cycle service level
dependent demand models
economic order quantity
EOQ
fixed order quantity
holding cost
independent demand models
inventory control
JIT
just-in-time
lead time
material requirements planning

MRP
newsboy problem
periodic review system
reorder cost
reorder level
safety stocks
service level
shortage cost
single period models
stock cycle
target stock level
two-bin system
unit cost

Case study

The Midland Pill Supply Company

In the United Kingdom, pharmaceuticals are supplied to around 12 000 retail pharmacies, hospitals, dispensing doctors and a few other outlets. Historically, deliveries were made directly by manufacturers, but during the 1960s the range of pharmaceuticals and related goods grew rapidly, and a wholesale industry developed to give an efficient delivery service from centralized warehouses.

There was a period of stability in this wholesale sector up to the mid-1970s when several hundred depots operated around the country. Then in 1978 retail price maintenance was removed from pharmaceuticals and:

● smaller retail pharmacies closed and were replaced by fewer, larger ones

● chains of national wholesalers developed

● wholesalers began to offer price discounts

● the government tightened its control on prices – through the National Health Service which was by far the biggest customer

● a limited list of acceptable drugs for National Health Service prescription was introduced in 1985

● some parallel imports of cheaper – usually lower quality – drugs started

● increasingly sophisticated computerized systems were developed.

The market was becoming increasingly competitive and a small number of national companies began to dominate the wholesale pharmaceutical market. The Midland Pill Supply Company (MPS) is a medium-sized private company which is run efficiently and, by offering a good service to customers in a relatively small area, is competing successfully with the national wholesalers. The three main activities of MPS are:

● order taking and processing

● stock holding and control

● delivery to customers.

To ensure its survival, MPS continuously looks for improvements to its performance. A short time ago the management were concerned that the cost of deliveries to customers was rising. The distribution system had been reviewed occasionally as the company grew, but it was essentially designed for a much smaller operation. As there was little expertise in transport planning within the company, MPS hired a management consultant to advise them on transport operations, vehicle schedules, and general materials management. This consultant did some work that saved the company a substantial amount. In his final report the consultant also suggested that the company might look at its stock holding policies, as this seemed an area where they could make more savings.

The company started to look at its inventory control system. They had introduced this 5 years earlier when they bought a new computer, and it seemed to be working quite well. But when they looked at the system in detail, they soon noticed that stock levels had been drifting upwards for the past 3 years. The purchasing department explained that the company was successful because it had a reputation for reliability and service. A customer could phone in an order at any time during the working day and delivery would normally be guaranteed within 3 hours. Unfortunately there had been occasions when they had run out of stock and had let down customers (their own lead time from manufacturers averaged about a week). To make sure this happened as infrequently as possible the purchasing department had adopted a policy of keeping 3 weeks' demand in reserve to cover for late deliveries from manufacturers or sudden, unexpectedly high demands from customers.

The stock in MPS was computer controlled, with the purchasing department setting parameters. They had decided the most important factor was the average demand for an item over the past 3 weeks. This value, F, was used as a forecast of future demand and a stock of 3 weeks' demand was held in reserve. Lead time averaged 1 week so the reorder level was set at $4*F*FACTOR1$, where FACTOR1 was a variable between 1 and 2 and gave a subjective view of the supplier's reliability.

Order quantities were based on the workload that could be handled by the purchasing department. The equivalent of four full-time people worked in the department and each could process up to 40 orders a day, so in 200 working days they could process 32 000 orders. As there were 3500 items in stock, each item could, on average, have 9.1 orders a year. To add an element of safety, each order was made big enough to last about 7 weeks, including a small, subjective allowance for the 'importance' of the item. The same inventory policy was used for all items.

The computer recorded all stock transactions for the past 13 weeks and although it was not set up to produce summarized reports, raw data was readily available. Management looked at a small sample of this, but they did not have time to make much progress. The following table shows some demand data collected for seven items:

				Item Number			
Week	132/75	741/33	884/65	884/92	331/21	175/88	303/18
1	252	27	145	1235	567	121	987
2	260	32	208	1098	664	87	777
3	189	23	177	987	548	223	743
4	221	22	195	1154	602	304	680
5	232	27	211	1559	530	76	634
6	195	30	179	1209	650	377	655
7	217	31	205	993	612	156	598
8	225	23	187	1313	608	198	603
9	186	28	156	1405	596	94	621
10	265	23	182	1009	637	355	564
11	245	25	171	985	555	187	559
12	212	28	169	1237	589	209	519
13	224	31	210	1119	601	304	485
ROL	1057	162	1121	6101	2517	893	4415
Q	1509	245	1443	7926	4517	1945	6432
UC	10.02	8.73	13.67	1.25	2.49	6.55	14.20

When the company accountant was asked for information on stocks he was reluctant to give advice and explained that he had little hard information. The unit cost varied from a few pence to several hundred pounds, and no-one had attempted to cost the stock holding or purchasing functions. Wages were slightly over agreed union rates for the industry; turnover of MPS was £750 000 a week, and the company expects to make a net profit of 2.5% – which is slightly above the average for similar companies.

Question

The management of MPS are keen to make progress in this area. They think that their initial examination has confirmed the consultant's report that they could make savings. What would you advise them to do?

Problems

11.1   The unit cost of an item is £24; reorder cost is £80 and holding cost is £8 a unit a year. Demand for the item is 1800 a year and lead time is three weeks. What is the optimal inventory policy for the item?

11.2 A wholesaler buys microwave cookers for £250 each and sells about 80 a week at £300 each. Each order sent to the manufacturers costs an average of £45 for administration, £445 for transport, £30 for testing and £20 for miscellaneous costs. Annual holding costs are £40 a cooker for warehouse space plus 15% for use of capital.

The wholesaler currently buys 1000 cookers at a time. What is the total cost of holding a stock of microwaves? How much does this add to the price of each cooker? What is the best policy for the stock of cookers? What savings would this policy give? What size of order would give variable costs within 15% of optimal?

11.3 Annual demand for an item is 2000 units, each order costs £10 to place and the annual holding cost is 40% of the unit cost. The unit cost depends on the quantity ordered as follows:

- for quantities less than 500, unit cost is £1
- for quantities between 500 and 1000, unit cost is £0.80
- for quantities of 1000 or more, unit cost is £0.60

What is the best ordering policy for the item?

11.4 In a small warehouse the demand for an item is constant at 100 units a year. The unit cost is £50, the cost of processing an order is £20 and the annual holding cost is £10 a unit. If the warehouse could be supplied at a finite rate of 10 units a week what is the best inventory policy for the item?

11.5 A manufacturer needs 1800 computer chips of a particular type over a 200-day working year. If there are any shortages production will be disrupted with very high costs. The holding cost for the chips is £2 a unit a year and the cost of placing an order is £40 an order. Find the economic order quantity, the number of orders a year, and the costs of running the system if the real interest rate is 20% a year. What is the effect on this inventory system if the supplier of chips will only supply them at a finite rate of 40 a day?

11.6 Demand for an item is steady at 20 units a week and the economic order quantity has been calculated at 50 units. What is the reorder level when the lead time is: (a) 1 week, (b) 3 weeks, (c) 5 weeks, (d) 7 weeks?

11.7 A company advertises a 95% cycle service level for all stock items. Stock is replenished from a single supplier who guarantees a lead time of 4 weeks. What reorder level should the company adopt for an item that has a normally distributed demand with mean 1000 units a week and standard deviation of 100 units? What is the reorder level if a 98% cycle service level is used?

11.8   A company assembles trolleys, each consisting of a body and four wheels. They must have six of these finished in the sixth week of a production cycle, and a further ten finished in the eighth week. Assembly takes 1 week.

- The bodies are bought from an outside supplier with an average lead time of 2 weeks. At the beginning of the production cycle there are four bodies already in stock.

- Wheels are made in another part of the company with a lead time of 2 weeks. At the beginning of the production cycle there are ten wheels in stock, but company policy is to keep at least eight wheels in stock.

Each wheel consists of two rims and a tyre that are bought from suppliers with lead times of 1 and 2 weeks respectively. There are opening stocks of six tyres but no rims, and the rim supplier will only deliver in batches of 100 units.

Use MRP to design a timetable for placing orders and starting production.

Discussion questions

11.1   Some organizations try to reduce their stocks by making to order, or guaranteeing delivery within a specified period. Do these systems really reduce inventory costs?

11.2   What costs are there for holding stocks? Are these easy to find? Why are shortage costs so difficult to find?

11.3   What is a service level? As customers will go to another supplier if, say, a supermarket runs out of stock, does it make sense to aim for less than 100% service level?

11.4   One of the problems with MRP is the amount of data needed. What does this include, and is it difficult to get? Does this limit the use of MRP?

11.5   When would you use independent demand systems rather than dependent demand systems?

11.6   Just-in-time systems are nothing new. Organizations have always tried to work this way, but computers now make it possible. Do you think that this is true?

Simulation and queues

Chapter outline	501
12.1 Queues at single servers	502
12.2 Multi-server queues	509
12.3 Simulation methods	515
12.4 Random sampling	521
12.5 Simulation flow charts	530

12.6 Benefits of simulation	540
Chapter review	542
Key terms	543
Case Study: City Assistance	543
Problems	546
Discussion questions	547

CHAPTER OUTLINE

This chapter talks about simulation. It introduces some ideas from queueing theory, and then shows how these problems, together with many others, can be tackled by simulation. Simulation is one of the most widely used management tools. After reading the chapter you should be able to:

- appreciate the scope of queueing problems
- find the operating characteristics of single-server queues
- find the operating characteristics of queues with multiple servers
- describe the characteristic approach of simulation
- do manual simulations for simple problems
- get random samples from a variety of distributions
- see how to tackle larger problems
- draw simulation flow charts to describe the logic of a process

| 12.1 | Queues at single servers

12.1.1 Background

We are all familiar with *queues*, which we meet when buying a train ticket, getting money from a bank, at the checkout of a supermarket, waiting for traffic lights to change, and in many other situations. But not all queues involve people – there can be queues of jobs waiting to be processed on a computer, items waiting to move along an assembly line, telephone calls waiting for equipment to become free, faulty equipment waiting for maintenance engineers, ships waiting for a berth, and so on.

All queues have some common features. By convention a **customer** is anyone or anything wanting a service, and a **server** is the person or thing giving that service.

> **Queues** are formed when customers want a service, but the server is busy and they have to wait.

Queues can take many forms:

- customers may form a single queue, or they may form separate queues for each server
- customers may arrive singly, or in batches (when, for example, a bus drops a batch of people to eat at motorway services)
- arrivals may be at random, or spread out by an appointment system
- customers may be served individually, or in batches (when, for example, a train picks up a batch of customers)
- servers may be in parallel (where each does the same job), or in series (where each gives part of the service and then passes the customer on to the next server)
- service time may be constant, or variable
- customers may be served in order of arrival, or some other order (hospitals admit patients in order of urgency, etc.).

As you know from experience, we often judge the service by the time customers have to wait. And the length of a queue depends on three factors:

- the rate at which customers arrive to be served
- the time taken for a server to deal with a customer
- the number of servers available.

If there are a lot of servers the queues will be short, but the cost of the service will be high; if there are only a few servers the cost will be low, but potential customers will see the long queues and go somewhere else. We need a balance that seems reasonable to everyone concerned. This differs according to circumstances. When you visit a doctor's surgery you often have to wait a long time. This is because a doctor's time is considered expensive, while patients' time is cheap. To make sure the doctor does not wait for patients, appointments are made close together and patients are expected to wait. On the other hand, you would not expect to wait long at a petrol station. The cost of servers (petrol pumps) is low and customers can drive to a competitor if there is a queue. So petrol stations have a lot of servers, and although the utilization of each is low, customers have a short wait in any queue.

IN SUMMARY

Queues arise in many situations, not all of which involve people. When managing queues, we need a balance between large numbers of servers and reasonable costs.

12.1.2 Describing single-server queues

The simplest type of queue has a single server dealing with a queue of customers. We can build a model of these *single-server queues*, assuming that there is:

- a single server
- a single queue
- random arrivals
- random service time
- service in the order 'first come first served'
- a steady state that the system can reach
- no limit to the number of customers allowed in the queue
- no limit on the number of customers who use the service
- all arrivals wait to be served

Random arrivals

Chapter 7 showed how random events follow a Poisson distribution. We can use this to describe customer arrivals. If the average number of customers arriving in unit time is λ, the probability of r arrivals in unit time is given by the Poisson distribution (see Figure 12.1):

$$P(r) = \frac{e^{-\lambda} * \lambda^r}{r!}$$

where: r = number of arrivals
         λ = mean number of arrivals
         e = exponential constant (2.71828 …)

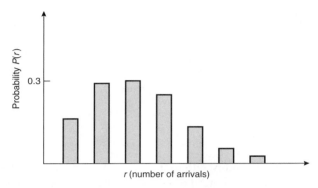

Figure 12.1   Random arrivals follow a Poisson distribution.

Random service time

Service time is also random, but it is continuous. We can describe this by a *negative exponential distribution*, which is related to the Poisson distribution (see Figure 12.2). This has the useful property that the probability of service time not exceeding some specified value, T, is:

$$P(t \le T) = 1 - e^{-\mu * T}$$

where: μ = mean service rate
         = the average number of customers served per unit of time

So the probability that service is not completed by time T is:

$$P(t > T) = 1 - P(t \le T) = e^{-\mu * T}$$

Now we have described the *random arrival* of customers in terms of λ, the mean *arrival rate*, and a *random service time* in terms of μ, the mean *service rate*. If the mean arrival rate is greater than the mean service rate, the system will never settle down to a steady state. More customers are arriving than are being served, so the queue will get longer and longer. Our analysis must assume a steady state has been reached with μ greater than λ (see Figure 12.3).

With these distributions, we can find the *operating characteristics* of a single-server queue. Some of these results are not obvious and you will have to think about them. Here we will quote them as standard results without a detailed derivation.

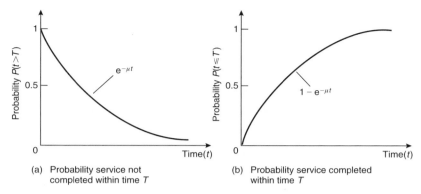

(a) Probability service not
    completed within time T

(b) Probability service completed
    within time T

Figure 12.2   Random service times follow a negative exponential distribution.

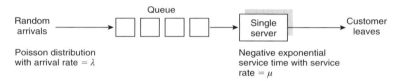

Figure 12.3   A single-server queue with $\mu > \lambda$.

On average, the system is busy a proportion of time λ/μ. Here 'busy' is defined as having at least one customer either being served or in the queue. This is also the average number of customers being served at any time. If, for example, the mean arrival rate is two an hour and the mean service rate is four an hour, we have $\lambda/\mu = 2/4 = 0.5$. This means the system is busy half the time or there is an average of half a customer in the system.

The probability that there is no customer in the system is:

$$P_0 = 1 - \frac{\lambda}{\mu}$$

This is the probability that a new customer can be served without any wait.

The probability that there are n customers in the system is:

$$P_n = P_0 * \left(\frac{\lambda}{\mu}\right)^n$$

This result – which may not be obvious but is generally true – allows us to calculate some other characteristics of the queue. To start with, the average number of customers in the system, L, is:

$$L = \sum_{n=0}^{\infty} n * P_n = \frac{\lambda}{\mu - \lambda}$$

The average number of customers in the queue, L_q, is equal to the average number in the system minus the average number being served:

$$L_q = L - \frac{\lambda}{\mu} = \frac{\lambda}{\mu - \lambda} - \frac{\lambda}{\mu} = \frac{\lambda^2}{\mu * (\mu - \lambda)}$$

With L as the average number of customers in the system and λ as the mean arrival rate, the average time any arriving customer has to spend in the system, W, is:

$$W = \frac{L}{\lambda} = \frac{1}{\mu - \lambda}$$

The average time spent in the queue, W_q, is the average time in the system minus the average service time:

$$W_q = W - \frac{1}{\mu} = \frac{\lambda}{\mu * (\mu - \lambda)}$$

WORKED EXAMPLE 12.1

People arrive randomly at a bank teller at an average rate of 30 an hour. How long is the queue if the teller takes an average of 0.5 minutes to serve each customer? What happens if the average service time changes to 1.0, 1.5 or 2.0 minutes? How long do customers spend in the system?

Solution

The average arrival rate is $\lambda = 30$. The teller takes an average of 0.5 minutes to serve each customer, and this is equivalent to a service rate of 120 an hour. Then the average number of customers in the queue (excluding anyone being served) is L_q:

$$L_q = \frac{\lambda^2}{\mu * (\mu - \lambda)} = \frac{30^2}{120 * (120 - 30)} = 0.083$$

The average time in the queue, W_q, is:

$$W_q = \frac{\lambda}{\mu * (\mu - \lambda)} = \frac{30}{120 * (120 - 30)} = 0.003 \text{ hours or } 0.18 \text{ minutes}$$

Similarly, substituting $\mu = 60$ and 40 (corresponding to average service times of 1 minute and 1.5 minutes respectively) gives:

$$\mu = 60: \quad L_q = 0.5 \qquad W_q = 0.017 \text{ hours or } 1.02 \text{ minutes}$$

$$\mu = 40: \quad L_q = 2.25 \qquad W_q = 0.075 \text{ hours or } 4.5 \text{ minutes}$$

If the average service time is raised to 2 minutes, the service rate is $\mu = 30$. This does not satisfy the condition that $\mu > \lambda$, so the system will not settle down to a steady state and the queue will continue to grow.

To find the average number of people in the system rather than the queue:

$$L = L_q + \frac{\lambda}{\mu}$$

and the average time in the system is:

$$W = W_q + \frac{1}{\mu}$$

Then:

with $\mu = 120$: $L = 0.083 + \dfrac{30}{120} = 0.333$

$W = 0.003 + \dfrac{1}{120} = 0.011$ hours $= 0.66$ minutes

with $\mu = 60$: $L = 0.5 + \dfrac{30}{60} = 1.0$

$W = 0.017 + \dfrac{1}{60} = 0.034$ hours $= 2.04$ minutes

with $\mu = 40$: $L = 2.25 + \dfrac{30}{40} = 3.0$

$W = 0.075 + \dfrac{1}{40} = 0.1$ hours $= 6.0$ minutes

WORKED EXAMPLE 12.2

Customers arrive randomly at a railway information desk at a mean rate of 20 an hour. The single server on the desk takes an average of 2 minutes with each customer. Find the operating characteristics of the queue.

Solution

The mean arrival rate, λ, is 20 an hour and the mean service rate, μ, is 30 an hour. So the probability that there is no one in the system is:

$$P_0 = 1 - \frac{\lambda}{\mu} = 1 - \frac{20}{30} = 0.33$$

This means that there is a probability of 0.67 that a customer has to wait to be served.

The probability of n customers in the system is:

$$P_n = P_0 * \left(\frac{\lambda}{\mu}\right)^n = 0.33 * (0.67)^n$$

so

$$P_1 = 0.22,\ P_2 = 0.15,\ P_3 = 0.10,\ P_4 = 0.07,\ P_5 = 0.04,\ P_6 = 0.03,\ \text{etc.}$$

The average number of customers in the system is:

$$L = \frac{\lambda}{\mu - \lambda} = \frac{20}{30 - 20} = 2$$

The average number of customers in the queue is:

$$L_q = \frac{\lambda^2}{\mu * (\mu - \lambda)} = \frac{20^2}{30 * 10} = 1.33$$

The average time a customer spends in the system is:

$$W = \frac{1}{\mu - \lambda} = \frac{1}{30 - 20} = 0.1 \text{ hours} = 6 \text{ minutes}$$

The average time a customer spends in the queue is:

$$W_q = \frac{\lambda}{\mu * (\mu - \lambda)} = \frac{20}{30 * 10} = 0.0667 \text{ hours} = 4 \text{ minutes}$$

IN SUMMARY

After making a number of assumptions, we can find the operating characteristics of a single-server queue. These include:

- **The probability the system is empty, $P_0 = 1 - \lambda/\mu$**
- **The probability there are n customers in the system, $P_n = P_0 * (\lambda/\mu)^n$**
- **The average number of customers in the system, $L = \lambda/(\lambda - \mu)$**
- **The average number of customers in the queue, $L_q = \lambda^2/(\mu * (\mu - \lambda))$**
- **The average time spent in the system, $W = 1/(\mu - \lambda)$**
- **The average time spent in the queue, $W_q = \lambda/(\mu * (\mu - \lambda))$**

Self-assessment questions

12.1 What causes a queue?

12.2 'Customers do not like to wait, so we should always provide enough servers to eliminate queues.' Do you think this is true?

12.3 What are the variables λ and μ in a queueing system?

12.4 What happens in a queue if $\lambda \geq \mu$?

12.2 | Multi-server queues

If the mean arrival rate is greater than mean service rate, or if queue lengths are too long, we can improve a service by using more servers. Consider a single queue of customers served by S servers in parallel – such as the queues in most banks and post offices. Here customers arrive and join a single queue, and whenever a server becomes free they serve the next customer in the line (see Figure 12.4).

Again we have to make a number of assumptions:

- there are S identical servers working in parallel
- there is a single queue
- there are random arrivals
- there is random service time
- service is in the order first come first served
- the system has reached its steady state
- there is no limit to the number of customers allowed in the queue
- there is no limit on the number of customers who use the service
- all customers wait to be served

If μ is the service rate for each of the servers, we must have $S * \mu > \lambda$, so the total service rate is greater than the total arrival rate. Unfortunately, the arithmetic now becomes a little more complicated, so rather than explaining the derivation we will simply state the results.

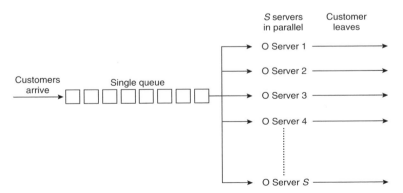

Figure 12.4 A multi-server queue.

The probability that all S servers are idle and there is no one in the system is:

$$P_0 = \frac{1}{\sum_{n=0}^{S-1} \frac{(\lambda/\mu)^n}{n!} + \frac{(\lambda/\mu)^S * \mu}{(S-1)! * (S*\mu - \lambda)}}$$

The probability of n customers in the system is:

$$P_n = \frac{(\lambda/\mu)^n}{S! * S^{n-S}} * P_0 \qquad \text{for } n > S$$

$$P_n = \frac{(\lambda/\mu)^n}{n!} * P_0 \qquad \text{for } 0 \le n \le S$$

The average number of customers waiting for service is:

$$L_q = \frac{(\lambda/\mu)^S * \lambda * \mu}{(S-1)! * (S*\mu - \lambda)^2} * P_0$$

The average number of customers in the system is:

$$L = L_q + \lambda/\mu$$

The average time a customer waits in the queue is:

$$W_q = L_q/\lambda$$

The average time a customer spends in the system is:

$$W = W_q + 1/\mu$$

WORKED EXAMPLE 12.3

A car exhaust centre has customers arriving randomly at a rate of 25 an hour. It has three service bays, each of which can handle 10 customers an hour. Find the operating characteristics of the queues.

Solution

The mean arrival rate is $\lambda = 25$ while the mean service rate for each channel is $\mu = 10$. The number of servers, S, is 3. Then the probability that all three service bays are idle and there is no one in the system is:

$$P_0 = \frac{1}{\sum_{n=0}^{S-1} \frac{(\lambda/\mu)^n}{n!} + \frac{(\lambda/\mu)^S * \mu}{(S-1)! * (S*\mu - \lambda)}}$$

so

$$P_0 = \frac{1}{\sum_{n=0}^{3-1} \frac{(25/10)^n}{n!} + \frac{(25/10)^3 * 10}{(3-1)! * (3*10 - 25)}}$$

Now $\displaystyle\sum_{n=0}^{2} \frac{(25/10)^n}{n!} = 1 + (25/10) + \frac{(25/10)^2}{2} = 1 + 2.5 + 3.125 = 6.625$

So $\displaystyle P_0 = \frac{1}{6.625 + 7.813 * 2} = 0.045$

The probability of n customers in the system is:

$$P_n = \frac{(\lambda/\mu)^n}{n!} * P_0 \quad \text{for } 0 \le n \le 3$$

So $P_1 = 25/10 * 0.045 = 0.113$

$$P_2 = \frac{(25/10)^2}{2} * 0.045 = 0.141$$

$$P_3 = \frac{(25/10)^3}{6} * 0.045 = 0.117$$

Then $\displaystyle P_n = \frac{(\lambda/\mu)^n}{S! * S^{n-S}} * P_0 \quad \text{for } n > 3$

So $\displaystyle P_4 = \frac{(25/10)^4}{6 * 3} * 0.045 = 0.098$

$$P_5 = \frac{(25/10)^5}{6*9} * 0.045 = 0.081$$

$$P_6 = \frac{(25/10)^6}{6 * 27} * 0.045 = 0.068$$

and so on for increasing values of n. The probability of more than 6 in the system is about 0.337.

The average number of customers waiting for service is:

$$L_q = \frac{(\lambda/\mu)^S * \lambda * \mu}{(S - 1)! * (S * \mu - \lambda)^2} * P_0$$

$$= \frac{(25/10)^3 * 25 * 10}{(3 - 1)! * (3 * 10 - 25)^2} * 0.045 = 3.51$$

The average number of customers in the system is:

$$L = L_q + \lambda/\mu = 3.51 + 25/10 = 6.01$$

The average time a customer waits in the queue is:

$$W_q = L_q/\lambda = 3.51/25 = 0.14 \text{ hours or } 8.4 \text{ minutes}$$

The average time a customer spends in the system is:

$$W = W_q + 1/\mu = 0.14 + 1/10 = 0.24 \text{ hours or } 14.4 \text{ minutes}$$

As you can see, it is much more difficult to solve problems with several servers than problems with a single server. If we remove some of the assumptions, the arithmetic becomes very difficult. There are two ways around this:

● use a computer

● use some other method of solution

In practice, it is always sensible to use a computer for these calculations. Figure 12.5 shows the printout from a typical package working with a single-server queue.

SINGLE SERVER QUEUEING SYSTEM – M/M/1 QUEUE

PROBLEM: Example 1   Date: 01-01-1111
                                      Time: 0000

Input Parameter Values:

   Arrival Distribution: Poisson
   Mean Customer Arrival Rate: lambda = 40

   Number of servers: S = 1
   Service Distribution: negative exponential
   Mean Customer Service Rate: mu = 60

   Queue Limit: infinity
   Customer Population: infinity
   List to: n = 10

Output Queueing Results:

   Mean service time: 0.017 hours
   Standard deviation: 0.017 hours

   Mean Number of Customers in System: L = 2
   Mean Customer Time Spent in System: W = .05
   Mean Number of Customers Waiting: Lq = 1.333333
   Mean Customer Waiting Time: Wq = 3.333334E-02
   Service Utilization Factor: rho = .6666667
   Probability that Customer Does Not Wait: P0 = .3333333
   Probability that Customer Waits: 1-P0 = 0.6666667

Number in System n	Probability Pn	Cumulative Probability
0	0.3333	0.3333
1	0.2222	0.5556
2	0.1481	0.7037
3	0.0988	0.8025
4	0.0658	0.8683
5	0.0439	0.9122
6	0.0293	0.9415
7	0.0195	0.9610
8	0.0130	0.9740
9	0.0087	0.9827
10	0.0058	0.9884

Figure 12.5 Computer printout for a single-server queue.

The title *M/M/1* uses a standard notation for queues, where the two letters show that arrivals and service times are both random – using M for Markovian or random – and there is one server. Figure 12.6 shows a printout for a multi-server

---

MULTIPLE SERVER QUEUEING SYSTEM – M/M/4

PROBLEM: Example 2   Date: 01-01-1111
                                            Time: 0000

Input Parameter Values:

   Arrival Distribution: Poisson
   Mean Customer Arrival Rate: lambda = 60

   Number of servers: S = 4
   Service Distribution: negative exponential
   Mean Customer Service Rate: mu = 20

   Queue Limit: infinity
   Customer Population: infinity
   List to: n = 15

Output Queueing Results:

   Mean service time: 0.050 hours
   Standard deviation: 0.050 hours

   Mean Number of Customers in System: L = 4.528302
   Mean Customer Time Spent in System: W = .0754717
   Mean Number of Customers Waiting: Lq = 1.528302
   Mean Customer Waiting Time: Wq = .0254717
   Service Utilization Factor: rho = .75
   Probability that All Servers Are Idle: P0 = 3.773585E-02
   Probability that Customer Waits: 1-P0 = .509434

Number in System n	Probability Pn	Cumulative Probability
0	0.0377	0.0377
1	0.1132	0.1509
2	0.1698	0.3208
3	0.1698	0.4906
4	0.1274	0.6179
5	0.0955	0.7134
6	0.0716	0.7851
7	0.0537	0.8388
8	0.0403	0.8791
9	0.0302	0.9093
10	0.0227	0.9320
11	0.0170	0.9490
12	0.0128	0.9617
13	0.0096	0.9713
14	0.0072	0.9785
15	0.0054	0.9839

Output Cost Analysis

   Customer Cost per Unit of Time = 20
   Server Cost per Unit of Time = 10

Servers	Wq	W	Server Cost	Customer Cost	Total Cost
4	0.03	0.08	40.00	90.57	130.57
5	0.01	0.06	50.00	67.08	117.08
6	0.00	0.05	60.00	61.98	121.98
7	0.00	0.05	70.00	60.56	130.56
8	0.00	0.05	80.00	60.16	140.16
9	0.00	0.05	90.00	60.04	150.04
10	0.00	0.05	100.00	60.01	160.01

Figure 12.6   Computer printout for a multi-server queue.

system with four servers, and random arrivals and service time – so the system is described as M/M/4. This printout also shows a cost analysis for different numbers of servers. When customer time is valued at £20 an hour, and server time is valued at £10 an hour, the best number of servers is 5, giving a total cost of £117.08 an hour.

The second alternative for doing the arithmetic uses a completely new approach to solving problems. This is simulation, which we will describe in the next sections.

IN SUMMARY

We can build models for queueing systems with many servers. The arithmetic in these models soon becomes difficult. Standard programs can do a variety of analyses.

Self-assessment questions

12.5   Why would a queueing system have multiple servers?

12.6   Why is the condition $\mu > \lambda$ not used for multi-server systems?

Case example

Management of queues

People do not like queueing. They view queues in a number of ways, most of which are unpleasant:

- inevitable result of varying demand
- waste of valuable time
- sign of inefficiency
- deliberate insult
- time to do some routine work
- time to relax and meet other people
- punishment.

Adding more servers will make queues shorter, but it also costs more money. An alternative is to make the time spent queueing more pleasant. This encourages the positive views, such as 'time to relax and meet other people' and plays down negative views. Ways of doing this include:

- offer entertainment – like buskers outside a theatre
- offer other services – like drinks in a lounge at a restaurant
- improve fittings and layout – so the surroundings are pleasant
- fit mirrors – so there are things to look at
- be courteous and attentive – so people are not left completely alone
- remove anxiety – telling people how long the queue will take
- use the time constructively – like preparing for the service by filling in forms
- break a service into stages – giving separate short queues rather than one long one

12.3 | Simulation methods

The queueing theory models in the last sections are *analytical models* – which means that we built models and substituted values for the variables to get solutions. Now we are going to describe another approach to solving problems. This does not use a series of equations to describe a situation, but **simulates** the operations.

> **Simulation** gives a dynamic view of problems. It imitates real operations over a typical period.

The main feature of simulation is that it imitates real operations, to give a dynamic view. An ordinary model for, say, stock control looks at the system, collects data for some fixed point of time and draws conclusions: simulation follows the operations of the system and sees exactly what happens over time. A simple analogy has an ordinary model giving a snapshot of the system at some fixed point, while a simulation model takes a video of the system. The following example illustrates this approach.

WORKED EXAMPLE 12.4

An item is made on a production line at a rate of one every 2 minutes (see Figure 12.7). At some point there is an inspection, which takes virtually no time. This inspection rejects 50% of units, and the remaining 50% continue along the line to the next process. This process takes 3 minutes per unit. What can you say about these operations?

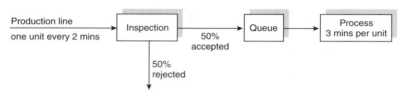

Figure 12.7 Operations for Worked Example 12.4.

Solution

We want to answer a number of questions here:

- How much space should be left for the queue between the inspection and the next process?
- How long will each unit stay in the system?
- What is the utilization of the processor?
- Are there any bottlenecks?

We could, of course, develop an analytical model for this problem and solve it using queueing theory. Alternatively, we could stand and watch the system working over a typical period to see what happens. We might follow a few units through the system and record information, perhaps using a table like the following:

Unit no.	Arrival time	Accept or reject	Time joins queue	No. in queue	Time process starts	Time in queue	Time process finish	Time in system
1	0	A	0	0	0	0	3	3
2	2	A	2	0	3	1	6	4
3	4	A	4	0	6	2	9	5
4	6	R	–	–	–	–	–	–
5	8	R	–	–	–	–	–	–
6	10	A	10	0	10	0	13	3

Here the first unit arrived for inspection at some time which was arbitrarily set to 0. The unit was accepted and moved straight to processing which took 3 minutes. The total time the unit was in the system – consisting of inspection, queue and processing – was 3 minutes.

The second unit arrived at time 2 from the arbitrary start time, was accepted and joined the queue. The fifth column shows the number already in the queue when the next customer joins it. Processing could only start on unit 2 when unit 1 was finished at time 3. This processing then took 3 minutes and unit 2 left the system at time 6.

We could stand and watch the process for as long as it takes to get a reliable view. Then we could analyse the observations, and get the information we are looking for.

Unfortunately, the observations described in this worked example have a number of disadvantages:

- it takes a long time to stand and watch the process
- it might take a lot of observations to get reliable figures
- we only watched one way of working; to compare different methods we would have to implement each and repeat the observations
- watching a system is unpopular with people working on it – as well as with those doing the observation
- watching a system might change its behaviour – to return to normal when the observer has left

We can avoid these disadvantages by using simulation to imitate the actual process. A simulation generates the sheet of observations without actually standing and watching the process.

The only uncertainty in the process is whether a unit is going to be accepted or rejected. We need some method of randomly making these decisions, and still giving a 50% chance of acceptance and a 50% chance of rejection. An obvious way of doing this is to spin a coin: if it comes down heads the unit is rejected, and if it comes down tails it is accepted. A more formal way of doing the same thing uses random numbers, which we described in Chapter 8. Given the following string of random digits

528477801694135675645547930177149431790465825

we could use even digits (including 0) for acceptance and odd digits for rejection. Then, the first unit is rejected (based on 5), the second is accepted (based on 2), the third is accepted (based on 8), and so on.

Now we can develop a typical set of results for the process without actually watching it. The following table shows one set of results using the random numbers above:

1	2	3	4	5	6	7	8	9	10
Unit no.	Arrival time	Random number	Accept or reject	Time joins queue	No. in queue	Time process starts	Time in queue	Time process finishes	Time in system
1	0	5	R	–	–	–	–	–	0
2	2	2	A	2	0	2	0	5	3
3	4	8	A	4	0	5	1	8	4
4	6	4	A	6	0	8	2	11	5
5	8	7	R	–	–	–	–	–	0
6	10	7	R	–	–	–	–	–	0
7	12	8	A	12	0	12	0	15	3
8	14	0	A	14	0	15	1	18	4
9	16	1	R	–	–	–	–	–	0
10	18	6	A	18	0	18	0	21	3

In this table each unit arriving is given an identifying number (in column 1). Then we know that one unit arrives for inspection every 2 minutes, so we can complete column 2. Column 3 shows the sequence of random numbers, with the corresponding decision given in column 4.

Units that are rejected leave the system, while the accepted units join the queue at their arrival time (as the inspection takes no time). This completes column 5. Column 6 shows the number already in the queue, while column 7 shows the time at which processing starts. If there is already a unit being processed, a queue is formed until the processor becomes free (shown in column 9): if there is no unit being processed work can start immediately (at the time shown in column 5).

Processing finishes 3 minutes after it starts (shown in column 9) and the time spent in the queue (column 8) is the difference between arrival time and time processing starts. Column 10 shows the total time in the system, which is the difference between arrival time and time processing finishes.

This gives the rules for calculating each column in the table as:

- column 1: number increases by 1 for each unit entering
- column 2: arrival time increases by 2 for each unit entering
- column 3: from the string of random numbers
- column 4: a unit is accepted if the corresponding random number is even and rejected if it is odd
- column 5: accepted units join the queue straight away (i.e. at arrival time) while rejected ones leave the system
- column 6: the number already in the queue is one more than it was for the last arrival, minus the number that have left since the last arrival
- column 7: processing starts at the arrival time if the equipment is already free, or when the equipment next becomes free (the previous entry in column 9)

- column 8: the time in the queue is the difference between the arrival time in the queue and the time processing starts (column 7 − column 5)
- column 9: processing finishes 3 minutes after it starts (column 7 + 3)
- column 10: the time in the system is the difference between the arrival time and the finish of the processing (column 9 − column 2)

The simulation has been run for ten units arriving and we can get some useful results. We can, for example, see that there was at most one unit in the queue. We could also find:

- number accepted = 6 (in the long run this would be 50% of units)
- number rejected = 4 (again this would be 50% in the long run)
- maximum time in queue = 2 minutes
- average time in queue = 4/6 minutes = 40 seconds
- maximum time in system = 5 minutes
- average time in system = 22/6 = 3.67 minutes
- average time in system including rejects = 22/10 = 2.2 minutes
- processor was busy for 18 minutes
- utilization of processor = 18/21 = 86%

We could find the distributions of time, and a range of other information. But it is important to ask how reliable these figures are. The simulation certainly shows the operations for a typical period, but we have used a very small number of observations. With such a small sample the results are not likely to be very accurate – or to represent the long-term operations. So the next step is to run the simulation for a much longer period. When we have information for a few thousand arrivals we can be fairly confident that the results are reliable.

The process includes a random element, so we can never be sure that the results are entirely correct, even with thousands of observations. We can only say that large numbers of repetitions should give a reasonable picture. Doing a simulation for thousands of observations requires a lot of simple, repetitive arithmetic, so real simulations are always done by computer.

WORKED EXAMPLE 12.5

One customer has an appointment at a reception desk (A) every 8 minutes. After answering some standard questions, which takes 2 minutes, customers are passed on to one of two areas (B or C). 50% of customers are passed to B for 5 minutes each, and 50% are passed to C for 10 minutes each. Finally, all customers go to area D when they fill in forms for 6 minutes before leaving. Simulate this system for ten arrivals and find the utilization of each area.

Solution

Figure 12.8 shows a summary of this problem.

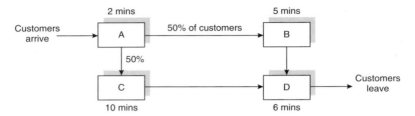

Figure 12.8 Operations for Worked Example 12.5.

We are only interested in the times spent in each area so we can do the simulation with the following table:

1	2	3	4	5	6	7	8	9	10
Arrival number	*Start A*	*Leave A*	*Random number*	*Start B*	*Leave B*	*Start C*	*Leave C*	*Start D*	*Leave D*
1	0	2	6	–	–	2	12	12	18
2	8	10	4	–	–	12	22	22	28
3	16	18	5	18	23	–	–	28	34
4	24	26	4	–	–	26	36	36	42
5	32	34	7	34	39	–	–	42	48
6	40	42	9	42	47	–	–	48	54
7	48	50	3	50	55	–	–	55	61
8	56	58	0	–	–	58	68	68	74
9	64	66	1	66	71	–	–	74	80
10	72	74	7	74	79	–	–	80	86

Column 1 gives the unit number arriving, while column 2 shows an arrival every 8 minutes starting from a notional time of zero. Column 3 adds 2 minutes for processing at A before each customer is ready to move to B or C. The random numbers in column 4 are from the sequence given before, starting at an arbitrary point about halfway along. Units corresponding to odd random digits are sent to area B while those corresponding to even digits are sent to area C. After leaving A, a customer can start immediately in areas B or C if they are empty – or must wait until the next time their area becomes empty (shown in columns 5 or 7). Columns 6 and 8 show the finishing times in areas B and C, found by adding 5 and 10 minutes respectively to the starting times. Column 9 shows the starting time in area D which is either the finishing time in B or C (if D is empty) or the next time D will be empty (if it is busy). Column 10 shows the finish time in area D by adding 6 to the start time.

The utilization of each area is the proportion of time each is busy. We should ignore unusual effects, and find the utilization from a typical period when the system has settled down. Taking the period between, say, minutes 20 and 80 gives utilizations of:

A: 14/60 = 23%   B: 28/60 = 47%

C: 22/60 = 37%   D: 48/60 = 80%

These figures are approximations and we need many more results to get reliable figures (actually 25%, 31%, 63% and 75% respectively).

| IN SUMMARY |

Simulation provides a way of dynamically modelling problems. The purpose of simulation is to imitate operations over a typical period, and collect relevant information. This gives realistic – but artificial – results.

Self-assessment questions

12.7   Simulation provides a 'dynamic' representation of problems. What does this mean?

12.8   'We can use simulation to tackle problems that are too difficult for analytical models.' Do you think this is true?

12.9   How can you deal with random events in simulation?

| 12.4 | Random sampling

12.4.1 Sampling from distributions

In the last section we used **random numbers** to simulate random events. But we only looked at situations where a variable could take two values, each with a probability of 0.5. Now we can show how to get random values from more complex patterns.

Suppose, for example, we want to get a probability of acceptance of 0.6. For this we can take random digits in the range 0 to 9, and say that the first six digits

– 0 to 5 – represent acceptance and the other four digits – 6 to 9 – represent rejection. Then the string:

52847780169413567564547930177149431790465825

represents accept, accept, reject, accept, reject, and so on.

Suppose that we want to accept 50% of units, rework 15%, reinspect 20%, and reject 15%. For this we can use the following approach:

- split the stream of random digits into pairs:

    52 84 77 80 16 94 13 56 75 64 54 79 30 17 71, etc.

- then let   00 to 49 (i.e. 50% of pairs) represent acceptance

    50 to 64 (i.e. 15% of pairs) represent reworking

    65 to 84 (i.e. 20% of pairs) represent reinspection

    85 to 99 (i.e. 15% of pairs) represent rejection

The stream of random digits then represents rework, reinspect, reinspect, reinspect, accept, and so on. In the long term we will get the correct proportion of outcomes, but in the short term there will obviously be random variations. Here three units out of the first four need reinspecting. You might be tempted to 'adjust' such figures – but you must not. Simulation is based on completely *random samples* and it needs a lot of repetitions to get typical figures. From time to time these will include some fairly unlikely occurrences.

We can extend this *sampling* to more complex patterns, including probability distributions. If the process we are simulating has a *Poisson distribution* with mean 1.0 we can find the probabilities of different numbers of events from Appendix C. Then:

$$P(0) = 0.3679 \quad P(1) = 0.3679 \quad P(2) = 0.1839 \quad P(4) = 0.0613$$
$$P(5) = 0.0031 \quad P(6) = 0.0005 \quad P(7) = 0.0001$$

To simulate this we could take random samples from this distribution by splitting the stream of random digits into groups of four:

    5284 7780 1694 1356 7564 5479 3017 7149 4317 9046, etc.

Then: the first 3679 numbers – 0000 to 3678 – represent 0 events

    the next 3679 numbers – 3679 to 7358 – represent 1 event

    the next 1839 numbers – 7359 to 9196 – represent 2 events

    the next 613 numbers   – 9197 to 9809 – represent 3 events

    the next 153 numbers   – 9810 to 9962 – represent 4 events

    the next 31 numbers   – 9963 to 9993 – represent 5 events

    the next 5 numbers   – 9994 to 9998 – represent 6 events

    the last number   – 9999   – represents 7 events

Then our random number string gives 2, 3, 1, 1, 3 events, and so on.

WORKED EXAMPLE 12.6

The stock of an item is checked at the beginning of each month and an order is placed so that:

$$\text{order size} = 100 - \text{opening stock}$$

Each order is equally likely to arrive in the month it is placed or one month later. Demand follows the pattern:

Monthly demand	10	20	30	40	50	60	70
Probability	0.1	0.15	0.25	0.25	0.15	0.05	0.05

Assuming there are 40 units in stock at the beginning of the first month, simulate the system for 10 months and say what results you can get.

Solution

The variables are delivery time and demand. Samples for these can be found using the following schemes.

Delivery time:
Use single digits with:

- even random digits mean delivery in current month
- odd random digits mean delivery in next month

Demand:
Use random digits in pairs with:

Demand	10	20	30	40	50	60	70
Probability	0.1	0.15	0.25	0.25	0.15	0.05	0.05
Random number	00–09	10–24	25–49	50–74	75–89	90–94	95–99

The results of this simulation are shown in the spreadsheet in Figure 12.9. Standard functions were used to generate the random numbers, and the other calculations were done automatically.

In month 1 the initial stock is 40, so 60 are ordered. The arrival random number sets this to arrive in the same month. The demand random number sets a demand of 50 in the month so the closing stock is:

$$\text{closing stock} = \text{opening stock} + \text{arrivals} - \text{demand} = 40 + 60 - 50 = 50$$

There are no shortages and the closing stock is transferred to the opening stock for month 2. These calculations are repeated for the following 10 months.

	A	B	C	D	E	F	G	H	I	J	K
1	**Stock simulation**										
2											
3	**Month**	1	2	3	4	5	6	7	8	9	10
4											
5	**Opening stock**	40	50	10	20	80	150	130	80	60	60
6	**Order**	60	50	90	80	20	–50	–30	20	40	40
7											
8	**Arrival RN**	2	5	9	1	0	7	3	8	4	6
9	**Arrival month**	1	3	4	5	5	7	8	8	9	10
10											
11	**Demand RN**	83	50	56	49	37	15	84	52	66	41
12	**Demand size**	50	40	40	30	30	20	50	40	40	30
13											
14	**Arrival**	60	0	50	90	100	0	0	20	40	40
15											
16	**Closing stock**	50	10	20	80	150	130	80	60	60	70
17											
18	**Shortages**	0	0	0	0	0	0	0	0	0	0

Figure 12.9 Spreadsheet showing simulation for Worked Example 12.6.

The results from this very limited simulation are not at all reliable. But if we ran it for longer, we could find the distribution of opening and closing stock levels (including mean, maximum and minimum), distribution of orders (mean, minimum and maximum), mean demand, shortages and mean lead time. Adding costs to the model would allow a range of other calculations.

Sampling from continuous distributions is a little more complicated, as we can see with a normal distribution. For this we need to:

● split the stream of random digits into pairs

● add 12 of these and subtract 600

● put a decimal point in front of the result to give a random value from a normal distribution with mean 0 and standard deviation 1

● translate this to a random value from a normal distribution with mean μ and standard deviation σ by multiplying the result by σ and adding μ

WORKED EXAMPLE 12.7

Use the stream of random digits to generate a random value from a normal distribution with mean 20 and standard deviation 5:

528477801694135675645479301771

Solution

Splitting the random digits into pairs, and adding the first 12 of these:

$$52 + 84 + 77 + 80 + 16 + 94 + 13 + 56 + 75 + 64 + 54 + 79 = 744$$

Subtracting 600 leaves 144. Then 0.144 is a random value from a normal distribution with mean 0 and standard deviation 1. To find a random value from a normal distribution with mean 20 and standard deviation 5 we calculate:

$$(\sigma * 0.144) + \mu = (5*0.144) + 20 = 20.72$$

WORKED EXAMPLE 12.8

Use the following stream of random digits to take random samples from:

(a) a binomial distribution for samples of size six and probability of success equal to 0.25

(b) a Poisson distribution with mean 1.5

(c) a normal distribution with mean 50 and standard deviation 10.

Random digits: 7299466015902564214167494453049

Solution

(a) Binomial tables in Appendix B show the probability of r successes with $n = 6$ and $p = 0.25$ as:

$$P(0) = 0.1780 \quad P(1) = 0.3560 \quad P(2) = 0.2966 \quad P(3) = 0.1318$$
$$P(4) = 0.0330 \quad P(5) = 0.0044 \quad P(6) = 0.0002$$

We can divide the random digits into groups of 4 with:

- the first 1780 numbers – 0000 to 1779 – representing 0 successes
- the next 3560 numbers – 1780 to 5339 – representing 1 success
- the next 2966 numbers – 5340 to 8305 – representing 2 successes
- the next 1318 numbers – 8306 to 9623 – representing 3 successes
- the next 330 numbers   – 9624 to 9953 – representing 4 successes

- the next 44 numbers – 9954 to 9997 – representing 5 successes
- the last 2 numbers – 9998 to 9999 – representing 6 successes

Then the string of random digits gives:

Random numbers	7299	4660	1590	2564	2141	6749	4453	0498
Sample value	2	1	0	1	1	2	1	0

(b) Poisson tables in Appendix C show the probability of r successes with mean = 1.5 as:

$$P(0) = 0.2231 \qquad P(1) = 0.3347 \qquad P(2) = 0.2510 \qquad P(3) = 0.1255$$
$$P(4) = 0.0471 \qquad P(5) = 0.0141 \qquad P(6) = 0.0035 \qquad P(7) = 0.0008$$
$$P(>8) = 0.0002$$

We can divide the random digits into groups of 4 with:

- the first 2231 numbers – 0000 to 2230 – representing 0 events
- the next 3347 numbers – 2231 to 5577 – representing 1 event
- the next 2510 numbers – 5578 to 8087 – representing 2 events
- the next 1255 numbers – 8088 to 9342 – representing 3 events
- the next 471 numbers – 9343 to 9813 – representing 4 events
- the next 141 numbers – 9814 to 9954 – representing 5 events
- the next 35 numbers – 9955 to 9989 – representing 6 events
- the next 8 numbers – 9990 to 9997 – representing 7 events
- the last 2 numbers – 9998 to 9999 – representing 8 events

The random string of digits gives:

Random numbers	7299	4660	1590	2564	2141	6749	4453	0498
Sample value	2	1	0	1	1	2	1	0

(c) To take samples from a normal distribution we need twelve pairs of random digits. Then, following the procedure described above:

The sum of the first twelve pairs of digits is:

- $72 + 99 + 46 + 60 + 15 + 90 + 25 + 64 + 21 + 41 + 67 + 49 = 649$
- subtracting 600 and putting in decimal point gives 0.049
- multiplying by 10 (σ) and adding 50 (μ) gives 50.49

We do not, of course, need to put in the effort shown in the last example. Spreadsheets, and many other packages, have standard functions for taking samples from many distributions. In Microsoft Excel, for example, if you use the 'data analysis tool' with the 'random number generation' option, you can select random samples from a range of distributions.

IN SUMMARY

We can use random numbers to find random values from a range of distributions. Standard functions in many packages will automatically find these values.

12.4.2 Number of repetitions

An important question in simulation is the number of repetitions we need to get reliable results. Generally, the more times you repeat a simulation, the more reliable are the results – but the more effort you need to get the results. So we need a compromise between effort and reliability.

Each simulation really gives a sample from possible solutions, so we can use the ideas of statistical sampling described in Chapter 8. Two important points to remember are:

- If we repeat a simulation a large number of times we can use the sampling distribution of the mean to give a point estimate for the population mean
- We can also find a confidence interval for the mean, using the standard error (which is the standard deviation of the sampling distribution of the mean)

WORKED EXAMPLE 12.9

Conway and Mallinson are extending their production facilities and want to know how profitable this will be. They estimate fixed and variable costs of £60 000 a year and £20 a unit. Production will be increased by 5000 units a year, and the selling price is £35. Unfortunately, the figures are uncertain and follow normal distributions with standard deviations of £8000 for fixed costs, £3 for variable costs, 500 for production and £5 for selling price. Use simulation to find the distribution of profits.

Solution

The simple solution to this ignores any variability and says:

Profit = (selling price − variable cost) * number produced − fixed costs

= (35 − 20) * 5000 − 60 000 = £15 000 a year

This point estimate seems quite attractive. But there is a lot of variability in the figures, and Conway and Mallinson could easily make a loss.

Simulation can use random values from the distributions to calculate the range of profits. Figure 12.10 (opposite) shows a spreadsheet with one simulation of the calculation. It has taken random values for:

- selling price = £40.13392
- variable cost = £23.11762
- number produced = 4879.554 (assuming fractional numbers are possible)
- fixed cost = £72 842.68

This gives one simulated profit of:

$$(40.13392 - 23.11762) * 4879.554 - 72 842.68 = £10 189.26$$

If we repeat this a large number of times, we can get more reliable results. You can see that after 100 repetitions the spreadsheet shows the mean profit is £13 842 with a standard deviation of £32 945. This shows a very large variation, and it is not surprising that the profit ranges from £101 678 to −£64 276.

With a sample of 100 simulated results, the 95% confidence interval for the population mean is:

$$\bar{x} - 1.96 * \sigma/\sqrt{n} \quad \text{to} \quad \bar{x} + 1.96 * \sqrt{n}$$
$$13 842 - 1.96 * 32 945/\sqrt{100} \quad \text{to} \quad 13 842 + 1.96 * 32 945/\sqrt{100}$$
$$7385 \quad \text{to} \quad 20 299$$

This compares with the actual mean, which we know to be £15 000.

When there is a lot of variability, we have to do a very large number of repetitions before we get reliable results. In the last worked example, we might have to do tens of thousands of repetitions before the results are reliable enough. The spreadsheet in Figure 12.11 (opposite) shows some typical results for different numbers of repetitions. As you can see, with up to 30 000 repetitions the confidence interval is still getting narrower, and the simulated value is approaching the actual value of £15 000.

One rule of thumb for the number of repetitions – which is only a subjective guideline – is to do a large number of repetitions. Then repeat this a few times and compare the results. If there is not much variation in the results and they have same patterns, you have probably done enough repetitions; if the results have significant differences, you should increase the number of repetitions.

IN SUMMARY

Generally, the more times you repeat a simulation, the more reliable are the results. We usually have to compromise between number of repetitions and effort needed.

	A	B	C	D	E	F	G	H
1	**Simulation of Company Profit**							
2								
3								
4	**One simulation**						**100 Simulations**	
5								
6	**Samples**				**Calculation**			
7	Selling price		40.13392		10189.26		Mean	13842.2
8	Variable cost		23.11762				Standard Error	3294.498
9	Number produced		4879.554				Median	11430.16
10	Fixed costs		72842.68				Standard Deviation	32944.98
11							Sample Variance	1.09E + 09
12							Kurtosis	0.158919
13							Skewness	0.388434
14							Range	165954.6
15							Minimum	–64276.2
16							Maximum	101678.4
17							Sum	1384220
18							Count	100
19							Confidence Level (95.0%)	6537

Figure 12.10　Spreadsheet showing simulation for Worked Example 12.9.

	A	B	C	D	E	F
1	**Simulation of Company Profits**					
2						
3					**95% Confidence Interval**	
4	**Number of Simulations**	**Mean profit**	**Standard deviation**	**Standard error**	**From**	**To**
5						
6	1	10189.26	0.00	0.00	10189.26	10189.26
7	10	7649.23	19649.08	6213.58	–4529.40	19827.86
8	100	13842.24	27401.25	2740.13	8471.60	19212.89
9	500	14810.71	30297.99	1354.97	12154.97	17466.45
10	1000	14155.51	30905.71	977.32	12239.95	16071.07
11	5000	14655.81	31319.29	442.92	13787.68	15523.94
12	10000	14884.07	31341.29	313.41	14269.78	15498.36
13	20000	15077.73	31324.61	221.50	14643.59	15511.87
12	30000	15028.88	31297.78	180.70	14674.71	15383.05

Figure 12.11　Spreadsheet showing results from different numbers of repetitions.

Self-assessment questions

12.10 Why are random numbers used in simulation?

12.11 'Random numbers can only be used to give sample values from certain distributions.' Is this true?

12.12 Why does it take so many repetitions for simulation to get reliable results?

12.5 | Simulation flow charts

The examples we have looked at so far are relatively simple and we can follow the logic in tables of simulated values. But this would be very difficult with more complex problems – so we need a way of clearly describing the steps. For this we will use simulation *flow charts*.

The first problem we simulated was an inspection on a production line, shown again in Figure 12.12.

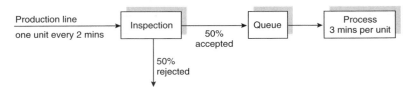

Figure 12.12 Initial example of simulation.

Some results for this simulation are shown in the following table:

1	2	3	4	5	6	7	8	9	10
Unit no.	Arrival time	Random number	Accept or reject	Time joins queue	No. in queue	Time process starts	Time in queue	Time process finishes	Time in system
1	0	5	R	–	–	–	–	–	0
2	2	2	A	2	0	2	0	5	3
3	4	8	A	4	0	5	1	8	4
4	6	4	A	6	0	8	2	11	5
5	8	7	R	–	–	–	–	–	0
6	10	7	R	–	–	–	–	–	0
7	12	8	A	12	0	12	0	15	3
8	14	0	A	14	0	15	1	18	4
9	16	1	R	–	–	–	–	–	0
10	18	6	A	18	0	18	0	21	3

The logic is described by the calculations for each column. As we are describing a series of events over time, this approach is called ***discrete event simulation***.

But we can look at the logic in another way. Suppose we start a clock at time zero and take a series of views of the system at one-minute intervals. At time 0 the first unit arrives at the inspector and is rejected. At time 1 nothing happens. At time 2 unit 2 arrives for inspection, is passed and moves on to processing. At time 3 nothing happens. At time 4 unit 3 arrives for inspection and joins the queue at the processor. At time 5 unit 2 finishes processing and leaves the system while unit 3 moves on to processing. So a timetable of events has:

Time	Event
0	unit 1 arrives
	unit 1 is inspected and rejected
1	nothing
2	unit 2 arrives
	unit 2 is inspected and accepted
	unit 2 moves and joins queue
	unit 2 leaves queue and starts processing
3	nothing
4	unit 3 arrives
	unit 3 is inspected and accepted
	unit 3 joins queue
5	unit 2 stops processing and leaves system
	unit 3 starts processing
6	unit 4 arrives
	unit 4 is inspected and joins queue
7	nothing
.	.
.	.
.	etc.

As you can see, the clock moves forward one period at a time and we note everything that happens in a period. This approach is sometimes called 'next time' simulation. We can describe the logic in a flow chart, shown in Figure 12.13.

Sometimes, when nothing happens in a period, we can save some effort by using ***next event simulation***. Then the clock moves forward to the next time when something happens. In our example nothing happened in times 1 and 3, so next event simulation ignores these and moves directly to the next time when something actually happens.

Complex simulations will give very complicated flow charts. The best way to draw these is to start with a simple view, and slowly add more details. Consider

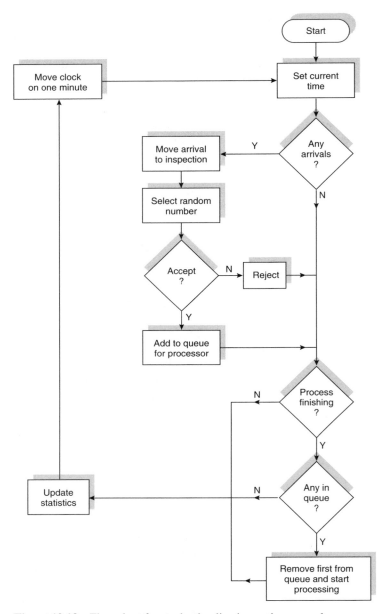

Figure 12.13   Flow chart for production line inspection example.

Worked Example 12.6, which described an inventory system. This simulation was relatively straightforward and we did the calculations in a table. Now we can describe the logic in the flow chart of Figure 12.14.

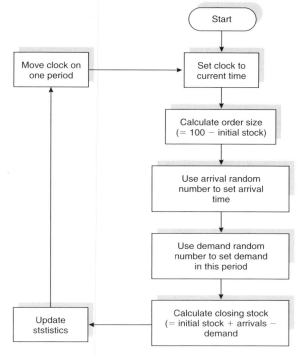

Figure 12.14 Flow chart for inventory example.

We can easily extend this flow chart to show more details. Figure 12.15 shows the same basic chart, but with a different ordering policy, shortages and costs. We could continue to extend this chart, adding more details and features. Perhaps the next steps would expand the forecasting procedures, then the order quantity and reorder level calculations. By continuing in this way, we would eventually get a detailed view of a complete inventory control system.

When we have a detailed flow chart for the whole process, we can transfer this to a computer. We can use an ordinary programming language – like Pascal, C, Visual Basic or Fortran – or one of the many specialized simulation languages – like Siman, Simscript and Slam. Figure 12.16 shows a typical printout for a simulation program tackling the inventory problem outlined in Figure 12.15. The simulation follows the inventory system for ten periods, and calculates the performance and costs over this very limited time.

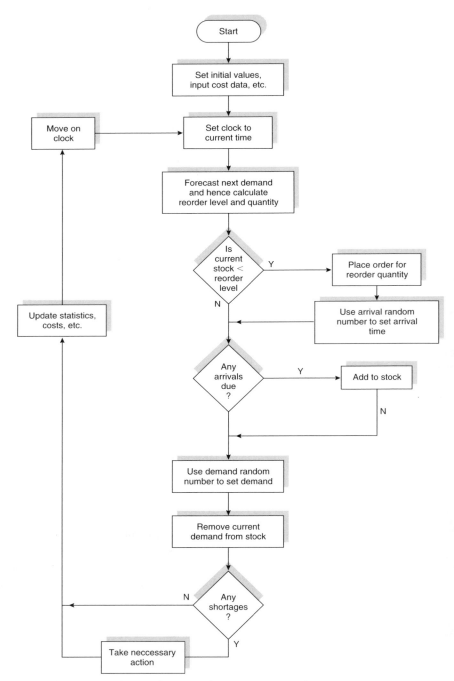

Figure 12.15 Extending the flow chart for inventory control.

SIMULATION PROGRAMME

PROBLEM TITLE: INVENTORY SIMULATION

Date	**01.01.11**
Time:	**1111**
Originator:	**xxxxxxxx**

SUMMARY OF DATA ENTERED

Order quantity:	Automatic EOQ
Reorder point:	Automatic ROL
Rounded to:	10
Opening stock:	1500
Carrying cost:	1
Reorder cost:	75
Shortage cost:	50
Demand distribution:	Uniform
Lowest demand value:	100
Highest demand value:	500
Lead time:	Variable
System parameters:	User defined
Orders arrive:	At end of Period
Number of periods:	10
Random number sequence:	Random
Calculated mean demand:	300
Calculated economic order quantity:	210
Calculated reorder point:	900

LOG OF EVENTS

Week	Opening Stock	Demand	Closing Stock	Shortages	Orders Placed	Orders Arrive
1	1500	331	1169			
2	1169	372	797		210	
3	797	229	568		210	
4	568	205	363		210	
5	363	397	0	34	210	
6	0	227	0	227	210	
7	0	215	0	215	210	210
8	210	326	0	116	210	210
9	210	329	0	119	210	210
10	210	336	0	126	210	210

SUMMARY OF SIMULATION RESULTS

Number of Periods:	10 weeks		
Average Stock:	396.2 units	Carrying Cost:	£76.19
Orders:	8	Reorder Cost:	£600.00
Shortages:	837 units	Shortage Cost:	£41,850.00
Average Demand:	296.7 units		
Average Lead Time:	5 weeks	Total Cost:	£42,526.19

Figure 12.16 Typical printout from simulation of inventory problem.

WORKED EXAMPLE 12.10

How would you use simulation to tackle an M/M/6 queueing problem?

Solution

This has a single queue formed in front of six servers. The 'M/M' mean that both arrivals and service times are random. The way to tackle this problem is to describe the logic in a flow chart, transfer this logic to a computer, run the programs to get results, and then analyse the results.

Figure 12.17 (opposite) gives a start for a simulation flow chart. More details must be added to this before it is transferred to a computer. Then we might get results of the type shown in Figure 12.18 (on pages 538–9). This printout summarizes the model, and shows that it simulates a six-server queue with mean arrival rate of 50 and mean service rate of 15. Then it does a simulation and prints summaries of results. These results show the proportion of times the system has different numbers of customers waiting, and histograms of arrival, service and waiting times. It also prints a complete log of the simulation for the requested 200 customers – but only the first 20 customers are shown.

IN SUMMARY

We can describe the logic for a simulation using a flow chart. These can then be transferred to a computer, using either a general language or a specialized simulation language.

Self-assessment questions

12.13 Why are flow charts used to represent simulation models?

12.14 'There is only one correct flow chart for a given situation.' Do you think this is true?

12.15 What are the benefits of using a specialized simulation language?

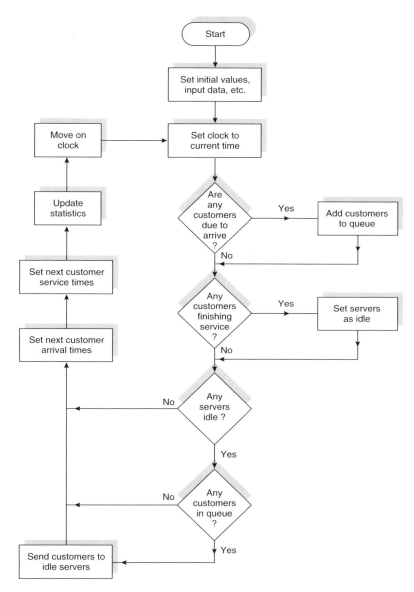

Figure 12.17 Simulation flow chart for M/M/6 queues.

```
-------------------------------------------------------------------------------
QUEUEING SIMULATION RESULTS
-------------------------------------------------------------------------------
PROBLEM: Simulation of Queues
```

Problem Parameters

Number of Servers = 6
Number of trials = 200

Exponential Distribution for Arrival Time:
    Mean rate (customers/unit of time) = 50

Exponential Distribution for Service Time:
    Mean rate (customers/unit of time) = 15

Mean Number of Customers in System: L   = 3.518901
Mean Customer Time Spent in System: W   = .073669
Mean Number of Customers Waiting: Lq = .3105177
Mean Customer Waiting Time: Wq = 6.396826E-03
Server Utilization Factor: rho = .5442595

Number of Customers	Proportion of Time in System	Proportion of Time Waiting
0	.0541	.9270
1	.1138	.0176
2	.1843	.0162
3	.2220	.0023
4	.1856	.0054
5	.1234	.0039
6	.0437	.0035
7	.0176	.0121
8	.0162	.0039
9	.0023	.0049
10	.0054	.0032
11	.0039	.0000
12	.0035	.0000
13	.0121	.0000
14	.0039	.0000
15	.0049	.0000
16	.0032	.0000

Arrival Time Histogram for Simulation Results

                                            * = 2 + : < 2   n = 200

                                            Fractile .01:   0.000121
  *   .05:   0.001146
    *   *   .10:   0.002567
  + +*   * *   .25:   0.006670
  * * * *   * * *   .50:   0.015429
  + * * * * * * * + * *   .75:   0.025753
  * * * * * * * * * * *   .90:   0.043592
  * * * * * * * * * * * * +   +   .95:   0.056931
  * * * * * * * * * * * * * * * + * *   + * *   +   .99:   0.074112
  * + * + * * * * *   + + +

  + - - - + - - - - + - - - - + - - - - + - - - - + - - - - + - - - - + - - - - + - - - - +   Minimum: 0.000034
  0   0.02   0.04   0.06   0.08   0.10   Maximum: 0.077059
                                                           Mean: 0.019423
  Nearest Arrival Time   S.Dev.:   0.016515
```

*Figure 12.18 continued opposite*
```

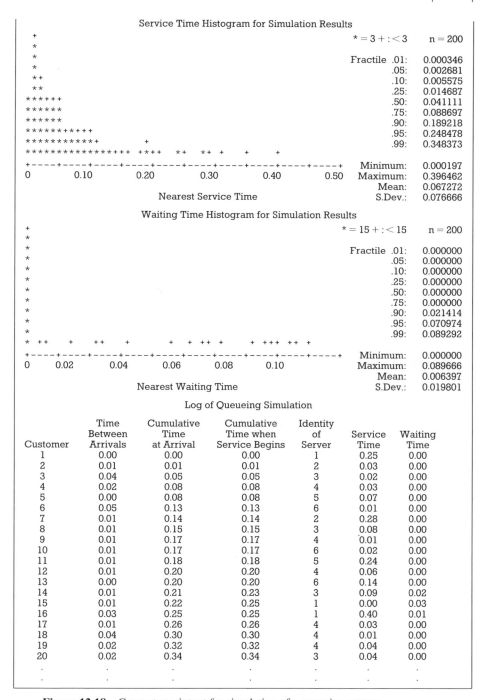

Service Time Histogram for Simulation Results

```
+                                                        * = 3 + : < 3      n = 200
*
*
*                                                        Fractile .01:     0.000346
*                                                                 .05:     0.002681
* +                                                               .10:     0.005575
* *                                                               .25:     0.014687
* * * + + +                                                       .50:     0.041111
* * * * *                                                         .75:     0.088697
* * * * *                                                         .90:     0.189218
* * * * * * + * + + +                                             .95:     0.248478
* * * * * * * * * * * +                 +                         .99:     0.348373
* * * * * * * * * * * * * * * + + +   + + + +    * +   * * +   +     +        +
+ - - - + - - - - + - - - - + - - - - + - - - - + - - - - + - - - - + - - - - + - - - - + - - - - +   Minimum:   0.000197
0          0.10        0.20        0.30        0.40        0.50    Maximum:   0.396462
                                                                  Mean:      0.067272
              Nearest Service Time                                S.Dev.:    0.076666
```

Waiting Time Histogram for Simulation Results

```
+                                                        * = 15 + : < 15     n = 200
*
*                                                        Fractile .01:     0.000000
*                                                                 .05:     0.000000
*                                                                 .10:     0.000000
*                                                                 .25:     0.000000
*                                                                 .50:     0.000000
*                                                                 .75:     0.000000
*                                                                 .90:     0.021414
*                                                                 .95:     0.070974
*                                                                 .99:     0.089292
* + +     +     + +     +           +     + + +  +     + + +  + +  +
+ - - - + - - - - + - - - - + - - - - + - - - - + - - - - + - - - - + - - - - + - - - - +   Minimum:   0.000000
0      0.02        0.04        0.06        0.08        0.10        Maximum:   0.089666
                                                                  Mean:      0.006397
            Nearest Waiting Time                                  S.Dev.:    0.019801
```

Log of Queueing Simulation

Customer	Time Between Arrivals	Cumulative Time at Arrival	Cumulative Time when Service Begins	Identity of Server	Service Time	Waiting Time
1	0.00	0.00	0.00	1	0.25	0.00
2	0.01	0.01	0.01	2	0.03	0.00
3	0.04	0.05	0.05	3	0.02	0.00
4	0.02	0.08	0.08	4	0.03	0.00
5	0.00	0.08	0.08	5	0.07	0.00
6	0.05	0.13	0.13	6	0.01	0.00
7	0.01	0.14	0.14	2	0.28	0.00
8	0.01	0.15	0.15	3	0.08	0.00
9	0.01	0.17	0.17	4	0.01	0.00
10	0.01	0.17	0.17	6	0.02	0.00
11	0.01	0.18	0.18	5	0.24	0.00
12	0.01	0.20	0.20	4	0.06	0.00
13	0.00	0.20	0.20	6	0.14	0.00
14	0.01	0.21	0.23	3	0.09	0.02
15	0.01	0.22	0.25	1	0.00	0.03
16	0.03	0.25	0.25	1	0.40	0.01
17	0.01	0.26	0.26	4	0.03	0.00
18	0.04	0.30	0.30	4	0.01	0.00
19	0.02	0.32	0.32	4	0.04	0.00
20	0.02	0.34	0.34	3	0.04	0.00
.	.	.	.	.	.	.
.	.	.	.	.	.	.

Figure 12.18 Computer printout for simulation of a queueing system.

12.6 | **Benefits of simulation**

We have outlined the approach of simulation, and you can see that it has the following steps:

- initial observation of the problem, identifying the important features and measuring the parameters
- detailed description of the problem, probably using a flow chart
- more detailed observation of the problem to check distributions for variables and find any more details needed by the model
- develop a program for the simulation and get some initial results
- check the results of the simulation and test these for accuracy and reliability
- make any adjustments needed to the model
- re-run the program enough times to get a reliable set of final results
- analyse the results, draw conclusions and present them

This is, of course, only a guideline, and the details will vary with the problem tackled. But you should remember that building a large simulation model can be a major undertaking.

Case example

Transporting coal across Canada

Many of Canada's largest coal mines are in the western province of Alberta. Unfortunately, the major demand for coal comes from power stations in the population centres of southern Ontario, over 3000 km to the East. Coal is currently moved by truck from the mines to rail terminals, by rail to the Great Lakes, and then by ship to lakeside power stations. Several million tonnes a year follow this route.

In the early 1990s the Alberta coal industry noticed several advantages. The international cost of oil was high; nuclear power and hydroelectricity caused environmental damage that was no longer acceptable; coal from other areas had a higher sulphur content, so it needed more expensive treatment of emissions. This combination of factors meant that demand for Alberta's coal was increasing. The only problem was the cost of transport, which accounted for $45 of the $72 delivered price.

The Alberta coal industry was understandably keen to reduce the cost of transport, and they looked at a large number of alternative routes, including:

- keep the present system of truck, train and laker

- use a train for the whole journey from mines in Alberta to power stations in Ontario

- travel south and use American trains rather than Canadian ones

- send coal to Vancouver in the west, then by ship down through the Panama Canals, and up into the Great Lakes via the St Lawrence seaway

- generate electricity near the mines in Alberta and move the electricity rather than the coal

- crush the coal and form a slurry with oil – which is also exported from Alberta – to travel through pipelines for some or all of the journey to the east

- crush the coal and form a slurry that moves west through pipelines to Vancouver, and then uses ships through the Panama canal

- build new larger, high efficiency trains for some or all of the journey

- mix the coal with heavy oil to increase its calorific value so that less weight has to be moved.

The only way of comparing these alternatives was to use simulation. A comprehensive model was built for each alternative, and this was run to find the effects of the route. The simulations were run with time horizons of 13 and 25 years, annual demands from 0.5 to 7 million tonnes, and a range of other variables. Overall, the route that gave the lowest cost per tonne was to use the current route, but replace ordinary trains by larger high efficiency ones. This would reduce costs by $1 a tonne, or about 1.5%. At the other extreme, moving a slurry to the west coast and then transporting the coal via the Panama Canal would raise costs to $127 a tonne. The obvious solution of moving electricity across the country is, in practice, not yet technically feasible.

However, the costs were only one part of the simulation results. These also showed the employment levels, facilities to be built, investment needed, effects on Prairie communities, Provincial taxes, grants, and so on. Reducing the use of the train, for example, would affect employment in the Prairies – where there is already significant unemployment. It would reduce Provincial incomes, create ill-feelings between western and central Canada, close some rail lines as the services became uneconomic, affect government grants, and so on.

You can begin to see the complications of these decisions when we list the interested parties, which include the coal producers in Alberta, competing coal companies, other energy companies, power stations in Ontario, other customers for coal, electricity users in Ontario, railway companies, other transport operators, Canadian national government, Provincial governments (particularly in Alberta and Ontario), research organizations (like the Alberta Coal Research and Technology Unit), other advisory organizations, and external organizations (like environmental groups).

Simulation is the only way of approaching such complicated problems.

The major advantage of simulation is that it can describe complex situations – it is the only feasible approach to many large problems. So it has the advantages of:

- modelling a wide range of problems
- getting solutions to complicated problems
- clearly showing interactions
- being fairly easy to understand
- allowing experiments to test alternatives
- following operations over a long period
- involving managers in the design and analysis of the model
- having specialized languages that make programming relatively easy.

On the other hand, simulation models have the disadvantages of:

- often being big, complicated and expensive to build
- needing a unique model for each situation
- not guaranteeing optimal solutions
- relying on managers' views and data.

IN SUMMARY

Simulation provides a powerful way of tackling complicated problems. It is often the only feasible way of approaching these.

Self-assessment questions

12.16 'You would only use simulation as a last resort when analytical methods fail.' Do you think this is true?

12. 17 What is the most difficult part of simulation?

CHAPTER REVIEW

This chapter described the approach of simulation. It started by looking at queueing theory, and then showed how simulation gave another way of tackling these, and other, problems. In particular it:

- discussed the general features of queues and the need to balance customer service and cost
- found the operating characteristics of a single-server queue

- looked at the operating characteristics of multi-server queues
- described the general approach of simulation
- did simple manual simulations
- showed how to get random samples from various distributions
- looked at the number of repetitions needed to get reliable results
- drew simulation flow charts
- showed how to tackle larger simulations
- outlined the advantages of simulation

KEY TERMS

analytical models   *queues*
arrival rate   *random arrival*
discrete event simulation   *random numbers*
flow charts   *random samples*
M/M/1   *random service time*
negative exponential distribution   *sampling*
next event simulation   *service rate*
operating characteristics   *simulation*
Poisson distribution   *single-server queues*

Case study

City Assistance

Jim Peters left university with a law degree and joined an international oil company. There he met David Bryant who had recently finished training to be a chartered accountant. Two years ago they ran a 'business advice stall' at a local charity fair. Anyone with a small business problem could pay £1 and get some instant advice. This stall was remarkably successful and at the end of the fair they had talked briefly to over 300 people.

A month after the fair a local businessman's club offered a small payment for the pair to give four evening sessions of the same kind. Large numbers of people turned up for these sessions, most of whom were self-employed or were employed by small companies which lacked expertise in some areas. The questions often concerned basic information about taxes, contracts, finances, liabilities, and so on.

These evening engagements became so successful – and requests for follow-up advice so time-consuming – that Jim Peters and David Bryant decided to leave their company and form 'City Assistance'. For the past 6 months this has operated from a shop near the commercial centre of the city. The clientele has widened a little, but is mainly people with a small business problem who want advice on a very informal basis. Typically the owner of a small company might receive a letter about Value Added Tax and will drop in to ask what the letter means and what is the best way to reply. A manager might have a letter from a dissatisfied customer and will drop into City Assistance for a few words of cheap, friendly and reliable advice.

The shop has an initial queue at a receptionist. This queue must be short or potential customers are discouraged and will go somewhere else for advice. The receptionist talks to the customer for a few minutes, decides who can best answer their question, and passes them either to Jim Peters for legal questions, David Bryant for financial questions, or both of them together for more complicated problems. A third consultant was hired to answer general management questions and he always works alone.

Ordinarily the office is quiet, but there are periods when business is brisk and fairly long queues form. Many people leave when there is an obvious queue, but others stay and wait their turn.

City Assistance aim to increase their business by 30% in the next 6 months and a further 50% in the following year. To cope with this they are thinking of making changes to the structure of the shop. Their current idea is to reduce the size of reception areas and free space for more employees.

To get some feeling for the numbers involved, everyone in the company kept a log of their activities during a typical week. Although there is no way of knowing whether these figures will apply to the future, they seem reasonable.

Summary of data collected during trial week

General:

The shop is open from 8.30 in the morning to 4.30 in the afternoon. No appointments are accepted, and if follow-up meetings are needed these must be outside normal working hours. They provide a quick efficient service for people who can walk in off the street.

The shop has a reception area with a single queue at the receptionist. There is plenty of space here, but there are only easy chairs for four people. Leading from the reception area are four waiting lounges for finance, law, joint finance and law and general questions. Each of these gives free coffee and snacks, and can comfortably seat 20 people. An office leads from each lounge.

Receptionist:

Arrivals come randomly at a mean rate of 22 an hour. The time spent with each customer is randomly distributed with mean of 3 minutes. None of the customers who came in stayed if there were more than three already in the queue, and only half of those who came in stayed when the queue was three long. 40% of those who stayed were directed to the finance lounge, 20% to the law lounge, 10% to the joint finance and law lounge, and 30% to the general lounge.

Finance office:

The time spent with a customer is randomly distributed with a mean of 10 minutes. 10% of customers have problems that are broader than finance alone, and a joint meeting with law is arranged. These happen when the current customer leaves the law office. Although there is enough space in the lounge for 20 customers, 60% of these customers leave if there are already four people queueing, and no one stays if there are already five in the queue.

Law office:

The time spent with a customer is randomly distributed with a mean of 15 minutes. 20% of customers arriving are referred to joint meetings with finance. These happen when the current customer leaves the finance office. 40% of customers passed into the law lounge leave if there are already three people waiting, and no one stays if there are already four people in the queue.

Joint finance and law meetings:

If either the finance or law office arrange these visits the duration is randomly distributed with a mean of 15 minutes. If meetings are arranged directly by the receptionist the duration is randomly distributed with a mean of 20 minutes. The priority of these customers is a little vague, but the aim is that they should not be kept waiting for more than 20 minutes. If either office becomes free they start talking to the customer and the meeting starts in earnest next time the other office is free. There is only a 10% chance that customers for joint meetings will wait if there are two other customers in the queue, and no chance of them waiting if there are three customers in the queue.

General office:

The duration of these meetings is randomly distributed with a mean of 20 minutes. 10% of customers are redirected to the law office and 15% to the finance office. Only 10% of customers wait if there are already three customers in the queue, and none wait if there are four in the queue.

Question

Bearing in mind the aims of City Assistance, how effective are the current arrangements? What changes would you suggest?

Problems

12.1 Describe the operating characteristics of a single-server queue where arrivals are random at an average rate of 100 an hour and service time is random at an average rate of 120 an hour.

12.2 A single-server queue has random arrivals at a rate of 30 an hour and random service time at a rate of 40 an hour. If it costs £20 for each hour a customer spends in the system and £40 for each hour of service time how much does the queue cost?

12.3 Describe the operating characteristics of a queueing system with one queue and five servers if arrivals are random at an average rate of 100 an hour and service time is randomly distributed with a mean of 2 minutes.

12.4 Check the results given in Figures 12.5 and 12.6.

12.5 Do a simulation to check the results in Worked Examples 12.9 and 12.10.

12.6 A self-employed plumber offers a 24-hour emergency service to deal with burst pipes. For most of the year calls arrive randomly at a rate of six a day. The time he takes to travel to a call and do the repair is randomly distributed with a mean of 90 minutes. Weather forecasts for February say that it will be cold, and the last time this happened emergency calls came in at a rate of 18 a day. Because of repeat business, the plumber is anxious not to lose a customer and wants average waiting time to be no longer in February than during a normal month. How many assistants should he employ to achieve this?

12.7 Use random numbers to find samples from:

(a) a binomial distribution for samples of size eight and probability of success equal to 0.3

(b) a Poisson distribution with mean 2.0

(c) a normal distribution with mean 1500 and standard deviation 125.

12.8 Customers arrive randomly at server A at a mean rate of 12 an hour. Service time is normally distributed with mean 4 minutes and standard deviation 1.25 minutes. After finishing with server A the customers are interviewed (which takes 3 minutes) and then 60% are passed to server B, 30% leave the system and 10% are returned to server A. Service time at server B is normally distributed with mean 7 minutes and standard deviation 2 minutes. After finishing with server B customers are again interviewed (which takes 3 minutes) and then 85% leave the system, 10% are returned to server B and 5% are returned to server A. Simulate this system and develop a table of typical observations.

12.9 Draw a flow chart for the system described in Problem 12.8.

Discussion questions

12.1 'Queueing theory is so complicated that it is never used in practice.' Do you think this is true? When might it be particularly useful?

12.2 Managers must decide how long customers are prepared to wait for service. This sets the number of servers they employ. Does this seem reasonable?

12.3 We have described simulation in terms of queues, but it is very widely used. What types of problem do you think it is most useful for?

12.4 Some people say that simulation is so powerful that it is by far the most widely used method of management science. Other people say that it is only used when you do not have enough information to build analytical models. What do you think about these views?

Appendix A

Solutions to self-assessment questions

This appendix lists the answers to the self-assessment questions at the end of each chapter.

Chapter 1
Introducing management science

1.1 The application of scientific methods to the problems met by managers.

1.2 Rational and objective analyses of problems.

1.3 No – some of management science uses quantitative ideas, but this is not necessary.

1.4 No – managers make decisions.

1.5 Increased use of computers, fiercer competition, need for better and faster decisions, development of new quantitative methods, more areas of application, good experiences with earlier analyses, better education of managers, etc.

1.6 A simplified view of reality.

1.7 To show relationships between variables, allow experiments without risk to actual operations, do experiments that are impossible in reality, see how sensitive operations are to change, and so on.

1.8 Symbolic models.

1.9 No. Models help with decisions, but are not meant to be perfect representations of reality.

1.10 Observation, modelling, experimentation and implementation – but there are several other versions of these.

Chapter 2
Financial models

2.1 The number of units made, or processed in some way.

2.2 The number of units that must be sold before an organization covers its costs and begins to make a profit.

2.3 The product is not recovering all the fixed costs and is making a loss.

2.4 No – there can also be diseconomies of scale.

2.5 (a) more than £1000 in 5 years' time.

2.6 No.

2.7 By reducing costs and revenues to present values, and finding the net present values.

2.8 An estimate of the proportional increase or decrease in the value of money in each time period.

2.9 Discounting where values are assumed to decline continuously over time rather than in discrete steps.

2.10 No.

2.11 (c), when the average annual cost is a minimum.

2.12 It would lower the optimal age of replacement.

2.13 The straight-line method reduces the value by a fixed amount each year: the reducing-balance method reduces the value by a fixed proportion each year.

2.14 A fund set up to collect enough money to replace some asset.

2.15 By adding a quantitative view, they allow qualitative ideas to be compared.

2.16 Yes.

Chapter 3
Linear programming

3.1 A problem that needs an optimal solution, but there are constraints on the possible values.

3.2 A means of tackling problems of constrained optimization.

3.3 This gives a description of the problem in a standard form.

3.4 The decision variables, constraints, objective function and non-negativity constraints.

3.5 The problem tackled is constrained optimization with linear constraints and objective function; there is proportionality and additivity of resources.

3.6 The area of a graph that contains all the solutions which satisfy the constraints.

3.7 It gives the measure by which solutions are judged, and allows us to identify the optimal solution.

3.8 The extreme points are the corners of the feasible region. The optimal solution always lies at an extreme point.

3.9 By moving the objective function line as far away from the origin as possible to identify the extreme point with the highest value – or moving the objective function line as near to the origin as possible to identify the extreme point with the lowest value.

3.10 This shows how changes in the data – particularly the coefficients in the objective function and the availability of resources – change the optimal solution.

3.11 Until the gradient of the objective function is no longer between the gradients of the limiting constraints.

3.12 The values of one extra unit of each resource – corresponding to the marginal values.

3.13 Until there are so many resources that the constraint is no longer limiting (or resources are reduced until a new constraint becomes limiting).

3.14 Real problems involve so much arithmetic that they can only be solved by computer.

3.15 The most usual information is a copy of the original problem, details of the optimal solution, limiting constraints, unused resources, shadow prices, ranges over which

these are valid, and variations in the objective function that will not change the position of the optimal solution.

Chapter 4
Extensions to linear programming

4.1 No.

4.2 Using appropriate software – but it is difficult to solve most types of non-linear programme.

4.3 Some or all of the variables must take integer values.

4.4 This is a method of solving problems like integer linear programmes, where the problem is divided into smaller parts (branching) to see which one contains the optimal solution (bounds).

4.5 An integer linear programme has tighter constraints than the equivalent linear programme, so the feasible region must be smaller.

4.6 Variables that can only take the values zero or one.

4.7 No.

4.8 It allows logical constraints.

4.9 Constraints are fixed and cannot be broken: goals are targets to be aimed for.

4.10 The solution gave 20 more than the target in the fourth constraint.

4.11 There is a mistake somewhere.

4.12 Some function of the deviations from target values.

4.13 Not really. Because each problem is different, there is little standard software for dynamic programming.

4.14 Because there is no standard model. In practice, dynamic-relationships can be very difficult to describe.

4.15 A relationship that links different stages in the solution.

Chapter 5
Scheduling and routing

5.1 Sequencing finds the order in which activities are done. Scheduling finds the times when activities are done. In practice, the two are very similar.

5.2 $n!$

5.3   For combinations the order of selection is not important; for permutations the order of selection is important.

5.4   More permutations.

5.5   A heuristic rule that gives the best sequence of jobs to achieve some objective.

5.6   Shortest first.

5.7   In order of increasing due date, i.e. most urgent first.

5.8   In a flow shop with two machines, and an object of minimizing total time in the system.

5.9   A problem where we want to find the minimum cost of assigning 'operators' to 'machines'.

5.10   Yes – using zero-one variables.

5.11   By finding the 'active' zero in each row and in each column.

5.12   Known demands at customers are met from sources with known capacity. There is a fixed cost of moving one unit of goods between any two points, and the objective is to minimize the total transportation cost.

5.13   The difference between the cheapest option in any row or column and the second cheapest.

5.14   All elements with positive entries.

5.15   It is the shadow price – the price we are willing to pay to move goods between i and j.

5.16 D_j is the shortest path found to node j, and n is the previous node in the path.

5.17   Each node is labelled with the previous node in the path, so working backwards gives the complete path.

5.18 F is the maximum flow into a node, and n is the node from which this flow comes.

5.19   This varies from problem to problem and there is no set number.

Chapter 6
Forecasting

6.1   Decisions are implemented at some point in the future, so the prevailing conditions must be forecast.

6.2   No. Forecasting may be done by experts but they should certainly not be working in isolation.

6.3   Judgemental, projective and causal forecasting.

6.4   Subjective views based on opinions and intuition rather than quantitative analysis.

6.5   Personal insight, panel consensus, market surveys, historical analogy and Delphi method.

6.6   Reliability.

6.7   Errors come from the random noise, incorrectly identifying the underlying pattern and changes in the system being forecast.

6.8   Mean error = $1/n * \sum[D(t) - F(t)]$. Positive and negative errors cancel each other.

6.9   By calculating the errors of each over a typical period.

6.10   A way of finding the equation of the line of best fit through a set of data.

6.11 X and Y are the independent and dependent variables respectively; a is the point where the line crosses the Y-axis, b is the gradient of the line; E is the noise.

6.12   The proportion of the total sum of squared error that is explained by the regression.

6.13 -1 to $+1$.

6.14   Because older data tends to swamp more recent (and more relevant) data.

6.15   By using a smaller value of N.

6.16   By making N equal the number of periods in a season.

6.17   Because the weight given to data declines exponentially with the age of the data, and the method smooths the effects of noise.

6.18   By using a higher value of α.

6.19 t = time period, $F(t)$ = forecast for time t, $U(t)$ = smoothed underlying value, $T(t)$ = smoothed trend, $I(n)$ = smoothed seasonal index for the period.

Chapter 7
Probability and probability distributions

7.1   Data is raw numbers that must be processed to give information.

7.2   It is easy to get swamped with detail and not appreciate the overall picture (trends, average, spread, and so on).

7.3 Graphically – using a bar chart, histogram, or some other diagram – or numerically.

7.4 Mean, median and mode.

7.5 Range, mean absolute deviation, variance and standard deviation.

7.6 Yes – describing the skewness, relative frequency, etc.

7.7 A measure of its likelihood or its relative frequency.

7.8 Events where the probability of one occurring is not affected by whether or not the other occurs.

7.9 Events that cannot both occur.

7.10 By adding the probabilities of each.

7.11 By multiplying the probabilities of each.

7.12 Events where the probability of one depends on whether the other has happened.

7.13 These use $P(a/b)$ to represent the probability of event a occurring given that event b has already occurred.

7.14 Bayes' theorem is used for calculating conditional probabilities. In particular it says that $P(a/b) = [P(b/a)*P(a)]/P(b)$.

7.15 To describe the relative frequency of events.

7.16 Empirical results are from actual observations; *a priori* results are derived theoretically.

7.17 1.

7.18 When a series of trials has two possible outcomes that are independent and mutually exclusive, with constant probabilities of p and $1 - p$.

7.19 Mean = $n*p$; standard deviation = $\sigma = \sqrt{n*p*q}$.

7.20 Looking at the entry in Appendix B under $n = 12$, $p = 0.2$ and $r = 2$ gives the probability of 0.2835.

7.21 When events occur infrequently and at random. The events must be independent, the probability of an event happening in an interval is proportional to the length of the interval, and an infinite number of events should be possible in an interval.

7.22 Mean = standard deviation = $n*p$.

7.23 $\mu = 0.8$ so looking up the value for $r = 2$ in Appendix C gives a value of 0.1438.

7.24 When the number of events is large and the probability of success is small, so that $n*p$ is less than 5.

7.25 In a wide range of applications, particularly when there is a large number of observations.

7.26 The binomial and Poisson distributions are discrete, while the normal distribution is continuous.

7.27 The mean and the standard deviation.

7.28 About 95% of observations are within one standard deviation of the mean.

7.29 A small correction to allow the continuous normal distribution to describe discrete data.

Chapter 8
Statistical sampling and testing

8.1 The probability that a piece of equipment continues to operate during a specified time period.

8.2 Increased.

8.3 No.

8.4 By higher costs, lower productivity, worse quality, more breakdowns, and so on.

8.5 No.

8.6 To take a sample of units from the population, measure the desired property (weight, length, etc.) and then estimate the value of the property for the population.

8.7 If we take a series of samples from a population, the mean values of a variable will follow some distribution. This distribution is the 'sampling distribution of the mean'.

8.8 If the sample size is more than about 30 the sampling distribution of the mean is normally distributed with mean μ and standard deviation $\sigma/\sqrt{n}$, where σ and μ are values for the population and n is sample size.

8.9 The range within which we are 95% confident the actual value lies.

8.10 Define a precise statement about the situation; test to see if the data supports the statement or if it is highly improbable; if the statement is highly improbable reject the original hypothesis, otherwise accept it.

8.11 Type 1 errors reject true hypotheses; type II errors accept false hypotheses.

8.12 The minimum acceptable probability that an observation is a random sample from the hypothesized population.

8.13 No (it does not **prove** it).

Chapter 9
Decision analysis

9.1 No – they describe the problem.

9.2 To give structure to decisions and present them in a useful form.

9.3 A decision maker, a number of alternatives one of which must be chosen, a number of events one of which will happen, a set of measurable outcomes for each combination of alternative and event, and an objective of choosing the best alternative.

9.4 There is only one event, and we know with certainty that this will occur.

9.5 No.

9.6 One of several events will occur, but there is no way of telling which events are more likely.

9.7 The three criteria described here are Laplace, Wald and Savage. There are many others.

9.8 Only the Laplace criterion.

9.9 Perfect information means that we know which event will occur. This allows better decisions. The extra benefit from the perfect information sets the maximum fee worth paying.

9.10 There are several events that may occur and we can give probabilities to each.

9.11 The sum of the probabilities multiplied by the values of the outcomes, $\sum P * V$.

9.12 Yes – provided you look carefully at the reliability of the results.

9.13 Bayes' theorem is used for updating conditional probabilities in situations of risk.

9.14 Because they describe the value of money more accurately.

9.15 Because the decisions are related – and a sequence of separate decisions could miss the interactions and give a poor solution.

9.16 Decision node, random node, terminal node.

9.17 The total cost or benefit of reaching that node; the best value of nodes reached by leaving alternative branches; the expected value of the leaving event branches.

9.18 By choosing the best alternative at each decision node.

Chapter 10
Project management

10.1 A self-contained piece of work that makes a unique product.

10.2 Planning, scheduling and controlling activities in a project to make sure the project runs on time and that resources are used efficiently.

10.3 No.

10.4 Planning and execution.

10.5 Nodes show events and arrows show activities.

10.6 A list of all activities in the project and the immediate predecessors of each activity. Durations, resources needed and other factors can be added but these are not essential.

10.7 Before an activity can begin all preceding activities must be finished; arrows only show precedence and neither the length nor orientation is important.

10.8 To make sure only one activity is directly between any two nodes; to make sure the logic of the dependence table is maintained in the network.

10.9 The earliest time of an event is the earliest time by which **all** preceding activities can be finished; the latest time is the latest time that allows **all** following activities to be started on time.

10.10 The amount it can move without affecting the project duration.

10.11 The amount of flexibility in an activity's timing.

10.12 The chain of activities that have no float and set the project duration.

10.13 CPM assumes a fixed activity duration; PERT allows some uncertainty.

10.14 A way of calculating the mean and variance of activity durations, assuming a beta distribution.

10.15 By adding the durations and variances of critical activities.

10.16 Critical activities.

10.17 By the total float of activities on parallel paths – after which another path becomes critical.

10.18 By the total float.

10.19 The shortest possible time using more resources.

10.20 No.

10.21 They emphasize the timing – so they can show the activities that should be in hand, as well as those that should have finished, those that are about to start, and so on.

10.22 By delaying non-critical activities to times when less resources are needed.

Chapter 11
Inventory control

11.1 To allow a buffer between supply and demand.

11.2 There are several classifications, and a useful one has raw materials, work in progress, finished goods, spare parts and consumables.

11.3 Unit, reorder, holding and shortage costs.

11.4 What to stock, when to order, how much to order.

11.5 It takes a single item with known demand, which is constant and continuous; costs are known exactly, replenishment is instantaneous, no shortages are allowed, and the lead time is constant.

11.6 The order size that minimizes inventory costs.

11.7 It gives higher total reorder costs, but lower total holding costs.

11.8 The stock level when it is time to place an order – it equals the lead time demand.

11.9 Yes.

11.10 Lower.

11.11 Larger.

11.12 There are several different definitions, but a useful one is the probability that a demand can be met from stock.

11.13 Extra stock that is kept for times when the demand is higher than average.

11.14 By increasing the safety stock – and reorder level.

11.15 By finding the difference between the stock on hand and the target stock level.

11.16 Periodic review system.

11.17 A problem where stock is bought for a single cycle.

11.18 The cumulative probability that demand is greater than or equal to n.

11.19 They show the effort worth putting into the control of each item.

11.20 B items.

11.21 Material requirements planning is a process that explodes production plans to show detailed parts requirements. These are scheduled to arrive just before they are needed.

11.22 Supplies are closely matched to demands, stocks are kept low, a valid production plan must be devised and maintained, early warning is given of shortages or other problems, priority areas are identified.

11.23 No.

Chapter 12
Simulation and queues

12.1 Customers who want a service at a time the server is busy.

12.2 No.

12.3 λ is the mean arrival rate and μ is the mean service rate.

12.4 Customers arrive faster than they are served and the queue continues to grow.

12.5 To give shorter queues and improve customer service.

12.6 Because it is replaced by $S * \mu > \lambda$.

12.7 Analytical models describe a problem at some point in time; simulation models follow the working of a process over time.

12.8 Yes.

12.9 By using random numbers.

12.10 To give typical (i.e. random) values to variables.

12.11 No.

12.12 If there is a lot of variability, it takes a lot of samples to reduce the standard error.

12.13 They provide convenient ways of describing the details of the logic. They also allow easy translation into computer programs.

12.14 No.

12.15 They have been specially developed to make programming of simulation models easy.

12.16 No.

12.17 Building an accurate model of the problem.

Appendix B

Probabilities for the binomial distribution

							p				
n	r	.05	.10	.15	.20	.25	.30	.35	.40	.45	.50
1	0	.9500	.9000	.8500	.8000	.7500	.7000	.6500	.6000	.5500	.5000
	1	.0500	.1000	.1500	.2000	.2500	.3000	.3500	.4000	.4500	.5000
2	0	.9025	.8100	.7225	.6400	.5625	.4900	.4225	.3600	.3025	.2500
	1	.0950	.1800	.2550	.3200	.3750	.4200	.4550	.4800	.4950	.5000
	2	.0025	.0100	.0225	.0400	.0625	.0900	.1225	.1600	.2025	.2500
3	0	.8574	.7290	.6141	.5120	.4219	.3430	.2746	.2160	.1664	.1250
	1	.1354	.2430	.3251	.3840	.4219	.4410	.4436	.4320	.4084	.3750
	2	.0071	.0270	.0574	.0960	.1406	.1890	.2389	.2880	.3341	.3750
	3	.0001	.0010	.0034	.0080	.0156	.0270	.0429	.0640	.0911	.1250
4	0	.8145	.6561	.5220	.4096	.3164	.2401	.1785	.1296	.0915	.0625
	1	.1715	.2916	.3685	.4096	.4219	.4116	.3845	.3456	.2995	.2500
	2	.0135	.0486	.0975	.1536	.2109	.2646	.3105	.3456	.3675	.3750
	3	.0005	.0036	.0115	.0256	.0469	.0756	.1115	.1536	.2005	.2500
	4	.0000	.0001	.0005	.0016	.0039	.0081	.0150	.0256	.0410	.0625
5	0	.7738	.5905	.4437	.3277	.2373	.1681	.1160	.0778	.0503	.0312
	1	.2036	.3280	.3915	.4096	.3955	.3602	.3124	.2592	.2059	.1562
	2	.0214	.0729	.1382	.2048	.2637	.3087	.3364	.3456	.3369	.3125
	3	.0011	.0081	.0244	.0512	.0879	.1323	.1811	.2304	.2757	.3125
	4	.0000	.0004	.0022	.0064	.0146	.0284	.0488	.0768	.1128	.1562
	5	.0000	.0000	.0001	.0003	.0010	.0024	.0053	.0102	.0185	.0312
6	0	.7351	.5314	.3771	.2621	.1780	.1176	.0754	.0467	.0277	.0156
	1	.2321	.3543	.3993	.3932	.3560	.3025	.2437	.1866	.1359	.0938
	2	.0305	.0984	.1762	.2458	.2966	.3241	.3280	.3110	.2780	.2344
	3	.0021	.0146	.0415	.0819	.1318	.1852	.2355	.2765	.3032	.3125
	4	.0001	.0012	.0055	.0154	.0330	.0595	.0951	.1382	.1861	.2344
	5	.0000	.0001	.0004	.0015	.0044	.0102	.0205	.0369	.0609	.0938
	6	.0000	.0000	.0000	.0001	.0002	.0007	.0018	.0041	.0083	.0516

						p					
n	r	.05	.10	.15	.20	.25	.30	.35	.40	.45	.50
7	0	.6983	.4783	.3206	.2097	.1335	.0824	.0490	.0280	.0152	.0078
	1	.2573	.3720	.3960	.3670	.3115	.2471	.1848	.1306	.0872	.0547
	2	.0406	.1240	.2097	.2753	.3115	.3177	.2985	.2613	.2140	.1641
	3	.0036	.0230	.0617	.1147	.1730	.2269	.2679	.2903	.2918	.2734
	4	.0002	.0026	.0109	.0287	.0577	.0972	.1442	.1935	.2388	.2734
	5	.0009	.0002	.0012	.0043	.0115	.0250	.0466	.0774	.1172	.1641
	6	.0000	.0000	.0001	.0004	.0013	.0036	.0084	.0172	.0320	.0547
	7	.0000	.0000	.0000	.0000	.0001	.0002	.0006	.0016	.0037	.0078
8	0	.6634	.4305	.2725	.1678	.1001	.0576	.0319	.0168	.0084	.0039
	1	.2793	.3826	.3847	.3355	.2670	.1977	.1373	.0896	.0548	.0312
	2	.0515	.1488	.2376	.2936	.3115	.2965	.2587	.2090	.1569	.1094
	3	.0054	.0331	.0839	.1468	.2076	.2541	.2786	.2787	.2568	.2188
	4	.0004	.0046	.0185	.0459	.0865	.1361	.1875	.2322	.2627	.2734
	5	.0000	.0004	.0026	.0092	.0231	.0467	.0808	.1239	.1719	.2188
	6	.0000	.0000	.0002	.0011	.0038	.0100	.0217	.0413	.0703	.1094
	7	.0000	.0000	.0000	.0001	.0004	.0012	.0033	.0079	.0164	.0312
	8	.0000	.0000	.0000	.0000	.0000	.0001	.0002	.0007	.0017	.0039
9	0	.6302	.3874	.2316	.1342	.0751	.0404	.0207	.0101	.0046	.0020
	1	.2985	.3874	.3679	.3020	.2253	.1556	.1004	.0605	.0339	.0176
	2	.0629	.1722	.2597	.3020	.3003	.2668	.2162	.1612	.1110	.0703
	3	.0077	.0446	.1069	.1762	.2336	.2668	.2716	.2508	.2119	.1641
	4	.0006	.0074	.0283	.0661	.1168	.1715	.2194	.2508	.2600	.2461
	5	.0000	.0008	.0050	.0165	.0389	.0735	.1181	.1672	.2128	.2461
	6	.0000	.0001	.0006	.0028	.0087	.0210	.0424	.0743	.1160	.1641
	7	.0000	.0000	.0000	.0003	.0012	.0039	.0098	.0212	.0407	.0703
	8	.0000	.0000	.0000	.0000	.0001	.0004	.0013	.0035	.0083	.0716
	9	.0000	.0000	.0000	.0000	.0000	.0000	.0001	.0003	.0008	.0020
10	0	.5987	.3487	.1969	.1074	.0563	.0282	.0135	.0060	.0025	.0010
	1	.3151	.3874	.3474	.2684	.1877	.1211	.0725	.0403	.0207	.0098
	2	.0746	.1937	.2759	.3020	.2816	.2335	.1757	.1209	.0763	.0439
	3	.0105	.0574	.1298	.2013	.2503	.2668	.2522	.2150	.1665	.1172
	4	.0010	.0112	.0401	.0881	.1460	.2001	.2377	.2508	.2384	.2051
	5	.0001	.0015	.0085	.0264	.0584	.1029	.1563	.2007	.2340	.2461
	6	.0000	.0001	.0012	.0055	.0162	.0368	.0689	.1115	.1596	.2051
	7	.0000	.0000	.0001	.0008	.0031	.0090	.0212	.0425	.0746	.1172
	8	.0000	.0000	.0000	.0001	.0004	.0014	.0043	.0106	.0229	.0439
	9	.0000	.0000	.0000	.0000	.0000	.0001	.0005	.0016	.0042	.0098
	10	.0000	.0000	.0000	.0000	.0000	.0000	.0000	.0001	.0003	.0010

						p					
n	r	.05	.10	.15	.20	.25	.30	.35	.40	.45	.50
11	0	.5688	.3138	.1673	.0859	.0422	.0198	.0088	.0036	.0014	.0005
	1	.3293	.3835	.3248	.2362	.1549	.0932	.0518	.0266	.0125	.0054
	2	.0867	.2131	.2866	.2953	.2581	.1998	.1395	.0887	.0513	.0269
	3	.0137	.0710	.1517	.2215	.2581	.2568	.2254	.1774	.1259	.0806
	4	.0014	.0158	.0536	.1107	.1721	.2201	.2428	.2365	.2060	.1611
	5	.0001	.0025	.0132	.0388	.0803	.1321	.1830	.2207	.2360	.2256
	6	.0000	.0003	.0023	.0097	.0268	.0566	.0985	.1471	.1931	.2256
	7	.0000	.0000	.0003	.0017	.0064	.0173	.0379	.0701	.1128	.1611
	8	.0000	.0000	.0000	.0002	.0011	.0037	.0102	.0234	.0462	.0806
	9	.0000	.0000	.0000	.0000	.0001	.0005	.0018	.0052	.0126	.0269
	10	.0000	.0000	.0000	.0000	.0000	.0000	.0002	.0007	.0021	.0054
	11	.0000	.0000	.0000	.0000	.0000	.0000	.0000	.0000	.0002	.0005
12	0	.5404	.2824	.1422	.0687	.0317	.0138	.0057	.0022	.0008	.0002
	1	.3413	.3766	.3012	.2062	.1267	.0712	.0368	.0174	.0075	.0029
	2	.0988	.2301	.2924	.2835	.2323	.1678	.1088	.0639	.0339	.0161
	3	.0173	.0852	.1720	.2362	.2581	.2397	.1954	.1419	.0923	.0537
	4	.0021	.0213	.0683	.1329	.1936	.2311	.2367	.2128	.1700	.1208
	5	.0002	.0038	.0193	.0532	.1032	.1585	.2039	.2270	.2225	.1934
	6	.0000	.0005	.0040	.0155	.0401	.0792	.1281	.1766	.2124	.2256
	7	.0000	.0000	.0006	.0033	.0115	.0291	.0591	.1009	.1489	.1934
	8	.0000	.0000	.0001	.0005	.0024	.0078	.0199	.0420	.0762	.1208
	9	.0000	.0000	.0000	.0001	.0004	.0015	.0048	.0125	.0277	.0537
	10	.0000	.0000	.0000	.0000	.0000	.0002	.0008	.0025	.0068	.0161
	11	.0000	.0000	.0000	.0000	.0000	.0000	.0001	.0003	.0010	.0029
	12	.0000	.0000	.0000	.0000	.0000	.0000	.0000	.0000	.0001	.0002
13	0	.5133	.2542	.1209	.0550	.0238	.0097	.0037	.0013	.0004	.0001
	1	.3512	.3672	.2774	.1787	.1029	.0540	.0259	.0113	.0045	.0016
	2	.1109	.2448	.2937	.2680	.2059	.1388	.0836	.0453	.0220	.0095
	3	.0214	.0997	.1900	.2457	.2517	.2181	.1651	.1107	.0660	.0349
	4	.0028	.0277	.0838	.1535	.2097	.2337	.2222	.1845	.1350	.0873
	5	.0003	.0055	.0266	.0691	.1258	.1803	.2154	.2214	.1989	.1571
	6	.0000	.0008	.0063	.0230	.0559	.1030	.1546	.1968	.2169	.2095
	7	.0000	.0001	.0011	.0058	.0186	.0442	.0833	.1312	.1775	.2095
	8	.0000	.0000	.0001	.0011	.0047	.0142	.0336	.0656	.1089	.1571
	9	.0000	.0000	.0000	.0001	.0009	.0034	.0101	.0243	.0495	.0873
	10	.0000	.0000	.0000	.0000	.0001	.0006	.0022	.0065	.0162	.0349
	11	.0000	.0000	.0000	.0000	.0000	.0001	.0003	.0012	.0036	.0095
	12	.0000	.0000	.0000	.0000	.0000	.0000	.0000	.0001	.0005	.0016
	13	.0000	.0000	.0000	.0000	.0000	.0000	.0000	.0000	.0000	.0001

p

n	r	.05	.10	.15	.20	.25	.30	.35	.40	.45	.50
14	0	.4877	.2288	.1028	.0440	.0178	.0068	.0024	.0008	.0002	.0001
	1	.3593	.3559	.2539	.1539	.0832	.0407	.0181	.0073	.0027	.0009
	2	.1229	.2570	.2912	.2501	.1802	.1134	.0634	.0317	.0141	.0056
	3	.0259	.1142	.2056	.2501	.2402	.1943	.1366	.0845	.0462	.0222
	4	.0037	.0348	.0998	.1720	.2202	.2290	.2022	.1549	.1040	.0611
	5	.0004	.0078	.0352	.0860	.1468	.1963	.2178	.2066	.1701	.1222
	6	.0000	.0013	.0093	.0322	.0734	.1262	.1759	.2066	.2088	.1833
	7	.0000	.0002	.0019	.0092	.0280	.0618	.1082	.1574	.1952	.2095
	8	.0000	.0000	.0003	.0020	.0082	.0232	.0510	.0918	.1398	.1833
	9	.0000	.0000	.0000	.0003	.0018	.0066	.0183	.0408	.0762	.1222
	10	.0000	.0000	.0000	.0000	.0003	.0014	.0049	.0136	.0312	.0611
	11	.0000	.0000	.0000	.0000	.0000	.0002	.0010	.0033	.0093	.0222
	12	.0000	.0000	.0000	.0000	.0000	.0000	.0001	.0005	.0019	.0056
	13	.0000	.0000	.0000	.0000	.0000	.0000	.0000	.0001	.0002	.0009
	14	.0000	.0000	.0000	.0000	.0000	.0000	.0000	.0000	.0000	.0001
15	0	.4633	.2059	.0874	.0352	.0134	.0047	.0016	.0005	.0001	.0000
	1	.3658	.3432	.2312	.1319	.0668	.0305	.0126	.0047	.0016	.0005
	2	.1348	.2669	.2856	.2309	.1559	.0916	.0476	.0219	.0090	.0032
	3	.0307	.1285	.2184	.2501	.2252	.1700	.1110	.0634	.0318	.0139
	4	.0049	.0428	.1156	.1876	.2252	.2186	.1792	.1268	.0780	.0417
	5	.0006	.0105	.0449	.1032	.1651	.2061	.2123	.1859	.1404	.0916
	6	.0000	.0019	.0132	.0430	.0917	.1472	.1906	.2066	.1914	.1527
	7	.0000	.0003	.0030	.0138	.0393	.0811	.1319	.1771	.2013	.1964
	8	.0000	.0000	.0005	.0035	.0131	.0348	.0710	.1181	.1647	.1964
	9	.0000	.0000	.0001	.0007	.0034	.0116	.0298	.0612	.1048	.1527
	10	.0000	.0000	.0000	.0001	.0007	.0030	.0096	.0245	.0515	.0916
	11	.0000	.0000	.0000	.0000	.0001	.0006	.0024	.0074	.0191	.0417
	12	.0000	.0000	.0000	.0000	.0000	.0001	.0004	.0016	.0052	.0139
	13	.0000	.0000	.0000	.0000	.0000	.0000	.0001	.0003	.0010	.0032
	14	.0000	.0000	.0000	.0000	.0000	.0000	.0000	.0000	.0001	.0005
	15	.0000	.0000	.0000	.0000	.0000	.0000	.0000	.0000	.0000	.0000

							p				
n	r	.05	.10	.15	.20	.25	.30	.35	.40	.45	.50
16	0	.4401	.1853	.0743	.0281	.0100	.0033	.0010	.0003	.0001	.0000
	1	.3706	.3294	.2097	.1126	.0535	.0228	.0087	.0030	.0009	.0002
	2	.1463	.2745	.2775	.2111	.1336	.0732	.0353	.0150	.0056	.0018
	3	.0359	.1423	.2285	.2463	.2079	.1465	.0888	.0468	.0215	.0085
	4	.0061	.0514	.1311	.2001	.2252	.2040	.1553	.1014	.0572	.0278
	5	.0008	.0137	.0555	.1201	.1802	.2099	.2008	.1623	.1123	.0667
	6	.0001	.0028	.0180	.0550	.1101	.1649	.1982	.1983	.1684	.1222
	7	.0000	.0004	.0045	.0197	.0524	.1010	.1524	.1889	.1969	.1746
	8	.0000	.0001	.0009	.0055	.0197	.0487	.0923	.1417	.1812	.1964
	9	.0000	.0000	.0001	.0012	.0058	.0185	.0442	.0840	.1318	.1746
	10	.0000	.0000	.0000	.0002	.0014	.0056	.0167	.0392	.0755	.1222
	11	.0000	.0000	.0000	.0000	.0002	.0013	.0049	.0142	.0337	.0667
	12	.0000	.0000	.0000	.0000	.0000	.0002	.0011	.0040	.0115	.0278
	13	.0000	.0000	.0000	.0000	.0000	.0000	.0002	.0008	.0029	.0085
	14	.0000	.0000	.0000	.0000	.0000	.0000	.0000	.0001	.0005	.0018
	15	.0000	.0000	.0000	.0000	.0000	.0000	.0000	.0000	.0001	.0002
	16	.0000	.0000	.0000	.0000	.0000	.0000	.0000	.0000	.0000	.0000
17	0	.4181	.1668	.0631	.0225	.0075	.0023	.0007	.0002	.0000	.0000
	1	.3741	.3150	.1893	.0957	.0426	.0169	.0060	.0019	.0005	.0001
	2	.1575	.2800	.2673	.1914	.1136	.0581	.0260	.0102	.0035	.0010
	3	.0415	.1556	.2359	.2393	.1893	.1245	.0701	.0341	.0144	.0052
	4	.0076	.0605	.1457	.2093	.2209	.1868	.1320	.0796	.0411	.0182
	5	.0010	.0175	.0668	.1361	.1914	.2081	.1849	.1379	.0875	.0472
	6	.0001	.0039	.0236	.0680	.1276	.1784	.1991	.1839	.1432	.0944
	7	.0000	.0007	.0065	.0267	.0668	.1201	.1685	.1927	.1841	.1484
	8	.0000	.0001	.0014	.0084	.0279	.0644	.1134	.1606	.1883	.1855
	9	.0000	.0000	.0003	.0021	.0093	.0276	.0611	.1070	.1540	.1855
	10	.0000	.0000	.0000	.0004	.0025	.0095	.0263	.0571	.1008	.1484
	11	.0000	.0000	.0000	.0001	.0005	.0026	.0090	.0242	.0525	.0944
	12	.0000	.0000	.0000	.0000	.0001	.0006	.0024	.0081	.0215	.0472
	13	.0000	.0000	.0000	.0000	.0000	.0001	.0005	.0021	.0068	.0182
	14	.0000	.0000	.0000	.0000	.0000	.0000	.0001	.0004	.0016	.0052
	15	.0000	.0000	.0000	.0000	.0000	.0000	.0000	.0001	.0003	.0010
	16	.0000	.0000	.0000	.0000	.0000	.0000	.0000	.0000	.0000	.0001
	17	.0000	.0000	.0000	.0000	.0000	.0000	.0000	.0000	.0000	.0000

Appendix C

Probabilities for the Poisson distribution

					μ					
r	.005	.01	.02	.03	.04	.05	.06	.07	.08	.09
0	.9950	.9900	.9802	.9704	.9608	.9512	.9418	.9324	.9231	.9139
1	.0050	.0099	.0192	.0291	.0384	.0476	.0565	.0653	.0738	.0823
2	.0000	.0000	.0002	.0004	.0008	.0012	.0017	.0023	.0030	.0037
3	.0000	.0000	.0000	.0000	.0000	.0000	.0000	.0001	.0001	.0001

					μ					
r	0.1	0.2	0.3	0.4	0.5	0.6	0.7	0.8	0.9	1.0
0	.9048	.8187	.7408	.6703	.6065	.5488	.4966	.4493	.4066	.3679
1	.0905	.1637	.2222	.2681	.3033	.3293	.3476	.3595	.3659	.3679
2	.0045	.0164	.0333	.0536	.0758	.0988	.1217	.1438	.1647	.1839
3	.0002	.0011	.0033	.0072	.0126	.0198	.0284	.0383	.0494	.0613
4	.0000	.0001	.0002	.0007	.0016	.0030	.0050	.0077	.0111	.0153
5	.0000	.0000	.0000	.0001	.0002	.0004	.0007	.0012	.0020	.0031
6	.0000	.0000	.0000	.0000	.0000	.0000	.0001	.0002	.0003	.0005
7	.0000	.0000	.0000	.0000	.0000	.0000	.0000	.0000	.0000	.0001

					μ					
r	1.1	1.2	1.3	1.4	1.5	1.6	1.7	1.8	1.9	2.0
0	.3329	.3012	.2725	.2466	.2231	.2019	.1827	.1653	.1496	.1353
1	.3662	.3614	.3543	.3452	.3347	.3230	.3106	.2975	.2842	.2707
2	.2014	.2169	.2303	.2417	.2510	.2584	.2640	.2678	.2700	.2707
3	.0738	.0867	.0998	.1128	.1255	.1378	.1496	.1607	.1710	.1804
4	.0203	.0260	.0324	.0395	.0471	.0551	.0636	.0723	.0812	.0902
5	.0045	.0062	.0084	.0111	.0141	.0176	.0216	.0260	.0309	.0361
6	.0008	.0012	.0018	.0026	.0035	.0047	.0061	.0078	.0098	.0120
7	.0001	.0002	.0003	.0005	.0008	.0011	.0015	.0020	.0027	.0034
8	.0000	.0000	.0001	.0001	.0001	.0002	.0003	.0005	.0006	.0009
9	.0000	.0000	.0000	.0000	.0000	.0000	.0001	.0001	.0001	.0002

r	2.1	2.2	2.3	2.4	μ 2.5	2.6	2.7	2.8	2.9	3.0
0	.1225	.1108	.1003	.0907	.0821	.0743	.0672	.0608	.0550	.0498
1	.2527	.2438	.2306	.2177	.2052	.1931	.1815	.1703	.1596	.1494
2	.2700	.2681	.2652	.2613	.2565	.2510	.2450	.2384	.2314	.2240
3	.1890	.1966	.2033	.2090	.2138	.2176	.2205	.2225	.2237	.2240
4	.0992	.1082	.1196	.1254	.1336	.1414	.1488	.1557	.1662	.1680
5	.0417	.0476	.0538	.0602	.0668	.0735	.0804	.0872	.0940	.1008
6	.0146	.0174	.0206	.0241	.0278	.0319	.0362	.0407	.0455	.0504
7	.0044	.0055	.0068	.0083	.0099	.0118	.0139	.0163	.0188	.0216
8	.0011	.0015	.0019	.0025	.0031	.0038	.0047	.0057	.0068	.0081
9	.0003	.0004	.0005	.0007	.0009	.0011	.0014	.0018	.0022	.0027
10	.0001	.0001	.0001	.0002	.0002	.0003	.0004	.0005	.0006	.0008
11	.0000	.0000	.0000	.0000	.0000	.0001	.0001	.0001	.0002	.0002
12	.0000	.0000	.0000	.0000	.0000	.0000	.0000	.0000	.0000	.0001

r	3.1	3.2	3.3	3.4	μ 3.5	3.6	3.7	3.8	3.9	4.0
0	.0450	.0408	.0369	.0334	.0302	.0273	.0247	.0224	.0202	.0183
1	.1397	.1304	.1217	.1135	.1057	.0984	.0915	.0850	.0789	.0733
2	.2165	.2087	.2008	.1929	.1850	.1771	.1692	.1615	.1539	.1465
3	.2237	.2226	.2209	.2186	.2158	.2125	.2087	.2046	.2001	.1954
4	.1734	.1781	.1823	.1858	.1888	.1912	.1931	.1944	.1951	.1954
5	.1075	.1140	.1203	.1264	.1322	.1377	.1429	.1477	.1522	.1563
6	.0555	.0608	.0662	.0716	.0771	.0826	.0881	.0936	.0989	.1042
7	.0246	.0278	.0312	.0348	.0385	.0425	.0466	.0508	.0551	.0595
8	.0095	.0111	.0129	.0148	.0169	.0191	.0215	.0241	.0269	.0298
9	.0033	.0040	.0047	.0056	.0066	.0076	.0089	.0102	.0116	.0132
10	.0010	.0013	.0016	.0019	.0023	.0028	.0033	.0039	.0045	.0053
11	.0003	.0004	.0005	.0006	.0007	.0009	.0011	.0013	.0016	.0019
12	.0001	.0001	.0001	.0002	.0002	.0003	.0003	.0004	.0005	.0006
13	.0000	.0000	.0000	.0000	.0001	.0001	.0001	.0001	.0002	.0002
14	.0000	.0000	.0000	.0000	.0000	.0000	.0000	.0000	.0000	.0001

r	4.1	4.2	4.3	4.4	μ 4.5	4.6	4.7	4.8	4.9	5.0
0	.0166	.0150	.0136	.0123	.0111	.0101	.0091	.0082	.0074	.0067
1	.0679	.0630	.0583	.0540	.0500	.0462	.0427	.0395	.0365	.0337
2	.1393	.1323	.1254	.1188	.1125	.1063	.1005	.0948	.0894	.0842
3	.1904	.1852	.1798	.1743	.1687	.1631	.1574	.1517	.1460	.1404
4	.1951	.1944	.1933	.1917	.1898	.1875	.1849	.1820	.1789	.1755
5	.1600	.1633	.1662	.1687	.1708	.1725	.1738	.1747	.1753	.1755
6	.1093	.1143	.1191	.1237	.1281	.1323	.1362	.1398	.1432	.1462
7	.0640	.0686	.0732	.0778	.0824	.0869	.0914	.0959	.1002	.1044
8	.0328	.0360	.0393	.0428	.0463	.0500	.0537	.0575	.0614	.0653
9	.0150	.0168	.0188	.0209	.0232	.0255	.0280	.0307	.0334	.0363
10	.0061	.0071	.0081	.0092	.0104	.0118	.0132	.0147	.0164	.0181
11	.0023	.0027	.0032	.0037	.0043	.0049	.0056	.0064	.0073	.0082
12	.0008	.0009	.0011	.0014	.0016	.0019	.0022	.0026	.0030	.0034
13	.0002	.0003	.0004	.0005	.0006	.0007	.0008	.0009	.0011	.0013
14	.0001	.0001	.0001	.0001	.0002	.0002	.0003	.0004	.0004	.0005
15	.0000	.0000	.0000	.0000	.0001	.0001	.0001	.0001	.0001	.0002

r	5.1	5.2	5.3	5.4	5.5 μ	5.6	5.7	5.8	5.9	6.0
0	.0061	.0055	.0050	.0045	.0041	.0037	.0033	.0030	.0027	.0025
1	.0311	.0287	.0265	.0244	.0225	.0207	.0191	.0176	.0162	.0149
2	.0793	.0746	.0701	.0659	.0618	.0580	.0544	.0509	.0477	.0446
3	.1348	.1293	.1239	.1185	.1133	.1082	.1033	.0985	.0938	.0892
4	.1719	.1681	.1641	.1600	.1558	.1515	.1472	.1428	.1383	.1339
5	.1753	.1748	.1740	.1728	.1714	.1697	.1678	.1656	.1632	.1606
6	.1490	.1515	.1537	.1555	.1571	.1584	.1594	.1601	.1605	.1606
7	.1086	.1125	.1163	.1200	.1234	.1267	.1298	.1326	.1353	.1377
8	.0692	.0731	.0771	.0810	.0849	.0887	.0925	.0962	.0998	.1033
9	.0392	.0423	.0454	.0486	.0519	.0552	.0586	.0620	.0654	.0668
10	.0200	.0220	.0241	.0262	.0285	.0309	.0334	.0359	.0386	.0413
11	.0093	.0104	.0116	.0129	.0143	.0157	.0173	.0190	.0207	.0225
12	.0039	.0045	.0051	.0058	.0065	.0073	.0082	.0092	.0102	.0113
13	.0015	.0018	.0021	.0024	.0028	.0032	.0036	.0041	.0046	.0052
14	.0006	.0007	.0008	.0009	.0011	.0013	.0015	.0017	.0019	.0022
15	.0002	.0002	.0003	.0003	.0004	.0005	.0006	.0007	.0008	.0009
16	.0001	.0001	.0001	.0001	.0001	.0002	.0002	.0002	.0003	.0003
17	.0000	.0000	.0000	.0000	.0000	.0001	.0001	.0001	.0001	.0001

r	6.1	6.2	6.3	6.4	6.5 μ	6.6	6.7	6.8	6.9	7.0
0	.0022	.0020	.0018	.0017	.0015	.0014	.0012	.0011	.0010	.0009
1	.0137	.0126	.0116	.0106	.0098	.0090	.0082	.0076	.0070	.0064
2	.0417	.0390	.0364	.0340	.0318	.0296	.0276	.0258	.0240	.0223
3	.0848	.0806	.0765	.0726	.0688	.0652	.0617	.0584	.0552	.0521
4	.1294	.1249	.1205	.1162	.1118	.1076	.1034	.0992	.0952	.0912
5	.1579	.1549	.1519	.1487	.1454	.1420	.1385	.1349	.1314	.1277
6	.1605	.1601	.1595	.1586	.1575	.1562	.1546	.1529	.1511	.1490
7	.1399	.1418	.1435	.1450	.1462	.1472	.1480	.1486	.1489	.1490
8	.1066	.1099	.1130	.1160	.1188	.1215	.1240	.1263	.1284	.1304
9	.0723	.0757	.0791	.0825	.0858	.0891	.0923	.0954	.0985	.1014
10	.0441	.0469	.0498	.0528	.0558	.0588	.0618	.0649	.0679	.0710
11	.0245	.0265	.0285	.0307	.0330	.0353	.0377	.0401	.0426	.0452
12	.0124	.0137	.0150	.0164	.0179	.0194	.0210	.0227	.0245	.0264
13	.0058	.0065	.0073	.0081	.0089	.0098	.0108	.0119	.0130	.0142
14	.0025	.0029	.0033	.0037	.0041	.0046	.0052	.0058	.0064	.0071
15	.0010	.0012	.0014	.0016	.0018	.0020	.0023	.0026	.0029	.0033
16	.0004	.0005	.0005	.0006	.0007	.0008	.0010	.0011	.0013	.0014
17	.0001	.0002	.0002	.0002	.0003	.0003	.0004	.0004	.0005	.0006
18	.0000	.0001	.0001	.0001	.0001	.0001	.0001	.0002	.0002	.0002
19	.0000	.0000	.0000	.0000	.0000	.0000	.0000	.0001	.0001	.0001

Appendix D

Probabilities for the normal distribution

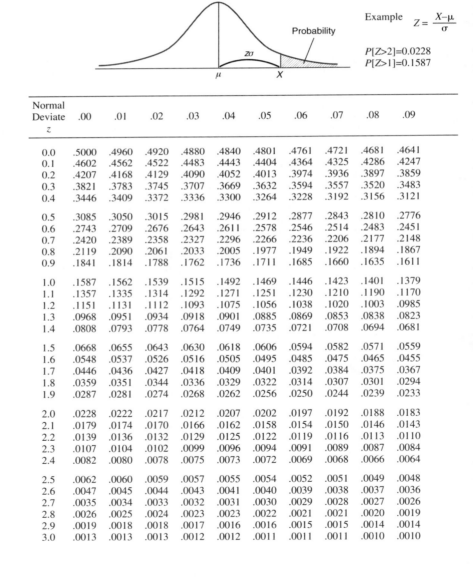

Example $Z = \dfrac{X-\mu}{\sigma}$

$P[Z>2]=0.0228$

$P[Z>1]=0.1587$

Normal Deviate z	.00	.01	.02	.03	.04	.05	.06	.07	.08	.09
0.0	.5000	.4960	.4920	.4880	.4840	.4801	.4761	.4721	.4681	.4641
0.1	.4602	.4562	.4522	.4483	.4443	.4404	.4364	.4325	.4286	.4247
0.2	.4207	.4168	.4129	.4090	.4052	.4013	.3974	.3936	.3897	.3859
0.3	.3821	.3783	.3745	.3707	.3669	.3632	.3594	.3557	.3520	.3483
0.4	.3446	.3409	.3372	.3336	.3300	.3264	.3228	.3192	.3156	.3121
0.5	.3085	.3050	.3015	.2981	.2946	.2912	.2877	.2843	.2810	.2776
0.6	.2743	.2709	.2676	.2643	.2611	.2578	.2546	.2514	.2483	.2451
0.7	.2420	.2389	.2358	.2327	.2296	.2266	.2236	.2206	.2177	.2148
0.8	.2119	.2090	.2061	.2033	.2005	.1977	.1949	.1922	.1894	.1867
0.9	.1841	.1814	.1788	.1762	.1736	.1711	.1685	.1660	.1635	.1611
1.0	.1587	.1562	.1539	.1515	.1492	.1469	.1446	.1423	.1401	.1379
1.1	.1357	.1335	.1314	.1292	.1271	.1251	.1230	.1210	.1190	.1170
1.2	.1151	.1131	.1112	.1093	.1075	.1056	.1038	.1020	.1003	.0985
1.3	.0968	.0951	.0934	.0918	.0901	.0885	.0869	.0853	.0838	.0823
1.4	.0808	.0793	.0778	.0764	.0749	.0735	.0721	.0708	.0694	.0681
1.5	.0668	.0655	.0643	.0630	.0618	.0606	.0594	.0582	.0571	.0559
1.6	.0548	.0537	.0526	.0516	.0505	.0495	.0485	.0475	.0465	.0455
1.7	.0446	.0436	.0427	.0418	.0409	.0401	.0392	.0384	.0375	.0367
1.8	.0359	.0351	.0344	.0336	.0329	.0322	.0314	.0307	.0301	.0294
1.9	.0287	.0281	.0274	.0268	.0262	.0256	.0250	.0244	.0239	.0233
2.0	.0228	.0222	.0217	.0212	.0207	.0202	.0197	.0192	.0188	.0183
2.1	.0179	.0174	.0170	.0166	.0162	.0158	.0154	.0150	.0146	.0143
2.2	.0139	.0136	.0132	.0129	.0125	.0122	.0119	.0116	.0113	.0110
2.3	.0107	.0104	.0102	.0099	.0096	.0094	.0091	.0089	.0087	.0084
2.4	.0082	.0080	.0078	.0075	.0073	.0072	.0069	.0068	.0066	.0064
2.5	.0062	.0060	.0059	.0057	.0055	.0054	.0052	.0051	.0049	.0048
2.6	.0047	.0045	.0044	.0043	.0041	.0040	.0039	.0038	.0037	.0036
2.7	.0035	.0034	.0033	.0032	.0031	.0030	.0029	.0028	.0027	.0026
2.8	.0026	.0025	.0024	.0023	.0023	.0022	.0021	.0021	.0020	.0019
2.9	.0019	.0018	.0018	.0017	.0016	.0016	.0015	.0015	.0014	.0014
3.0	.0013	.0013	.0013	.0012	.0012	.0011	.0011	.0011	.0010	.0010

Appendix E

Selected references

There are many books on management science. The following list is not comprehensive, but illustrates some of the books available.

General books on management science

Anderson D.R., Sweeney D.J. and Williams T.A. (1994).
  An Introduction to Management Science (7th edn). St Paul, MN: West Publishing Co.
Cook T.M. and Russell R. A. (1993).
  Management Science (5th edn). Englewood Cliffs, NJ: Prentice Hall.
Dennis T.L. and Dennis L.B. (1991).
  Management Science. St Paul, MN: West Publishing Co.
Eppen G.D., Gould F.J. and Schmidt C.P. (1993).
  Introductory Management Science (4th edn). Englewood Cliffs, NJ: Prentice Hall.
Plane D. (1997).
  Management Science (2nd edn). Danvers, MA: Boyd and Fraser.
Render B. and Stair R.M. (1991).
  Quantitative Analysis for Managers (4th edn). Boston, MA: Allyn & Bacon.
Taylor B.W. (1993).
  Introduction to Management Science (4th edn). Needham Heights, MA: Allyn & Bacon.
Turban E. and Meredith J.R. (1991).
  Fundamentals of Management Science (5th edn). Homewood, IL: Irwin.
Waters D. (1997).
  Quantitative Methods for Business. Harlow: Addison Wesley.

Mathematical programming

Bazaraa M.S., Jarvis J.J. and Sherali H.D. (1989).
  Linear Programming and Network Flows. New York: John Wiley.
Bunday B. (1984).
  Basic Linear Programming. London: Edward Arnold.
Schrage L. (1991).
  LINDO: an optimization modelling system (4th edn). San Francisco: Scientific Press.
Shapiro R.O. (1984).
  Optimisation for Planning and Allocation. New York: John Wiley.
Williams H.P. (1993).
  Model Building in Mathematical Programming (3rd edn). Chichester: John Wiley & Sons.

Scheduling and routing

Baker K.R. (1984).
   Introduction to Sequencing and Scheduling. New York: John Wiley.
Fogarty D.W. and Hoffman T.R. (1983).
   Production and Inventory Management. Cincinnati: South-Western Publishing.
Green J.H. (1987).
   Production and Inventory Control Handbook (2nd edn). New York: McGraw-Hill.
McLeavey D. and Narasimhan (1985).
   Production Planning and Inventory Control. Boston, MA: Allyn & Bacon.
Vollman T.E., Berry W.L. and Whybark D.C. (1992).
   Manufacturing Planning and Control Systems (3rd edn). Homewood, IL: Irwin.

Regression and forecasting

Hanke J.E. and Reitsch A.G. (1986).
   Business Forecasting (2nd edn). Boston, MA: Allyn & Bacon.
Makridakis S. and Wheelwright S.C. (1989).
   Forecasting Methods for Management (5th edn). New York: John Wiley.
Thomopoulos N.T. (1980).
   Applied Forecasting Methods. New Jersey: Prentice Hall.
Willis R.E. (1987).
   A Guide to Forecasting for Planners and Managers. New Jersey: Prentice Hall.

Statistics

Daniel W.W. and Terrell J.C. (1986).
   Business Statistics. Boston: Houghton Mifflin Company.
Freund J.E. and Williams F.J. (1984).
   Elementary Business Statistics: the modern approach (4th edn). New Jersey:
   Prentice Hall.
Harnett D.L. and Soni A.K. (1991).
   Statistical Methods for Business and Economics. Reading, MA: Addison Wesley.
Kennedy G. (1983).
   Invitation to Statistics. Oxford: Martin Robertson.
Lawson M., Hubbard S. and Pugh P. (1995).
   Maths and Statistics for Business. Harlow: Addison Wesley.
Mann P.S. (1995).
   Statistics for Business and Economics. New York: John Wiley.
McClave J.T. and Benson P.G. (1988).
   Statistics for Business and Economics (4th edn). San Francisco, CA: Dellen–Macmillan.
Triola M.F. and Franklin L.A. (1994).
   Business Statistics. Reading, MA: Addison Wesley.

Decision analysis

Buchanan J.T. (1982).
   Discrete and Dynamic Decision Analysis. Chichester: John Wiley & Sons.
Bunn D. (1984).
   Applied Decision Analysis. New York: McGraw-Hill.

Daellanbach H.G. (1994).
   Systems and Decision Making. New York: John Wiley.
Golub A. (1997).
   Decision Analysis. New York: John Wiley.
Lindley D.V. (1985).
   Making Decisions. Chichester: John Wiley & Sons.
Samson D. (1988).
   Managerial Decision Analysis. Homewood, IL: Irwin.

Project network analysis

Cleland D.I. (1994).
   Project Management (2nd edn). New York: McGraw-Hill.
Kerzner H. (1984).
   Project Management for Executives. New York: Van Nostrand Reinhold.
Kerzner H. and Thamhain H. (1984).
   Project Management for Small and Medium-Sized Business. New York: Van Nostrand
   Reinhold.
Meredith J.R. and Mantel S.J. (1985).
   Project Management. New York: John Wiley.
Nicholas J.M. (1990).
   Managing Business and Engineering Projects. Englewood Cliffs, NJ: Prentice Hall.
Shtub A., Bard J.F. and Globerson S. (1994).
   Project Management. Englewood Cliffs, NJ: Prentice Hall.

Inventory control

Silver E.A. and Peterson R. (1985).
   Decision Systems for Inventory Management and Production Planning (2nd edn).
   New York: John Wiley.
Tersine R.J. (1987).
   Principles of Inventory and Materials Management (3rd edn). New York: Elsevier
   North-Holland.
Waters C.D.J (1992).
   Inventory Control and Management. Chichester: John Wiley & Sons.

Simulation and queues

Banks J. and Carson J.S. (1984).
   Discrete-Event Simulation. New Jersey: Prentice Hall.
Law A.M. and Kelton W.D. (1982).
   Simulation Modelling and Analysis. New York: McGraw-Hill.
Payne J.A. (1982).
   Introduction to Simulation: Programming Techniques and Methods of Analysis.
   New York: McGraw-Hill.
Pidd M. (1988).
   Computer Simulation in Management Science (2nd edn). Chichester: John Wiley &
   Sons.
Soloman S.L. (1983).
   Simulation of Waiting-Line Systems. New Jersey: Prentice Hall.

Index